AN INTRODUCTION
TO LITERARY CRITICISM

An Introduction to Literary Criticism

An Anthology

Edited, Selected, and with Introductions by

LAILA GROSS

CAPRICORN BOOKS, *New York*

Copyright © 1971 by Educational Resources Corporation

Library of Congress Catalog
Card Number: 71–151206

CAPRICORN EDITION, 1972

PRINTED IN THE UNITED STATES OF AMERICA

801.95
Int

CONTENTS

INTRODUCTION   1

1. ARISTOTLE   *Poetics*   22

2. LONGINUS   *On the Sublime*   53

3. DANTE   *De Vulgari Eloquentia*   78

4. SIDNEY   *An Apologie for Poetrie*   93

5. DRYDEN   "An Essay of Dramatic Poesy"   137

6. WORDSWORTH   "Observations Prefixed to
                  Lyrical Ballads"   189

7. ARNOLD   "The Study of Poetry"   212

8. JAMES   "The Art of Fiction"   237

9. TAINE   Introduction to
                  History of English Literature   259

10. JUNG   "Psychology and Literature"   275

11. BROOKS   "The Language of Paradox"   284

12. AUERBACH   "Odysseus' Scar"   300

13. FRYE   "The Archetypes of Literature"   327

    Suggestions for Further Reading   341

INTRODUCTION

What is literary criticism? An apparently simple question to which most of us would rush to answer, "Why, criticism of course is . . . . Well, criticism . . . ," and find that although we were perfectly certain what it was before, we now find it difficult to form an acceptable definition. When one turns to the men called critics, one usually finds them very silent on the subject. It is a question that never seems to have occurred to most of them, or if it did, they answered it silently.

However, in this century there have been a few attempts to raise and to answer this question. Following are some thoughtful, some crotchety, some vague, and some reasonable reflections on criticism by twentieth-century critics:

> Criticism . . . is pretty much the same thing as the reasoned exercise of Literary Taste—the attempt, by examination of literature, to find out what it is that makes literature pleasant, and therefore good—the discovery, classification, and as far as possible tracing to their sources, of the qualities of poetry and prose, of style and metre, the classification of literary kinds, the examination and "proving," as arms are proved, of literary means and weapons, not neglecting the observation of literary fashions and the like.—GEORGE SAINTSBURY, *A History of Criticism*, p. 4.

> The office of criticism is to discern and to point out exactly where lies the poetical motive.—CROCE, *Ariosto, Shakespeare and Corneille*, p. 147.

> . . . [Literary] criticism ought to be . . . a history of man's ideas and imaginings in the setting of the conditions which have shaped them.—EDUMUND WILSON, *Axel's Castle*, "Dedication to Christian Gauss."

> Criticism is an attitude of mind, not simply a method of elucidation. It is what remains when literature itself has begun to expire. Criticism flourishes when literature has failed . . . .—KARL SHAPIRO, *In Defense of Ignorance*, p. 6.

> He [the critic] must translate his experience of literature into intellectual terms, assimilate it to a coherent scheme which must be rational if it is to be knowledge.—WELLEK and WARREN, *Theory of Literature*, p. 15.

> . . . [B]y criticism I mean the whole work of scholarship and taste concerned with literature which is a part of what is variously called liberal education, culture, or the study of the humanities. I start from the principle that criticism is not simply part of this larger activity, but an essential part of it.—NORTHROP FRYE, *Anatomy of Criticism*, p. 3.

> The criterion [of a critical theory] is not the scientific verifiability of its single propositions, but the scope, precision, and coherence of the insights that it yields into the properties of single works of art and the adequacy with which it accounts for diverse kinds of art.— M. H. ABRAMS, *The Mirror and the Lamp*, pp. 4–5.

> What then is the role of criticism? The answer is that *a good work of criticism is a work of art about another work of art*. Anything short of that is failure.—KARL SHAPIRO, *In Defense of Ignorance*, p. 31.

> From the beginning criticism has exhibited two aspects. In one it has compared and judged; it has attempted to isolate the values of literature and to determine whether the specimens it appraises are good or bad.— H. CAIRNS, Introduction, *Lectures in Criticism* (Harper and Brothers, 1961, p. 1.)

Although Huntington Cairns gives one of the most acceptable definitions of criticism, he himself is not satisfied. The definition was offered at the Symposium on Criticism held at Johns Hopkins in 1948, when some of the accepted great, living critics assembled to discuss previous critics and possibly to evolve some definition of criticism. Cairns ended his introduction with these words, however:

All this is to say that criticism for twenty-three hundred years has lacked a volume which might have begun:

> *Our subject is criticism, and I propose to speak not only of the art in general, but also of the various kinds and their respective capacities; of the principles required for good criticism; and whatever else is proper to this same inquiry. Let us follow the natural order and begin first with first principles. . . .*

These words, alas, are not the opening words of a *Kritike* by Aristotle. . . . [However] . . . it would have stated the theory of criticism in a form of the utmost generality, but one which would, nevertheless, allow the future to add to or subtract from it as the novelties of creative activity indicated. Criticism has always stood in need of such a *Kritike*, and no more so than at the present.—CAIRNS, pp. 11–12.

The difficulties concerning a definition suggest that we consider a rough outline of the history of criticism. By history of criticism, I mean simply an account of main ideas of critics considered important in our culture, and whose writings therefore are presented in this volume.

The importance of criticism is usually judged according to one or both of two factors: (1) custom—the work has endured and has been considered important through the ages; (2) influence on later thought—sometimes, especially when one deals with modern criticism, the factor of representativeness has to be considered.

It is with Aristotle that criticism begins. His *Poetics* is the first work we have which critically evaluates the nature of literature and it has been taken as the point of departure for most critical concerns for 2300 years. It, therefore, demands especially careful consideration.

Aristotle lays down the very important premise that art is imitation of nature. He maintains that men desire to imitate nature in art for two reasons: (1) the desire for imitation is instinctive in men, and (2) there is a pleasure in contemplating imitation. In poetry the object of imitation is men in action, who may be better than the readers, worse, or as they are. The manner of imitation may be narrative (as in a modern novel) or dramatic (as in an acted play).

The importance of this premise of art as imitation of nature can hardly be exaggerated. It forms the basis for most later discussions, reactions to, and appreciations of art. It also emphasizes the classical conception of nature, which is behind the premise. As W. J. Bate points out: "Moreover, if art is said to imitate nature, then the character of art is governed by one's conception of what it imitates. The classical theory of art, therefore, is firmly based upon the far more important conception of what constitutes nature itself. In this sense, the foundation of the classical tradition is its confidence in a rationally *ordered and harmonious universe*, working according to fixed laws, principles, and forms." (*Criticism: The Major Texts* [Harcourt, Brace & World, 1952], pp. 3–4.)

After offering his far-reaching definition of art, Aristotle concentrates on what he considers to be the most important genre in literature:

tragedy. Tragedy, first of all, ". . . is an imitation of an action that is serious, complete, and of a certain magnitude. . . ." By "serious" he simply means that the action is not comic and is one which involves men who are slightly better than we, depicted as going from good to bad fortune. By "complete" he points out that he means "having a beginning, middle, and end," and then proceeds to define each of the terms. "Certain magnitude" is a more difficult concept by which he means whole and proper within the circumstances; thus an exceedingly small or large picture cannot be beautiful, and a plot should be of "a length which can be easily embraced by the memory."

Behind the concept of "certain magnitude" is not only the ordered and harmonious universe but also the whole notion that beauty consists in order and harmony. Order and harmony necessitate all the parts to form a whole, to have unity. Thus unity of plot is required, by which Aristotle means that only one complete action should be imitated. Besides unity of plot, there should be a certain unity of time. In fairness to Aristotle one must point out that he never uses this phrase; he simply says: "Tragedy endeavors, as far as possible, to confine itself to a single revolution of the sun, or but slightly to exceed this limit. . . ." We will see later what critics after him did with this statement and the whole notion of "unity."

A consequence to Aristotle's "imitation of an action of certain magnitude" are the concerns of probability and necessity. Events should be presented according to the laws of probability and necessity. This does not mean, however, that the poet should depict what has happened; rather, he should show us what may happen. Thus, Aristotle's concern is not with real life or history. As a matter of fact, he points out that poetry is more philosophical than history because it concerns itself not only with what should be but also with the universal rather than the particular.

In order to achieve the most effective imitation of nature, the poet's diction should be most proper and interesting. The importance of diction (which includes the proper use of poetic devices, such as metaphors) to Aristotle is so great that he devotes more attention to it than to any other element. However, because most of the discussion and examples cited are not valuable to a modern-English-speaking reader, they have been omitted from the text.

From the consideration of what poetry or, specifically, tragedy is, Aristotle turns to what it does or should do—in other words, the effects of poetry. Through pity and fear the action imitated should, accordingly, effect "the proper purgation of these emotions." What exactly is meant by purgation (*katharsis*) is still a matter of controversy. But it does bring us to the question of the involvement of emotions in art—a notion that again has the greatest consequence for later critical thought. Furthermore, this notion also fits in with the conception of an ordered universe so that, as W. J. Bate shows "beneath the theory of *katharsis* lies the general Greek premise that art, in presenting a heightened and harmonious 'imitation' of reality, is formative; that, in enlarging, exercising, and refining one's feelings, and in leading them outward, art possesses a unique power to form the 'total man,' in whom emotion has been reconciled to intelligence and harmoniously integrated with it." (*Criticism*, p. 19.)

In summary, there are six main influential concerns and implications to be seen in Aristotle's *Poetics*. (1) The work of art is imitation of nature. This idea is still central for any discussion of art; consequently, such things as found art, driftwood, and happenings cannot be considered as art. An important implication here is the fact that imitation requires an imitator—an artist. (2) The concern with form and unity (harmony, whole, magnitude). (3) Emphasis on probability rather than real life or history has the corollary that the universal rather than the particular should be stressed. (4) There is an implication of the pleasure principle in art, since, according to Aristotle, we value imitation because it gives us pleasure. He is silent on the didactic values of art. (5) We see also the concern with language—specifically, what words do and how they are effectively used. (6) Also urged is concern with the emotions or the emotional effect of a work of art.

This concern with emotion is developed much further by the second classical critic (both in time and importance): Longinus. His influence begins much later than Aristotle's, but is one that perhaps is more strongly felt today. Unlike Aristotle, Longinus is not preoccupied with the whole work in all its elements; he focuses on what is great, or "sublime," in a work and the reader's necessary enthusiastic response to the sublime. Like Aristotle, however, Longinus also stresses the importance of unity and harmony.

Longinus is the first to focus on single elements in a literary work, on the emotional response and transport of the reader. Longinus also is the first in a long line of critics who attempt to define what is sublime or great in literature: "For that is really great which bears a repeated examination, and which it is difficult or rather impossible to withstand, and the memory of which is strong and hard to efface." What Longinus is attempting to define is what we would call a "classic" today.

For about a thousand years after Longinus critical activity for various historical and social reasons was negligible. However, with Dante, who had definitely not read Longinus' *On the Sublime* or Aristotle's *Poetics*, we find a similar concern: proper language for poetry. For the previous two critics language was but one of the concerns; for Dante, in the particular work presented, it is the only one.

His preoccupation with language can be well understood when we look to the thirteenth century. At that time those who wished to write important works wrote them as a matter of course in the universal language—Latin. Only works meant for popular consumption, such as romances and lyrics, were written in the "vulgar tongue" (tongue of the people, the vernacular). Important works, such as philosophical treatises, Church hymns, and histories, could only be rendered in the language of the Church and the law. To explain and to justify the use of the vernacular in his important work, *The Divine Comedy*, Dante wrote *De Vulgari Eloquentia*. The work is as passionate as it is timely; it is also the first to establish the usefulness, excellence, and expressibility of the vulgar tongues. Therefore, the significance of *De Vulgari Eloquentia* for its own age and later ones cannot be overestimated. As George Saintsbury declares: "For myself, I am prepared to claim for it, not merely the position of the most important critical document between Longinus and the seventeenth century at least, but one of intrinsic importance on a line with that of the very greatest critical documents of all history." (*A History of Criticism and Literary Taste in Europe*, Vol. I [William Blackwood & Sons, 1949], p. 431.)

After the long centuries with almost no critical activity the Renaissance makes up for the silence with an abundance of critical writing. And of all the critics writing in England and on the continent, Sir Philip Sidney is the most influential and the most representative anywhere. J. E. Spingarn in his *Literary Criticism in the Renaissance* makes this strong claim: "His [Sidney's] *Defence of Poesy* [another title for the essay included in this volume] is a veritable epitome of the literary criticism of the Italian Renaissance; and so thoroughly is it imbued with this spirit, that no other work, Italian, French, or English, can be said to give so complete and so noble a conception of the temper and the principles of Renaissance criticism." ([Harcourt, Brace & World, 1963], p. 170)

Sidney is not only the epitome of Renaissance critics; he is also the first in a long line of English poet-critics. This line extends to our day: from Ben Jonson, Dryden, Pope, Wordsworth, Coleridge, Shelley, Arnold, and Poe, to Eliot, Auden, Yeats, Pound, and Shapiro. So much a part of our thinking is the notion of writer-critic that many people argue that only a practitioner of the art is qualified to have critical judgment. Alexander Pope summarized this view in his usual concise manner:

> Let such teach others who themselves excel,
> And censure freely, who have written well.
> *An Essay on Criticism*, Part I, pp. 15–16.

Sidney brought Aristotle's *Poetics* to England by way of his deep reading of Italian criticism. As all other classical writings and themes, Aristotle's thought was refashioned and tempered by the Renaissance. But changed though it was, Sidney's thoughts recognizably stem from the *Poetics*. First, the underlying premise of his criticism is that art is imitation of nature. "Poesie therefore is an arte of imitation, for so Aristotle termeth it in his word *Mimesis* that is to say, a representing, counterfetting, or figuring foorth: to speake metaphorically, a speaking picture. . . ." Secondly, Sidney echoes his master by concerning himself with the relative values of history and poetry. Like Aristotle, though for some different reasons, Sidney proclaims the superiority of poetry over history. He argues with Aristotle that poetry is more universal and that the universal is to be preferred over the particular. He even goes much further and declares that poetry embodies truth.

Being a true proponent of the Renaissance, Sidney's attitude also differs from the classical. Where Aristotle simply defines, analyzes, and classifies, Sidney, along with other Renaissance critics, prescribes and legislates. Aristotle shows his concern with genres by discussing tragedy and the epic; Sidney makes distinctions between genres. He disapproves of tragicomedy, for example, calling it "mongrell," and, Shakespeare's dramas notwithstanding, later critics have echoed Sidney's contempt for the mixing of genres. Aristotle dealt with the unity of action and declared that one revolution of the sun was a preferable time span for a tragedy. Sidney, again along with his fellow critics, especially in France, insists on three Aristotelian unities: of action, time, and place. Finally, Aristotle was greatly preoccupied with what is probable, but Sidney introduces "poetic justice." According to this notion, "we see virtue exalted and vice punished." Clearly, Aristotle would have frowned upon this highly improbable attitude.

Thus Classic thought is reinterpreted, very often with a shift toward rigidity. Literature has become an extremely serious social matter and it is now expected both to teach and delight. It is, however, to Sidney's credit that while he insists on all the weighty arguments for the didactic value of literature, unlike most of his narrow-minded colleagues and successors, he, almost despite himself, proclaims the function of delight of literature. Finally, when all learned arguments, historical examples, and logic have been put forward, *An Apologie for Poetrie* emerges as a plea for poetry and an ecstatic affirmation of it. Thus he ends his serious tract with an emotional, outrageous, and moving curse on those who will not love poetry: ". . . if . . . you be borne so neere the dull making Cataphract of Nilus, that you cannot heare the Plannet-like Musick of Poetrie, if you have so earth-creeping a mind, that it cannot lift it selfe up, to looke to the sky of Poetry . . . then, though I will not wish unto you, the Asses eares of Midas, nor to bee driven by a Poets verses . . . to hang himselfe, nor to be rimed to death, as is sayd to be doone in Ireland: yet thus much curse I must send you in the behalfe of all Poets, that while you live, you live in love, and never get favour, for lacking skill of a Sonnet: and when you die, your memory die from the earth, for want of an Epitaph." In England this kind of passionate, illogical, and eloquent defense of poetry is often part of accepted criticism. In the nineteenth century especially critics such as Shelley wrote in this tradition.

What the Renaissance critics began to codify and prescribe, the Neoclassic (1650–1800) Age carried farther, and poets strove to do their best within strictly marked and delineated critical boundaries. Where the Renaissance critics took much from Aristotle, often distorting his ideas and forgetting to give him credit, the Neoclassicists insisted they were the true interpreters of the Classics. In their often rigid approach, however, they distorted more what the Renaissance had lightly taken as its own.

The English and continental writings are remarkably similar (this fact is brought out by the English critics often simply translating the

French critical works). But perhaps because most of the English critics were also poets, perhaps because of the annoying example of Shakespeare who had not followed the rules and had yet written better than anyone else, or perhaps simply because of the traditional English questioning of authority, the English critics are much more tolerant than their continental colleagues. John Dryden, poet, dramatist, and critic, best exemplifies the Neoclassic Age and at the same time exhibits a tolerance his French contemporary, Du Bellay, for example, was never capable of. "In Dryden, as in Sidney, the disputes of his time are gathered." (Smith and Parks, Introduction, *The Great Critics* [W. W. Norton & Co., 1967], p. xviii.)

Among Aristotelian ideas still flourishing in the seventeenth and eighteenth centuries is that of art being imitation of nature. This is a dictum that forms the premise of all discussion of literature. However, imitation of nature could be done in two different ways: first, imitating it directly, and, secondly, imitating the ancient writers who, it was felt, had imitated nature best. Thus, nature could be imitated twice removed, as it were. The various advantages of these two different approaches, called "imitation of ancients" and "original composition," were argued with tenacity and emotion that are hard to imagine these days. Dryden, in his usual peaceful manner, presents the advantages of both.

Of all the genres in literature, drama was singled out as being most noble and significant for the imitation of nature. It is, of course, no coincidence that Aristotle also emphasized drama. However, drama now had to be of a certain kind: pure and without a mixture of tragedy and comedy, just as Sidney had already recommended, and it had to keep the three unities. By this time the three unities are not even questioned: without them drama is unthinkable.

Another by now well-known Aristotelian concern is that with language, but now the stress is on "proper" diction. A concomitant concern here, as for Aristotle, is the rhythm of verse. Again the emphasis is on "proper," so Chaucer's verse shows his "bad ear." Metaphors, similes, as well as other poetic devices using language, are also examined at length.

Aside from the Aristotelian concerns, Dryden's works also embody the other preoccupations and even attitudes of the age. "Refinement," "correctness," "order," "good sense," and "wit" occur over and over again in Dryden's pages, as these terms do in Du Bellay's, Voltaire's, Pope's, and Johnson's. Literature emerges as a rational and ordered activity in a witty, urbane, and refined society. Emotions have been made orderly and talent is regulated as much as possible. No wonder a later generation rebelled against this view of literature!

Already in the beginning of the eighteenth century there is some chafing against the emphasis on reason and the neglect of emotions. Psychological theories begin to appear and, together with the translation in French of Longinus' *On the Sublime* in 1694, to contribute towards a complete change in critical thinking. Looking back through scholarly glasses, it seems that the change was not sudden, and yet to the people living then and readers now there seems to have occurred one of those revolutions in thought and feeling toward literature that are often proclaimed but rarely happen.

This revolution was slowly heralded in Germany, and then it seemed to come suddenly to England with the publications of the *Lyrical Ballads* by Wordsworth and Coleridge in 1798. This volume of poetry, despite all its ties to previous literature, was obviously something new. Then two years later Wordsworth affixed his manifesto on poetry to the second edition. It is no exaggeration to say that neither poetry nor criticism has been the same since then. Other Romantic poets and critics took up the cry for change; frantic critical activity followed, and we have not yet seen the end. Before, only a few men reflected on literature; now just about everyone considered himself a critic.

What is remarkable about Wordsworth's document, "Preface to the *Lyrical Ballads*" (also called "Observations Prefixed to *Lyrical Ballads*"), and the new era it ushered in is that the premise for literature stayed the same, but what followed from it differed so much. Although Wordsworth introduces new terminology, the similarities to and differences from the previous ages are illuminated if one keeps in mind the Aristotelian terminology, which is definitely not used by Wordsworth. Wordsworth's object of poetry and the reason for its pleasing provide a starting point in the illustration of new and old elements in the manifesto:

> The principal object, then, proposed in these Poems was to choose incidents and situations from common life, and to relate or describe them, throughout, as far as was possible in a selection of language really used by men, and, at the same time, to throw over them a certain colouring of imagination, whereby ordinary things should be presented to the mind in an unusual aspect; and, further, and above all, to make

these incidents and situations interesting by tracing in them, truly though not ostentatiously, the primary laws of our nature: chiefly, as far as regards the manner in which we associate ideas in a state of excitement. Humble and rustic life was generally chosen, because, in that condition, the essential passions of the heart find a better soil in which they can attain their maturity, are less under restraint, and speak a plainer and more emphatic language. . . .

He explains why poetry should please: "Among the chief of these causes is to be reckoned a principle which must be well known to those who have made any of the Arts the object of accurate reflection; namely, the pleasure which the mind derives from the perception of similitude in dissimilitude." The Aristotelian emphases come through very strongly here: the reason why men like imitation is the pleasure principle.

The principal object of poetry is still imitation of nature. The word "nature" still means vaguely the same thing it did to Aristotle, Sidney and Dryden: "life" or "world." Specifically, however, the concept has undergone change. "Nature" now means common, everyday situations and people. Also the concept involves another meaning of nature: mountains, rivers, etc., in short, natural sights. The change in focus is profound and crucial to the development of literature and our reaction to it.

Wordsworth is concerned with not only language but the *proper* language of poetry, and we recall that Aristotle, Longinus, Dante, Sidney, and Dryden were also concerned with it. But again Wordsworth's focus is changed. He wants to use "language really used by men" and these men do not speak in closed couplets, *terza rima*, or elaborate poetic metaphors. (In all fairness, or unfairness, it should be pointed out that Wordsworth wrote excellent sonnets and used rhymes, personifications, apostrophes, and all other poetic devices very skillfully and effectively.)

There are also other shifts and even complete changes in emphases. First, there is the reaction against the Neoclassic rules. This reaction took the form of stressing the spontaneous and free in poetry (even poetry itself, according to one of Wordsworth's definitions, is "the spontaneous overflow of feelings"). In place of "poetic language" one uses the language heard anywhere or picked up at random. In place of perfect iambic pentameters the rhythm of natural speech is sought to be imitated. In place of proper or correct subjects the strange, original, or commonplace are depicted. Also there is a shift, which in some ways is a natural consequence of the first, from reason to emotion. Not only are emotional states sought and portrayed, but the less rational faculty of the mind, imagination, is cultivated and extolled. A consequence of both these changes is the desirable selection of objects for imitation. Children, primitive people (the noble savage), and rural people become the fit subjects for verse.

An important change in the role of the poet also comes about. The poet should suffer and feel as much as possible what he describes others suffering or feeling. Thus Wordsworth writes: "The Poet is chiefly distinguished from other men by a greater promptness to think and feel without immediate external excitement." Whereas before it was taken for granted that the poet was like other men and a member of the society, here is the beginning of the setting apart of the poet from other men. The result of this distance is to make the poet endowed with uncommon, unusual talents and personality traits. Subsequently, the poet's personality and biography become important per se as well as important for the clues they give to his work.

All these shifts really indicate the underlying change from the universal to the concrete. Before, the critics and poets advised poets to seek and to present objectively that which is true for all times and all men. Now, as a consequence of looking for the unusual, the original, and the spontaneous, necessarily the unique experience, the strange, the once-in-a-lifetime feeling or occurrence is depicted, and depicted subjectively.

And yet, even while this change from the universal to the concrete is taking place, Wordsworth draws attention to the Aristotelian notion concerning the philosophical nature and truth of poetry: "Aristotle, I have been told, has said, that Poetry is the most philosophic of all writing: . . . its object is truth, not individual and local, but general, and operative. . . ."

Perhaps the main responsibility for these shifts in critical approaches rests on the different conception of the universe. From Classical through Neoclassical ages, despite the controversies and disputes, the universe was seen as basically an ordered and harmonious entity. Now, if it possesses any order at all, it is an organic one.

It is perhaps typical of human affairs and thought that to any kind of freedom and innovation reaction sets in almost immediately. After the Romantic revolution followed the more conservative period that in

England was called Victorian. During this period Wordsworth's suggested approaches to literature were tentatively explored, and other new approaches—expecially scientific—were formulated; but many critics went back to some pre-Wordsworthian critical notions.

Among these was Matthew Arnold, a very important spokesman for and educator of his age. W. J. Bate shows that Arnold's importance lies ". . . in his constant support of the dignity of critical thinking; his attempt to lift the view of the English-speaking reader toward a wider, more cosmopolitan range; his reapplication of classical criteria; and, above all, his courageous attempt, in an increasingly hostile environment, to reassert the traditional value of literature." (p. 438.)

For the traditional values of literature Arnold goes back to Aristotle and Longinus. He takes Aristotle's observation that the best poetry possesses "higher truth and seriousness" and then in a Longinian fashion, by examining the excellence of particular lines, he determines the higher truth and seriousness of the whole (his famous "touchstone" theory). Like Longinus, he also endeavors to define a classic. His definition is one which echoes the concerns of his age: a classic work is one belonging to the best class. Like both Longinus and Aristotle, he insists on the great importance of diction.

While Arnold looks back, he also looks forward and both influenced later thinking as well as suggested future concerns and pitfalls in criticism. He is among the first who redefines the role of the critic. The critic had been the analyzer, defender, and leader for literature; with Arnold the critic emerges in the now familiar role of arbiter, guide, and authority of literary taste and values. In his writing he also points to future concerns and attitudes. First, he has an ecstatic view of poetry, so it becomes the most important human achievement and end. In fact, it seems to take the place of or is confused with religion. He also sets poetry against science and begins the unfortunate hostility that continues to our day. By considering science, however, he also points to its importance in later critical approaches. Finally, he sees already the danger of historical investigations as well as personal estimates of poetry and therefore pleads not to set them up at the expense of the work of art. Later ages show that his fear was well founded: so much that goes by the name of criticism has led us away from rather than to the work of art.

Thus Arnold, more perhaps than any other critic, stands at the crossroads of criticism. He points both back and forward in critical concerns; he is also the last individual to command an age's respect and to have authority. After Arnold the field of criticism becomes fragmented. No one man can be called a spokesman and no one work can be called representative. If one were to attempt to sum up criticism after Arnold, it would be possible only in terms of diversity and variety.

In what follows, we can see a few of the diverse approaches or concerns of "modern" criticism. In a sense, the modern variety can be seen as a necessary development of the nineteenth-century tendency toward the emphasis on the concrete and particular rather than the universal. Modern critics seldom attempt to assess literature as a whole; they usually examine one or a few specific literary works in terms of one theory or approach.

Typical in that the particular rather than the universal is stressed is Henry James' criticism dealing with just one genre—a genre that the ancients knew nothing about—the novel. It became really respectable only in the nineteenty century, and thus the preoccupation with it is a peculiarly modern one from a nineteenth-century legacy. The concern with this genre can be seen in the great preponderance of criticism of specific novels, the fact that today most people think of the novel when they think of literature, that most young writers choose that as their métier, and the number of critical works devoted to this genre in particular.

Henry James, himself a very fine practitioner in the field, is among the first to attempt to assess the importance of its elements and to form some criteria for judging it. His implied premise could not be more familiar now: art as imitation of nature. Much of his work basically deals with the problem of realism and what is believable (shades of probability and necessity again!) and desirable in fiction. A further Aristotelian echo is found in his reflections on unity and harmony in a work of prose fiction.

Another change from the universal to the particular is seen in the challenge of science that was already taken up in the nineteenth century and continues to be felt to our day. A good example of one who tried to apply the scientific method to literature, even tried to treat literature as science, is Hippolyte Taine. Although he lived in the nineteenth century, his concerns and influence belong to twentieth or modern criticism. He analyzes a work of literature according to three criteria—race, moment, and milieu—and sees the work as a document shaped by and illustrating the three criteria.

Taine was by no means the only one concerned with the scientific method. Zola, for example, attempted to apply the specific methods of medicine to both the writing and the criticizing of a literary work. Today the concern is far from being forgotten. One of the most influential and important contemporary critics, Northrop Frye, begins the essay "Archetypes of Literature" (included in this volume): ". . . while no one expects literature itself to behave like a science, there is surely no reason why criticism, as a systematic and organized study, should not be, at least partly, a science. Not a 'pure' or 'exact' science, perhaps, but these phrases form part of a 19th century cosmology which is no longer with us."

Not only the scientific method but specific sciences have been utilized in literary criticism. Anthropology, linguistics, and biology (especially in connection with the theory of evolution) have had and still have their adherents. Of all of them however, psychology has been found to be the most interesting when applied to a work of art and to the artistic creation itself. Both Freud and Jung showed the way by examining literature from psychological standpoints, and there are few critics who have been completely untouched by the psychological approach or at least its jargon; there are many who deal with it exclusively. The Jung essay included here is an excellent introduction to the problems and aims of the psychological approach to literature. This essay also happens to be an unusually calm and objective consideration of both the artist and the work of art.

The change from the universal to the concrete can nowhere be seen better than in the approach called New Criticism, which perhaps is still today most controversial and influential. It is typical of its concreteness that nowhere is there a general exposition of the method; the method is applied to particular works. Basically, the New Critic examines in detail a specific work. He attempts to examine minutely the work in terms of itself without appealing to outside criteria or values. As far as possible, he even attempts to disregard the temporal period of the literary work. Cleanth Brooks, one of the spokesmen and proponents of this approach, explains: ". . . . what must be sought is an instrument which will allow for some critical precision, and yet one which may be used in the service, not of Romantic poetry or of metaphysical poetry, but of *poetry*." (*The Well-Wrought Urn*, p. 218.) The scientific connotations of "precision" are not accidental in this statement. Although Brooks states specifically that we employ different faculties when doing scientific thinking and reading poetry, this kind of "precision method" inevitably places the approach with most other modern ones strongly influenced by science.

The terms used for looking at poems (the New Critics say that one can examine any literary work in this fashion, but, as a matter of fact, they deal with poetry almost exclusively) are "explication" and "analysis." The first and main step in an explication is a minute examination of the familiar, age-old element: language. To begin with, a practitioner of New Criticism analyzes diction and points out words that are especially rich in connotations; these connotations lead him to comment on their inherent ambiguities and paradoxes. Then the critic will usually turn his attention to various poetic devices employing language, such as metaphor, simile, personification, apostrophe, and the like. A second step, after the examination of the language, may be an analysis of rhythmical and metrical elements. Here the critic will point out variations in rhymes and in meter as well as alliteration and onomatopoeic lines. Thirdly, he may turn his attention to the overall effect of a part or the whole poem: its tone, irony, and imagery.

When practiced by a fine, imaginative critic, such as Cleanth Brooks, this approach can be exciting, suggestive, and emotionally as well as aesthetically satisfying. It can also be practiced by a beginner reader of poetry because the approach provides him with a vocabulary and tools to apply to the poem without any previous knowledge. Herein lies the tremendous influence of this approach. The professor of literature has specific elements to teach or to discuss, and nowadays he is aided by the fact that most college anthologies and introductory as well as advanced college texts are organized and arranged along the line of New Criticism. Chapter headings or division titles in textbooks usually read: "Diction," "Metaphor and Simile," "The Tone of the Poem," etc.; these headings are then followed by a group of poems especially rich in or illustrative of that one element.

This pedagogic value is one reason for the influence and prevalence of this approach. As Northrop Frye remarks: ". . . the criticism of literature is all that can be directly taught. Literature is not a subject of study, but an object of study." (*The Anatomy of Criticism*, p. 11.) Adherents to this approach also feel that by turning to the poem itself, instead of criteria outside it, the reader can finally appreciate the poem and even judge it according to ". . . its coherence, sensitivity, depth, richness, and tough-mindedness." (Brooks, *The Well-Wrought Urn*, p. 256.) Thus each reader becomes a sophisticated critic and combines in his own person the two functions of a critic: to analyze and to evaluate.

Needless to say, so popular and so different an approach from many previous and contemporary ones collects adversaries. They feel that this method is too mechanical, too dry, too unimaginative. The poet, critic, and teacher Karl Shapiro obviously has New Criticism in mind when he makes the following charge: "Textbooks designed for the 'understanding' or 'exploration' of poetry [the best-known and best-selling New Criticism textbook is by Brooks and Warren called *Understanding Poetry*!] have probably done more to warp the literary judgment of college students than the Collected Comic Books of the Twentieth Century. Because they are based on the 'depersonalized' view of literature and life, they all tend toward the extinction of the faculty of judgment, one of man's most vital characteristics. My experience with students who have been subjected to these dry and terrible tomes, the very paper of which seems impregnated with lead, is that they are utterly and permanently stunned into literary insensibility." (*In Defense of Ignorance* [Vintage Books, 1965], p. 12.)

Another very influential and controversial contemporary approach goes by the names of "mythic" or "archetypal" criticism. This approach is by no means new; a version of it was already practiced in the nineteenth century, so it is really another nineteenth-century legacy to our century. However, it seems novel because of some forceful, cogent, and productive spokesmen for it, among them Northrop Frye. Archetypal criticism has also gained in respectability as more and more modern writers' utilization of and dependence on myth have been recognized.

Like the New Criticism, this approach attempts to be scientific when dealing with literature by analyzing elements that are present in all literature and thereby introducing as much precision as possible into the discussion of literature. As in New Criticism, so in archetypal criticism particular, concrete examples are examined in terms of universal elements present in all literature. If the mention of "universal" recalls Aristotle again, this is no coincidence. Frye continually refers to Aristotle and, in fact, founds his theories on "art as imitation of nature," "proper magnitude," and a work having "beginning, middle, and end."

The universal elements present in all literature are called archetypes by Northrop Frye and his adherents. "An archetypal symbol is usually a natural object with a human meaning, and it forms part of the critical

view of art as a civilized product, a vision of the goals of human work."
(*Anatomy of Criticism* [Princeton U. Press, 1957], p. 113.) Let us take
the particular, concrete example of a natural object, water—an object,
by the way, that W. H. Auden has examined in an extremely interesting
manner in *The Enchafèd Flood*. Now water has meaning and specific
associations in our culture which are primarily learned from myths and
figure consciously and unconsciously in a literary work; some of the
associations with water are: life, rebirth, purity. Writers have always
utilized these associations (Milton in *Lycidas*, for example, calls up all
the associations with water), but it is especially in modern literature
that writers, such as Yeats, Joyce, Pound, Auden, Eliot, have consciously
counted on them when introducing a natural object (here T. S. Eliot's
The Waste Land quickly comes to mind).

Archetypal criticism provides a framework within which to discuss all
literature without reference to personalities or periods and helps make
some kind of order out of the myriad concerns and themes of literature.
T. S. Eliot makes this claim for the mythic critical method: "It is
simply a way of controlling, of ordering, of giving a shape and a significance to the immense panorama of futility and anarchy which is
contemporary history. . . . It is, I seriously believe, a step toward making
the modern world possible for art. . . ." ("'Ulysses,' Order, and Myth.")
Eliot's words bring us back to an Aristotelian concern that we have not
met since the Neoclassic age: order.

The last approach presented in this volume defies accurate labeling,
but for lack of a better word I call it the "stylistic" approach. Erich
Auerbach is the most important and influential critic of this kind.
In his major work *Mimesis*, he examines specific texts for different
periods from the standpoint of style. "Style" is used in a very loose
sense, as the summary at the end of his discussion of Homer's *Odyssey*
and the Old Testament shows:

> We have compared these two texts, and, with them, the two kinds
> of style they embody, in order to reach a starting point for an investi-
> gation into the literary representation of reality in European culture.
> The two styles, in their opposition, represent basic types: on the one
> hand fully externalized description, uniform illumination, uninterrup-
> ted connection, free expression, all events in the foreground, displaying
> unmistakable meanings, few elements of historical development and of
> psychological perspective; on the other hand, certain parts brought into
> high relief, others left obscure, abruptness, suggestive influence of the

unexpressed, "background" quality, multiplicity of meanings and the need for interpretation, universal-historical claims, development of the concept of the historically becoming, and preoccupation with the problematic.

"Representation of reality," which is also the subtitle of *Mimesis*, is another way of expressing Aristotle's dictum of art as imitation of nature. Like Frye, Auerbach begins with this dictum. What they have to say follows as a consequence of examining how literature actually imitates nature. So we have come full circle.

We have really come so completely full circle that the concerns of Aristotle can still be seen as the important and guiding ones. Despite the hoarse cries of "now" and "today," we see that while sometimes terminology and emphases may change—let us say from "proper language" to "language really used by men"—the concerns remain the same. Thus one can agree with Allen Tate: "The permanent critics do not settle the question. They compel us to ask it again. They are the rotating chairmen of a debate only the rhetoric of which changes from time to time." (*Lectures in Criticism*, p. 70.)

Although the basic concerns do not change, there are changes in general tendencies over the hundreds of years. These can be generally summarized. First, there is the movement of emphasis from general and universal to specific and particular. There is a change from viewing all literature, even all art, forming a whole to a minute examination of a work, even one stanza or one word, as is done in the scholarly journals and in the New Critics' writings. A concomitant result of this tendency can be seen as the change from the objective to the subjective examination of a literary work.

This trend from objective to subjective is also related to another change from the implied or expressed assumptions of rational bases of art to emphasis on emotion or nonrationality. Except for Longinus, from Aristotle to the end of the eighteenth-century critics, the rational foundation of art was never questioned. Since the Romantics, exemplified by Wordsworth, however, we have become accustomed to thinking of literature as not involving reason so much as emotion. Especially in the twentieth century the feeling has been strong that the writing and appreciation of literature involve other faculties—associative, subconscious, inspirational—that are taken as the very opposites of the rational.

Besides these two important critical trends, there is a change in the concept of a critic and therefore criticism. Here Matthew Arnold again stands at the midpoint of the change. This trend has gone from a prescriptive role (the critic explains what a literary work should have or be) to an analytic role (what a work is or has). For many hundreds of years the critic was one who laid down the rules for literature and then evaluated and judged according to these rules. In a sense the critic had an important social function to perform as the judge and arbiter of culture. Today, while some critics still assume these functions, the stress is on the subjective and individual discussions of a particular work. He may still judge but primarily to evaluate; he may arbitrate but mainly to put forward his appreciation of or insights into a literary work.

The essays selected for this volume illustrate these trends. The essays also should, of course, illustrate and explain in detail the important critical concerns that have been traced and summarized here. Actually the essays were chosen because they have been held important and because they have influenced other critics or other literature. That they finally form a coherent whole, concerned with many of the same critical ideas, is a testimony to the basic unity of our culture.

Selecting the "classics" of criticism up to the end of the nineteenth century was relatively easy, then. The critics really chose themselves or were already chosen by the judgment through the ages. This is not to say that other critics could not have been chosen—that these in the volume were the only possible choices. Goethe or the Schlegel brothers could have been included instead of Wordsworth, Sainte-Beuve instead of Arnold, Corneille instead of Dryden, just to mention a few possible substitutions. However, because it is possible to have important English works rather than translations, the English critical writings seem preferable. Most readers are probably more familiar with the English critics, especially since many of them are well-known writers too. The reader may also have knowledge of the English literature which the critics use to illustrate their points.

The classics are the representatives of their centuries; the modern would-be classics are representative of the current concerns. Here again no attempt was made to select the critics who would best illustrate the overriding and emphatic critical concerns I have outlined before. Many could have been chosen who are much closer descendants of Aristotle or Wordsworth. The choice finally rests again on the considerations of importance, influence, and some representativeness. These choices, however, more than the ones before late nineteenth century, are, I confess, subjective.

One has to make a choice among the myriad of approaches in the twentieth century. Besides the ones included in the anthology, concerns, named at random and without any attempt to be exhaustive, that could have also been included are: historical, biographical, textual, religious, moral, symbolic, linguistic, Neo-Aristotelian, generic (genre criticism), appreciative, and traditional (such as T. S. Eliot's criticism). Each of these has dozens of offshoots and variations; this is especially true for two approaches I have included: socio-historical (Taine) and scientific (Taine and Jung). Actually the great variety of approaches possible today is reflected in this volume by the much larger number of modern critics included, as compared with the critics of previous ages.

Finally, the points I have made in this introductory essay are the following. (1) There is no very good or agreed upon definition of criticism. (2) Aristotle is not only the founder of literary criticism, but has had the greatest influence throughout its history. (3) Critics write not only with respect to literature but also with respect and in reaction to each other. (4) There has been a trend since the nineteenth century away from the universal concerns in literature toward concrete particulars. (5) This trend has in modern times fragmented critical responses, so simple critical descriptions of criticism are difficult, if not impossible, to give.

1. ARISTOTLE

Poetics

Aristotle (384–322 B.C.), one of the greatest philosophers, was born in Stagira, where his father was court physician to Amyntas II, the father of Philip. When Aristotle was seventeen years old, he became a student of Plato in Athens, where he stayed until Plato's death (347 B.C.). Afterward he taught in Assus in Asia Minor at a colony of Platonists. From 342 B.C. he taught Philip's son, Alexander of Macedon, until his accession to power in 336 B.C.

Aristotle possessed one of the greatest minds of all time. There is hardly a field of human knowledge to which he did not apply his acute intelligence, and there are few areas of thought which were not originally based on his investigations. He was as profound as he was prolific: the complete translated works of Aristotle comprise eleven volumes in the Oxford edition. The variety of his interests can be seen from some titles of his important works: *Physics, Politics, Metaphysics, Rhetoric, Nicomachean Ethics, Organon, On Generation and Corruption, On the Soul.*

Many of his works are also believed to be lost. According to ancient authorities, among these were early literary works, which were heavily influenced by Plato. His serious interest in literature is demonstrated by the incomplete *Poetics* in which he cites literally hundreds of lines of poetry and mentions many tragedies and poems with which he seems thoroughly familiar.

Much concerning the *Poetics* is unknown or controversial. For example, some modern authorities think that the *Poetics*, like Aristotle's other works, is a later compilation of students' lecture notes. It is not even known how influential the work was in antiquity. Later, in the tenth century, most of his works were translated and wielded tremendous influence; the *Poetics*, however, seems to have been forgotten until Petrarch's time. "The beginning of the Aristotelian influence on modern literary theory may be said to date from the year 1536, in which year Trincaveli published a Greek text of the *Poetics*, Pazzi his edition and Latin version, and Daniello his own *Poetica*." (Spingarn, p. 85.)

In the *Poetics* Aristotle deals with what poetry is, its essential quality, origin, types, structure, necessary parts, and anything else that may be appropriate. Important and influential elements of the essay have already been discussed generally in the Introduction, but some particulars should be noted. Aristotle finds that tragedy and epic are the most important genres; however, the first and main portion of the work, as it has come down to us, deals with tragedy. Consequently, his ideas concerning this genre are most important for us. After his definition of tragedy he lists the six necessary parts of it: plot, character, diction, thought, spectacle, and song. The plot he calls "the soul of tragedy," character holds second place, while he defines "thought" as "the faculty of saying what is possible and pertinent in given circumstances." He also says that he will not talk much about it because he has dealt with it sufficiently in the *Rhetoric*. How important he considered diction can be seen from the length of the discussion: four long chapters. These chapters have been omitted almost in their entirety because an understanding of them depends on the knowledge of the Greek language and literature and its rhythm. Spectacle, which included elaborate stage machinery and props on the Greek stage, he does not have much to say about. His most important reflection on the subject, and one really dealing with the plot is that the conflict should not be resolved by a *deus ex machina*, literally, "god from the machine." By this he means that very common epic device whereby a character is rescued from a difficult situation by a god (for example, in the *Iliad* Aphrodite gathers Paris up in a cloud and places him in his bedroom when it looks as if he might die in single combat with Menelaus). The last of the six elements, song or music, was very important in the Greek theatre, but none of it has survived and Aristotle has little to say about it anyway.

Let us look at the "soul of tragedy"—plot. A tragedy should contain events according to the "law of probability and necessity" and should present a change from good to bad fortune, or vice versa. Plots may be divided into two different kinds: complex and simple. A complex plot is one in which the change is accompanied by a reversal of the situation, or by recognition, or by both. When explaining the reversal of a situation, Aristotle begins to use Sophocles' *Oedipus the*

King as a paradigm, which he seems to consider the best of tragedies and one which certainly fits best the Aristotelian view of tragedy. Reversal is simply that: action goes to the opposite (from king to beggar; the messenger comes to calm, but actually upsets everything, etc.). Recognition is a specific kind of reversal: change from ignorance to knowledge. It may be of actions or objects but is best of persons. Both recognition and reversal will produce pity and fear, which are then purged (this notion of purgation, *katharsis*, was mentioned already in the Introduction). It is clear that a tragedy is better with a complex plot rather than a simple one, which lacks reversal and recognition.

From plot we are easily led into character. The change of fortune should occur to a man "who is not eminently good or just, yet whose misfortune is brought about not by vice or depravity, but by some error or frailty" (some translators use the word "flaw" for "error" or "frailty"). It is best if the tragedy presents a man who is slightly better than we are. Besides being good, he must be presented with propriety, he must be true to life, and he must be consistent. The aim should always be at the necessary and the probable.

Finally, he turns to the structure of tragedy. A tragedy should fall into two parts: complication and unraveling. Complication is "all that extends from the beginning of the action to the part which marks the turning-point to good or bad fortune. The unraveling is that which extends from the beginning of the change to the end."

Aristotle's remaining discussion of the epic is not as important. Basically, the epic is very much like a tragedy, except that it is narrative rather than dramatic; it is longer; it may have several lines of action. He considers it inferior to tragedy because tragedy "attains its end within narrower limits; for the concentrated effect is more pleasurable than one which is spread over a long time and diluted." Finally, and perhaps most importantly, an epic has less unity than a tragedy. "Unity," "order," "harmony" are the guiding lights for Aristotle. A work which has them has everything; a work which lacks them completely lacks everything.

This selection is taken from the translation by Henry Butcher.*

I propose to treat of Poetry in itself and of its various kinds, noting the essential quality of each; to inquire into the structure of the plot as requisite to a good poem; into the number and nature of the parts of which a poem is composed; and similarly into whatever else falls within the same inquiry. Following, then, the order of nature, let us begin with the principles which come first.

2. Epic poetry and Tragedy, Comedy also and Dithyrambic poetry,

* London, Macmillan, 1902, third ed.

and the music of the flute and of the lyre in most of their forms, are all in their general conception modes of imitation. 3. They differ, however, from one another in three respects,—the medium, the objects, the manner or mode of imitation, being in each case distinct.

4. For as there are persons who, by conscious art or mere habit, imitate and represent various objects through the medium of colour and form, or again by the voice; so in the arts above mentioned, taken as a whole, the imitation is produced by rhythm, language, or "harmony," either singly or combined.

Thus in the music of the flute and of the lyre, "harmony" and rhythm alone are employed; also in other arts, such as that of the shepherd's pipe, which are essentially similar to these. 5. In dancing, rhythm alone is used without "harmony"; for even dancing imitates character, emotion, and action, by rhythmical movement.

6. There is another art which imitates by means of language alone, and that either in prose or verse—which verse, again, may either combine different metres or consist of but one kind—but this has hitherto been without a name. 7. For there is no common term we could apply to the mimes of Sophron and Xenarchus and the Socratic dialogues on the one hand; and, on the other, to poetic imitations in iambic, elegiac, or any similar metre. People do, indeed, add the word "maker" or "poet" to the name of the metre, and speak of elegiac poets, or epic (that is, hexameter) poets, as if it were not the imitation that makes the poet, but the verse that entitles them all indiscriminately to the name. 8. Even when a treatise on medicine or natural science is brought out in verse, the name of poet is by custom given to the author; and yet Homer and Empedocles have nothing in common but the metre, so that it would be right to call the one poet, the other physicist rather than poet. 9. On the same principle, even if a writer in his poetic imitation were to combine all metres, as Chaeremon did in his Centaur, which is a medley composed of metres of all kinds, we should bring him too under the general term poet. So much then for these distinctions.

10. There are, again, some arts which employ all the means above mentioned,—namely, rhythm, tune and metre. Such are Dithyrambic and Nomic poetry, and also Tragedy and Comedy; but between them the difference is, that in the first two cases these means are all employed in combination, in the latter, now one means is employed, now another.

Such, then, are the differences of the arts with respect to the medium of imitation.

2

Since the objects of imitation are men in action, and these men must be either of a higher or a lower type (for moral character mainly answers to these divisions, goodness and badness being the distinguishing marks of moral differences), it follows that we must represent men either as better than in real life, or as worse, or as they are. It is the same in painting: Polygnotus depicted men as nobler than they are, Pauson as less noble, Dionysius drew them true to life.

2. Now it is evident that each of the modes of imitation above mentioned will exhibit these differences, and become a distinct kind in imitating objects that are thus distinct. 3. Such diversities may be found even in dancing, flute-playing, and lyre-playing. So again in language, whether prose or verse unaccompanied by music. Homer, for example, makes men better than they are; Cleophon as they are; Hegemon the Thasian, the inventor of parodies, and Nicochares, the author of the Deiliad, worse than they are. 4. The same thing holds good of Dithyrambs and Nomes; here too one may portray different types, as Timotheus and Philoxenus differed in representing their Cyclopes. The same distinction marks off Tragedy from Comedy; for Comedy aims at representing men as worse, Tragedy as better than in actual life.

3

There is still a third difference—the manner in which each of these objects may be imitated. For the medium being the same, and the objects the same, the poet may imitate by narration—in which case he can either take another personality as Homer does, or speak in his own person, unchanged—or he may present all his characters as living and moving before us.

2. These, then, as we said at the beginning, are the three differences which distinguish artistic imitation—the medium, the objects and the manner. So that from one point of view, Sophocles is an imitator of the same kind as Homer—for both imitate higher types of character; from another point of view, of the same kind as Aristophanes—for both imitate persons acting and doing. 3. Hence, some say, the name of "drama" is given to such poems, as representing action. . . .

4. This may suffice as to the number and nature of the various modes of imitation.

4

Poetry in general seems to have sprung from two causes, each of them lying deep in our nature. 2. First, the instinct of imitation is implanted in man from childhood, one difference between him and other animals being that he is the most imitative of living creatures, and through imitation he learns his earliest lessons; and no less universal is the pleasure felt in things imitated. 3. We have evidence of this in the facts of experience. Objects which in themselves we view with pain, we delight to contemplate when reproduced with minute fidelity: such as the forms of the most ignoble animals and of dead bodies. 4. The cause of this again is, that to learn gives the liveliest pleasure, not only to philosophers but to men in general; whose capacity, however, of learning is more limited. 5. Thus the reason why men enjoy seeing a likeness is, that in contemplating it they find themselves learning or inferring, and saying perhaps, "Ah, that is he." For if you happen not to have seen the original, the pleasure will be due not to the imitation as such, but to the execution, the colouring, or some such other cause.

6. Imitation, then, is one instinct of our nature. Next, there is the instinct for "harmony" and rhythm, metres being manifestly sections of rhythm. Persons, therefore, starting with this natural gift developed by degrees their special aptitudes, till their rude improvisations gave birth to Poetry.

7. Poetry now diverged in two directions, according to the individual character of the writers. The graver spirits imitated noble actions, and the actions of good men. The more trivial sort imitated the actions of meaner persons, at first composing satires, as the former did hymns to the gods and the praises of famous men. 8. A poem of the satirical kind cannot indeed be put down to any author earlier than Homer; though many such writers probably there were. But from Homer onward, instances can be cited,—his own Margites, for example, and other similar compositions. The appropriate metre was also here introduced; hence the measure is still called the iambic or lampooning measure, being that in which people lampooned one another. 9. Thus the older poets were distinguished as writers of heroic or of lampooning verse.

As, in the serious style, Homer is pre-eminent among poets, for he alone combined dramatic form with excellence of imitation, so he too first laid down the main lines of Comedy, by dramatising the ludicrous instead of writing personal satire. His Margites bears the same relation to Comedy that the Iliad and Odyssey do to Tragedy. 10. But when Tragedy and Comedy came to light, the two classes of poets still followed their natural bent: the lampooners became writers of Comedy, and the Epic poets were succeeded by Tragedians, since the drama was a larger and higher form of art.

11. Whether Tragedy has as yet perfected its proper types or not; and whether it is to be judged in itself, or in relation also to the audience,—this raises another question. 12. Be that as it may, Tragedy—as also Comedy—was at first mere improvisation. The one originated with the authors of the Dithyramb, the other with those of the phallic songs, which are still in use in many of our cities. Tragedy advanced by slow degrees; each new element that showed itself was in turn developed. Having passed through many changes, it found its natural form, and there it stopped.

13. Aeschylus first introduced a second actor; he diminished the importance of the Chorus, and assigned the leading part to the dialogue. Sophocles raised the number of actors to three, and added scene-painting. 14. Moreover, it was not till late that the short plot was discarded for one of greater compass, and the grotesque diction of the earlier satyric form for the stately manner of Tragedy. The iambic measure then replaced the trochaic tetrameter, which was originally employed when the poetry was of the satyric order, and had greater affinities with dancing. Once dialogue had come in, Nature herself discovered the appropriate measure. For the iambic is, of all measures, the most colloquial: we see it in the fact that conversational speech runs into iambic form more frequently than into any other kind of verse; rarely into hexameters, and only when we drop the colloquial intonation. 15. The additions to the number of "episodes" or acts, and the other accessories of which tradition tells, must be taken as already described; for to discuss them in detail would, doubtless, be a large undertaking.

5

Comedy is, as we have said, an imitation of characters of a lower type—not, however, in the full sense of the word bad, the Ludicrous being merely a subdivision of the ugly. It consists in some defect or ugliness which is not painful or destructive. To take an obvious example, the comic mask is ugly and distorted, but does not imply pain.

2. The successive changes through which Tragedy passed, and the authors of these changes are well known, whereas Comedy has had no history, because it was not at first treated seriously. It was late before the Archon granted a comic chorus to a poet; the performers were till then voluntary. Comedy had already taken definite shape when comic poets, distinctively so called, are heard of. 3. Who introduced masks, or prologues, or increased the number of actors,—these and other similar details remain unknown. As for the plot, it came originally from Sicily; but of Athenian writers Crates was the first who, abandoning the "iambic" or lampooning form, generalised his themes and plots.

4. Epic poetry agrees with Tragedy in so far as it is an imitation in verse of characters of a higher type. They differ in that Epic poetry admits but one kind of metre and is narrative in form. They differ, again, in their length: for Tragedy endeavours, as far as possible, to confine itself to a single revolution of the sun, or but slightly to exceed this limit; whereas the Epic action has no limits of time. This, then, is a second point of difference; though at first the same freedom was admitted in Tragedy as in Epic poetry.

5. Of their constituent parts some are common to both, some peculiar to Tragedy. Whoever, therefore, knows what is good or bad Tragedy, knows also about Epic poetry. All the elements of an Epic poem are found in Tragedy, but the elements of a Tragedy are not all found in the Epic poem.

6

Of the poetry which imitates in hexameter verse, and of Comedy, we will speak hereafter. Let us now discuss Tragedy, resuming its formal definition, as resulting from what has been already said.

2. Tragedy, then, is an imitation of an action that is serious, complete, and of a certain magnitude; in language embellished with each kind of artistic ornament, the several kinds being found in separate parts of the play; in the form of action, not of narrative; through pity and fear effecting the proper purgation of these emotions. 3. By "language embellished," I mean language into which rhythm, "harmony," and song enter. By "the several kinds in separate parts," I mean, that some parts are rendered through the medium of verse alone, others again with the aid of song.

4. Now as tragic imitation implies persons acting, it necessarily

follows, in the first place, that Spectacular equipment will be a part of Tragedy. Next, Song and Diction, for these are the medium of imitation. By "Diction" I mean the mere metrical arrangement of the words: as for "Song," it is a term whose sense every one understands.

5. Again, Tragedy is the imitation of an action; and an action implies personal agents, who necessarily possess certain distinctive qualities both of character and thought; for it is by these that we qualify actions themselves, and these—thought and character—are the two natural causes from which actions spring, and on actions again all success or failure depends. 6. Hence, the Plot is the imitation of the action:—for by plot I here mean the arrangement of the incidents. By Character I mean that in virtue of which we ascribe certain qualities to the agents. Thought is required wherever a statement is proved, or, it may be, a general truth enunciated. 7. Every Tragedy, therefore, must have six parts, which parts determine its quality—namely, Plot, Character, Diction, Thought, Spectacle, Song. Two of the parts constitute the medium of imitation, one the manner, and three the objects of imitation. And these complete the list. 8. These elements have been employed, we may say, by the poets to a man; in fact, every play contains Spectacular elements as well as Character, Plot, Diction, Song, and Thought.

9. But most important of all is the structure of the incidents. For Tragedy is an imitation, not of men, but of an action and of life, and life consists in action, and its end is a mode of action, not a quality. 10. Now character determines men's qualities, but it is by their actions that they are happy or the reverse. Dramatic action, therefore, is not with a view to the representation of character: character comes in as subsidiary to the actions. Hence the incidents and the plot are the end of a tragedy; and the end is the chief thing of all. 11. Again, without action there cannot be a tragedy; there may be without character. The tragedies of most of our modern poets fail in the rendering of character; and of poets in general this is often true. It is the same in painting; and here lies the difference between Zeuxis and Polygnotus. Polygnotus delineates character well: the style of Zeuxis is devoid of ethical quality. 12. Again, if you string together a set of speeches expressive of character, and well finished in point of diction and thought, you will not produce the essential tragic effect nearly so well as with a play which, however deficient in these respects, yet has a plot and artistically constructed incidents. 13. Besides which, the most powerful elements of emotional interest in Tragedy—Peripeteia or Reversal of the situation,

and Recognition scenes—are parts of the plot. 14. A further proof is, that novices in the art attain to finish of diction and precision of portraiture before they can construct the plot. It is the same with almost all the early poets.

The Plot, then, is the first principle, and, as it were, the soul of a tragedy: Character holds the second place. 15. A similar fact is seen in painting. The most beautiful colours, laid on confusedly, will not give as much pleasure as the chalk outline of a portrait. Thus Tragedy is the imitation of an action, and of the agents mainly with a view to the action.

16. Third in order is Thought,—that is, the faculty of saying what is possible and pertinent in given circumstances. In the case of oratory, this is the function of the political art and of the art of rhetoric: and so indeed the older poets make their characters speak the language of civic life; the poets of our time, the language of the rhetoricians.

17. Character is that which reveals moral purpose, showing what kind of things a man chooses or avoids. Speeches, therefore, which do not make this manifest, or in which the speaker does not choose or avoid anything whatever, are not expressive of character. Thought, on the other hand, is found where something is proved to be or not to be, or a general maxim is enunciated.

18. Fourth among the elements enumerated comes Diction; by which I mean, as has been already said, the expression of the meaning in words; and its essence is the same both in verse and prose.

19. Of the remaining elements Song holds the chief place among the embellishments.

The Spectacle has, indeed, an emotional attraction of its own, but, of all the parts, it is the least artistic, and connected least with the art of poetry. For the power of Tragedy, we may be sure, is felt even apart from representation and actors. Besides, the production of spectacular effects depends more on the art of the stage machinist than that of the poet.

7

These principles being established, let us now discuss the proper structure of the Plot, since this is the first and most important thing in Tragedy.

2. Now, according to our definition, Tragedy is an imitation of an action that is complete, and whole, and of a certain magnitude; for

there may be a whole that is wanting in magnitude. 3. A whole is that which has a beginning, a middle, and an end. A beginning is that which does not itself follow anything by causal necessity, but after which something naturally is or comes to be. An end, on the contrary, is that which itself naturally follows some other thing, either by necessity, or as a rule, but has nothing following it. A middle is that which follows something as some other thing follows it. A well constructed plot, therefore, must neither begin nor end at haphazard, but conform to these principles.

4. Again, a beautiful object, whether it be a picture of a living organism or any whole composed of parts, must not only have an orderly arrangement of parts, but must also be of a certain magnitude; for beauty depends on magnitude and order. Hence an exceedingly small picture cannot be beautiful; for the view of it is confused, the object being seen in an almost imperceptible moment of time. Nor, again, can one of vast size be beautiful; for as the eye cannot take it all in at once, the unity and sense of the whole is lost for the spectator; as for instance if there were one a thousand miles long. 5. As, therefore, in the case of animate bodies and organisms a certain magnitude is necessary, and a magnitude which may be easily embraced in one view; so in the plot, a certain length is necessary, and a length which can be easily embraced by the memory. 6. The limit of length in relation to dramatic competition and sensuous presentment, is no part of artistic theory. For had it been the rule for a hundred tragedies to compete together, the performance would have been regulated by the water-clock,—as indeed we are told was formerly done. 7. But the limit as fixed by the nature of the drama itself is this:—the greater the length, the more beautiful will the piece be by reason of its size, provided that the whole be perspicuous. And to define the matter roughly, we may say that the proper magnitude is comprised within such limits, that the sequence of events, according to the law of probability or necessity, will admit of a change from bad fortune to good, or from good fortune to bad.

8

Unity of plot does not, as some persons think, consist in the unity of the hero. For infinitely various are the incidents in one man's life, which cannot be reduced to unity; and so, too, there are many actions of one man out of which we cannot make one action. 2. Hence, the error as it appears, of all poets who have composed a Heracleid, a Theseid, or other poems of the kind. They imagine that as Heracles was one man, the story of Heracles must also be a unity. 3. But Homer, as in all else he is of surpassing merit, here too—whether from art or natural genius—seems to have happily discerned the truth. In composing the Odyssey he did not include all the adventures of Odysseus—such as his wound on Parnassus, or his feigned madness at the mustering of the host—incidents between which there was no necessary or probable connexion: but he made the Odyssey, and likewise the Iliad, to centre round an action that in our sense of the word is one. 4. As therefore, in the other imitative arts, the imitation is one when the object imitated is one, so the plot, being an imitation of an action, must imitate one action and that a whole, the structural union of the parts being such that, if any one of them is displaced or removed, the whole will be disjointed and disturbed. For a thing whose presence or absence makes no visible difference, is not an organic part of the whole.

9

It is, moreover, evident from what has been said, that it is not the function of the poet to relate what has happened, but what may happen,—what is possible according to the law of probability or necessity. 2. The poet and the historian differ not by writing in verse or in prose. The work of Herodotus might be put into verse, and it would still be a species of history, with metre no less than without it. The true difference is that one relates what has happened, the other what may happen. 3. Poetry, therefore, is a more philosophical and a higher thing than history: for poetry tends to express the universal, history the particular. 4. By the universal I mean how a person of a certain type will on occasion speak or act, according to the law of probability or necessity; and it is this universality at which poetry aims in the names she attaches to the personages. The particular is—for example—what Alcibiades did or suffered. 5. In Comedy this is already apparent: for here the poet first constructs the plot on the lines of probability, and then inserts characteristic names;—unlike the lampooners who write about particular individuals. 6. But tragedians still keep to real names, the reason being that what is possible is credible: what has not happened we do not at once feel sure to be possible: but what has happened is manifestly possible: otherwise it would not have happened. 7. Still there are some tragedies in which there are only one or two well known names, the rest being fictitious. In others, none are well known,—as in Agathon's Antheus, where incidents and names alike are fictitious, and yet they give none the less pleasure. 8. We must not, therefore, at all costs keep to the received legends, which are the usual subjects of Tragedy. Indeed, it would be absurd to attempt it; for even subjects that are known are known only to a few, and yet give pleasure to all. 9. It clearly follows that the poet or "maker" should be the maker of plots rather than of verses; since he is a poet because he imitates, and what he imitates are actions. And even if he chances to take an historical subject, he is none the less a poet; for there is no reason why some events that have actually happened should not conform to the law of the probable and possible, and in virtue of that quality in them he is their poet or maker.

10. Of all plots and actions the epeisodic are the worst. I call a plot "epeisodic" in which the episodes or acts succeed one another without probable or necessary sequence. Bad poets compose such pieces by their own fault, good poets, to please the players; for, as they write show pieces for competition, they stretch the plot beyond its capacity, and are often forced to break the natural continuity.

11. But again, Tragedy is an imitation not only of a complete action, but of events inspiring fear or pity. Such an effect is best produced when the events come on us by surprise; and the effect is heightened when, at the same time, they follow as cause and effect. 12. The tragic wonder will then be greater than if they happened of themselves or by accident; for even coincidences are most striking when they have an air of design. We may instance the statue of Mitys at Argos, which fell upon his murderer while he was a spectator at a festival, and killed him. Such events seem not to be due to mere chance. Plots, therefore, constructed on these principles are necessarily the best.

10

Plots are either Simple or Complex, for the actions in real life, of which the plots are an imitation, obviously show a similar distinction. 2. An action which is one and continuous in the sense above defined, I call Simple, when the change of fortune takes place without Reversal of the Situation and without Recognition.

A Complex action is one in which the change is accompanied by such Reversal, or by Recognition, or by both. 3. These last should arise from the internal structure of the plot, so that what follows should be the necessary or probable result of the preceding action. It makes all the difference whether any given event is a case of *propter hoc* or *post hoc* ["because of this" or "after this."].

11

Reversal of the Situation is a change by which the action veers round to its opposite, subject always to our rule of probability or necessity. Thus in the Oedipus, the messenger comes to cheer Oedipus and free him from his alarms about his mother, but by revealing who he is, he produces the opposite effect. Again in the Lynceus, Lynceus is being led away to his death, and Danaus goes with him, meaning to slay him; but the outcome of the action is, that Danaus is killed and Lynceus saved.

2. Recognition, as the name indicates, is a change from ignorance to knowledge, producing love or hate between the persons destined by the poet for good or bad fortune. The best form of recognition is coincident with a Reversal of the Situation, as in the Oedipus. 3. There are indeed other forms. Even inanimate things of the most trivial kind may sometimes be objects of recognition. Again, we may recognise or discover whether a person has done a thing or not. But the recognition which is most intimately connected with the plot and action is, as we have said, the recognition of persons. 4. This recognition, combined with Reversal, will produce either pity or fear; and actions producing these effects are those which, by our definition, Tragedy represents. Moreover, it is upon such situations that the issues of good or bad fortune will depend. 5. Recognition, then, being between persons, it may happen that one person only is recognised by the other—when the latter is already known—or it may be necessary that the recognition should be on both sides. Thus Iphigenia is revealed to Orestes by the sending of the letter; but another act of recognition is required to make Orestes known to Iphigenia.

6. Two parts, then, of the Plot—Reversal of the Situation and Recognition—turn upon surprises. A third part is the Scene of Suffering. The Scene of Suffering is a destructive or painful action, such as death on the stage, bodily agony, wounds, and the like. . . .

13

As the sequel to what has already been said, we must proceed to consider what the poet should aim at, and what he should avoid, in constructing his plots; and by what means the specific effect of Tragedy will be produced.

2. A perfect tragedy should, as we have seen, be arranged not on the simple but on the complex plan. It should, moreover, imitate actions which excite pity and fear, this being the distinctive mark of tragic imitation. It follows plainly, in the first place, that the change of fortune presented must not be the spectacle of a virtuous man brought from prosperity to adversity: for this moves neither pity nor fear; it merely shocks us. Nor, again, that of a bad man passing from adversity to prosperity: for nothing can be more alien to the spirit of Tragedy; it possesses no single tragic quality; it neither satisfies the moral sense, nor calls forth pity or fear. Nor, again, should the downfall of the utter villain be exhibited. A plot of this kind would, doubtless, satisfy the moral sense, but it would inspire neither pity nor fear; for pity is aroused by unmerited misfortune, fear by the misfortune of a man like ourselves. Such an event, therefore, will be neither pitiful nor terrible. 3. There remains, then, the character between these two extremes,—that of a man who is not eminently good and just, yet whose misfortune is brought about not by vice or depravity, but by some error or frailty. He must be one who is highly renowned and prosperous,—a personage like Oedipus, Thyestes, or other illustrious men of such families.

4. A well constructed plot should, therefore, be single in its issue, rather than double as some maintain. The change of fortune should be not from bad to good, but, reversely, from good to bad. It should come about as the result not of vice, but of some great error or frailty, in a character either such as we have described, or better rather than worse. 5. The practice of the stage bears out our view. At first the poets recounted any legend that came in their way. Now, the best tragedies are founded on the story of a few houses,—on the fortunes of Alcmaeon, Oedipus, Orestes, Meleager, Thyestes, Telephus, and those others who have done or suffered something terrible. A tragedy, then, to be perfect according to the rules of art should be of this construction. 6. Hence they are in error who censure Euripides just because he follows this principle in his plays, many of which end unhappily. It is, as we

have said, the right ending. The best proof is that on the stage and in dramatic competition, such plays, if well worked out, are the most tragic in effect; and Euripides, faulty though he may be in the general management of his subject, yet is felt to be the most tragic of the poets.

7. In the second rank comes the kind of tragedy which some place first. Like the Odyssey, it has a double thread of plot, and also an opposite catastrophe for the good and for the bad. It is accounted the best because of the weakness of the spectators; for the poet is guided in what he writes by the wishes of his audience. 8. The pleasure, however, thence derived is not the true tragic pleasure. It is proper rather to Comedy, where those who, in the piece, are the deadliest enemies—like Orestes and Aegisthus—quit the stage as friends at the close, and no one slays or is slain.

14

Fear and pity may be aroused by spectacular means; but they may also result from the inner structure of the piece, which is the better way, and indicates a superior poet. For the plot ought to be so constructed that, even without the aid of the eye, he who hears the tale told will thrill with horror and melt to pity at what takes place. This is the impression we should receive from hearing the story of the Oedipus. 2. But to produce this effect by the mere spectacle is a less artistic method, and dependent on extraneous aids. Those who employ spectacular means to create a sense not of the terrible but only of the monstrous, are strangers to the purpose of Tragedy; for we must not demand of Tragedy any and every kind of pleasure, but only that which is proper to it. 3. And since the pleasure which the poet should afford is that which comes from pity and fear through imitation, it is evident that this quality must be impressed upon the incidents.

Let us then determine what are the circumstances which strike us as terrible or pitiful.

4. Actions capable of this effect must happen between persons who are either friends or enemies or indifferent to one another. If an enemy kills an enemy, there is nothing to excite pity either in the act or the intention,—except so far as the suffering in itself is pitiful. So again with indifferent persons. But when the tragic incident occurs between those who are near or dear to one another—if, for example, a brother kills, or intends to kill, a brother, a son his father, a mother her son, a

son his mother, or any other deed of the kind is done—these are the situations to be looked for by the poet. 5. He may not indeed destroy the framework of the received legends—the fact, for instance, that Clytemnestra was slain by Orestes and Eriphyle by Alcmaeon—but he ought to show invention of his own, and skilfully handle the traditional material. Let us explain more clearly what is meant by skilful handling.

6. The action may be done consciously and with knowledge of the persons, in the manner of the older poets. It is thus too that Euripides makes Medea slay her children. Or, again, the deed of horror may be done, but done in ignorance, and the tie of kinship or friendship be discovered afterwards. The Oedipus of Sophocles is an example. Here, indeed, the incident is outside the drama proper; but cases occur where it falls within the action of the play: one may cite the Alcmaeon of Astydamas, or Telegonus in the Wounded Odysseus. 7. Again, there is a third case,—⟨to be about to act with knowledge of the persons and then not to act. The fourth case is⟩ when some one is about to do an irreparable deed through ignorance, and makes the discovery before it is done. These are the only possible ways. For the deed must either be done or not done,—and that wittingly or unwittingly. But of all these ways, to be about to act knowing the persons, and then not to act, is the worst. It is shocking without being tragic, for no disaster follows. It is, therefore, never, or very rarely, found in poetry. One instance, however, is in the Antigone, where Haemon threatens to kill Creon. 8. The next and better way is that the deed should be perpetrated. Still better, that it should be perpetrated in ignorance, and the discovery made afterwards. There is then nothing to shock us, while the discovery produces a startling effect. 9. The last case is the best, as when in the Cresphontes Merope is about to slay her son, but, recognising who he is, spares his life. So in the Iphigenia, the sister recognises the brother just in time. Again in the Helle, the son recognises the mother when on the point of giving her up. This, then, is why a few families only, as has been already observed, furnish the subjects of tragedy. It was not art, but happy chance, that led poets to look for such situations and so impress the tragic quality upon their plots. They are compelled, therefore, to have recourse to those houses whose history contains moving incidents like these.

Enough has now been said concerning the structure of the incidents, and the proper constitution of the plot.

15

In respect of Character there are four things to be aimed at. First, and most important, it must be good. Now any speech or action that manifests moral purpose of any kind will be expressive of character: the character will be good if the purpose is good. This rule is relative to each class. Even a woman may be good, and also a slave; though the woman may be said to be an inferior being, and the slave quite worthless. 2. The second thing to aim at is propriety. There is a type of manly valour; but valour in a woman, or unscrupulous cleverness, is inappropriate. 3. Thirdly, character must be true to life: for this is a distinct thing from goodness and propriety, as here described. 4. The fourth point is consistency: for though the subject of the imitation, who suggested the type, be inconsistent, still he must be consistently inconsistent. 5. As an example of motiveless degradation of character, we have Menelaus in the Orestes: of character indecorous and inappropriate, the lament of Odysseus in the Scylla, and the speech of Melanippe: of inconsistency, the Iphigenia at Aulis,—for Iphigenia the suppliant in no way resembles her later self.

6. As in the structure of the plot, so too in the portraiture of character, the poet should always aim either at the necessary or the probable. Thus a person of a given character should speak or act in a given way, by the rule either of necessity or of probability; just as this event should follow that by necessary or probable sequence. 7. It is therefore evident that the unravelling of the plot, no less than the complication, must arise out of the plot itself, it must not be brought about by the *Deus ex Machina*—as in the Medea, or in the Return of the Greeks in the Iliad. The *Deus ex Machina* should be employed only for events external to the drama,—for antecedent or subsequent events, which lie beyond the range of human knowledge, and which require to be reported or foretold; for to the gods we ascribe the power of seeing all things. Within the action there must be nothing irrational. If the irrational cannot be excluded, it should be outside the scope of the tragedy. Such is the irrational element in the Oedipus of Sophocles.

8. Again, since Tragedy is an imitation of persons who are above the common level, the example of good portrait-painters should be followed. They, while reproducing the distinctive form of the original, make a likeness which is true to life and yet more beautiful. So too the poet, in representing men who are irascible or indolent, or have other defects

of character, should preserve the type and yet ennoble it. In this way Achilles is portrayed by Agathon and Homer.

9. These then are rules the poet should observe. Nor should he neglect those appeals to the senses, which, though not among the essentials, are the concomitants of poetry; for here too there is much room for error. But of this enough has been said in our published treatises.

16

What Recognition is has been already explained. We will now enumerate its kinds.

First, the least artistic form, which, from poverty of wit, is most commonly employed—recognition by signs. 2. Of these some are congenital,—such as "the spear which the earth-born race bear on their bodies," or the stars introduced by Carcinus in his Thyestes. Others are acquired after birth; and of these some are bodily marks, as scars; some external tokens, as necklaces, or the little ark in the Tyro by which the discovery is effected. 3. Even these admit of more or less skilful treatment. Thus in the recognition of Odysseus by his scar, the discovery is made in one way by the nurse, in another by the swineherds. The use of tokens for the express purpose of proof—and, indeed, any formal proof with or without tokens—is a less artistic mode of recognition. A better kind is that which comes about by a turn of incident, as in the Bath Scene in the Odyssey.

4. Next come the recognitions invented at will by the poet, and on that account wanting in art. For example, Orestes in the Iphigenia reveals the fact that he is Orestes. She, indeed, makes herself known by the letter; but he, by speaking himself, and saying what the poet, not what the plot requires. This, therefore, is nearly allied to the fault above mentioned:—for Orestes might as well have brought tokens with him. Another similar instance is the "voice of the shuttle" in the Tereus of Sophocles.

5. The third kind depends on memory when the sight of some object awakens a feeling: as in the Cyprians of Dicaeogenes, where the hero breaks into tears on seeing the picture; or again in the "Lay of Alcinous," where Odysseus, hearing the minstrel play the lyre, recalls the past and weeps; and hence the recognition.

6. The fourth kind is by process of reasoning. Thus in the Choëphori: —"Some one resembling me has come: no one resembles me but Orestes: therefore Orestes has come.". . .

8. But, of all recognitions, the best is that which arises from the incidents themselves, where the startling discovery is made by natural means. Such is that in the Oedipus of Sophocles, and in the Iphigenia; for it was natural that Iphigenia should wish to dispatch a letter. These recognitions alone dispense with the artificial aid of tokens or amulets. Next come the recognitions by process of reasoning.

17

In constructing the plot and working it out with the proper diction, the poet should place the scene, as far as possible, before his eyes. In this way, seeing everything with the utmost vividness, as if he were a spectator of the action, he will discover what is in keeping with it, and be most unlikely to overlook inconsistencies. The need of such a rule is shown by the fault found in Carcinus. Amphiaraus was on his way from the temple. This fact escaped the observation of one who did not see the situation. On the stage, however, the piece failed, the audience being offended at the oversight.

2. Again, the poet should work out his play, to the best of his power, with appropriate gestures; for those who feel emotion are most convincing through natural sympathy with the characters they represent; and one who is agitated storms, one who is angry rages, with the most life-like reality. Hence poetry implies either a happy gift of nature or a strain of madness. In the one case a man can take the mould of any character; in the other, he is lifted out of his proper self.

3. As for the story, whether the poet takes it ready made or constructs it for himself, he should first sketch its general outline, and then fill in the episodes and amplify in detail. The general plan may be illustrated by the Iphigenia. A young girl is sacrificed; she disappears mysteriously from the eyes of those who sacrificed her; she is transported to another country, where the custom is to offer up all strangers to the goddess. To this ministry she is appointed. Some time later her own brother chances to arrive. The fact that the oracle for some reason ordered him to go there, is outside the general plan of the play. The purpose, again, of his coming is outside the action proper. However, he comes, he is seized, and, when on the point of being sacrificed, reveals who he is. The mode of recognition may be either that of Euripides or of Polyidus, in whose play he exclaims very naturally:—"So it was not my sister only, but I too, who was doomed to be sacrificed"; and by that remark he is saved.

4. After this, the names being once given, it remains to fill in the episodes. We must see that they are relevant to the action. In the case of Orestes, for example, there is the madness which led to his capture, and his deliverance by means of the purificatory rite. 5. In the drama, the episodes are short, but it is these that give extension to Epic poetry. Thus the story of the Odyssey can be stated briefly. A certain man is absent from home for many years; he is jealously watched by Poseidon, and left desolate. Meanwhile his home is in a wretched plight—suitors are wasting his substance and plotting against his son. At length, tempest-tost, he himself arrives; he makes certain persons acquainted with him; he attacks the suitors with his own hand, and is himself preserved while he destroys them. This is the essence of the plot; the rest is episode.

18

Every tragedy falls into two parts,—Complication and Unravelling or *Dénouement*. Incidents extraneous to the action are frequently combined with a portion of the action proper, to form the Complication; the rest is the Unravelling. By the Complication I mean all that extends from the beginning of the action to the part which marks the turning-point to good or bad fortune. The Unravelling is that which extends from the beginning of the change to the end. Thus, in the Lynceus of Theodectes, the Complication consists of the incidents presupposed in the drama, the seizure of the child, and then again ⟨The Unravelling⟩ extends from the accusation of murder to the end.

2. There are four kinds of Tragedy, the Complex, depending entirely on Reversal of the Situation and Recognition; the Pathetic (where the motive is passion),—such as the tragedies on Ajax and Ixion; the Ethical (where the motives are ethical),—such as the Phthiotides and the Peleus. The fourth kind is the Simple. ⟨We here exclude the purely spectacular element⟩, exemplified by the Phorcides, the Prometheus, and scenes laid in Hades. 3. The poet should endeavour, if possible, to combine all poetic elements; or failing that, the greatest number and those the most important; the more so, in face of the cavilling criticism of the day. For whereas there have hitherto been good poets, each in his own branch, the critics now expect one man to surpass all others in their several lines of excellence.

In speaking of a tragedy as the same or different, the best test to take is the plot. Identity exists where the Complication and Unravelling are the same. Many poets tie the knot well, but unravel it ill. Both arts, however, should always be mastered.

4. Again, the poet should remember what has been often said, and not make an Epic structure into a Tragedy—by an Epic structure I mean one with a multiplicity of plots—as if, for instance, you were to make a tragedy out of the entire story of the Iliad. In the Epic poem, owing to its length, each part assumes its proper magnitude. In the drama the result is far from answering to the poet's expectation. 5. The proof is that the poets who have dramatised the whole story of the Fall of Troy, instead of selecting portions, like Euripides; or who have taken the whole tale of Niobe, and not a part of her story, like Aeschylus, either fail utterly or meet with poor success on the stage. Even Agathon has been known to fail from this one defect. In his Reversals of the Situation, however, he shows a marvellous skill in the effort to hit the popular taste,—to produce a tragic effect that satisfies the moral sense. 6. This effect is produced when the clever rogue, like Sisyphus, is outwitted, or the brave villain defeated. Such an event is probable in Agathon's sense of the word: "it is probable," he says, "that many things should happen contrary to probability."

7. The Chorus too should be regarded as one of the actors; it should be an integral part of the whole, and share in the action, in the manner not of Euripides but of Sophocles. As for the later poets, their choral songs pertain as little to the subject of the piece as to that of any other tragedy. They are, therefore, sung as mere interludes,—a practice first begun by Agathon. Yet what difference is there between introducing such choral interludes, and transferring a speech, or even a whole act, from one play to another?

19

It remains to speak of Diction and Thought, the other parts of Tragedy having been already discussed. Concerning Thought, we may assume what is said in the Rhetoric, to which inquiry the subject more strictly belongs. 2. Under Thought is included every effect which has to be produced by speech, the subdivisions being,—proof and refutation; the excitation of the feelings, such as pity, fear, anger, and the like; the suggestion of importance or its opposite. 3. Now, it is evident that the dramatic incidents must be treated from the same points of view as the dramatic speeches, when the object is to evoke the sense of pity, fear, importance, or probability. The only difference is, that the incidents should speak for themselves without verbal exposition; while the effects aimed at in speech should be produced by the speaker, and as a result of the speech. For what were the business of a speaker, it the Thought were revealed quite apart from what he says?

4. Next, as regards Diction. One branch of the inquiry treats of the Modes of Utterance. But this province of knowledge belongs to the art of Delivery and to the masters of that science. It includes, for instance,—what is a command, a prayer, a statement, a threat, a question, an answer, and so forth. 5. To know or not to know these things involves no serious censure upon the poet's art. For who can admit the fault imputed to Homer by Protagoras,—that in the words, "Sing, goddess, of the wrath," he gives a command under the idea that he utters a prayer? For to tell some one to do a thing or not to do it is, he says, a command. We may, therefore, pass this over as an inquiry that belongs to another art, not to poetry. . . .

22

The perfection of style is to be clear without being mean. The clearest style is that which uses only current or proper words; at the same time it is mean:—witness the poetry of Cleophon and Sthenelus. That diction, on the other hand, is lofty and raised above the commonplace which employs unusual words. By unusual, I mean strange (or rare) words, metaphorical, lengthened,—anything, in short, that differs from the normal idiom. 2. Yet a style wholly composed of such words is either a riddle or a jargon; a riddle, if it consists of metaphors; a jargon, if it consists of strange (or rare) words. For the essence of a riddle is to express true facts under impossible combinations. Now this cannot be done by any arrangement of ordinary words, but by the use of metaphor it can. Such is the riddle:—"A man I saw who on another man had glued the bronze by aid of fire," and others of the same kind. A diction that is made up of strange (or rare) terms is a jargon. 3. A certain infusion, therefore, of these elements is necessary to style; for the strange (or rare) word, the metaphorical, the ornamental, and the other kinds above mentioned, will raise it above the commonplace and mean, while the use of proper words will make it perspicuous. 4. But nothing contributes more to produce a clearness of diction that is remote from commonness than the lengthening, contraction, and alteration of words. For by deviating in exceptional cases from the normal idiom, the language will gain distinction; while, at the same time, the partial conformity with usage will give perspicuity. 5. The critics, therefore, are in error who censure these licenses of speech, and hold the author up to ridicule. Thus Eucleides, the elder, declared that it would be an easy matter to be a poet if you might lengthen syllables at will. . . . 6. To employ such license at all obtrusively is, no doubt, grotesque; but in any mode of poetic diction there must be moderation. Even metaphors, strange (or rare) words, or any similar forms of speech, would produce the like effect if used without propriety, and with the express purpose of being ludicrous. 7. How great a difference is made by the appropriate use of lengthening, may be seen in Epic poetry by the insertion of ordinary forms in the verse. So, again, if we take a strange (or rare) word, a metaphor, or any similar mode of expression, and replace it by the current or proper term, the truth of our observation will be manifest. . . .

9. It is a great matter to observe propriety in these several modes of expression as also in compound words, strange (or rare) words, and so forth. But the greatest thing by far is to have a command of metaphor. This alone cannot be imparted by another; it is the mark of genius, for to make good metaphors implies an eye for resemblances.

10. Of the various kinds of words, the compound are best adapted to dithyrambs, rare words to heroic poetry, metaphors to iambic. In heroic poetry, indeed, all these varieties are serviceable. But in iambic verse, which reproduces, as far as may be, familiar speech, the most appropriate words are those which are found even in prose. These are,—the current or proper, the metaphorical, the ornamental.

Concerning Tragedy and imitation by means of action this may suffice.

23

As to that poetic imitation which is narrative in form and employs a single metre, the plot manifestly ought, as in a tragedy, to be constructed on dramatic principles. It should have for its subject a single action, whole and complete, with a beginning, a middle, and an end. It will thus resemble a living organism in all its unity, and produce the pleasure proper to it. It will differ in structure from historical compositions, which of necessity present not a single action, but a single period, and all that happened within that period to one person or to many, little connected together as the events may be. 2. For as the sea-fight at Salamis and the battle with the Carthaginians in Sicily took place at the same time, but did not tend to any one result, so in the sequence of events, one thing sometimes follows another, and yet no single result is thereby produced. Such is the practice, we may say, of most poets. 3. Here again, then, as has been already observed, the transcendent excellence of Homer is manifest. He never attempts to make the whole war of Troy the subject of his poem, though that war had a beginning and an end. It would have been too vast a theme, and not easily embraced in a single view. If, again, he had kept it within moderate limits, it must have been overcomplicated by the variety of the incidents. As it is, he detaches a single portion, and admits as episodes many events from the general story of the war—such as the Catalogue of the ships and others—thus diversifying the poem. All other poets take a single hero, a single period, or an action single indeed, but with a multiplicity of parts. Thus did the author of the Cypria and of the Little Iliad. 4. For this reason the Iliad and the Odyssey each furnish the subject of one tragedy, or, at most, of two; while the Cypria supplies materials for many, and the Little Iliad for eight—the Award of the Arms, the Philoctetes, the Neoptolemus, the Eurypylus, the Mendicant Odysseus, the Laconian Women, the Fall of Ilium, the Departure of the Fleet.

24

Again, Epic poetry must have as many kinds as Tragedy: it must be simple, or complex, or "ethical," or "pathetic." The parts also, with the exception of song and spectacle, are the same; for it requires Reversals of the Situation, Recognitions, and Scenes of Suffering. 2. Moreover, the thoughts and the diction must be artistic. In all these respects Homer is our earliest and sufficient model. Indeed each of his poems has a twofold character. The Iliad is at once simple and "pathetic," and the Odyssey complex (for Recognition scenes run through it), and at the same time "ethical." Moreover, in diction and thought they are supreme.

3. Epic poetry differs from Tragedy in the scale on which it is constructed, and in its metre. As regards scale or length, we have already laid down an adequate limit:—the beginning and the end must be capable of being brought within a single view. This condition will be satisfied by poems on a smaller scale than the old epics, and answering in length to the group of tragedies presented at a single sitting.

4. Epic poetry has, however, a great—a special—capacity for en-

larging its dimensions, and we can see the reason. In Tragedy we cannot imitate several lines of actions carried on at one and the same time; we must confine ourselves to the action on the stage and the part taken by the players. But in Epic poetry, owing to the narrative form, many events simultaneously transacted can be presented; and these, if relevant to the subject, add mass and dignity to the poem. The Epic has here an advantage, and one that conduces to grandeur of effect, to diverting the mind of the hearer, and relieving the story with varying episodes. For sameness of incident soon produces satiety, and makes tragedies fail on the stage.

5. As for the metre, the heroic measure has proved its fitness by the test of experience. If a narrative poem in any other metre or in many metres were now composed, it would be found incongruous. For of all measures the heroic is the stateliest and the most massive; and hence it most readily admits rare words and metaphors, which is another point in which the narrative form of imitation stands alone. On the other hand, the iambic and the trochaic tetrameter are stirring measures, the latter being akin to dancing, the former expressive of action. 6. Still more absurd would it be to mix together different metres, as was done by Chaeremon. Hence no one has ever composed a poem on a great scale in any other than heroic verse. Nature herself, as we have said, teaches the choice of the proper measure.

7. Homer, admirable in all respects, has the special merit of being the only poet who rightly appreciates the part he should take himself. The poet should speak as little as possible in his own person, for it is not this that makes him an imitator. Other poets appear themselves upon the scene throughout, and imitate but little and rarely. Homer, after a few prefatory words, at once brings in a man, or woman, or other personage; none of them wanting in characteristic qualities, but each with a character of his own.

8. The element of the wonderful is required in Tragedy. The irrational, on which the wonderful depends for its chief effects, has wider scope in Epic poetry, because there the person acting is not seen. Thus, the pursuit of Hector would be ludicrous if placed upon the stage—the Greeks standing still and not joining in the pursuit, and Achilles waving them back. But in the Epic poem the absurdity passes unnoticed. Now the wonderful is pleasing: as may be inferred from the fact that every one tells a story with some addition of his own, knowing that his hearers like it. 9. It is Homer who has chiefly taught other poets

the art of telling lies skilfully. The secret of it lies in a fallacy. For, assuming that if one thing is or becomes, a second is or becomes, men imagine that, if the second is, the first likewise is or becomes. But this is a false inference. Hence, where the first thing is untrue, it is quite unnecessary, provided the second be true, to add that the first is or has become. For the mind, knowing the second to be true, falsely infers the truth of the first. There is an example of this in the Bath Scene of the Odyssey.

10. Accordingly, the poet should prefer probable impossibilities to improbable possibilities. The tragic plot must not be composed of irrational parts. Everything irrational should, if possible, be excluded; or, at all events, it should lie outside the action of the play (as, in the Oedipus, the hero's ignorance as to the manner of Laius' death); not within the drama,—as in the Electra, the messenger's account of the Pythian games; or, as in the Mysians, the man who comes from Tegea to Mysia and is still speechless. The plea that otherwise the plot would have been ruined, is ridiculous; such a plot should not in the first instance be constructed. But once the irrational has been introduced and an air of likelihood imparted to it, we must accept it in spite of the absurdity. Take even the irrational incidents in the Odyssey, where Odysseus is left upon the shore of Ithaca. How intolerable even these might have been would be apparent if an inferior poet were to treat the subject. As it is, the absurdity is veiled by the poetic charm with which the poet invests it.

11. The diction should be elaborated in the pauses of the action, where there is no expression of character or thought. For, conversely, character and thought are merely obscured by a diction that is over brilliant.

25

With respect to critical difficulties and their solutions, the number and nature of the sources from which they may be drawn may be thus exhibited.

The poet being an imitator, like a painter or any other artist, must of necessity imitate one of three objects,—things as they were or are, things as they are said or thought to be, or things as they ought to be. 2. The vehicle of expression is language,—either current terms or, it may be, rare words or metaphors. There are also many modifications of language, which we concede to the poets. 3. Add to this, that the standard of correctness is not the same in poetry and politics, any more than in poetry and any other art. Within the art of poetry itself there are two kinds of faults,—those which touch its essence, and those which are accidental. 4. If a poet has chosen to imitate something, ⟨but has imitated it incorrectly⟩ through want of capacity, the error is inherent in the poetry. But if the failure is due to a wrong choice—if he has represented a horse as throwing out both his off legs at once, or introduced technical inaccuracies in medicine, for example, or in any other art—the error is not essential to the poetry. These are the points of view from which we should consider and answer the objections raised by the critics.

5. First as to matters which concern the poet's own art. If he describes the impossible, he is guilty of an error; but the error may be justified, if the end of the art be thereby attained (the end being that already mentioned),—if, that is, the effect of this or any other part of the poem is thus rendered more striking. A case in point is the pursuit of Hector. If, however, the end might have been as well, or better, attained without violating the special rules of the poetic art, the error is not justified: for every kind of error should, if possible, be avoided.

Again, does the error touch the essentials of the poetic art, or some accident of it? For example,—not to know that a hind has no horns is a less serious matter than to paint it inartistically.

6. Further, if it be objected that the description is not true to fact, the poet may perhaps reply,—"But the objects are as they ought to be": just as Sophocles said that he drew men as they ought to be; Euripides, as they are. 7. In this way the objection may be met. If, however, the representation be of neither kind, the poet may answer,— "This is how men say the thing is." This applies to tales about the gods. It may well be that these stories are not higher than fact nor yet true to fact: they are, very possibly, what Xenophanes says of them. But anyhow, "this is what is said." Again, a description may be no better than the fact: "still, it was the fact"; as in the passage about the arms: "Upright upon their butt-ends stood the spears." This was the custom then, as it now is among the Illyrians.

8. Again, in examining whether what has been said or done by some one is poetically right or not, we must not look merely to the particular act or saying, and ask whether it is poetically good or bad. We must also consider by whom it is said or done, to whom, when, by what means, or

for what end; whether, for instance, it be to secure a greater good, or avert a greater evil.

9. Other difficulties may be resolved by due regard to the usage of language. . . .

17. In general, the impossible must be justified by reference to artistic requirements, or to the higher reality, or to received opinion. With respect to the requirements of art, a probable impossibility is to be preferred to a thing improbable and yet possible. Again, it may be impossible that there should be men such as Zeuxis painted. "Yes," we say, "but the impossible is the higher thing; for the ideal type must surpass the reality." To justify the irrational, we appeal to what is commonly said to be. In addition to which, we urge that the irrational sometimes does not violate reason; just as "it is probable that a thing may happen contrary to probability."

18. Things that sound contradictory should be examined by the same rules as in dialectical refutation—whether the same thing is meant, in the same relation, and in the same sense. We should therefore solve the question by reference to what the poet says himself, or to what is tactitly assumed by a person of intelligence.

19. The element of the irrational, and, similarly, depravity of character, are justly censured when there is no inner necessity for introducing them. Such is the irrational element in the introduction of Aegeus of Euripides, and the badness of Menelaus in the Orestes.

20. Thus, there are five sources from which critical objections are drawn. Things are censured either as impossible, or irrational, or morally hurtful, or contradictory, or contrary to artistic correctness. The answers should be sought under the twelve heads above mentioned.

26

The question may be raised whether the Epic or Tragic mode of imitation is the higher. If the more refined art is the higher, and the more refined in every case is that which appeals to the better sort of audience, the art which imitates anything and everything is manifestly most unrefined. The audience is supposed to be too dull to comprehend unless something of their own is thrown in by the performers, who therefore indulge in restless movements. Bad flute-players twist and twirl, if they have to represent "the quoit-throw," or hustle the coryphaeus when they perform the "Scylla." 2. Tragedy, it is said, has this same defect. We may compare the opinion that the older actors entertained of their successors. Mynniscus used to call Callippides "ape" on account of the extravagance of his action, and the same view was held of Pindarus. Tragic art, then, as a whole, stands to Epic in the same relation as the younger to the elder actors. So we are told that Epic poetry is addressed to a cultivated audience, who do not need gesture; Tragedy, to an inferior public. 3. Being then unrefined, it is evidently the lower of the two.

Now, in the first place, this censure attaches not to the poetic but to the histrionic art; for gesticulation may be equally overdone in epic recitation, as by Sosistratus, or in lyrical competition, as by Mnasitheus the Opuntian. Next, all action is not to be condemned—any more than all dancing—but only that of bad performers. Such was the fault found in Callippides, as also in others of our own day, who are censured for representing degraded women. Again, Tragedy like Epic poetry produces its effect even without action; it reveals its power by mere reading. If, then, in all other respects it is superior, this fault, we say, is not inherent in it.

4. And superior it is, because it has all the epic elements—it may even use the epic metre—with the music and spectacular effects as important accessories; and these produce the most vivid of pleasures. Further, it has vividness of impression in reading as well as in representation. 5. Moreover, the art attains its end within narrower limits; for the concentrated effect is more pleasurable than one which is spread over a long time and so diluted. What, for example, would be the effect of the Oedipus of Sophocles, it if were cast into a form as long as the Iliad? 6. Once more, the Epic imitation has less unity; as is shown by this, that any Epic poem will furnish subjects for several tragedies. Thus if the story adopted by the poet has a strict unity, it must either be concisely told and appear truncated; or, if it conform to the Epic canon of length, it must seem weak and watery. ⟨Such length implies some loss of unity,⟩ if, I mean, the poem is constructed out of several actions, like the Iliad and the Odyssey, which have many such parts, each with a certain magnitude of its own. Yet these poems are as perfect as possible in structure; each is, in the highest degree attainable, an imitation of a single action.

7. If, then, Tragedy is superior to Epic poetry in all these respects,

and, moreover, fulfils its specific function better as an art—for each art ought to produce, not any chance pleasure, but the pleasure proper to it, as already stated—it plainly follows that Tragedy is the higher art, as attaining its end more perfectly.

8. Thus much may suffice concerning Tragic and Epic poetry in general; their several kinds and parts, with the number of each and their differences; the causes that make a poem good or bad; the objections of the critics and the answers to these objections.

2. LONGINUS

On the Sublime

Neither the author nor the date of composition is known of the very important and influential late classical work *On the Sublime*. In the earliest known manuscript of the tenth century, which was first published by Robertello in 1554, the author is said to be "Dionysius or Longinus." There was a famous rhetorician, Dionysius of Halicarnassus, who lived during the first century; there was also a Cassius Longinus of Palmyra who lived during the third century. Most scholars agree today that it is very unlikely either of the two was the author of the treatise. Then why assign the work to the first century? The answer is simple: the treatise sets out to refute a work by Caecilius who did write in the first century. So the name Longinus is used merely for convenience's sake.

After the edition of 1554 a few more editions and some translations appeared. John Hall translated it into English in 1652 under the title *Of the Height of Eloquence*—a title that many modern critics prefer to the traditional *On the Sublime*. But it was not until Boileau's French translation in 1674 that the treatise began to attract notice.

After some introductory remarks to the recipient of the letter on Caecilius' treatise ("my dear Postumius Terentianus"), Longinus gives a working definition of the sublime: "The effect of elevated language upon an audience is not persuasion but transport. At every time and in every way imposing speech, with the spell it throws over us, prevails over that which aims at persuasion and gratification." Quickly he dismisses the two "ugly growths"—tumidity and frigidity—that hinder greatness in literature, and then launches into the necessary five elements for greatness. The rest of the work really considers these elements.

The elements or sources of the sublime are the following: (1) the power of forming great conceptions; (2) vehement and inspired passion; (3) formation of figures—those of thought and those of expression; (4) noble diction (this includes such figures as metaphors); (5) dignified and elevated composition. All these elements are painstakingly illustrated by numerous lines possessing the particular element. (Most of these examples are left out of this edition because the appreciation of them depends upon the knowledge of Greek.) Thus, unlike Aristotle but like later critics, Longinus concentrates on parts of literature instead of stressing continually either the literary work or even literature itself as a whole.

Although these five sources of the sublime are somewhat confusing and perhaps overlapping, three main emphases emerge from them: importance of what Aristotle would call "thought"; importance of emotional transport; and importance of language. It is especially the second important emphasis that was responsible for Longinus' influence during the eighteenth and nineteenth centuries. Interestingly Boileau says in his preface to the French translation: "By the *sublime* in Longinus, then, we must understand the extraordinary, the surprising, and, as I have translated it, the marvelous in discourse," (*Selected Criticism of Boileau*, trans. by E. Dilworth [Bobbs-Merrill, 1965], p. 50.) The extraordinary, the surprising, the marvelous, plus the emotional transport also add up to the Romantic emphases.

If Longinus spoke so well for future ages, he, nevertheless, also spoke for antiquity. As Aristotle, he is concerned with order and harmony. Even his way of expressing the concern is in terms of a classical analogy: "Among the chief causes of the sublime in speech, as in the structure of the human body, is the collocation of members, a single one of which if severed from another possesses in itself nothing remarkable, but all united together make a full and perfect organism. So the constituents of grandeur, when separated from one another, carry with them sublimity in distraction this way and that, but when formed into a body by association and when further encircled in a chain of harmony they become sonorous by their very rotundity. . . ."

The selection is taken from the translation by W. Rhys Roberts.*

I

You will remember, my dear Postumius Terentianus, that when we examined together the treatise of Caecilius, On the Sublime, we found that it fell below the dignity of the whole subject, while it failed signally to grasp the essential points, and conveyed to its readers but little of

* Cambridge University Press, 1899.

that practical help which it should be a writer's principal aim to give. In every systematic treatise two things are required. The first is a statement of the subject; the other, which although second in order ranks higher in importance, is an indication of the methods by which we may attain our end. Now Caecilius seeks to show the nature of the sublime by countless instances as though our ignorance demanded it, but the consideration of the means whereby we may succeed in raising our own capacities to a certain pitch of elevation he has, strangely enough, omitted as unnecessary. 2. However, it may be that the man ought not so much to be blamed for his shortcomings as praised for his happy thought and his enthusiasm. But since you have urged me, in my turn, to write a brief essay on the sublime for your special gratification, let us consider whether the views I have formed contain anything which will be of use to public men. You will yourself, my friend, in accordance with your nature and with what is fitting, join me in appraising each detail with the utmost regard for truth; for he answered well who, when asked in what qualities we resemble the Gods, declared that we do so in benevolence and truth. 3. As I am writing to you, my good friend, who are well versed in literary studies, I feel almost absolved from the necessity of premising at any length that sublimity is a certain distinction and excellence in expression, and that it is from no other source than this that the greatest poets and writers have derived their eminence and gained an immortality of renown. 4. The effect of elevated language upon an audience is not persuasion but transport. At every time and in every way imposing speech, with the spell it throws over us, prevails over that which aims at persuasion and gratification. Our persuasions we can usually control, but the influences of the sublime bring power and irresistible might to bear, and reign supreme over every hearer. Similarly, we see skill in invention, and due order and arrangement of matter, emerging as the hard-won result not of one thing nor of two, but of the whole texture of the composition, whereas sublimity flashing forth at the right moment scatters everything before it like a thunderbolt, and at once displays the power of the orator in all its plenitude. But enough; for these reflexions, and others like them, you can, I know well, my dear Terentianus, yourself suggest from your own experience.

II

First of all, we must raise the question whether there is such a thing as an art of the sublime or lofty. Some hold that those are entirely in error who would bring such matters under the precepts of art. A lofty tone, says one, is innate, and does not come by teaching; nature is the only art that can compass it. Works of nature are, they think, made worse and altogether feebler when wizened by the rules of art. 2. But I maintain that this will be found to be otherwise if it be observed that, while nature as a rule is free and independent in matters of passion and elevation, yet is she wont not to act at random and utterly without system. Further, nature is the original and vital underlying principle in all cases, but system can define limits and fitting seasons, and can also contribute the safest rules for use and practice. Moreover, the expression of the sublime is more exposed to danger when it goes its own way without the guidance of knowledge—when it is suffered to be unstable and unballasted—when it is left at the mercy of mere momentum and ignorant audacity. It is true that it often needs the spur, but it is also true that it often needs the curb. 3. Demosthenes expresses the view, with regard to human life in general, that good fortune is the greatest of blessings, while good counsel, which occupies the second place, is hardly inferior in importance, since its absence contributes inevitably to the ruin of the former. This we may apply to diction, nature occupying the position of good fortune, art that of good counsel. Most important of all, we must remember that the very fact that there are some elements of expression which are in the hands of nature alone, can be learnt from no other source than art. If, I say, the critic of those who desire to learn were to turn these matters over in his mind, he would no longer, is seems to me, regard the discussion of the subject as superfluous or useless. . . .

III

> Quell they the oven's far-flung splendour-glow!
> Ha, let me but one hearth-abider mark—
> One flame-wreath torrent-like I'll whirl on high;
> I'll burn the roof, to cinders shrivel it!—
> Nay, now my chant is not of noble strain.
>
> Aeschylus, tr. by A. S. Way.

Such things are not tragic but pseudo-tragic—"flame-wreaths," and "belching to the sky," and Boreas represented as a "flute-player," and all the rest of it. They are turbid in expression and confused in imagery rather than the product of intensity, and each one of them, if examined in the light of day, sinks little by little from the terrible into the contemptible. But since even in tragedy, which is in its very nature stately and prone to bombast, tasteless tumidity is unpardonable, still less, I presume, will it harmonise with the narration of fact. 2. And this is the ground on which the phrases of Gorgias of Leontini are ridiculed when he describes Xerxes as the "Zeus of the Persians" and vultures as "living tombs." So is it with some of the expressions of Callisthenes which are not sublime but high-flown, and still more with those of Cleitarchus, for the man is frivolous and blows, as Sophocles has it,

> On pigmy hautboys: mouthpiece have they none.
>
> Tr. by A. S. Way.

Other examples will be found in Amphicrates and Hegesias and Matris, for often when these writers seem to themselves to be inspired they are in no true frenzy but are simply trifling. 3. Altogether, tumidity seems particularly hard to avoid. The explanation is that all who aim at elevation are so anxious to escape the reproach of being weak and dry that they are carried, as by some strange law of nature, into the opposite extreme. They put their trust in the maxim that "failure in a great attempt is at least a noble error." 4. But evil are the swellings, both in the body and in diction, which are inflated and unreal, and threaten us with the reverse of our aim; for nothing, say they, is drier than a man who has the dropsy. While tumidity desires to transcend the limits of the sublime, the defect which is termed puerility is the direct antithesis of elevation, for it is utterly low and mean and in real truth the most ignoble vice of style. What, then, is this puerility? Clearly, a pedant's thoughts, which begin in learned trifling and end in frigidity. Men slip into this kind of error because, while they aim at the uncommon and elaborate and most of all at the attractive, they drift unawares into the tawdry and affected. 5. A third, and closely allied, kind of defect in matters of passion is that which Theodorus used to call *parenthyrsus*. By this is meant unseasonable and empty passion, where no passion is required, or immoderate, where moderation is needed. For men are often carried away, as if by intoxication, into displays of emotion which are not caused by the nature of the subject, but are purely personal and wearisome. In consequence they seem to hearers who are in no wise affected to act in an ungainly way. And no wonder; for they are beside themselves, while their hearers are not. But the question of the passions we reserve for separate treatment.

IV

Of the second fault of which we have spoken—frigidity—Timaeus supplies many examples. Timaeus was a writer of considerable general ability, who occasionally showed that he was not incapable of elevation of style. He was learned and ingenious, but very prone to criticise the faults of others while blind to his own. Through his passion for continually starting novel notions, he often fell into the merest childishness. 2. I will set down one or two examples only of his manner, since the greater number have been already appropriated by Caecilius. In the course of a eulogy on Alexander the Great, he describes him as "the man who gained possession of the whole of Asia in fewer years than it took Isocrates to write his Panegyric urging war against the Persians." Strange indeed is the comparison of the man of Macedon with the rhetorician. How plain it is, Timaeus, that the Lacedaemonians, thus judged, were far inferior to Isocrates in prowess, for they spent thirty years in the conquest of Messene, whereas he composed his Panegyric in ten. . . . 6. Yes, and Plato (usually so divine) when he means simply *tablets* says, "They shall write and preserve *cypress memorials* in the temples."[1]

And again, "As touching walls, Megillus, I should hold with Sparta that they be suffered to lie asleep in the earth and not summoned to arise."[2] The expression of Herodotus to the effect that beautiful women are "eye-smarts" is not much better.[3] This, however, may be condoned in some degree since those who use this particular phrase in his narrative are barbarians and in their cups, but not even in the mouths of such characters is it well that an author should suffer, in the judgment of posterity, from an unseemly exhibition of triviality.

V

All these ugly and parasitical growths arise in literature from a single cause, that pursuit of novelty in the expression of ideas which may be regarded as the fashionable craze of the day. Our defects usually spring for the most part, from the same sources as our good points. Hence, while beauties of expression and touches of sublimity, and charming elegances withal, are favourable to effective composition, yet these

[1] *Laws*, V, 741c.
[2] *Ibid.*, VI, 778d.
[3] V, 18.

very things are the elements and foundation, not only of success, but also of the contrary. Something of the kind is true also of variations and hyperboles and the use of the plural number, and we shall show subsequently the dangers to which these seem severally to be exposed. It is necessary now to seek and to suggest means by which we may avoid the defects which attend the steps of the sublime.

VI

The best means would be, my friend, to gain, first of all, clear knowledge and appreciation of the true sublime. The enterprise is, however, an arduous one. For the judgment of style is the last and crowning fruit of long experience. None the less, if I must speak in the way of precept, it is not impossible perhaps to acquire discrimination in these matters by attention to some such hints as those which follow.

VII

You must know, my dear friend, that it is with the sublime as in the common life of man. In life nothing can be considered great which it is held great to despise. For instance, riches, honours, distinctions, sovereignties, and all other things which possess in abundance the external trappings of the stage, will not seem, to a man of sense, to be supreme blessings, since the very contempt of them is reckoned good in no small degree, and in any case those who could have them, but are high-souled enough to disdain them, are more admired than those who have them. So also in the case of sublimity in poems and prose writings, we must consider whether some supposed examples have not simply the appearance of elevation with many idle accretions, so that when analysed they are found to be mere vanity—objects which a noble nature will rather despise than admire. 2. For, as if instinctively, our soul is uplifted by the true sublime; it takes a proud flight, and is filled with joy and vaunting, as though it had itself produced what it has heard. 3. When, therefore, a thing is heard repeatedly by a man of intelligence, who is well versed in literature, and its effect is not to dispose the soul to high thoughts, and it does not leave in the mind more food for reflexion than the words seem to convey, but falls, if examined carefully through and through, into disesteem, it cannot rank as true sublimity because it does not survive a first hearing. For that is really great which bears a repeated examination, and which it is difficult or rather impossible to withstand, and the memory of which is strong and hard to efface. 4. In general, consider those examples of sublimity to be fine and genuine which please all and always. For when men of different pursuits, lives, ambitions, ages, languages, hold identical views on one and the same subject, then that verdict which results, so to speak, from a concert of discordant elements makes our faith in the object of admiration strong and unassailable.

VIII

There are, it may be said, five principal sources of elevated language. Beneath these five varieties there lies, as though it were a common foundation, the gift of discourse, which is indispensable. First and most important is the power of forming great conceptions, as we have elsewhere explained in our remarks on Xenophon. Secondly, there is vehement and inspired passion. These two components of the sublime are for the most part innate. Those which remain are partly the product of art. The due formation of figures deals with two sorts of figures, first those of thought and secondly those of expression. Next there is noble diction, which in turn comprises choice of words, and use of metaphors, and elaboration of language. The fifth cause of elevation—one which is the fitting conclusion of all that have preceded it—is dignified and elevated composition. Come now, let us consider what is involved in each of these varieties, with this one remark by way of preface, that Caecilius has omitted some of the five divisions, for example, that of passion. 2. Surely he is quite mistaken if he does so on the ground that these two, sublimity and passion, are a unity, and if it seems to him that they are by nature one and inseparable. For some passions are found which are far removed from sublimity and are of a low order, such as pity, grief and fear; and on the other hand there are many examples of the sublime which are independent of passion, such as the daring words of Homer with regard to the Aloadae, to take one out of numberless instances,

> Yea, Ossa in fury they strove to upheave on Olympus on high,
> With forest-clad Pelion above, that thence they might step to the sky.[4]

And so of the words which follow with still greater force:

> Ay, and the deed had they done.[5]

[4] *Odyssey*, XI, 315–16.
[5] *Ibid.*, XI, 317.

3. Among the orators, too, eulogies and ceremonial and occasional addresses contain on every side examples of dignity and elevation, but are for the most part void of passion. This is the reason why passionate speakers are the worst eulogists, and why, on the other hand, those who are apt in encomium are the least passionate. 4. If, on the other hand, Caecilius thought that passion never contributes at all to sublimity, and if it was for this reason that he did not deem it worthy of mention, he is altogether deluded. I would affirm with confidence that there is no tone so lofty as that of genuine passion, in its right place, when it bursts out in a wild gust of mad enthusiasm and as it were fills the speaker's words with frenzy.

IX

Now the first of the conditions mentioned, namely elevation of mind, holds the foremost rank among them all. We must, therefore, in this case also, although we have to do rather with an endowment than with an acquirement, nurture our souls (as far as that is possible) to thoughts sublime, and make them always pregnant, so to say, with noble inspiration. 2. In what way, you may ask, is this to be done? Elsewhere I have written as follows: "Sublimity is the echo of a great soul." Hence also a bare idea, by itself and without a spoken word, sometimes excites admiration just because of the greatness of soul implied. Thus the silence of Ajax in the Underworld is great and more sublime than words.[6] 3. First, then, it is absolutely necessary to indicate the source of this elevation, namely, that the truly eloquent must be free from low and ignoble thoughts. For it is not possible that men with mean and servile ideas and aims prevailing throughout their lives should produce anything that is admirable and worthy of immortality. Great accents we expect to fall from the lips of those whose thoughts are deep and grave. 4. Thus it is that stately speech comes naturally to the proudest spirits. [You will remember the answer of] Alexander to Parmenio when he said "For my part I had been well content."[7]. . .

. . . the distance from earth to heaven; and this might well be considered the measure of Homer no less than of Strife. 5. How unlike to this the expression which is used of Sorrow by Hesiod, if indeed the Shield is to be attributed to Hesiod:

Rheum from her nostrils was trickling.[8]

[6] *Ibid.*, XI, 543.
[7] Quotation from Arrian.
[8] *Shield of Heracles*, 267.

The image he has suggested is not terrible but rather loathsome. Contrast the way in which Homer magnifies the higher powers:

> And far as a man with his eyes through the sea-line haze may discern,
> On a cliff as he sitteth and gazeth away o'er the wine-dark deep,
> So far at a bound do the loud-neighing steeds of the Deathless leap.[9]

He makes the vastness of the world the measure of their leap. The sublimity is so overpowering as naturally to prompt the exclamation that if the divine steeds were to leap thus twice in succession they would pass beyond the confines of the world. 6. How transcendent also are the images in the Battle of the Gods:

> Far round wide heaven and Olympus echoed his clarion of thunder;
> And Hades, king of the realm of shadows, quaked thereunder.
> And he sprang from his throne, and he cried aloud in the dread of his heart
> Lest o'er him earth-shaker Poseidon should cleave the ground apart,
> And revealed to Immortals and mortals should stand those awful abodes,
> Those mansions ghastly and grim, abhorred of the very Gods.[10]

You see, my friend, how the earth is torn from its foundations, Tartarus itself is laid bare, the whole world is upturned and parted asunder, and all things together—heaven and hell, things mortal and things immortal—share in the conflict and the perils of that battle!

7. But although these things are awe-inspiring, yet from another point of view, if they be not taken allegorically, they are altogether impious, and violate our sense of what is fitting. Homer seems to me, in his legends of wounds suffered by the gods, and of their feuds, reprisals, tears, bonds, and all their manifold passions, to have made, as far as lay within his power, gods of the men concerned in the Siege of Troy, and men of the gods. But whereas we mortals have death as the destined haven of our ills if our lot is miserable, he portrays the gods as immortal not only in nature but also in misfortune. 8. Much superior to the passages respecting the Battle of the Gods are those which represent the divine nature as it really is—pure and great and undefiled; for example, what is said of Poseidon in a passage fully treated by many before ourselves:

---

[9] *Iliad*, V, 770.
[10] *Ibid.*, XXI, 388; XX, 61–65.

> Her far-stretching ridges, her forest-trees, quaked
> in dismay,
>
> And her peaks, and the Trojans' town, and the ships
> of Achaia's array,
> Beneath his immortal feet, as onward Poseidon
> strode.
> Then over the surges he drave: leapt sporting before
> the God
> Sea-beasts that uprose all around from the depths,
> for their king they knew,
> And for rapture the sea was disparted, and onward
> the car-steeds flew.[11]

9. Similarly, the legislator of the Jews,[12] no ordinary man, having formed and expressed a worthy conception of the might of the Godhead, writes at the very beginning of his Laws, "God said"—what? "Let there be light, and there was light; let there be land, and there was land.". . .

He shows, however, in the Odyssey (and this further observation deserves attention on many grounds) that, when a great genius is declining, the special token of old age is the love of marvellous tales. 12. It is clear from many indications that the Odyssey was his second subject. A special proof is the fact that he introduces in that poem remnants of the adventures before Ilium as episodes, so to say, of the Trojan War. And indeed, he there renders a tribute of mourning and lamentation to his heroes as though he were carrying out a long-cherished purpose. In fact, the Odyssey is simply an epilogue to the Iliad:

> There lieth Ajax the warrior wight, Achilles is there,
> There is Patroclus, whose words had weight as a
> God he were;
> There lieth mine own dear son.[13]

13. It is for the same reason, I suppose, that he has made the whole structure of the Iliad, which was written at the height of his inspiration, full of action and conflict, while the Odyssey for the most part consists of narrative, as is characteristic of old age. Accordingly, in the Odyssey

[11] *Ibid.*, XIII, 18; XX, 60; XIII, 19, 27–29.
[12] Moses.
[13] *Odyssey*, III, 109–11.

Homer may be likened to a sinking sun, whose grandeur remains
without its intensity. He does not in the Odyssey maintain so high a
pitch as in those poems of Ilium. His sublimities are not evenly sustained and free from the liability to sink; there is not the same profusion
of accumulated passions, nor the supple and oratorical style, packed
with images drawn from real life. You seem to see henceforth the ebb and
flow of greatness, and a fancy roving in the fabulous and incredible, as
though the ocean were withdrawing into itself and were being laid bare
within its own confines. 14. In saying this I have not forgotten the
tempests in the Odyssey and the story of the Cyclops and the like. If
I speak of old age, it is nevertheless the old age of Homer. The fabulous
element, however, prevails throughout this poem over the real. The
object of this digression has been, as I said, to show how easily great
natures in their decline are sometimes diverted into absurdity, as in
the incident of the wine-skin and of the men who were fed like swine by
Circe (*whining porkers*, as Zoilus called them), and of Zeus like a
nestling nurtured by the doves, and of the hero who was without food
for ten days upon the wreck, and of the incredible tale of the slaying of
the suitors.[14] For what else can we term these things than veritable
dreams of Zeus? 15. These observations with regard to the Odyssey
should be made for another reason—in order that you may know that
the genius of great poets and prose-writers, as their passion declines,
finds its final expression in the delineation of character. For such are
the details which Homer gives, with an eye to characterisation, of life
in the home of Odysseus; they form as it were a comedy of manners.

X

Let us next consider whether we can point to anything further that
contributes to sublimity of style. Now, there inhere in all things by
nature certain constituents which are part and parcel of their substance.
It must needs be, therefore, that we shall find one source of the sublime
in the systematic selection of the most important elements, and the
power of forming, by their mutual combination, what may be called one
body. The former process attracts the hearer by the choice of the ideas,
the latter by the aggregation of those chosen. For instance, Sappho
everywhere chooses the emotions that attend delirious passion from its
accompaniments in actual life. Wherein does she demonstrate her

[14] *Ibid.*, IX, 182; X, 17, 237; XII, 62, 447; XXII, 79.

supreme excellence? In the skill with which she selects and binds together the most striking and vehement circumstances of passion:

2.   Peer of Gods he seemeth to me, the blissful
          Man who sits and gazes at thee before him.
          Close beside thee sits, and in silence hears thee
             Silverly speaking,

          Laughing love's low laughter. Oh this, this only
          Stirs the troubled heart in my breast to tremble!
          For should I but see thee a little moment,
             Straight is my voice hushed;

          Yea, my tongue is broken, and through and through me
          'Neath the flesh impalpable fire runs tingling;
          Nothing see mine eyes, and a noise of roaring
             Waves in my ear brands;

          Sweat runs down in rivers, a tremor seizes
          All my limbs, and paler than grass in autumn,
          Caught by pains of menacing death, I falter,
             Lost in the love-trance.

3. Are you not amazed how at one instant she summons, as though they were all alien from herself and dispersed, soul, body, ears, tongue, eyes, colour? Uniting contradictions, she is at one and the same time hot and cold, in her senses and out of her mind, for she is either terrified or at the point of death. The effect desired is that not one passion only should be seen in her, but a concourse of the passions. All such things occur in the case of lovers, but it is, as I said, the selection of the most striking of these and their combination into a single whole that has produced the singular excellence of the passage. . . .

XI

    An allied excellence to those already set forth is that which is termed *amplification*. This figure is employed when the narrative or the course of a forensic argument admits, from section to section, of many starting-points and many pauses, and elevated expressions follow, one after the other, in an unbroken succession and in an ascending order. 2. And this may be effected by way of the rhetorical treatment of commonplaces, or by way of intensification (whether events or arguments are to be strongly presented), or by the orderly arrangement of facts or of passions; indeed, there are innumerable kinds of amplification. Only, the orator must in every case remember that none of these methods by itself, apart from sublimity, forms a complete whole, unless indeed where pity is to be excited or an opponent to be disparaged. In all other cases of amplification, if you take away the sublime, you will remove as it were the soul from the body. For the vigour of the amplification at once loses its intensity and its substance when not resting on a firm basis of the sublime. 3. Clearness, however, demands that we should define concisely how our present precepts differ from the point under consideration a moment ago, namely the marking-out of the most striking conceptions and the unification of them; and wherein, generally, the sublime differs from amplification.

XII

Now the definition given by the writers on rhetoric does not satisfy me. Amplification is, say they, discourse which invests the subject with grandeur. This definition, however, would surely apply in equal measure to sublimity and passion and figurative language, since they too invest the discourse with a certain degree of grandeur. The point of distinction between them seems to me to be that sublimity consists in elevation, while amplification embraces a multitude of details. Consequently, sublimity is often comprised in a single thought, while amplification is universally associated with a certain magnitude and abundance. 2. Amplification (to sum the matter up in a general way) is an aggregation of all the constituent parts and topics of a subject, lending strength to the argument by dwelling upon it. . . .

XIV

Accordingly it is well that we ourselves also, when elaborating anything which requires lofty expression and elevated conception, should shape some idea in our minds as to how perchance Homer would have said this very thing, or how it would have been raised to the sublime by Plato or Demosthenes or by the historian Thucydides. For those personages, presenting themselves to us and inflaming our ardour and as it were illumining our path, will carry our minds in a mysterious way to the high standards of sublimity which are imaged within us. 2. Still more effectual will it be to suggest this question to our thoughts,

"What sort of hearing would Homer, had he been present, or Demosthenes have given to this or that when said by me, or how would they have been affected by the other?" For the ordeal is indeed a severe one, if we presuppose such a tribunal and theatre for our own utterances, and imagine that we are undergoing a scrutiny of our writings before these great heroes, acting as judges and witnesses. 3. A greater incentive still will be supplied if you add the question, "In what spirit will each succeeding age listen to me who have written thus?" But if one shrinks from the very thought of uttering aught that may transcend the term of his own life and time, the conceptions of his mind must necessarily be incomplete, blind, and as it were untimely born, since they are by no means brought to the perfection needed to ensure a futurity of fame.

XV

Images, moreover, contribute greatly, my young friend, to dignity, elevation, and power as a pleader. In this sense some call them mental representations. In a general way the name of *image* or *imagination* is applied to every idea of the mind, in whatever form it presents itself, which gives birth to speech. But at the present day the word is predominantly used in cases where, carried away by enthusiasm and passion, you think you see what you describe, and you place it before the eyes of your hearers. 2. Further, you will be aware of the fact that an image has one purpose with the orators and another with the poets, and that the design of the poetical image is enthralment, of the rhetorical— vivid description. Both, however, seek to stir the passions and the emotions.

> Mother!—'beseech thee, hark not them on me
> Yon maidens gory-eyed and snaky-haired!
> Lo there!—lo there!—they are nigh—they leap on me!
>> Euripides, *Orestes*, 255.

And:

> Ah! she will slay me! whither can I fly?
>> Euripides, *Iphigenia in Tauris*, 291.

In these scenes the poet himself saw Furies, and the image in his mind he almost compelled his audience also to behold. 3. Now, Euripides is most assiduous in giving the utmost tragic effect to these two motions—fits of love and madness. Herein he succeeds more, perhaps, than in any other respect, although he is daring enough to invade all the other regions of the imagination. Notwithstanding that he is by nature anything but elevated, he forces his own genius, in many passages, to tragic heights, and everywhere in the matter of sublimity it is true of him (to adopt Homer's words) that

> The tail of him scourgeth his ribs and his flanks to
>   left and to right,
> And he lasheth himself into frenzy, and spurreth
>   him on to the fight. . . .

Iliad, XX, 170.

7. Magnificent are the images which Sophocles has conceived of the death of Oedipus, who makes ready his burial amid the portents of the sky.[15] Magnificent, too, is the passage where the Greeks are on the point of sailing away and Achilles appears above his tomb to those who are putting out to sea—a scene which I doubt whether anyone has depicted more vividly than Simonides. But it is impossible to cite all the examples that present themselves. 8. It is no doubt true that those which are found in the poets contain, as I said, a tendency to exaggeration in the way of the fabulous and that they transcend in every way the credible, but in oratorical imagery the best feature is always its reality and truth. Whenever the form of a speech is poetical and fabulous and breaks into every kind of impossibility, such digressions have a strange and alien air. For example, the clever orators forsooth of our day, like the tragedians, see Furies, and—fine fellows that they are—cannot even understand that Orestes when he cries,

> Unhand me!—of mine Haunting Fiends thou art—
> Dost grip my waist to hurl me into hell![16]

has these fancies because he is mad. 9. What, then, can oratorical imagery effect? Well, it is able in many ways to infuse vehemence and passion into spoken words, while more particularly when it is combined with the argumentative passages it not only persuades the hearer but actually makes him its slave. Here is an example. "Why, if at this very moment," says Demosthenes, "a loud cry were to be heard in front of the courts, and we were told that the prisonhouse lies open and the prisoners are in full flight, no one, whether he be old or young, is so

[15] 1586.
[16] Euripides, *Orestes*, 264.

heedless as not to lend aid to the utmost of his power; aye, and if anyone came forward and said that yonder stands the man who let them go, the offender would be promptly put to death without a hearing."[17] 10. In the same way, too, Hyperides on being accused, after he had proposed the liberation of the slaves subsequently to the great defeat, said, "This proposal was framed, not by the orator, but by the battle of Chaeroneia." The speaker has here at one and the same time followed a train of reasoning and indulged a flight of imagination. He has, therefore, passed the bounds of mere persuasion by the boldness of his conception. 11. By a sort of natural law in all such matters we always attend to whatever possesses superior force; whence it is that we are drawn away from demonstration pure and simple to any startling image within whose dazzling brilliancy the argument lies concealed. And it is not unreasonable that we should be affected in this way, for when two things are brought together, the more powerful always attracts to itself the virtue of the weaker. 12. It will be enough to have said thus much with regard to examples of the sublime in thought, when produced by greatness of soul, imitation, or imagery.

XVI

Here, however, in due order comes the place assigned to Figures; for they, if handled in the proper manner, will contribute, as I have said, in no mean degree to sublimity. But since to treat thoroughly of them all at the present moment would be a great, or rather an endless task, we will now, with the object of proving our proposition, run over a few only of those which produce elevation of diction. 2. Demosthenes is bringing forward a reasoned vindication of his public policy. What was the natural way of treating the subject? It was this. "You were not wrong, you who engaged in the struggle for the freedom of Greece. You have domestic warrant for it. For the warriors of Marathon did no wrong, nor they of Salamis, nor they of Plataea."[18] When, however, as though suddenly inspired by heaven and as it were frenzied by the God of Prophecy, he utters his famous oath by the champions of Greece ("assuredly ye did no wrong; I swear it by those who at Marathon stood in the forefront of the danger"), in the public view by this one Figure of Adjuration, which I here term *Apostrophe*, he deifies his

[17] *Against Timocrates*, 208.
[18] *On the Crown*, 208.

ancestors. He brings home the thought that we ought to swear by those who have thus nobly died as we swear by Gods, and he fills the mind of the judges with the high spirit of those who there bore the brunt of the danger, and he has transformed the natural course of the argument into transcendent sublimity and passion and that secure belief which rests upon strange and prodigious oaths. He instils into the minds of his hearers the conviction—which acts as a medicine and an antidote—that they should, uplifted by these eulogies, feel no less proud of the fight against Philip than of the triumph at Marathon and Salamis. By all these means he carries his hearers clean away with him through the employment of a single figure. 3. It is said, indeed, that the germ of the oath is found in Eupolis:

> For, by the fight I won at Marathon,
> No one shall vex my soul and rue it not.

But it is not sublime to swear by a person in any chance way; the sublimity depends upon the place and the manner and the circumstances and the motive. Now in the passage of Eupolis there is nothing but the mere oath, addressed to the Athenians when still prosperous and in no need of comfort. Furthermore, the poet in his oath has not made divinities of the men in order so to create in his hearers a worthy conception of their valour, but he has wandered away from those who stood in the forefront of the danger to an inanimate thing—the fight. In Demosthenes the oath is framed for vanquished men, with the intention that Chaeroneia should no longer appear a failure to the Athenians. He gives them at one and the same time, as I remarked, a demonstration that they have done no wrong, an example, the sure evidence of oaths, a eulogy, an exhortation. 4. And since the orator was likely to be confronted with the objection, "You are speaking of the *defeat* which has attended your administration, and yet you swear by *victories*," in what follows he consequently measures even individual words, and chooses them unerringly, showing that even in the revels of the imagination sobriety is required. "Those," he says, "who stood in the forefront of danger at Marathon, and those who fought by sea at Salamis and Artemisium, and those who stood in the ranks at Plataea." Nowhere does he use the word "conquered," but at every turn he has evaded any indication of the result, since it was fortunate and the opposite of what happened at Chaeroneia. So he at once rushes forward and carries his hearer off his feet. "All of whom," says he, "were accorded a public burial by the state, Aeschines, and not *the successful only*."‡

XXXIX

The fifth of those elements contributing to the sublime which we mentioned, my excellent friend, at the beginning, still remains to be dealt with, namely the arrangement of the words in a certain order. In regard to this, having already in two treatises sufficiently stated such results as our inquiry could compass, we will add, for the purpose of our present undertaking, only what is absolutely essential, namely the fact that harmonious arrangement is not only a natural source of persuasion and pleasure among men but also a wonderful instrument of lofty utterance and of passion. 2. For does not the flute instil certain emotions into its hearers and as it were make them beside themselves and full of frenzy, and supplying a rhythmical movement constrain the listener to move rhythmically in accordance therewith and to conform himself to the melody, although he may be utterly ignorant of music? Yes, and the tones of the harp, although in themselves they signify nothing at all, often cast a wonderful spell, as you know, over an audience by means of the variations of sounds, by their pulsation against one another, and by their mingling in concert. 3. And yet these are mere semblances and spurious copies of persuasion, not (as I have said) genuine activities of human nature. Are we not, then, to hold that composition (being a harmony of that language which is implanted by nature in man and which appeals not to the hearing only but to the soul itself), since it calls forth manifold shapes of words, thoughts, deeds, beauty, melody, all of them born at our birth and growing with our growth, and since by means of the blending and variation of its own tones it seeks to introduce into the minds of those who are present the emotion which affects the speaker and since it always brings the audience to share in it and by the building of phrase upon phrase raises a sublime and harmonious structure: are we not, I say, to hold that harmony by these selfsame means allures us and invariably disposes us to stateliness and dignity and elevation and every emotion which it contains within itself, gaining absolute mastery over our minds? But it is folly to dispute concerning matters which are generally admitted, since experience is proof sufficient. 4. An example of a conception which is usually thought sub-

‡ Sections on technical detail are omitted here.

lime and is really admirable is that which Demosthenes associates with
the decree: "This decree caused the danger which then beset the city to
pass by just-as a cloud."[19] But it owes its happy sound no less to the
harmony than to the thought itself. For the thought is expressed
throughout in dactylic rhythms, and these are most noble and productive
of sublimity; and therefore it is that they constitute the heroic, the
finest metre that we know. For if you derange the words of the sentence
and transpose them in whatever way you will, as for example "This
decree just-as a cloud caused the danger of the time to pass by";
nay, if you cut off a single syllable only and say "caused to pass by as a
cloud," you will perceive to what an extent harmony is in unison with
sublimity. For the very words "just-as a cloud" begin with a long
rhythm, which consists of four metrical beats; but if one syllable is cut
off and we read "as a cloud," we immediately maim the sublimity by
the abbreviation. Conversely, if you elongate the word and write
"caused to pass by just-as-if a cloud," it means the same thing, but no
longer falls with the same effect upon the ear, inasmuch as the abrupt
grandeur of the passage loses its energy and tension through the
lengthening of the concluding syllables.

XL

Among the chief causes of the sublime in speech, as in the structure of
the human body, is the collocation of members, a single one of which if
severed from another possesses in itself nothing remarkable, but all
united together make a full and perfect organism. So the constituents of
grandeur, when separated from one another, carry with them sublimity
in distraction this way and that, but when formed into a body by association and when further encircled in a chain of harmony they become
sonorous by their very rotundity; and in periods sublimity is, as it were,
a contribution made by a multitude. 2. We have, however, sufficiently
shown that many writers and poets who possess no natural sublimity
and are perhaps even wanting in elevation have nevertheless, although
employing for the most part common and popular words with no striking associations of their own, by merely joining and fitting these together,
secured dignity and distinction and the appearance of freedom from
meanness. Instances will be furnished by Philistus among many others,
by Aristophanes in certain passages, by Euripides in most. . . .

[19] *Ibid.*, 188.

XLII

Further, excessive concision of expression tends to lower the sublime, since grandeur is marred when the thought is brought into too narrow a compass. Let this be understood not of proper compression, but of what is absolutely petty and cut into segments. For concision curtails the sense, but brevity goes straight to the mark. It is plain that, *vice versa*, prolixities are frigid, for so is everything that resorts to unseasonable length.

XLIII

Triviality of expression is also apt to disfigure sublimity. In Herodotus, for example, the tempest is described with marvellous effect in all its details, but the passage surely contains some words below the dignity of the subject. The following may serve as an instance—"when the sea seethed."[20] The word "seethed" detracts greatly from the sublimity because it is an ill-sounding one. Further, "the wind," he says, "grew fagged," and those who clung to the spars met "an unpleasant end."[21] The expression "grew fagged" is lacking in dignity, being vulgar; and the word "unpleasant" is inappropriate to so great a disaster. 2. Similarly when Theopompus had dressed out in marvellous fashion the descent of the Persian king upon Egypt, he spoilt the whole by some petty words. "For which of the cities (he says) or which of the tribes in Asia did not send envoys to the Great King? Which of the products of the earth or of the achievements of art was not, in all its beauty or preciousness, brought as an offering to his presence? Consider the multitude of costly coverlets and mantles, in purple or white or embroidery; the multitude of pavilions of gold furnished with all things useful; the multitude, too, of tapestries and costly couches. Further, gold and silver plate richly wrought, and goblets and mixing-bowls, some of which you might have seen set with precious stones, and others finished with care and at great price. In addition to all this, countless myriads of Greek and barbaric weapons, and beasts of burden beyond all reckoning and victims fattened for slaughter, and many bushels of condiments, and many bags and sacks and sheets of papyrus and all other useful things, and an equal number of pieces of salted flesh from all manner of victuals, so that the piles of them were so great that those who were approaching

[20] VII, 188.
[21] VII, 191; VIII, 13.

from a distance took them to be hills and eminences confronting them."
3. He runs off from the more elevating to the more lowly, whereas he
should, on the contrary, have risen higher and higher. With his wonderful description of the whole outfit he mixes bags and condiments and
sacks, and conveys the impression of a confectioner's shop! For just as
if, in the case of those very adornments, between the golden vessels and
the jewelled mixing-bowls and the silver plate and the pavilions of pure
gold and the goblets, a man were to bring and set in the midst paltry
bags and sacks, the proceeding would have been offensive to the eye, so
do such words when introduced out of season constitute deformities
and as it were blots on the diction. 4. He might have described the scene
in broad outline just as he says that hills blocked their way, and with
regard to the preparations generally have spoken of "waggons and
camels and the multitude of beasts of burden carrying everything that
ministers to the luxury and enjoyment of the table," or have used some
such expression as "piles of all manner of grain and things which conduce preeminently to good cookery and comfort of body," or if he must
necessarily put it in so uncompromising a way, he might have said that
"all the dainties of cooks and caterers were there." 5. In lofty passages
we ought not to descend to sordid and contemptible language unless
constrained by some overpowering necessity, but it is fitting that we
should use words worthy of the subject and imitate nature the artificer
of man, for she has not placed in full view our grosser parts or the means
of purging our frame, but has hidden them away as far as was possible,
and as Xenophon says has put their channels in the remotest background, so as not to sully the beauty of the entire creature. 6. But
enough; there is no need to enumerate, one by one, the things which
produce triviality. For since we have previously indicated those qualities
which render style noble and lofty, it is evident that their opposites will
for the most part make it low and base.

XLIV

It remains however (as I will not hesitate to add, in recognition of
your love of knowledge) to clear up, my dear Terentianus, a question
which a certain philosopher has recently mooted. "I wonder," he says,
"as no doubt do many others, how it happens that in our time there are
men who have the gift of persuasion to the utmost extent, and are well
fitted for public life, and are keen and ready, and particularly rich in all

the charms of language, yet there no longer arise really lofty and transcendent natures unless quite exceptionally. So great and world-wide a dearth of high utterance attends our age." 2. "Can it be," he continued, "that we are to accept the trite explanation that democracy is the kind nursing-mother of genius, and that literary power may be said to share its rise and fall with democracy and democracy alone? For freedom, it is said, has power to feed the imaginations of the lofty-minded and to inspire hope, and where it prevails there spreads abroad the eagerness of mutual rivalry and the emulous pursuit of the foremost place. 3. Moreover, owing to the prizes which are open to all under popular government, the mental excellences of the orator are continually exercised and sharpened, and as it were rubbed bright, and shine forth (as it is natural they should) with all the freedom which inspires the doings of the state. To-day," he went on, "we seem in our boyhood to learn the lessons of a righteous servitude, being all but enswathed in its customs and observances, when our thoughts are yet young and tender, and never tasting the fairest and most productive source of eloquence (by which," he added, "I mean freedom), so that we emerge in no other guise than that of sublime flatterers." 4. This is the reason, he maintained, why no slave ever becomes an orator, although all other faculties may belong to menials. In the slave there immediately burst out signs of fettered liberty of speech, of the dungeon as it were, of a man habituated to buffetings. 5. "For the day of slavery," as Homer has it, "takes away half our manhood." [22] "Just as," he proceeded, "the cages (if what I hear is true) in which are kept the Pygmies, commonly called *nani*, not only hinder the growth of the creatures confined within them, but actually attenuate them through the bonds which beset their bodies, so one has aptly termed all servitude (though it be most righteous) the cage of the soul and a public prison-house." 6. I answered him thus: "It is easy, my good sir, and characteristic of human nature, to find fault with the age in which one lives. But consider whether it may not be true that it is not the world's peace that ruins great natures, but far rather this war illimitable which holds our desires in its grasp, aye, and further still those passions which occupy as with troops our present age and utterly harry and plunder it. For the love of money (a disease from which we all now suffer sorely) and the love of pleasure make us their thralls, or rather, as one may say, drown us body and soul in the depths, the

[22] *Odyssey*, XVII, 322.

love of riches being a malady which makes men petty, and the love of pleasure one which makes them most ignoble. 7. On reflexion I cannot discover how it is possible for us, if we value boundless wealth so highly, or (to speak more truly) deify it, to avoid allowing the entrance into our souls of the evils which are inseparable from it. For vast and unchecked wealth is accompanied, in close conjunction and step for step as they say, by extravagance, and as soon as the former opens the gates of cities and houses, the latter immediately enters and abides. And when time has passed the pair build nests in the lives of men, as the wise say, and quickly give themselves to the rearing of offspring, and breed ostentation, and vanity, and luxury, no spurious progeny of theirs, but only too legitimate. If these children of wealth are permitted to come to maturity, straightway they beget in the soul inexorable masters—insolence, and lawlessness, and shamelessness. 8. This must necessarily happen, and men will no longer lift up their eyes or have any further regard for fame, but the ruin of such lives will gradually reach its complete consummation and sublimities of soul fade and wither away and become contemptible, when men are lost in admiration of their own mortal parts and omit to exalt that which is immortal. 9. For a man who has once accepted a bribe for a judicial decision cannot be an unbiassed and upright judge of what is just and honourable (since to the man who is venal his own interests must seem honourable and just), and the same is true where the entire life of each of us is ordered by bribes, and huntings after the death of others, and the laying of ambushes for legacies, while gain from any and every source we purchase—each one of us—at the price of life itself being the slaves of pleasure. In an age which is ravaged by plagues so sore, is it possible for us to imagine that there is still left an unbiassed and incorruptible judge of works that are great and likely to reach posterity, or is it not rather the case that all are influenced in their decisions by the passion for gain? 10. Nay, it is perhaps better for men like ourselves to be ruled than to be free, since our appetites, if let loose without restraint upon our neighbours like beasts from a cage, would set the world on fire with deeds of evil. 11. Summing up, I maintained that among the banes of the natures which our age produces must be reckoned that half-heartedness in which the life of all of us with few exceptions is passed, for we do not labour or exert ourselves except for the sake of praise and pleasure, never for those solid benefits which are a worthy object of our own efforts and the respect of others. 12. But "'tis best to leave these riddles unresolved,"[23] and to proceed to what next presents itself, namely the subject of the Passions, about which I previously undertook to write in a separate treatise. These form, as it seems to me a material part of discourse generally and of the Sublime itself. . . .

[23] Euripides, *Electra*, 37.

3. DANTE

De Vulgari Eloquentia

Dante Alighieri (1265–1321), the great Italian poet, was born into an aristocratic family in Florence. He studied contemporary philosophy, wrote poetry, and served in state affairs and on diplomatic missions. He was exiled from Florence in 1301 and died in Ravenna twenty years later.

Although Dante is best known for one work, he did write others: in 1292 *La Vita Nuova*, a collection of poems in Italian; in 1304, *De Vulgari Eloquentia;* in 1304–7 *Convivio*, a prose commentary on three *canzoni;* in 1313 *De Monarchia* in Latin prose; and in 1312 (all dates are approximate) the *Divine Comedy*. There also remain other poems and letters. Among the latter and of the greatest critical interest is Epistola X to Can Grande della Scala, although the controversy still exists regarding its authenticity. Dante explains the levels of meaning and symbolism in his *Divine Comedy*, outlining and commenting upon this very important medieval method of reading literature in general.

The incomplete *De Vulgari Eloquentia* originally seems to have been intended to contain four books. No reason is known for Dante's not having finished it, and editors even believe that what we have is an early draft of the work. Only three manuscripts of the treatise are extant, one of which, now considered the best, came to light only in 1917. Even the date of composition is unknown. A. Margio, the editor of the Italian edition (Florence, 1938), assigns the work to 1303 or 1304. The treatise was first published in modern Italian by Trissino in 1529. Only in 1577 was it published in the original Latin by Jacopo Corbinelli in Paris.

Since Dante's *Divine Comedy* was immediately hailed as a masterpiece and widely studied, one would expect a lively interest in a work which discusses the writing of poetry in the vernacular. But judging from the lateness and the paucity of editions, the work's importance seems to have been considered slight. The *De Vulgari Eloquentia* has fared no better in modern times. The first "modern" Italian edition was published in 1896; the next, still standard edition, is Margio's in 1938. The *De Vulgari Eloquentia* was translated into English by A. G. Ferrers Howells in a Temple Classic edition in 1904. This translation is out of print, and I have never come across reprinted excerpts from the text.

Thus this very important document has suffered a strange fate and continues to suffer it—perhaps because of its unavailability. Yet those who have read it and thought about it are extremely enthusiastic. In the Introduction I have quoted Saintsbury—a very influential critic and one whose *History of Criticism* was considered the undoubted standard for almost fifty years—on the extreme importance of the treatise. Vernon Hall in his *A Short History of Literary Criticism* also states: "His *De vulgari eloquentia* largely disregarded the question of genres which so dominated classical criticism and concerned itself with language and style, the main interest of modern poets. It gave the highest place to the new subjects the Middle Ages had introduced into literature and praised above all forms the *canzone*, a lyric poem. And when today we think of poetry we, like Dante, think of the lyric before we think of the dramatic and narrative forms, tragedy and the epic. In several ways, then, Dante was the first modern critic." (p. 25.) And Kenneth Burke, a critic who seldom praises or even seems to notice other critics, declares that "the greatest attempt at a poetics of sound is Dante's *De Vulgari Eloquenti. . . ."* (*The Philosophy of Literary Form*, p. 13.)

In good classical and medieval fashion Dante proceeds from the genus to the species in the treatise. Book I, chapters 1–5 contain the basic definitions of human speech, 6–9 a discussion of languages and their change, 10–15 an examination of Italian dialects, on which Thomas Bergin remarks, "Reading between the lines, it is clear that Tuscan is the only base that will really satisfy Dante, and further that he is not looking for language alone but for poetic diction." (*Dante* [Houghton Mifflin, 1965], p. 161.) The book's last chapters, 16–18, attempt to evolve an Italian standard and to establish the elements of that standard. In Book II, chapters 1–2 deal with the proper use of and the proper subjects for the Vulgar tongue; the remaining chapters (Dante breaks off in the middle of Chapter 14) contain an incomplete discussion of the specific genre, *canzone* (what we would call a lyric today, but Dante defines it in Chapter 8 as "the action or passion of singing"). Among the elements of the *canzone* which he discusses are: the proper style, diction, meter, construction, principal parts and their arrangement, musical setting, and rhymes. In the last chapter he intends to treat the number of lines and syllables in the stanza. In this edition I have left out certain technical chapters, such as forms of the *canzone*, etc.

By discussing the Vulgar tongue or the vernacular at all, Dante breaks completely with medieval tradition and for the first time insists on not just the serviceability of the vernacular but its potential for the very best literature. His definition is simple: ". . . we say that the Vulgar Tongue is that which we acquire without any rule, by imitating our nurses." (p. 2.) What emerges from this simple definition and the unusual raising to prominence of the vernacular is also most tradition-breaking. As he proceeds one becomes aware that Dante is working toward a kind of nationalism: Italian is considered as an entity above all the local dialects.

By way of expounding the Vulgar tongue Dante deals with critical concerns that point forward as well as backward in time, although, as I have mentioned before, he probably had not read Aristotle's *Poetics* and had definitely not read Longinus' *On the Sublime*. Dante's main concern is obviously with diction. He finds the Italian "illustrious," "cardinal" (basic), "courtly," and "curial" (balanced), and therefore a fit medium for both prose and poetry. He further distinguishes between different kinds of words and their proper or admissible use. Thus he finds and illustrates some words as childish, feminine, manly, sylvan, urban, combed-out, glossy, shaggy, or rumpled (I am using the terms from the English translation). Obviously the use of each kind of word will depend very greatly on the subject matter. Thus, like Aristotle before him and Dryden after him, Dante feels that the best subjects alone should be handled. What things are the greatest? Those that are useful, pleasurable, and right, or put differently: Safety (Arms), Love, and Virtue. The subjects most concerned with them are "prowess in Arms, the fire of Love, and the right direction of the Will."

Dante's advice on writing poetry also often harks back to the classical age. This advice also is of great interest, of course, because he is one of the best poets of all time. His advice, like all good advice, is simple: (1) emulate the great poets; (2) follow Horace's dictum of taking up a subject suited to your strength; (3) keep the distinctions between "lower," "higher," and "intermediate" styles depending on whether the subject is a comedy, tragedy, or elegy. The concern with proper styles was of great importance during the Renaissance and after (in Milton's work, for example). (4) Finally he reaffirms the greatness of art and warns poets against trusting "genius" alone: "And here let the folly of those stand confessed who, innocent of art and knowledge, and trusting to genius alone, rush forward to sing of the highest subjects in the highest style. Let them cease from such presumption, and if, in

their natural sluggishness they are but geese, let them abstain from
imitating the eagle soaring to the stars."

The selection is taken from the translation by A. G. Ferrers Howell.*

BOOK FIRST./CHAPTER I. WHAT THE VULGAR TONGUE IS, AND WHEREIN
IT DIFFERS FROM GRAMMAR (1).

Since we do not find that any one before us had treated of the science
of the Vulgar Tongue, while, in fact, we see that this tongue is highly
necessary for all, inasmuch as not only men, but even women and
children, strive, in so far as Nature allows them, to acquire it; and since
it is our wish to enlighten to some little extent the discernment (2) of
those who walk through the streets like blind men, generally fancying
that those things which are [really] in front of them are behind them (3);
we will endeavour, by the aid of the Wisdom which breathes from
Heaven (4), to be of service to the speech of the common people, not
only by drawing the water for such a draught from our own understanding, but by taking or compiling from others, mixing the most useful
information from each [with our own], so that we may then be able to
give draughts of the sweetest hydromel (5). But as the business of every
science is not to prove but to explain its subject (6), in order that men
may know what that is with which the science is concerned, we say at
once that we call the Vulgar Tongue that to which children are accustomed by those who are about them when they first begin to distinguish
sounds; or, to put it more shortly, we say that the Vulgar Tongue is
that which we acquire without any rule, by imitating our nurses. We
afterwards have another secondary speech, which the Romans called
Grammar. And this secondary speech the Greeks also have, as well as
others, but not all. Few, however, acquire the use of this secondary
speech, because we can only be guided and instructed in it by the
expenditure of much time, and by assiduous study. Of these two kinds of
speech also, the Vulgar Tongue is the nobler, as well because it was the
first employed by the human race, as because the whole world makes
use of it, though it has been divided into different forms of utterance
and words. It is also the nobler as being natural to us, whereas the other
is rather of an artificial kind; and it is of this nobler form of speech that
we intend to treat (7). . . .

CHAPTER XVI. OF THE EXCELLENCE OF THE HIGHEST FORM OF THE VULGAR
TONGUE: AND HOW IT IS COMMON TO ALL ITALIANS.

* London, Kegan Paul, Trench, Trübner & Co., 1890.

After having scoured the heights and pastures of Italy without having found that panther which we are in pursuit of (1), let us now track her out in a more rational manner, in order that we may with skilful efforts completely enclose within our toils her who is everywhere felt but nowhere seen (2). Resuming, then, our hunting-spears, we say that in every genus of things there must be some standard by which all the things of that genus may be compared and weighed, so that from it (3) we may obtain the measure of all the rest: just as in numbers all are measured by unity (4), and are said to be more or fewer according as they are distant from or near to unity: so also in colours all are measured by white, for they are said to be more or less visible according as they approach or recede from it. And what we say of those things which display quantity and quality, we think may also be said of all the categories (5) and of substance (6): namely, that everything in a genus is measurable by that which is simplest in the same genus. Wherefore in our actions, however many may be the species into which they are divided, we have to discover this standard by which they may be measured: thus, in what concerns our actions as human beings simply, we have Virtue, in order that we may have insight into the nature of our actions generally, for according to it we judge a man to be good or bad: in what concerns our actions as citizens, we have the Law, according to which a citizen is said to be good or bad: in what concerns our actions as Italians, we have certain very simple standards of manners, customs, and language, by which our actions as Italians are weighed and measured. Now, the noblest of those actions which belong to us as Italians are peculiar to no one town in Italy but are common to all: and among these we can now distinguish that Vulgar Tongue which we were pursuing above, and which is perceptible in every town, but abiding in none. It may, however, be more perceptible in one than in another, just like the simplest of substances (7), which is God, who is more perceptible in a man than in a brute, in an animal than in a plant, in a plant than in a mineral; in heaven than in the elements, in fire than in earth (8). And the simplest quantity, which is unity, is more perceptible in an odd than in an even number; and the simplest colour, which is white, is more perceptible in orange than in green. Having, then, found what we were looking for, we declare that the Illustrious, Cardinal, Courtly, and Curial Vulgar Tongue in Italy is that which belongs to all the towns in Italy, but does not appear to belong to any one of them; and is that by which all the local dialects of the Italians are measured, weighed, and compared.

Chapter XVII. why this language is called illustrious.

We must now set forth in order why it is that we call this language we have found by the epithets Illustrious, Cardinal, Courtly, and Curial; and by doing this we shall more clearly explain the nature of the language itself. First, then, let us lay bare what we mean by the epithet Illustrious, and why we call the language Illustrious. Now, whatever we call Illustrious we understand to be something which shines forth illuminating and illuminated: and in this way we call men illustrious, either because, being illuminated by authority, they illuminate others by [the display of] Justice and Charity; or else because, having been excellently trained, they in turn give excellent training, like Seneca and Numa Pompilius. And the Vulgar Tongue of which we are speaking has both been exalted by training and authority, and also exalts its followers by honour and glory. Now, it appears to have been exalted by training, inasmuch as we see it [purified] from so many rude Italian words, involved constructions, faulty expressions, and rustic accents, and brought to such a degree of excellence, clearness, completeness, and polish, as is displayed by Cino of Pistoja and his friend in their *Canzoni*. And that it has been exalted by authority is plain; for what is of greater authority than that which can sway the hearts of men, so as to make an unwilling man willing, and a willing man unwilling, just as this language has done and is doing? Now, that it exalts its followers by honour is evident. Do not they surpass in renown kings, marquises, counts, and all other magnates? This has no need at all of proof. But we ourselves know how glorious it makes its friends, for the sweetness of this glory makes us cast even our exile behind our back. Wherefore we ought deservedly to proclaim this language as Illustrious.

Chapter XVIII. why this language is called cardinal, courtly, and curial.

It is not without reason that we adorn this Illustrious Vulgar Tongue with a second epithet; that is, that we call it Cardinal: because, as the whole door follows its hinge, and whither the hinge turns the door also turns, whether it be moved inwards or outwards; so the whole herd of local dialects turns and returns, moves and pauses, according as this [Illustrious language does], which really seems to be the father of a family. Does it not daily root out the thorny bushes from the Italian wood? Does it not daily insert cuttings or plant young trees? What else have its foresters to do but to bring in and take away as has been said? Wherefore it surely deserves to be adorned with so great a name as this.

Now, the reason we call it Courtly is as follows: if we Italians had a Court it would be an Imperial one; and if a Court is a common home of all the realm, and an august ruler of all parts of the realm, it would be fitting that whatever is of such a character as to be common to all [parts] without being peculiar to any should frequent this Court and dwell there: nor is there any other abode worthy of so great an inmate. Such, in fact, seems to be that Vulgar Tongue of which we are speaking; and hence it is that those who frequent all the royal palaces always speak the Illustrious Vulgar Tongue. Hence, also, it happens that our Illustrious Language wanders about like a wayfarer, and is welcomed in humble shelters, seeing we have no Court.

This language is also deservedly to be styled Curial because Curiality is nothing else but the justly balanced rule of things which have to be done; and, because the scales required for this kind of balancing are only wont to be found in the most excellent Courts of Justice (1), it follows that whatever is well balanced in our actions is called Curial. Wherefore, since this Illustrious language has been weighed in the balances of the most excellent Court of Justice of the Italians, it deserves to be called Curial. But it seems mere trifling to say that it has been weighed in the balances of the most excellent Court of Justice of the Italians, because we have no [Imperial] Court of Justice. To this the answer is easy. For, though we have no Court of Justice in Italy in the sense of the one [Supreme] Court of the King of Germany, still the members of such a Court are not wanting. And just as the members of the German Court are united under one Prince, so the members of ours have been united by the gracious light of Reason. Wherefore, it would be false to assert that the Italians have no such Court of Justice, though we have no Prince (2), because we have a Court, though, as a body, it is scattered.

CHAPTER XIX. THAT THE LOCAL ITALIAN DIALECTS ARE REDUCIBLE TO ONE WHICH IS CALLED ITALIAN.

Now we declare that this Vulgar Tongue, which we have shown to be

Illustrious, Cardinal, Courtly, and Curial, is that which is called the Vulgar Italian. For just as a Vulgar Tongue is to be found belonging to Cremona, so can one be found belonging to Lombardy; and just as one can be found belonging to Lombardy, so one can be found belonging to the whole of the left side of Italy. And just as all these can be found, so also can that which belongs to the whole of Italy. And just as the first is called Cremonese, the second Lombard, and the third Semi-Italian, so that which belongs to the whole of Italy is called the Italian Vulgar Tongue. For this has been used by the illustrious writers who have written poetry in the vernacular throughout Italy; as Sicilians, Apulians, Tuscans, natives of Romagna, Lombardy, and both the Marches. And because our intention is, as we promised in the beginning of this work, to give instruction concerning the Vulgar Tongue, we will begin with this Illustrious Italian as being the most excellent; and treat, in the following books, of those whom we think worthy to use it; and for what, and how, and also where, when, and to whom, it ought to be used. And after making all this clear, we will make it our business to throw light on the lower forms of the Vulgar Tongue, gradually coming down to that which belongs to a single family.

BOOK SECOND./CHAPTER I. FOR WHOM THE USE OF THE POLISHED AND ORNATE VULGAR TONGUE IS FITTING, AND FOR WHOM IT IS NOT FITTING.

Promising once more to display the activity of our mental power, and taking up again the pen of useful work, we declare in the first place that the Illustrious Italian Vulgar Tongue is equally fit for use in prose and in verse. But because prose-writers get this language especially from poets, and because poetry remains a fixed pattern to prose-writers, and not the contrary, inasmuch as certain [definite] things appear to confer a supremacy on verse (1): therefore, according as this language is [primarily] metrical, let us carefully disentangle it, treating of it in the order we set forth at the end of the first book. Let us, then, first inquire whether those who write verse in the Vulgar Tongue should use this Illustrious language; and, so far as a superficial consideration of the matter goes, it would seem that they should, because every one who writes verse ought to adorn his verse as far as he is able. Wherefore, as nothing affords so great an adornment as the Illustrious Vulgar Tongue does, it would seem that every writer of verse ought to employ it. Besides, if that which is best in its kind be mixed with things inferior to itself, it not only appears not to detract anything from them, but even to improve them. Wherefore, if any writer of verse, even though his verse be poor in thought (2), mixes the Illustrious Vulgar Tongue with his poverty of thought, not only will he improve his poverty of thought, but he actually appears to be obliged to take this course. Things of small power require much more assistance than things of great power; and thus it appears that all writers of verse are at liberty to use this Illustrious language. But this is quite false, because not even poets of the highest order ought always to assume it, as will appear from a consideration of what is discussed farther on. This Illustrious language, then, just like our behaviour in other matters and our dress, demands men of like quality to its own; for great magnificence demands men of power, and the purple, men of noble character (3): and, in the same way, this Illustrious language seeks for men who excel in genius and knowledge, and despises others, as will appear from what is said below. For everything which is suited to us is so either in respect of the Genus, or of the Species, or of the Individual, as Sensation, Laughter (4), War: but this Illustrious language is not suited to us in respect of our Genus, for then it would also be suited to the brutes; nor in respect of our Species, for then it would be suited to all men,—and as to this there is no question, for no one will say that this language is suited to dwellers in the mountains; because the best thoughts cannot exist except where knowledge and genius are found: therefore the best language is suitable in respect of the Individual (5). But nothing is suited to an Individual except on account of his particular merit, as, for instance, Commerce, War, and Government. Wherefore, if things are suitable according to merit, that is, according to individual worth (and some men are worthy, other worthier, and others worthiest), it is plain that good things are suited to the worthy, better things to the worthier, and the best things to the worthiest. And as language is the instrument of our thought (6), just as a horse is the instrument of a soldier, and as the best horses are suited to the best soldiers, so the best language will, as has been said, be suited to the best thoughts. But the best thoughts cannot exist except where knowledge and genius are found; therefore the best language is only suitable in those in whom knowledge and genius are found: and so the best language is not suited to all who write verse, since a great many write without knowledge and genius: and consequently neither is the best Vulgar Tongue [suited to all who write verse]. Wherefore, if it is not suited to all, all ought not to use it, because no one ought to act in an unsuitable manner. And as to our statement that every one ought to adorn his verse as far as he can, we declare that it is true: but we should not describe an ox with a saddle or a swine with a belt as adorned, nay, rather we should laugh at them as disfigured; for adornment is the addition of some suitable thing. As to our statement that superior things mixed with inferior produce a perfect thing, we say that it is true if the blending is complete, as when we mix gold and silver together; but if it is not, the inferior things appear worse, as when beautiful women are mixed with ugly ones. Wherefore, since the theme of those who write verse always persists as an ingredient separate from the words; it will not, unless of the highest quality, appear better when associated with the best Vulgar Tongue, but worse; like an ugly woman if dressed out in gold or silk.

CHAPTER II. FOR WHAT SUBJECTS THE ORNATE VULGAR TONGUE OUGHT TO BE USED.

After having proved that not all those who write verse, but only those of the highest excellence ought to use the Illustrious Vulgar Tongue, we must in the next place establish whether every subject ought to be handled in it, or not; and if not, we must show separately what subjects are worthy of it. And, in reference to this, we must first find out what we understand by that which we call *worthy*. *Worthy* is that which has *worthiness*, just as *noble* is that which has *nobility*; and as, when the qualifying term is known, the qualified term is [also] known in so far as it is qualified by the other (1), if we know what *worthiness* is, we shall know also what *worthy* is. Now, *worthiness* is an effect or end of deserts: so that when any one has deserved well, we say that he has arrived at worthiness of good; but when he has deserved ill, at worthiness of evil. Thus we say that a soldier who has fought well has arrived at worthiness of victory; one who has ruled well, at worthiness of a kingdom; also, that a liar has arrived at worthiness of shame, and a robber at worthiness of death. But inasmuch as [further] comparisons are made among those who deserve well, as also among those who deserve ill, so that some deserve well, some better, and some best, some badly, some worse, and some worst; while such comparisons are only made with respect to the end of deserts, which (as has been mentioned before) we call *worthiness*, it is plain that worthinesses are compared together according as they are greater or less, so that some are great, some greater, and some greatest; and, consequently, it is obvious that one thing is worthy, another worthier, and another worthiest. And because there can be no such comparison of worthinesses with regard to the same object [of desert], but [only] with regard to different objects, so that we call *worthier* that which is worthy of greater objects, and *worthiest* that which is worthy of the greatest, because no thing can be more worthy than another of the same object: it is evident that the best things are worthy of the best [objects of desert], according to the requirement of the things (2). Whence it follows that, since the language we call Illustrious is the best of all the other forms of the Vulgar Tongue, the best subjects alone are worthy of being handled in it, and these we call the *worthiest* of those subjects which can be handled: and now let us hunt out what they are. And, in order to make this clear, it must be observed that, as man has been endowed with a threefold life, namely, Vegetable, Animal, and Rational, he journeys along a threefold road (3): for in so far as he is Vegetable (4), he seeks for what is useful in that which he has in common with plants; in so far as he is Animal (4), he seeks for what is pleasurable in that which he has in common with the brutes; in so far as he is Rational (4), he seeks for what is right (5),—and in this he stands alone, or is a partaker of the nature of the Angels. It is by these three kinds of life that we appear to carry out whatever we do: and because in each one of them some things are greater, some greatest, it follows that those which are greatest appear the ones which ought most to be treated of, and, consequently, in the greatest Vulgar Tongue.

But we must discuss what things are greatest; and first in respect of what is useful. Now, in this matter, if we carefully consider the object of all those who are in search of what is useful, we shall find that it is nothing else but Safety (6). Secondly, in respect of what is pleasurable: and here we say that that is most pleasurable which gives pleasure by the most exquisite object of appetite, and this is Love. Thirdly, in respect of what is right: and here no one doubts that Virtue has the first place. Wherefore these three things, Safety, Love, and Virtue, appear to be those capital matters which ought most to be treated of,—I mean the things which are most closely connected with them (7), as prowess in Arms, the fire of Love, and the right direction of the Will. And, if we duly consider, we shall find that the illustrious writers have written poetry in the Vulgar Tongue on these subjects exclusively, namely, Bertram of Born on Arms (8); Arnauld Daniel on Love (8); Gerard of Borneil on Righteousness; Cino of Pistoja on Love; his friend on Righteousness. . . . I do not find, however, that any Italian has as yet written poetry on the subject of Arms.

Having then arrived at this point, we know what are the proper subjects to be sung in the highest Vulgar Language. . . .

CHAPTER IV. OF THE VARIETY OF STYLE OF THOSE WHO WRITE POETRY.

Having, then, proved by a process of disentangling what persons and things are worthy of the Courtly Vulgar Tongue, as well as the form of verse which we deem worthy of such honour as alone is fitted for the highest Vulgar Tongue, before going off to other topics, let us explain the form of the *Canzone*, which many appear to adopt rather by chance than by design; and let us display that, of which a knowledge has been hitherto casually assumed, I mean the teaching of [the practice of] this art (1); omitting the form of *Ballate* and Sonnets, because we intend to explain this in the fourth book of this work, when we treat of the Intermediate Vulgar Tongue. Reviewing, therefore, what has been said, we remember that we have for the most part given the name of poets to those who write verse in the Vulgar Tongue; and this we have doubtless ventured to say with good reason, because they are in fact poets, if we take a right view of poetry, which is nothing else but *a rhetorical composition set to music* (2). But these poets differ from the great poets— that is, the Regular ones,—for these last have written poetry with stately language and regular art, whereas the others, as has been said, write by chance. It therefore happens that the nearer we approach to the great poets, the more correct is the poetry we write; whence it behoves us, by devoting somewhat of our work to teaching [the rules of the art], to emulate their poetic teaching.

In the first place, then, we say that each one ought to take up a subject of such weight as to be a fair burden for his own shoulders, so that their strength may not be too heavily taxed and he be forced to tumble into the mud. This is the advice our master Horace gives us when he says, in the beginning of his "Art of Poetry" (3), "Ye who write, take up a subject suited to your strength."

Next, we ought to possess a sound judgment as to those things which suggest themselves to us as fit to be uttered, so as to decide whether they ought to be sung in the way of Tragedy, Comedy, or Elegy. By Tragedy we understand the Higher style, by Comedy, the Intermediate style, by Elegy we understand the Lower style (4). If our subject appears fit to be sung in the Tragic style we must then assume the Illustrious Vulgar Tongue, and consequently we must write a properly constructed *Canzone*. If it appears fit to be sung in the Comic style, sometimes the Illustrious (5) and sometimes the Lower Vulgar Tongue should be used, and the judgment to be exercised in this case we reserve for treatment in the Fourth Book. If our subject appears fit to be sung in the Elegiac style we must adopt the Lower Vulgar Tongue alone.

But let us omit the other styles, and now, as is fitting, let us treat of the Tragic style. We are said, then, to make use of the Tragic style when the Stateliness (6) of the Lines as well as the Loftiness of the Construction and the Excellence of the Words agree with the Weight of the Subject. But, because, if we remember rightly, it has already been proved that the highest things are worthy of the highest, and because the style which we call Tragic appears to be the highest style, those things which we have distinguished as being worthy of the highest song are to be sung in that style alone, namely, Safety, Love, and Virtue, and those other things, our conceptions of which arise from these: provided that they be not degraded by any accident (7). Let every one, therefore, beware, and discern what we say; and, when he purposes to sing of these three subjects, simply, or of those things which directly and simply follow after them, let him first drink of Helicon (8), and then, after adjusting the strings, boldly take up his *plectrum* (9) and begin in the proper manner. But it is just here, in the due composition of the *Canzone* and in the exercise of this judgment that the real difficulty lies; for the proper result can never be attained without strenuous efforts of genius, constant practice in the art, and fully available knowledge. And it is those [so equipped] whom the Poet in the Sixth Book of the *Aeneid* describes (10) as Beloved of God, raised by glowing virtue to the sky, and Sons of the Gods, though he is speaking figuratively. And here let the folly of those stand confessed (11) who, innocent of art and knowledge, and trusting to genius alone, rush forward to sing of the highest subjects in the highest style. Let them cease from such presumption, and if, in their natural sluggishness they are but geese, let them abstain from imitating the eagle soaring to the stars (12)....

CHAPTER VII. WHAT WORDS ARE TO BE PUT [INTO "CANZONI"] AND WHAT WORDS ARE INADMISSIBLE INTO VERNACULAR METRE.

The next division of our progress demands that an explanation be given as to those words which are of such grandeur (1) as to be worthy of being admitted into that style to which we have awarded the first place. We declare, therefore, to begin with, that the due selection of words involves not the smallest labour of our reason, because we see that a great many sorts (2) of them can be found. For some words are *childish*, some *feminine*, some *manly:* and of these last some are *sylvan*, others *urban:* and of those we call urban we feel that some are *combed-out* and *glossy*, some *shaggy* and *rumpled*. Now, among these urban words, the combed-out and the shaggy are those we call *grand:* whilst we call the glossy and the rumpled those whose sound is superfluous, just as among great (3) works some are works of magnanimity, others of smoke (4); and as to these last, although when superficially looked at there may be thought to be a kind of ascent, still, [when they are viewed] by sound reason no ascent will be found, but rather a headlong fall down giddy precipices, because the marked-out path of virtue is departed from. Consider then, Reader, how much it behoves thee to use the sieve (5) in selecting noble words: for if thou hast regard to the Illustrious Vulgar Tongue, which (as has been said above) poets ought to use when writing in the Tragic style in the vernacular (and these are the persons to whom we intend to give information), thou wilt take care that the noblest words alone are left in thy sieve. And among these thou wilt not be able in anywise to place childish words, because of their simplicity, as *mamma* and *babbo*, *mate* and *pate*; nor feminine words because of their softness, as *dolciada* and *placevole:* nor sylvan words, because of their roughness, as *greggia* and the rest; nor the glossy nor rumpled urban words as *femina* and *corpo*. Therefore thou wilt see that only the combed-out and the shaggy urban words will be left to thee, which are the noblest, and members of the Illustrious Vulgar Tongue. Now, we call those words *combed-out* which have three, or as nearly as possible three syllables, without aspirate, without acute or circumflex accent, without the double consonants *z* or *x*, without double liquids (6) or liquids placed immediately after a doubled mute (7); and which, so to say, leave the speaker with a certain sweetness, like *amore*, *donna*, *disio*, *virtute*, *donare*, *litiria*, *salute*, *securitate*, *difesa* (8). We call *shaggy* all words beside these which appear either necessary or ornamental to the Illustrious Vulgar Tongue. We call *necessary* those which we cannot change, as certain monosyllables like *sì*, *vo*, *me*, *te*, *se*, *a*, *e*, *i*, *o*, *u*, the interjections, and many more. We describe as *ornamental* all polysyllables which, when mixed with combed-out words produce a fair harmony of structure though they may have the roughness of aspirate, accent, double [*s* or *z*], [double] liquids and length as *terra*, *honore*, *spezza* (9), *gravitate*, *alleviato*, *impossibilitate*, *benavventuratissimo*, *avventuratissimamente*, *disavventuratissimamente*, *sovramagnificantissimamente*, which last has eleven syllables. A name or word might yet be found with more syllables still; but as it would exceed the capacity of all our lines it does not appear to fall into the present discussion; such a word is *onorificabilitudinitate*, which runs in Italian to twelve syllables, and in Latin to thirteen, in two of the oblique cases. In what way shaggy words of this kind are to be harmonized in metres with the combed-out words, we leave to be taught further on. And what has been said here on the preeminent nature of the words to be used may suffice for every one of inborn discernment. . . .

4. SIDNEY

An Apologie for Poetrie

Sir Philip Sidney (1554–86), the oldest son of Sir Henry Sidney, was born in Penshurst, England. He was educated at Oxford, served on diplomatic missions, and was killed fighting the Spanish. He was a true example of a Renaissance man: a courtier, diplomat, soldier, lover, critic, and poet.

He is perhaps best known as poet. Certainly his sonnet sequence, *Astrophel and Stella*, is a great work; so is his prose, *Arcadia*. However, *An Apologie for Poetrie* is a major critical milestone. It was written in answer to Stephen Gosson's *The Schoole of Abuse*, a puritan attack on poetry, dedicated, without permission, to Sidney. At first Sidney's treatise was circulated among friends; then in 1595 two texts of it came out under different titles by two publishers: Ponsonby's *The Defence of Poesie* and Olney's *An Apologie for Poetrie*.

By way of answer to Gosson, Sidney not only rebuts the whole narrow-mindedness of *The Schoole of Abuse* but also assesses the history and the value of poetry. It is classical in subject matter and in style; as K. Myrick points out, it is really a moving oration. Thus its seven parts are those of a classical oration: "(1) the *exordium*, or the winning of the hearer's attention to what follows; (2) the *narratio*, in which Sidney offers a historical survey of the role of poetry; (3) the *propositio*, or resolving of what has been said, with Sidney's definition of poetry, drawn primarily from Aristotle; (4) the *partitio*, or dividing up and stating of what arguments remain to be answered; (5) the *confirmatio*, or proving of the case; (6) the *reprehensio*, or final refutation in the form of reproof or censure of the other side; and lastly (7) the *peroratio*, or final summing up." (Bate's summary, pp. 78–79 of Myrick chapter "The *Defence* as a Classical Oration.")

Examined from another point of view, Sidney's essay can also be seen to fall into three structural parts: (1) history of poetry, (2) aim of poetry, (3) the moral value of poetry. Although the "historical" beginning is valuable, it is the last two parts that are of particular interest. From them poetry emerges as the most valuable human activity: it surpasses nature, it embodies truth, and finally teaches and delights man. It is even better than all other teachers because it first moves man to wish to be taught; as Sidney soberly observes: "For who will be taught, if hee bee not mooved with desire to be taught?"

The selection uses the complete essay as published by Olney under the title *An Apologie for Poetrie*.

When the right vertuous Edward Wotton, and I, were at the Emperors Court together, wee gave our selves to learne horsemanship of John Pietro Pugliano: one that with great commendation had the place of an Esquire in his stable. And hee, according to the fertilnes of the Italian wit, did not onely afoord us the demonstration of his practise, but sought to enrich our mindes with the contemplations therein, which hee thought most precious. But with none I remember mine eares were at any time more loden, then when (either angred with slowe paiment, or mooved with our learner-like admiration,) he exercised his speech in the prayse of his facultie. Hee sayd, Souldiours were the noblest estate of mankinde, and horsemen, the noblest of Souldiours. Hee sayde, they were the Maisters of warre, and ornaments of peace: speedy goers, and strong abiders, triumphers both in Camps and Courts. Nay, to so unbeleeved a poynt hee proceeded, as that no earthly thing bred such wonder to a Prince, as to be a good horseman. Skill of government, was but a Pedanteria in comparison: then would hee adde certaine prayses, by telling what a peerlesse beast a horse was. The onely serviceable Courtier without flattery, the beast of most beutie, faithfulnes, courage, and such more, that if I had not beene a peece of a Logician before I came to him, I think he would have perswaded mee to have wished my selfe a horse. But thus much at least with his no fewe words hee drave into me, that selfe-love is better than any building to make that seeme gorgious, wherein our selves are parties. Wherein, if Pugliano his strong affection and weake arguments will not satisfie you, I wil give you a neerer example of my selfe, who (I knowe not by what mischance) in these my not old yeres and idelest times, having slipt into the title of a Poet, am provoked to say somthing unto you in the defence of that my unelected vocation, which if I handle with more good will then good reasons, beare with me, sith the scholler is to be pardoned that foloweth the steppes of his Maister. And yet I must say, that as I have just cause to make a pittiful defence of poore Poetry, which from almost the highest estimation of learning, is fallen to be the laughingstocke of children. So have I need to bring some more availeable proofes: sith the former is by no man barred of his deserved credite, the silly latter hath had even the names of Philosophers used to the defacing of it, with great danger of civill war among the Muses. And first, truly to al them that professing learning inveigh against Poetry, may justly be objected, that they goe very neer to ungratfulnes, to seek to deface that, which in the noblest nations and languages that are knowne, hath been the first light-giver to ignorance, and first Nurse, whose milk by little and little enabled them to feed afterwards of tougher knowledges: and will they now play the Hedghog, that being received into the den, drave out his host? or rather the Vipers, that with theyr birth kill their Parents? Let learned Greece in any of her manifold Sciences, be able to shew me one booke, before Musæus, Homer, and Hesiodus, all three nothing els but Poets. Nay, let any historie be brought, that can say any Writers were there before them, if they were not men of the same skil, as Orpheus, Linus, and some other are named: who having beene the first of that Country, that made pens deliverers of their knowledge to their posterity, may justly challenge to bee called their Fathers in learning: for not only in time they had this priority (although in it self antiquity be venerable) but went before them, as causes to drawe with their charming sweetnes, the wild untamed wits to an admiration of knowledge. So as Amphion was sayde to move stones with his Poetrie, to build Thebes. And Orpheus to be listened to by beastes, indeed, stony and beastly people. So among the Romans were Livius, Andronicus, and Ennius. So in the Italian language, the first that made it aspire to be a Treasure-house of Science, where the Poets Dante, Boccace, and Petrarch. So in our English were Gower and Chawcer.

After whom, encouraged and delighted with theyr excellent foregoing, others have followed, to beautifie our mother tongue, as wel in the same kinde as in other Arts. This did so notably shewe it selfe, that the Phylosophers of Greece, durst not a long time appeare to the worlde but under the masks of Poets. So Thales, Empedocles, and Parmenides, sange their naturall Phylosophie in verses: so did Pythagoras and Phocilides their morrall counsells: so did Tirteus in war matters, and Solon in matters of policie: or rather, they beeing Poets, dyd exercise their delightful vaine in those points of highest knowledge, which before them lay hid to the world. For that wise Solon was directly a Poet, it is manifest, having written in verse, the notable fable of the Atlantick Iland, which was continued by Plato.

And truely, even Plato, whosoever well considereth, shall find, that in the body of his work, though the inside and strength were Philosophy, the skinne as it were and beautie, depended most of Poetrie: for all standeth upon Dialogues, wherein he faineth many honest Burgesses of Athens to speake of such matters, that if they had been sette on the racke, they would never have confessed them. Besides, his poetical describing the circumstances of their meetings, as the well ordering of a banquet, the delicacie of a walke, with enterlacing meere tales, as Giges Ring, and others, which who knoweth not to be flowers of Poetrie, did never walke into Appolos Garden.

And even Historiographers (although theyr lippes sounde of things doone, and veritie be written in theyr fore-heads,) have been glad to borrow both fashion, and perchance weight of Poets. So Herodotus entituled his Historie, by the name of the nine Muses: and both he and all the rest that followed him, either stole or usurped of Poetrie, their passionate describing of passions, the many particularities of battalles, which no man could affirme: or if that be denied me, long Orations put in the mouthes of great Kings and Captaines, which it is certaine be never pronounced. So that truely, neither Phylosopher nor Historiographer, coulde at the first have entred into the gates of populer judgements, if they had not taken a great pasport to Poetry, which in all Nations at this day where learning florisheth not, is plaine to be seen by all which they have some feeling of Poetry. In Turky, besides their lawegiving Divines, they have no other Writers but Poets. In our neihbour Countrey Ireland, where truelie learning goeth very bare, yet are theyr Poets held in a devoute reverence. Even among the most barbarous and simple Indians where no writing is, yet have they their Poets, who make and sing songs which they call Areytos, both of theyr Auncestors deedes, and praises of theyr Gods. A sufficient probabilitie, that if ever learning comes among them, it must be by having theyr hard dull wits softened and sharpened with the swete delights of Poetrie. For untill they find a pleasure in the exercises of the minde, great promises of much knowledge, will little perswade them, that knowe not the fruites of knowledge. In Wales, the true remnant of the auncient Britons, as there are good authorities to shewe the long time they had Poets, which they called Bardes: so thorough all the conquests of Romaines, Saxons, Danes, and Normans, some of whom did seeke to ruine all memory of learning from among them, yet doo their Poets even to this day, last; so as it is not more notable if soone beginning then in long continuing. But since the Authors of most of our Sciences were the Romans, and before them the Greekes, in us a little stand uppon their authorities, but even so farre as to see, what names they have given unto this now scorned skill.

Among the Romans a Poet was called Vates which is as much as a Diviner, Fore-seer, or Prophet, as by his conjoyned wordes Vaticiniare and Vaticinari, is manifest: so heavenly a title did that excellent people bestow upon his part ravishing knowledge. And so farre were they carried into the admiration thereof, that they thought in the chaunceable hitting uppon any such verses great fore-tokens of their following fortunes were placed. Whereupon grew the worde of Sortes Virgilianæ, when by suddaine opening Virgils booke, they lighted upon any verse of hys making, whereof the histories of the Emperors lives are full, as of Albinus the Governour of our Iland, who in his childehoode mette with this verse.

> *Arma amens capio nec sat rationis in armis.*
> ["In my frenzy I take up arms, but I am not in control of my senses]."

And in his age performed it, which although it were a very vaine, and godles superstition, as also it was to think that spirits were commaunded by such verses, whereupon this word charmes, derived of Carmina commeth, so yet serveth it to shew the great reverence those wits were helde in. And altogether not without ground, since both the Oracles of *Delphos* and Sibillas prophecies, were wholy delivered in verses. For that same exquisite observing of number and measure in words, and that high dying liberty of conceit proper to the Poet, did seeme to have some dyvine force in it.

And may not I presume a little further, to shew the reasonablenes of this worde Vates? And say that the holy Davids Psalmes are a divine Poem? If I doo, I shall not do it without the testimonie of great learned men, both auncient and moderne: but even the name Psalmes will speake for mee, which being interpreted, is nothing but songes; then that it is fully written in meeter, as all learned Hebricians agree, although the rules be not yet fully found. Lastly and principally, his handeling his prophecy, which is meerely poetical. For what els is the awaking his musicall instruments? The often and free changing of persons? His notable Prosopoeias, when he maketh you as it were, see

God comming in his Majestie. His telling of the Beastes joyfulnes and hills leaping, but a heavenlie poesie: wherein almost hee sheweth himself a passionate lover, of that unspeakable and everlasting beautie to be seen by the eyes of the minde, onely cleered by fayth. But truely nowe having named him, I feare mee I seeme to prophane that holy name, applying it to Poetrie, which is among us throwne downe to so ridiculous an estimation: but they that with quiet judgements will looke a little deeper into it, shall finde the end and working of it such, as beeing rightly applyed, deserveth not to bee scourged out of the Church of God.

But now, let us see how the Greekes named it, and howe they deemed of it. The Greekes called him a Poet, which name, hath as the most excellent, gone thorough other Languages. It commeth of this word *Poiein*, which is, to make: wherein I know not whether by lucke or wisedome, wee Englishmen have mette with the Greekes, in calling him a maker: which name, how high and incomparable a title it is, I had rather were knowne by marking the scope of other Sciences, then by my partiall allegation.

There is no Arte delivered to mankinde, that hath not the wordes of Nature for his principall object, without which they could not consist, and on which they so depend, as they become Actors and Players as it were, of what Nature will have set foorth. So doth the Astronomer looke upon the starres, and by that he seeth, setteth downe what order Nature hath taken therein. So doe the Geometrician, and Arithmetician, in their diverse sorts of quantities. So doth the Musitian in times, tel you which by nature agree, which not. The naturall Philosopher thereon hath his name, and the Morrall Philosopher standeth upon the natural vertues, vices, and passions of man; and followe Nature (saith hee) therein, and thou shalt not erre. The Lawyer sayth what men have determined. The Historian what men have done. The Grammarian speaketh onely of the rules of speech, and the Rethorician, and Logitian, considering what in Nature will soonest prove and perswade, thereon give artificiall rules, which still are compassed within the circle of a question, according to the proposed matter. The Phisition waigheth the nature of a mans bodie, and the nature of things helpeful, or hurtefull into it. And the Metaphisick, though it be in the seconde and abstract notions, and therefore be counted supernaturall: yet doth hee indeede builde upon the depth of Nature: onely the Poet, disdayning to be tied to any such subjection, lifted up with the vigor of his owne invention, dooth growe in effect, another nature, in making things either better than Nature bringeth forth, or quite a newe formes such as never were in Nature, as the Heroes, Demigods, Cyclops, Chimeras, Furies, and such like: so as hee goeth hand in hand with Nature, not inclosed within the narrow warrant of her guifts, but freely ranging onely within the Zodiack of his owne wit.

Nature never set forth the earth in so rich tapistry, as divers Poets have done, neither with plesant rivers, fruitful trees, sweet smelling flowers: nor whatsoever els may make the too much loved earth more lovely. Her world is brasen, the Poets only deliver a golden: but let those things alone and goe to man, for whom as the other things are, so it seemeth in him her uttermost cunning is imployed, and knowe whether shee have brought foorth so true a lover as Theagines, so constant a friende as Pilades, so valiant a man as Orlando, so right a Prince as Xenophons Cyrus: so excellent a man every way, as Virgils Aeneas: neither let this be jestingly conceived, because the works of the one be essentiall: the other, in imitation or fiction, for any understanding knoweth the skil of the Artificer: standeth in that Idea or foreconceite of the work, and not in the work it selfe. And that the Poet hath that Idea, is manifest, by delivering them forth in such excellencie as hee hath imagined them. Which delivering forth also, is not wholie imaginative, as we are wont to say by them that build Castles in the ayre: but so farre substantially it worketh, not onely to make a Cyrus, which had been but a particuler excellencie, as Nature might have done, but to bestow a Cyrus upon the worlde, to make many Cyrus's, if they wil learne aright, why, and how that Maker made him.

Neyther let it be deemed too sawcie a comparison to ballance the highest poynt of mans wit with the efficacie of Nature: but rather give right honor to the heavenly Maker of that maker: who having made man to his owne likenes, set him beyond and over all the workes of that second nature, which in nothing hee sheweth so much as in Poetrie: when with the force of a divine breath, he bringeth things forth far surpassing her dooings, with no small argument to the incredulous of that first accursed fall of Adam: sith our erected wit, maketh us know what perfection is, and yet our infected will, keepeth us from reaching unto it. But these arguments wil by fewe be understood, and by fewer granted. Thus much (I hope) will be given me, that the Greekes with some probabilitie of reason, gave him the name above all names of learning. Now let us goe to a more ordinary opening of him, that the trueth may be more palpable: and so I hope, though we get not so unmatched a praise as the Etimologie of his names wil grant, yet his very description, which no man will denie, shall not justly be barred from a principall commendation.

Poesie therefore is an arte of imitation, for so Aristotle termeth it in his word *Mimesis* that is to say, a representing, counterfetting, or figuring foorth: to speake metaphorically, a speaking picture: with this end, to teach and delight; of this have beene three severall kindes. The chiefe both in antiquitie and excellencie, were they that did imitate the inconceivable excellencies of GOD. Such were, David in his Psalmes, Salomon in his song of Songs, in his Ecclesiastes, and Proverbs: Moses and Bebora in theyr Hymnes, and the writer of Job; which beside other, the learned Emanuell Tremilius and Franciscus Junius, doe entitle the poeticall part of the Scripture. Against these none will speake that hath the holie Ghost in due holy reverence.

In this kinde, though in a full wrong divinitie, were Orpheus, Amphion, Homer in his hymes, and many other, both Greekes and Romaines: and this Poesie must be used, by whosoever will follow S. James his counsell, in singing Psalmes when they are merry: and I knowe is used with the fruite of comfort by some, when in sorrowfull pangs of their death-bringing sinnes, they find the consolation of the never-leaving goodnesse.

The second kinde, is of them that deale with matters Philosophicall; eyther morrall, as Tirteus, Phocilides and Cato, or naturall, as Lucretius and Virgils Georgicks: or Astronomicall, as Manilius, and Pontanus: or historical, as Lucan: which who mislike, the faulte is in their judgements quite out of taste, and not in the sweet foode of sweetly uttered knowledge. But because thys second sorte is wrapped within the folde of the proposed subject, and takes not the course of his owne invention, whether they properly be Poets or no, let Gramarians dispute: and goe to the thyrd, indeed right Poets, of whom chiefly this question ariseth; betwixt whom, and these second is such a kinde of difference, as betwixt the meaner sort of Painters, (who counterfet onely such faces as are sette before them) and the more excellent: who having no law but wit, bestow that in cullours upon you which is fittest for the eye to see: as the constant, though lamenting looke of Lucrecia, when she punished in her selfe an others fault.

Wherein he painteth not Lucrecia whom he never sawe, but painteth the outwarde beauty of such a vertue: for these third be they which most properly do imitate to teach and delight, and to imitate, borrow nothing of what is, hath been, or shall be: but range onely rayned with learned discretion, into the divine consideration of what may be, and should be. These bee they, that as the first and most noble sorte, may justly bee termed *Vates*, so these are waited on in the excellen[te]st languages and best understandings, with the fore described name of Poets: for these indeede doo meerely make to imitate: and imitate both to delight and teach: and delight to move men to take that goodnes in hande, which without delight they would flye as from a stranger. And teach, to make them know that goodnes whereunto they are mooved, which being the noblest scope to which ever any learning was directed, yet want there not idle tongues to barke at them. These be subdivided into sundry more speciall denominations. The most notable bee the Heroick, Lirick, Tragick, Comick, Satirick, Iambick, Elegiack, Pastorall, and certaine others. Some of these being termed according to the matter they deale with, some by the sorts of verses they liked best to write in, for indeede the greatest part of Poets have apparelled their poeticall inventions in that numbrous kinde of writing which is called verse: indeed but apparelled, verse being by an ornament and no cause to Poetry: sith there have beene many most excellent Poets, that never versified, and now swarme many versifiers that neede never aunswere to the name of Poets. For Xenophon, who did imitate so excellently, as to give us *effigiem justi imperij*, the portraiture of a just Empire under the name of Cyrus, (as Cicero sayth of him) made therein an absolute heroicall Poem.

So did Heliodorus in his sugred invention of that picture of love in Theagines and Cariclea, and yet both these writ in Prose: which I speak to shew, that it is not riming and versing that maketh a Poet, no more then a long gowne maketh an Advocate: who though he pleaded in armor should be an Advocate and no Souldier. But it is that fayning notable images of vertues, vices or what els, with that delightfull teaching which must be the right describing note to know a Poet by: although indeed the Senate of Poets hath chosen verse as their fittest rayment, meaning, as in matter they passed all in all, so in maner to goe beyond them: not speaking (table talke fashion or like men in a dreame,) words as they chanceably fall from the mouth, but peyzing each sillable of each worde by just proportion according to the dignitie of the subject.

Nowe therefore it shall not bee amisse first to waigh this latter sort of Poetrie by his works, and then by his partes; and if in neyther of these

Anatomies hee be condemnable, I hope wee shall obtaine a more favourable sentence. This purifing of wit, this enritching of memory, enabling of judgment, and enlarging of conceyt, which commonly we call learning, under what name soever it com forth, or to what immediat end soever it be directed, the final end is, to lead and draw us to as high a perfection, as our degenerate soules made worse by theyr clayey lodgings, can be capable of. This according to the inclination of the man, bred many formed impressions, for some that thought this felicity principally to be gotten by knowledge, and no knowledge to be so high and heavenly, as acquaintance with the starres, gave themselves to Astronomie; others, perswading themselves to be Demigods if they knewe the causes of things, became naturall and supernaturall Philosophers, some an admirable delight drew to Musicke: and some, the certainty of demonstration, to the Mathematickes. But all, one, and other, having this scope to knowe, and by knowledge to lift up the mind from the dungeon of the body, to the enjoying his owne divine essence. But when by the ballance of experience it was found, that the Astronomer looking to the starres might fall into a ditch, that the enquiring Philosopher might be blinde in himselfe, and the Mathematician might draw foorth a straight line with a crooked hart: then loe, did proofe the over ruler of opinions, make manifest, that all these are but serving Sciences, which as they have each a private end in themselves, so yet are they all directed to the highest end of the mistres Knowledge, by the Greekes called *Arkitecktonike*, which stands, (as I thinke) in the knowledge of a mans selfe, in the Ethicke and politick consideration, with the end of well dooing and not of well knowing onely; even as the Sadlers next end is to make a good saddle: but his farther end, to serve a nobler facultie, which is horsemanship, so the horsemans to souldiery, and the Souldier not onely to have the skill, but to performe the practise of a Souldier: so that the ending end of all earthly learning, being vertuous action, those skilles that most serve to bring forth that, have a most just title to bee Princes over all the rest: wherein if wee can shewe the Poets noblenes, by setting him before his other Competitors, among whom as principall challengers step forth the morrall Philosophers, whom me thinketh, I see comming towards me with a sullen gravity, as though they could not abide vice by day light, rudely clothed for to witnes outwardly their contempt of outward things, with bookes in their hands agaynst glory, whereto they sette theyr names, sophistically speaking against subtility, and angry with any man in whom they see the foule fault of anger: these men casting larges as they goe, of Definitions, Divisions, and Distinctions, with a scornefull interogative, doe soberly aske, whether it bee possible to finde any path, so ready to leade a man to vertue, as that which teacheth what vertue is? and teacheth it not only by delivering forth his very being, his causes, and effects: but also, by making known his enemie vice, which must be destroyed, and his combersome servant Passion, which must be maistered, by shewing the generalities that contayneth it, and the specialities that are derived from it. Lastly, by playne setting downe, how it extendeth it selfe out of the limits of a mans own little world, to the government of families, and maintayning of publique societies.

The Historian, scarcely giveth leysure to the Moralist, to say so much, but that he loden with old Mouse-eaten records, authorising himselfe (for the most part) upon other histories, whose greatest authorities, are built upon the notable foundation of Heare-say, having much a-doe to accord differing Writers, and to pick trueth out of partiality, better acquainted with a thousande yeeres a goe, then with the present age: and yet better knowing how this world goeth, then how his owne wit runneth: curious for antiquities, and inquisitive of novelties, a wonder to young folkes, and a tyrant in table talke, denieth in a great chafe, that any man for teaching of vertue, and vertuous actions, is comparable to him. I am *Lux vitæ, Temporum Magistra, Vita memoriæ, Nuncia vetustatis, &c.* ["The light of life, the instructress of the ages, the life of memory, the messenger of antiquity."]

The Phylosopher (sayth hee) teacheth a disputative vertue, but I doe an active: his vertue is excellent in the dangerlesse Academie of Plato, but mine sheweth foorth her honorable face, in the battailes of Marathon, Pharsalia, Poitiers, and Agincourt. Hee teacheth vertue by certaine abstract considerations, but I onely bid you follow the footing of them that have gone before you. Olde-aged experience, goeth beyond the fine-witted Phylosopher, but I give the experience of many ages. Lastly, if he make the Song-booke, I put the learners hande to the Lute: and if hee be the guide, I am the light.

Then woulde hee alledge you innumerable examples, conferring storie by storie, how much the wisest Senatours and Princes, have beene directed by the credite of history, as Brutus, Alphonsus of Aragon, and who not, if need bee? At length, the long lyne of theyr disputation maketh a poynt in thys, that the one giveth the precept, and the other the example.

Nowe, whom shall wee finde (sith the question standeth for the highest forme in the Schoole of learning) to bee Moderator? Trulie, as me seemeth, the Poet; and if not a Moderator, even the man that ought to carrie the title from them both, and much more from all other serving Sciences. Therefore compare we the Poet with the Historian, and with the Morrall Phylosopher, and, if hee goe beyond them both, no other humaine skill can match him. For as for the Divine, with all reverence it is ever to be excepted, not only for having his scope as far beyonde any of these, as eternitie exceedeth a moment, but even for passing each of these in themselves.

And for the Lawyer, though Jus bee the Daughter of Justice, and Justice the chiefe of Vertues, yet because hee seeketh to make men good, rather *Formidine pœnæ*, then *Virtutis amore* ["Through fear of punishment" (rather than) "through love of virtue."], or to say righter, dooth not indevour to make men good, but that their evill hurt not others: having no care so hee be a good Cittizen; how bad a man he be. Therefore, as our wickedness maketh him necessarie, and necessitie maketh him honorable, so is hee not in the deepest trueth to stande in rancke with these; who all indevour to take naughtines away, and plant goodnesse even in the secretest cabinet of our soules. And these foure are all, that any way deale in that consideration of mens manners, which being the supreme knowledge, they that best breed it, deserve the best commendation.

The Philosopher therfore and the Historian, are they which would win the gole: the one by precept, the other by example. But both not having both, doe both halte. For the Philosopher, setting downe with thorny argument the bare rule, is so hard of utterance, and so mistie to bee conceived, that one that hath no other guide but him, shall wade in him till hee be olde, before he shall finde sufficient cause to bee honest: for his knowledge standeth so upon the abstract and generall, that happie is that man who may understande him, and more happie, that can applye what hee dooth understand.

On the other side, the Historian wanting the precept, is so tyed, not to what shoulde bee, but to what is, to the particular truth of things, and not to the general reason of things, that hys example draweth no necessary consequence and therefore a lesse fruitfull doctrine.

Nowe dooth the peerelesse Poet performe both: for whatsoever the Philosopher sayth should be doone, hee giveth a perfect picture of it in some one, by whom hee presupposeth it was done. So as hee coupleth the generall notion with the particuler example. A perfect picture I say, for hee yeeldeth to the powers of the minde, an image of that whereof the Philosopher bestoweth but a woordish description: which dooth neyther strike, pierce, nor possesse the sight of the soule, so much as that other dooth.

For as in outward things, to a man that had never seene an Elephant or a Rinoceros, who should tell him most exquisitely all theyr shapes, cullour, bignesse, and perticular markes: or of a gorgeous Pallace, the Architecture, with declaring the full beauties, might well make the hearer able to repeate as it were by rote, all hee had heard, yet should never satisfie his inward conceits, with being witnesse to it self of a true lively knowledge: but the same man, as soone as he might see those beasts well painted, or the house wel in moddel, should straightwaies grow without need of any description, to a judicial comprehending of them, so no doubt the Philosopher with his learned definition, bee it of vertue, vices, matters of publick policie, or privat government, replenisheth the memory with many infallible grounds of wisdom: which notwithstanding, lye darke before the imaginative and judging powre, if they bee not illuminated or figured foorth by the speaking picture of Poesie.

Tullie taketh much paynes and many times not without poeticall helpes, to make us knowe the forces love of our Country hath in us. Let us but heare old Anchises speaking in the middest of Troyes flames, or see Ulisses in the fulnes of all Calipso's delights, bewayle his absence from barraine and beggerly Ithaca. Anger the Stoicks say, was a short maddnes, let but Sophocles bring you Ajax on a stage, killing and whipping Sheepe and Oxen, thinking them the Army of Greeks, with theyr Chiefetaines Agamemnon and Menelaus, and tell mee if you have not a more familiar insight into anger, then finding in the Schoolemen his Genus and difference. See whether wisdome and temperance in Ulisses and Diomedes, valure in Achilles, friendship in Nisus and Eurialus, even to an ignoraunt man, carry not an apparent shyning: and contrarily, the remorse of conscience in Oedipus, the soone repenting pride of Agamemnon, the selfe-devouring crueltie in his Father Atreus, the violence of ambition in the two Theban brothers, the sowresweetnes of revenge in Medæa, and to fall lower, the Terentian Gnato and our Chaucers Pandar, so exprest, that we nowe use their names to signifie their trades. And finally, all vertues, vices, and passions, so in their own naturall seates layd to the viewe, that wee seeme not to heare of them, but cleerely to see through them. But even in the most excellent determination of goodnes, what Philosophers counsell can so redily direct a Prince, as the fayned Cyrus in Xenophon? or a vertuous man in all fortunes, as Aeneas in Virgill? or a whole Common-wealth, as the way of Sir Thomas Moores *Eutopia?* I say the way, because where Sir Thomas Moore erred, it was the fault of the man and not of the Poet, for that way of patterning a Common-wealth was most absolute, though hee perchaunce hath not so absolutely perfourmed it: for the question is, whether the fayned image of Poesie, or the regular instruction of Philosophy, hath the more force in teaching: wherein if the Philosophers have more rightly shewed themselves Philosophers, then the Poets have obtained to the high top of their profession as in truth,

> ——*Mediocribus esse poetis,*
> *Non Diji, non homines, non concessere Columnæ:*
> ["Neither gods, nor men, nor booksellers have granted poets the right to be mediocre."]

It is I say againe, not the fault of the Art, but that by fewe men that Arte can bee accomplished.

Certainly, even our Saviour Christ could as well have given, the morrall common places of uncharitablenes and humblenes, as the divine narration of Dives and Lazarus: or of disobedience and mercy, as that heavenly discourse of the lost Child and the gratious Father; but that hys through-searching wisdom, knewe the estate of Dives burning in hell, and of Lazarus being in Abrahams bosome, would more constantly (as it were) inhabit both the memory and judgment. Truly, for my selfe, mee seemes I see before my eyes the lost Childes disdainefull prodigality, turned to envie a Swines dinner: which by the learned Divines, are thought not historicall acts, but instructing Parables. For conclusion, I say the Philosopher teacheth, but he teacheth obscurely, so as the learned onely can understande him: that is to say, he teacheth them that are already taught, but the Poet is the foode for the tenderest stomacks, the Poet is indeed the right Popular Philosopher, whereof Esops tales give good proofe: whose pretty Allegories, stealing under the formall tales of Beastes, make many, more beastly then Beasts, begin to heare the sound of vertue from these dumbe speakers.

But now may it be alledged, that if this imagining of matters be so fitte for the imagination, then must the Historian needs surpasse, who bringeth you images of true matters, such as indeede were doone, and not such as fantastically or falsely may be suggested to have been doone. Truely Aristotle himselfe in his discourse of Poesie, plainely determineth this question, saying, that Poetry is *Philosophoteron* and *Spoudaioteron*, that is to say, it is more Philosophicall, and more studiously serious, then history. His reason is, because Poesie dealeth with *Katholon*, that is to say, with the universall consideration; and the history with *Kathekaston*, the perticuler; nowe sayth he, the universall wayes what is fit to bee sayd or done, eyther in likelihood or necessity, (which the Poesie considereth in his imposed names), and the perticuler, onely mark's whether Alcibiades did, or suffered, this or that. Thus farre Aristotle: which reason of his, (as all his) is most full of reason. For indeed, if the question were whether it were better to have a perticuler acte truly or falsly set down: there is no doubt which is to be chosen, no more then whether you had rather have Vespasians picture right as hee was, or at the Painters pleasure nothing resembling. But if the question be for your owne use and learning, whether it be better to have it set downe as it should be, or as it was: then certainely is more doctrinable the fained Cirus of Xenophon then the true Cyrus in Justine: and the fayned Aeneas in Virgil, then the right Aeneas in Dares Phrigius.

As to a Lady that desired to fashion her countenance to the best grace, a Painter should more benefite her to portrait a most sweet face, wryting Canidia upon it, then to paynt Canidia as she was, who Horace sweareth, was foule and ill favoured.

If the Poet doe his part a-right, he will shew you in Tantalus, Atreus, and such like, nothing that is not to be shunned. In Cyrus, Aeneas, Ulisses, each thing to be followed; where the Historian, bound to tell things as things were, cannot be liberall (without hee will be poeticall) of a perfect patterne; but as in Alexander or Scipio himselfe, shew dooings, some to be liked, some to be misliked. And then how will you discerne, what to followe but by your owne discretion, which you had without reading Quintus Curtius? And whereas a man may say, though in universall consideration of doctrine the Poet prevaileth; yet that the historie, in his saying such a thing was doone, doth warrant a man more in that hee shall follow.

The aunswere is manifest, that if hee stande upon that was; as if hee should argue, because it rayned yesterday, therefore it shoulde rayne today, then indeede it hath some advantage to a grose conceite: but if he know an example onlie, informes a conjectural likelihood, and so goe by reason, the Poet dooth so farre exceede him, as hee is to frame his example to that which is most reasonable: be it in warlike, politick, or private matters; where the Historian in his bare *Was*, hath many times that which wee call fortune, to over-rule the best wisdome. Manie times, he must tell events, whereof he can yeelde no cause: or if hee doe, it must be poeticall; for that a fayned example, hath as much force to teach, as a true example: (for as for to moove, it is cleere, sith the fayned may bee tuned to the highest key of passion) let us take one example, wherein a Poet and a Historian doe concur.

Herodotus and Justine do both testifie, that Zopirus, King Darius faithful servaunt, seeing his Maister long resisted by the rebellious Babilonians, fayned himselfe in extreame disgrace of his King: for verifying of which, he caused his owne nose and eares to be cut off: and so flying to the Babylonians, was received: and for his knowne valour, so far credited, that hee did finde meanes to deliver them over to Darius. Much like matter doth Livie record of Tarquinius and his sonne. Xenophon excellently faineth such another stratagem, performed by Abradates in Cyrus behalfe. Now would I fayne know, if occasion bee presented unto you, to serve your Prince by such an honest dissimulation, why you doe not as well learne it of Xenophons fiction, as of the others verity: and truely so much the better, as you shall save your nose by the bargaine: for Abradates did not counterfet so far. So then the best of the Historian, is subject to the Poet; for whatsoever action, or faction, whatsoever counsell, pollicy, or warre stratagem, the Historian is bound to recite, that may the Poet (if he list) with his imitation make his own; beautifying it both for further teaching, and more delighting, as it pleaseth him: having all, from Dante his heaven, to hys hell, under the authoritie of his penne. Which if I be asked what Poets have done so, as I might well name some, yet say I, and say againe, I speak of the Arte, and not of the Artificer.

Nowe, to that which commonly is attributed to the prayse of histories, in respect of the notable learning is gotten by marking the successe, as though therein a man should see vertue exalted, and vice punished. Truely that commendation is peculiar to Poetrie, and farre off from History. For indeede Poetrie ever setteth vertue so out in her best cullours, making Fortune her wel-wayting hand-mayd, that one must needs be enamored of her. Well may you see Ulisses in a storme, and in other hard plights; but they are but exercises of patience and magnanimitie, to make them shine the more in the neere-following prosperitie. And of the contrarie part, if evill men come to the stage, they ever goe out (as the Tragedie Writer answered, to one that misliked the shew of such persons) so manacled, as they little animate folkes to followe them. But the Historian, beeing captived to the trueth of a foolish world, is many times a terror from well dooing, and an incouragement to unbrideled wickednes.

For, see wee not valiant Milciades rot in his fetters? The just Phocion, and the accomplished Socrates, put to death like Traytors? The cruell Severus live prosperously? The excellent Severus miserably murthered? Sylla and Marius dying in theyr beddes? Pompey and Cicero slaine then, when they would have thought exile a happinesse?

See wee not vertuous Cato driven to kyll himselfe? and rebell Cæsar so advaunced, that his name yet after 1600 years, lasteth in the highest honor? And marke but even Cæsars own words of the fore-named Sylla, (who in that onely did honestly, to put downe his dishonest tyrannie,) *Literas nescivit* ["He was ignorant of letters."] as if want of learning caused him to doe well. Hee meant it not by Poetrie, which not content with earthly plagues, deviseth new punishments in hel for Tyrants; nor yet by Philosophie, which teacheth *Occidendos esse* ["(that) they are to be killed."], but no doubt by skill in Historie: for that indeede can affoord your Cipselus, Periander, Phalaris, Dionisius, and I know not how many more of the same kennell, that speede well enough in theyr abhominable unjustice or usurpation. I conclude therefore, that hee excelleth Historie, not onely in furnishing the minde with knowledge, but in setting it forward, to that which deserveth to be called and accounted good: which setting forward, and mooving to well dooing, indeed setteth the Lawrell crowne upon the Poet as victorious, not onely of the Historian, but over the Phylosopher: howsoever in teaching it may bee questionable.

For suppose it be granted, (that which I suppose with great reason may be denied,) that the Philosopher in respect of his methodical proceeding, doth teach more perfectly then the Poet: yet do I thinke, that no man is so much *Philophilosophos*, as to compare the Philosopher in mooving, with the Poet.

And that mooving is of a higher degree then teaching, it may by this appeare: that is wel nigh the cause and the effect of teaching. For who will be taught, if hee bee not mooved with desire to be taught? and what so much good doth that teaching bring forth, (I speak still of morall doctrine) as that it mooveth one to doe that which it dooth teach? for as Aristotle sayth, it is not *Gnosis*, but *Praxis* must be the fruit. And howe *Praxis* cannot be, without being mooved to practise, it is no hard matter to consider.

The Philosopher sheweth you the way, hee informeth you of the particularities, as well of the tediousnes of the way, as of the pleasant lodging you shall have when your journey is ended, as of the many byturnings that may divert you from your way. But this is to no man but to him that will read him, and read him with attentive studious painfulnes. Which constant desire, whosoever hath in him, hath already past halfe the hardnes of the way, and therefore is beholding to the Philosopher but for the other halfe. Nay truely, learned men have learnedly thought, that where once reason hath so much overmastred passion, as that the minde hath a free desire to doe well, the inward light each minde hath in it selfe, is as good as a Philosophers booke; seeing in nature we know it is wel, to doe well, and what is well, and what is evill, although not in the words of Arte, which Philosophers bestowe upon us. For out of naturall conceit, the Philosophers drew it, but to be moved to doe that which we know, or to be mooved with desire to knowe, *Hoc opus: Hic labor est.* ["In this the task and mighty labor lies."]

Nowe therein of all Sciences, (I speak still of humane, and according to the humane conceits) is our Poet the Monarch. For he dooth not only show the way, but giveth so sweete a prospect into the way, as will intice any man to enter into it. Nay, he dooth as if your journey should lye through a fayre Vineyard, at the first give you a cluster of Grapes: that full of that taste, you may long to passe further. He beginneth not with obscure definitions, which must blur the margent with interpretations, and load the memory with doubtfulnesse: but hee commeth to you with words sent in delightfull proportion, either accompanied with, or prepared for the well inchaunting skill of Musicke; and with a tale forsooth he commeth unto you: with a tale which holdeth children from play, and old men from the chimney corner. And pretending no more, doth intende the winning of the mind from wickednesse to vertue: even as the childe is often brought to take most wholsom things, by hiding them in such other as have a pleasant tast: which if one should beginne to tell them, the nature of Aloes, or Rubarb they shoulde receive, woulde sooner take their Phisicke at their eares, then at their mouth. So is it in men (most of which are childish in the best things, till they bee cradled in their graves,) glad they will be to heare the tales of Hercules, Achilles, Cyrus, and Aeneas: and hearing them, must needs heare the right description of wisdom, valure, and justice; which, if they had been barely, that is to say, Philosophically set out, they would sweare they bee brought to schoole againe.

That imitation whereof Poetry is, hath the most conveniency to Nature of all other, in somuch, that as Aristotle sayth, those things which in themselves are horrible, as cruell battailes, unnaturall Monsters, are made in poeticall imitation delightfull. Truely I have knowen men, that even with reading *Amadis de Gaule*, (which God knoweth wanteth much of a perfect Poesie) have found their harts mooved to the exercise of courtesie, liberalitie, and especially courage.

Who readeth Aeneas carrying olde Anchises on his back, that wisheth not it were his fortune to perfourme so excellent an acte? Whom doe not the words of Turnus moove? (the tale of Turnus, having planted his image in the imagination,)

> ————————*Fugientem hæc terra videbit,*
> *Usque adeone mori miserum est?*————
> ["Will this land see him fleeing? Is it then such a wretched thing
> to die?"]

Where the Philosophers, as they scorne to delight, so must they bee content little to moove: saving wrangling, whether Vertue bee the chiefe, or the the onely good: whether the contemplative, or the active life doe excell: which Plato and Boethius well knew, and therefore made Mistres Philosophy, very often borrow the masking rayment of Poesie. For even those harde harted evill men, who thinke vertue a schoole name, and knowe no other good, but *indulgere genio* ["to indulge their inclination(s)."], and therefore despise the austere admonitions of the Philosopher, and feele not the inward reason they stand upon; yet will be content to be delighted: which is all the good felow Poet seemeth to promise: and so steale to see the forme of goodnes (which seene they cannot but love) ere themselves be aware, as if they tooke a medicine of Cherries. Infinite proofes of the strange effects of this poeticall invention might be alledged, onely two shall serve, which are so often remembred, as I thinke all men knowe them.

The one of Menenius Agrippa, who when the whole people of Rome had resolutely devided themselves from the Senate, with apparent shew of utter ruine: though hee were (for that time) an excellent Oratour, came not among them, upon trust of figurative speeches, or cunning insinuations: and much lesse, with farre set Maximes of Phylosophie, which (especially if they were Platonick,) they must have learned Geometrie before they could well have conceived: but forsooth he behaves himselfe, like a homely, and familiar Poet. Hee telleth them a tale, that there was a time, when all the parts of the body made a mutinous conspiracie against the belly, which they thought devoured the fruits of each others labour: they concluded they would let so unprofitable a spender starve. In the end, to be short, (for the tale is notorious, and as notorious that it was a tale,) with punishing the belly, they plagued themselves. This applied by him, wrought such effect in the people, as I never read, that ever words brought forth but then, so suddaine and so good an alteration: for upon reasonable conditions, a perfect reconcilement ensued. The other is of Nathan the Prophet, who when the holie David had so far forsaken God, as to confirme adulterie with murther: when hee was to doe the tenderest office of a friende, in laying his owne shame before his eyes, sent by God to call againe so chosen a servant: how doth he it? but by telling of a man, whose beloved Lambe was ungratefullie taken from his bosome: the applycation most divinely true, but the discourse itselfe, fayned: which made David, (I speake of the second and instrumentall cause) as in a glasse, to see his own filthines, as that heavenly Psalme of mercie wel testifieth.

By these therefore examples and reasons, I think it may be manifest, that the Poet with that same hand of delight, both draw the mind more effectually, then any other Arte dooth, and so a conclusion not unfitlie ensueth: that as vertue is the most excellent resting place for all worldlie learning to make his end of: so Poetrie, beeing the most familiar to teach it, and most princelie to move towards it, in the most excellent work, is the most excellent workman. But I am content, not onely to decipher him by his workes, (although works in commendation or disprayse, must ever holde an high authority,) but more narrowly will examine his parts: so that (as in a man) though altogether may carry a presence ful of majestie and beautie, perchance in some one defectious peece, we may find a blemish: now in his parts, kinds, or *Species*, (as you list to terme them) it is to be noted that some Poesies have coupled together two or three kindes, as Tragicall and Comicall, wher-upon is risen, the Tragi-comicall. Some in the like manner have mingled Prose and Verse, as Sanazzar and Boetius. Some have mingled matters Heroical and Pastorall. But that commeth all to one in this question, for if severed they be good, the conjunction cannot be hurtfull. Therefore perchaunce forgetting some, and leaving some as needlesse to be remembred, it shall not be amisse in a worde to cite the speciall kindes, to see what faults may be found in the right use of them.

Is it then the Pastorall Poem which is misliked? (for perchance, where the hedge is lowest, they will soonest leape over.) Is the poore pype disdained, which sometime out of Melibeus mouth, can shewe the miserie of people, under hard Lords, or ravening Souldiours? And again, by Titirus, what blessednes is derived to them that lye lowest from the goodnesse of them that sit highest? Sometimes, under the prettie tales of Wolves and Sheepe, can include the whole considerations of wrong dooing and patience. Sometimes shew, that contention for trifles, can get but a trifling victorie. Where perchaunce a man may see, that even Alexander and Darius, when they strave who should be Cocke of this worlds dunghill, the benefit they got, was, that the after-livers may say,

> *Hæc memini et victum frustra contendere Thirsin:*
> *Ex illo Coridon, Coridon est tempore nobis.*
> ["I remember these things, and that Thirsis competed in vain and was defeated: From that time Coridon has to us been Coridon."]

Or is it the lamenting Elegiack, which in a kinde hart would moove rather pitty then blame, who bewailes with the great Philosopher Heraclitus, the weakenes of man-kind, and the wretchednes of the world: who surely is to be praysed, either for compassionate accompanying just causes of lamentation, or for rightly paynting out how weake be the passions of wofulnesse. Is it the bitter, but wholesome Iambick, which rubs the galled minde, in making shame the trumpet of villanie, with bolde and open crying out against naughtines; Or the Satirick, who

> *Omne vafer vitium, ridenti tangit amico?*
> ["In his cleverness he touches upon every fault of his laughing friend."]

who sportingly never leaveth, until hee make a man laugh at folly, and at length ashamed, to laugh at himselfe: which he cannot avoyd, without avoyding the follie. Who while

> *Circum præcordia ludit,*
> ["He plays about the heart."]

giveth us to feele, how many head-aches a passionate life bringeth us to. How when all is done,

Est ulubris animus si nos non deficit æquus?
["(What we are looking for) is at Ulubrae if we do not lack a tranquil mind."]

No perchance it is the Comick, whom naughtie Play-makers and Stage-keepers, have justly made odious. To the argument of abuse, I will answer after. Onely thus much now is to be said, that the Comedy is an imitation of the common errors of our life, which he representeth, in the most ridiculous and scornefull sort that may be. So as it is impossible, that any beholder can be content to be such a one.

Now, as in Geometry, the oblique must be knowne as well as the right: and in Arithmetick the odde as well as the even, so in the actions of our life, who seeth not the filthines of evil, wanteth a great foile to perceive the beauty of vertue. This doth the Comedy handle so in our private and domestical matters, as with hearing it, we get as it were an experience, what is to be looked for of a nigardly Demea: of a crafty Danus: of a flattering Gnato: of a vaine glorious Thraso: and not onely to know what effects are to be expected, but to know who be such, by the signifying badge given them by the Comedian. And little reason hath any man to say, that men learne evill by seeing it so set out: sith as I sayd before, there is no man living, but by the force trueth hath in nature, no sooner seeth these men play their parts, but wisheth them in *Pistrinum:* although perchance the sack of his owne faults, lye so behinde his back, that he seeth not himselfe daunce the same measure: whereto, yet nothing can more open his eyes, then to finde his own actions contemptibly set forth. So that the right use of Comedy will (I thinke) by no body be blamed, and much lesse of the high and excellent Tragedy, that openeth the greatest wounds, and sheweth forth the Vlcers, that are covered with Tissue: that maketh Kinges feare to be Tyrants, and Tyrants manifest their tirannicall humors: that with sturring the affects of admiration and commiseration, teacheth, the uncertainty of this world, and upon how weake foundations guilden roofes are builded. That maketh us knowe,

Qui sceptra sævus, duro imperio regit,
Timet timentes, metus in authorem redit.
["He who wields a scepter harshly and severely fears those who fear, and dread turns back upon its author."]

But how much it can moove, Plutarch yeeldeth a notable testimonie, of the abhominable Tyrant, Alexander Pheræus; from whose eyes, a

Tragedy wel made, and represented, drewe aboundance of teares: who without all pitty, had murthered infinite nombers, and some of his owne blood. So as he, that was not ashamed to make matters for Tragedies, yet coulde not resist the sweet violence of a Tragedie.

And if it wrought no further good in him, it was, that he in despight of himselfe, withdrewe himselfe from harkening to that, which might mollifie his hardened heart. But it is not the Tragedy they doe mislike: For it were too absurd to cast out so excellent a representation of whatsoever is most worthy to be learned. Is it the Liricke that most displeaseth, who with his tuned Lyre, and well accorded voyce, giveth praise, the reward of vertue, to vertuous acts? who gives morall precepts, and naturall Problemes, who sometimes rayseth up his voice to the height of the heavens, in singing the laudes of the immortall God. Certainly I must confesse my own barbarousness, I never heard the olde song of Percy and Duglas, that I found not my heart mooved more then with a Trumpet: and yet is it sung but by some blinde Crouder, with no rougher voyce, then rude stile: which being so evill apparrelled in the dust and cobwebbes of that uncivill age, what would it worke trymmed in the gorgeous eloquence of Pindar? In Hungary I have seene it the manner at all Feasts, and other such meetings, to have songes of their Auncestours valour; which that right Souldierlike Nation thinck the chiefest kindlers of brave courage. The incomparable Lacedemonians, did not only carry that kinde of Musicke ever with them to the field, but even at home, as such songs were made, so were they all content to bee the singers of them when the lusty men were to tell what they dyd, the olde men, what they had done, and the young men what they wold doe. And where a man may say, that Pindar many times prayseth highly victories of small moment, matters rather of sport then vertue: as it may be aunswered, it was the fault of the Poet, and not of the Poetry; so indeede, the chiefe fault was in the tyme and custome of the Greekes, who set those toyes at so high a price, that Phillip of Macedon reckoned a horserace wonne at Olimpus, among hys three fearefull felicities. But as the unimitable Pindar often did, so is that kinde most capable and most fit, to awake the thoughts from the sleep of idlenes, to imbrace honorable enterprises.

There rests the Heroicall, whose very name (I thinke) should daunt all back-biters; for by what conceit can a tongue be directed to speak evill of that, which draweth with it, no lesse Champions then Achilles, Cyrus, Aeneas, Turnus, Tideus, and Rinaldo? who doth not onely teach and move to a truth, but teacheth and mooveth to the most high and excellent truth. Who maketh magnanimity and justice shine, throughout all misty fearefulnes and foggy desires. Who, if the saying of Plato and Tullie bee true, that who could see Vertue, would be wonderfully ravished with the love of her beauty: this man sets her out to make her more lovely in her holyday apparell, to the eye of any that will daine, not to disdaine, untill they understand. But if anything be already sayd in the defence of sweete Poetry, all concurreth to the maintaining the Heroicall, which is not onely a kinde, but the best, and most accomplished kinde of Poetry. For as the image of each action styrreth and instructeth the mind, so the loftie image of such Worthies, most inflameth the mind with desire to be worthy, and informes with counsel how to be worthy. Only let Aeneas be worne in the tablet of your memory, how he governeth himselfe in the ruine of his Country, in the preserving his old Father, and carrying away his religious ceremonies: in obeying the Gods commandement to leave Dido, though not onely all passionate kindenes, but even the humane consideration of vertuous gratefulnes, would have craved other of him. How in storms, howe in sports, howe in warre, howe in peace, how a fugitive, how victorious, how besiedged, how besiedging, howe to strangers, howe to allyes, how to enemies, howe to his owne: lastly, how in his inward selfe, and how in his outward government. And I thinke, in a minde not prejudiced with a prejudicating humor, hee will be found in excellencie fruitefull: yea, even as Horace sayth

Melius Chrisippo et Crantore.
["Better than Chrisippo and Crantor."]

But truely I imagine, it falleth out with these Poet-whyppers, as with some good women, who often are sicke, but in fayth they cannot tel where. So the name of Poetrie is odious to them, but neither his cause, nor effects, neither the sum that containes him, nor the particularities descending from him, give any fast handle to their carping disprayse.

Sith then Poetrie is of all humane learning the most auncient, and of most fatherly antiquitie, as from whence other learnings have taken theyr beginnings: sith it is so universall, that no learned Nation dooth despise it, nor no barbarous Nation is without it: sith both Roman and Greek gave divine names unto it: the one of prophecying, the other of making. And that indeede, that name of making is fit for him; considering, that where as other Arts retaine themselves within their subject, and receive as it were, their beeing from it: the Poet onely, bringeth his owne stuffe, and dooth not learne a conceite out of a matter, but maketh matter for a conceite: Sith neither his description, nor his ende, contayneth any evill, the thing described cannot be evill: Sith his effects be so good as to teach goodnes and to delight the learners: Sith therein, (namely in morrall doctrine, the chiefe of all knowedges,) hee dooth not onely farre passe the Historian, but for instructing, is well nigh comparable to the Philosopher: and for moving, leaves him behind him: Sith the holy scripture (wherein there is no un-cleannes) hath whole parts in it poeticall. And that even our Saviour Christ, vouchsafed to use the flowers of it: Sith all his kindes are not onlie in their united formes, but in their severed dissections fully commendable, I think, (and think I thinke rightly) and Lawrell crowne appointed for tryumphing Captaines, doth worthilie (of al other learnings) honor the Poets tryumph. But because wee have eares aswell as tongues, and that the lightest reasons that may be, will seeme to weigh greatly, if nothing be put in the counter-balance: let us heare, and aswell as wee can ponder, what objections may bee made against this Arte, which may be worthy, eyther of yeelding, or answering.

First truely I note, not onely in these *Mysomousoi* Poet-haters, but in all that kinde of people, who seek a prayse by dispraysing others, that they doe prodigally spend a great many wandering wordes, in quips, and scoffes; carping and taunting at each thing, which by styrring the Spleene, may stay the braine from a thorough beholding the worthines of the subject.

Those kinde of objections, as they are full of very idle easines, sith there is nothing of so sacred a majestie, but that an itching tongue may rubbe it selfe upon it: so deserve they no other answer, but in steed of laughing at the jest, to laugh at the jester. Wee know a playing wit, can prayse the discretion of an Asse; the comfortablenes of being in debt, and the jolly commoditie of beeing sick of the plague. So of the contrary side, if we will turne Ovids verse,

Ut lateat virus, proximitate mali,

that good lye hid in neerenesse of the evill: Agrippa will be as merry in showing the vanitie of Science, as Erasmus was in commending of follie. Nether shall any man or matter escape some touch of these smyling raylers. But for Erasmus and Agrippa, they had another foundation then the superficiall part would promise. Mary, these other pleasant Fault-finders, who wil correct the Verbe, before they understande the Noune, and confute others knowledge before they confirme theyr owne: I would have them onely remember, that scoffing commeth not of wisedom. So as the best title in true English they gette with their merriments, is to be called good fooles: for so have our grave Forefathers ever termed that humorous kinde of jesters: but that which gyveth greatest scope to their scorning humors, is ryming and versing. It is already sayde (and as I think, trulie sayde) it is not ryming and versing, that maketh Poesie. One may bee a Poet without versing, and a versifier without Poetry. But yet, presuppose it were inseparable (as indeede it seemeth Scaliger judgeth) truelie it were an inseparable commendation. For if *Oratio*, next to *Ratio*, Speech next to Reason, bee the greatest gyft bestowed upon mortalitie: that can not be praiselesse, which dooth most pollish that blessing of speech, which considers each word, not only (as a man may say) by his forcible qualitie, but by his best measured quantitie, carrying even in themselves, a Harmonie: (without (perchaunce) Number, Measure, Order, Proportion, be in our time growne odious.) But lay a side the just prayse it hath, by beeing the onely fit speech for Musick (Musick I say, the most divine striker of the sences:) thus much is undoubtedly true, that if reading bee foolish, without remembring, memories being the onely treasurer of knowled[g]e, those words which are fittest for memory, are likewise most convenient for knowledge.

Now, that Verse farre exceedeth Prose in the knitting up of the memory, the reason is manifest. The words, (besides theyr delight which hath a great affinitie to memory,) beeing so set, as one word cannot be lost, but the whole worke failes: which accuseth it selfe, calleth the remembrance backe to it selfe, and so most strongly confirmeth it; besides, one word so as it were begetting another, as be it in ryme or measured verse, by the former a man shall have a neere gesse to the follower: lastly, even they that have taught the Art of memory, have shewed nothing so apt for it, as a certaine roome devided into many places well and throughly knowne. Now, that hath the verse in effect perfectly; every word having his naturall seate, which seate, must needes make the words remembred. But what needeth more in a thing so knowne to all men? who is it that ever was a scholler, that doth not carry away some verses of Virgill, Horace, or Cato, which in his youth he learned, and even to his old age serve him for howrely lessons? but the fitnes it hath for memory, is notably proved by all delivery of Arts:

wherein for the most part, from Grammar, to Logick, Mathematick, Phisick, and the rest, the rules chiefely necessary to bee borne away, are compiled in verses. So that, verse being in it selfe sweete and orderly, and beeing best for memory, the onely handle of knowledge, it must be in jest that any man can speake against it. Nowe then goe wee to the most important imputations laid to the poore Poets, for ought I can yet learne, they are these, first, that there beeing many other more fruitefull knowledges, a man might better spend his tyme in them, then in this. Secondly, that it is the mother of lyes. Thirdly, that it is the Nurse of abuse, infecting us with many pestilent desires: with a Syrens sweetnes, drawing the mind to the Serpents tayle of sinfull fancy. And heerein especially, Comedies give the largest field to erre, as Chaucer sayth: howe both in other Nations and in ours before Poets did soften us, we were full of courage, given to martiall exercises; the pillers of manlyke liberty, and not lulled a sleepe in shady idelenes with Poets pastimes. And lastly, and chiefely, they cry out with an open mouth, as if they out shot Robin Hood, that Plato banished them out of hys Commonwealth. Truely, this is much, if there be much truth in it. First to the first: that a man might better spend his time, is a reason indeede: but it doth (as they say) but *Petere principium* ["Revert to the beginning."]: for if it be as I affirme that no learning is so good, as that which teacheth and mooveth to vertue; and that none can both teach and move thereto so much as Poetry: then is the conclusion manifest, that Incke and Paper cannot be to a more profitable purpose employed. And certainly, though a man should graunt their first assumption, it should followe (me thinkes) very unwillingly, that good is not good, because better is better. But I still and utterly denye, that there is sprong out of earth a more fruitefull knowledge. To the second therefore, that they should be the principall lyars; I aunswere paradoxically, but truely, I thinke truely; that of all Writers under the sunne, the Poet is the least lier; and though he would, as a Poet can scarcely be a lyer, the Astronomer, with his cosen the Geometrician, can hardly escape, when they take upon them to measure the height of the starres.

How often, thinke you, doe the Phisitians lye, when they aver things, good for sicknesses, which afterwards send Charon a great number of soules drown[e]d in a potion before they come to his Ferry. And no lesse of the rest, which take upon them to affirme. Now, for the Poet, he nothing affirmes, and therefore never lyeth. For, as I take it, to lye, is to affirme that to be true which is false. So as the other Artists, and especially the Historian, affirming many things, can in the cloudy knowledge of mankinde, hardly escape from many lyes. But the Poet (as I sayd before) never affirmeth. The Poet never maketh any circles about your imagination, to conjure you to beleeve for true what he writes. Hee citeth not authorities of other Histories, but even for hys entry, calleth the sweete Muses to inspire into him a good invention: in troth, not labouring to tell you what is, or is not, but what should or should not be: and therefore, though he recount things not true, yet because hee telleth them not for true, he lyeth not, without we will say, that Nathan, lyed in his speech, before alledged to David. Which as a wicked man durst scarce say, so think I none so simple would say, that Esope lyed in the tales of his beasts: for who thinks that Esope writ it for actually true, were well worthy to have his name c[h]ronicled among the beastes hee writeth of.

What childe is there, that comming to a Play, and seeing Thebes written in great Letters upon an olde doore, doth beleeve that it is Thebes? If then, a man can arive, at that childs age, to know that the poets persons and dooings, are but pictures what should be, and not stories what have beene, they will never give the lye, to things not affirmatively, but allegorically, and figurativelie written. And therefore, as in Histories, looking for trueth, they goe away full fraught with falsehood: so in Poesie, looking for fiction, they shal use the narration, but as an imaginative groundplot of a profitable invention.

But heereto is replyed, that the Poets gyve names to men they write of, which argueth a conceite of an actuall truth, and so, not being true, prooves a falsehood. And doth the Lawyer lye then, when under the names of *John a stile* and *John a noakes*, hee puts his case? But that is easily answered. Theyr naming of men, is but to make theyr picture the more lively, and not to builde any historie: paynting men, they cannot leave men namelesse. We see we cannot play at Chesse, but that wee must give names to our Chesse-men; and yet mee thinks, hee were a very partiall Champion of truth, that would say we lyed, for giving a peece of wood, the reverend title of a Bishop. The Poet nameth Cyrus or Aeneas, no other way, then to shewe, what men of theyr fames, fortunes, and estates, should doe.

Their third is, how much it abuseth mens wit, trayning it to wanton sinfulness, and lustfull love: for indeed that is the principall, if not the onely abuse I can heare alledged. They say, the Comedies rather teach, then reprehend, amorous conceits. They say, the Lirick, is larded with

passionate Sonnets. The Elegiack, weepes the want of his mistresse. And
that even to the Heroical, Cupid hath amibitiously climed. Alas Love, I
would, thou couldest as well defende thy selfe, as thou canst offende
others. I would those, on whom thou doost attend, could eyther put
thee away, or yeelde good reason, why they keepe thee. But grant love
of beautie, to be a beastlie fault, (although it be very hard, sith onely man,
and no beast, hath that gyft, to discerne beauty.) Grant, that lovely
name of Love, to deserve all hatefull reproches: (although even some of
my Maisters the Phylosophers, spent a good deale of theyr Lamp-oyle,
in setting foorth the excellencie of it.) Grant, I say, whatsoever they will
have granted; that not onely love, but lust, but vanitie, but, (if they list)
scurrilitie, possesseth many leaves of the Poets bookes: yet thinke I,
when this is granted, they will finde, theyr sentence may with good
manners, put the last words foremost: and not say, that Poetrie abuseth
mans wit, but that, mans wit abuseth Poetrie.

For I will not denie, but that mans wit may make Poesie, (which
should be *Eikastike*, which some learned have defined, figuring foorth
good things,) to be *Phantastike:* which doth contrariwise, infect the
fancie with unworthy objects. As the Painter, that shoulde give to
the eye, eyther some excellent perspective, or some fine picture, fit for
building or fortification: or contayning in it some notable example, as
Abraham, sacrificing his Sonne Isaack, Judith killing Holofernes, David
fighting with Goliath, may leave those, and please an ill-pleased eye,
with wanton shewes of better hidden matters. But what, shall the abuse
of a thing, make the right use odious? Nay truely, though I yeeld, that
Poesie may not onely be abused, but that beeing abused, by the reason
of his sweete charming force, it can doe more hurt than any other
Armie of words: yet shall it be so far from concluding, that the abuse,
should give reproch to the abused, that contrariwise it is a good reason,
that whatsoever being abused, dooth most harme, beeing rightly used:
(and upon the right use each thing conceiveth his title) doth most good.

Doe wee not see the skill of Phisick, (the best rampire to our often-
assaulted bodies) beeing abused, teach poyson the most violent de-
stroyer? Dooth not knowledge of Law, whose end is, to even and right
all things being abused, grow the crooked fosterer of horrible injuries?
Doth not (to goe to the highest) Gods word abused, breed heresie? and
his Name abused, become blasphemie? Truely, a needle cannot doe
much hurt, and as truely, (with leave of Ladies be it spoken) it cannot
doe much good. With a sword, thou maist kill thy Father, and with a

sword thou maist defende thy Prince and Country. So that, as in their calling Poets the Fathers of lyes, they say nothing: so in this theyr argument of abuse, they proove the commendation.

They alledge heere-with, that before Poets beganne to be in price, our Nation, hath set their harts delight upon action, and not upon imagination: rather doing things worthy to bee written, then writing things fitte to be done. What that before tyme was, I thinke scarcely Sphinx can tell: Sith no memory is so auncient, that hath the precedence of Poetrie. And certaine it is, that in our plainest homelines, yet never was the Albion Nation without Poetrie. Mary, thys argument, though it bee leaveld against Poetrie, yet is it indeed, a chaine-shot against all learning, or bookishnes, as they commonly tearme it. Of such minde were certaine Goethes, of whom it is written, that having in the spoile of a famous Citie, taken a fayre librarie: one hangman (bee like fitte to execute the fruites of their wits) who had murthered a great number of bodies, would have set fire on it: no sayde another, very gravely, take heede what you doe, for whyle they are busie about these toyes, wee shall with more leysure conquer their Countries.

This indeede is the ordinary doctrine of ignorance, and many wordes sometymes I have heard spent in it: but because this reason is generally against all learning, aswell as Poetrie; or rather, all learning but Poetry: because it were too large a digression, to handle, or at least, too superfluous: (sith it is manifest, that all government of action, is to be gotten by knowledg, and knowledge best, by gathering many knowledges, which is, reading,) I onely with Horace, to him that is of that opinion,

> *Iubeo stultum esse libenter;*
> ["I order him to be stupid, and gladly so."]

for as for Poetrie it selfe, it is the freest from thys objection. For Poetrie is the companion of the Campes.

I dare undertake, *Oralndo Furioso*, or honest King Arthur, will never displease a Souldier: but the quiddity of *Ens*, and *Prima materia*, will hardly agree with a Corslet: and therefore, as I said in the beginning, even Turks and Tartares are delighted with Poets. Homer, a Greek, florished, before Greece flourished. And if to a slight conjecture, a conjecture may be opposed: truly it may seeme, that as by him, their learned men, tooke almost their first light of knowledge, so their active men, received their first notions of courage. Onlie Alexanders example may serve, who by Plutarch is accounted of such vertue, that Fortune was not his guide, but his footestoole: whose acts speake for him, though Plutarch did not: indeede, the Phœnix of warlike Princes. This Alexander, left his Schoolemaister, living Aristotle, behinde him, but tooke deade Homer with him: he put the Philosopher Calisthenes to death, for his seeming philosophicall, indeed mutinous stubburnnes. But the chiefe thing he ever was heard to wish for, was, that Homer had been alive. He well found he received more graverie of minde, bye the patterne of Achilles, then by hearing the definition of Fortitude: and therefore, if Cato misliked Fulvius, for carying Ennius with him to the fielde, it may be aunswered, that if Cato misliked it, the noble Fulvius liked it, or els he had not doone it: for it was not the excellent Cato Uticensis, (whose authority I would much more have reverenced,) but it was the former: in truth, a bitter punisher of faults, but else, a man that had never wel sacrificed to the Graces. Hee misliked and cryed out upon all Greeke learning, and yet being 80. yeeres olde, began to learne it. Be-like, fearing that Pluto understood not Latine. Indeede, the Romaine lawes allowed, no person to be carried to the warres, but hee that was in the Souldiers role: and therefore, though Cato misliked his unmustered person, hee misliked not his worke. And if hee had, Scipio Nasica judged by common consent, the best Romaine, loved him. Both the other Scipio Brothers, who had by their vertues no lesse surnames, then of Asia, and Affrick, so loved him, that they caused his body to be buried in their Sepulcher. So as Cato, his authoritie being but against his person, and that aunswered, with so farre greater then himselfe, is heerein of no validitie. But now indeede my burthen is great; now Plato his name is layde upon mee, whom I must confesse, of all Philosophers, I have ever esteemed most worthy of reverence, and with great reason: Sith of all Philosophers, he is the most poeticall. Yet if he will defile the Fountaine, out of which his flowing streames have proceeded, let us boldly examine with what reasons hee did it. First truly, a man might maliciously object, that Plato being a Philosopher was a naturall enemie of Poets: for indeede, after the Philosophers, had picked out of the sweete misteries of poetrie, the right discerning true points of knowledge, they forthwith putting it in method, and making a Schoole-arte of that which the Poets did onely teach, by a divine delightfulnes, beginning to spurne at their guides, like ungratefull Prentises, were not content to set up shops for themselves, but sought by all meanes to discredit their Maisters. Which by the force of delight being barred them, the lesse they could overthrow them, the more they hated them. For indeede, they found for Homer, seaven Cities strove, who should have him for their Citizen: where many Citties banished Philosophers, as not fitte members to live among them. For onely repeating certaine of Euripides verses, many Athenians had their lyves saved of the Siracusians: when the Athenians themselves, thought many Philosophers, unwoorthie to live.

Certaine Poets, as Simonides, and Pindarus had so prevailed with Hiero the first, that of a Tirant they made him a just King, where Plato could do so little with Dionisius, that he himself, of a Philosopher, was made a slave. But who should doe thus, I confesse, should requite the objections made against Poets, with like cavillation against Philosophers, as likewise one should doe, that should bid one read Phædrus, or Symposium in Plato, or the discourse of love in Plutarch, and see whether any Poet doe authorize abhominable filthines, as they doe. Againe, a man might aske out of what Commonwealth Plato did banish them? insooth, thence where he himselfe alloweth communitie of women: So as belike, this banishment grewe not for effeminate wantonnes, sith little should poeticall Sonnets be hurtfull, when a man might have what woman he listed. But I honor philosophicall instructions, and blesse the wits which bred them: so as they be not abused, which is likewise stretched to Poetrie.

S. Paule himselfe, (who yet for the credite of Poets) alledgeth twise two Poets, and one of them by the name of a Prophet, setteth a watchword upon Philosophy, indeede upon the abuse. So dooth Plato, upon the abuse, not upon Poetrie. Plato found fault, that the Poets of his time, filled the worlde, with wrong opinions of the Gods, making light tales of that unspotted essence; and therefore, would not have the youth depraved with such opinions. Heerin may much be said, let this suffice: the Poets did not induce such opinions, but dyd imitate those opinions already induced. For all the Greek stories can well testifie, that the very religion of that time, stoode upon many, and many-fashioned Gods, not taught so by the Poets, but followed, according to their nature of imitation. Who list, may reade in Plutarch, the discourses of Isis and Osiris, of the cause why Oracles ceased, of the divine providence; and see, whether the Theologie of that nation, stood not upon such dreames, which the Poets indeed supersticiously observed, and truly, (sith they had not the light of Christ,) did much better in it than the Philosophers, who shaking off superstition brought in Atheisme. Plato therefore, (whose authoritie I had much rather justly conster, then unjustly resist,) meant not in general of Poets, in those words of which Julius Scaliger saith *Qua authoritate, barbari quidam, atque hispidi, abuti velint, ad Poetas é republica exigendo* ["Which authority certain crude barbarians wished to abuse in order to drive poets out of the state."]; but only meant, to drive out those wrong opinions of the Deitie (whereof now, without further law, Christianity hath taken away all the hurtful beliefe,) perchance (as he thought) norished by the then esteemed Poets. And a man need goe no further then to Plato himselfe, to know his meaning: who in his Dialogue called Ion, giveth high, and rightly divine commendation to Poetrie. So as Plato, banishing the abuse, not the thing, not banishing it, but giving due honor unto it, shall be our Patron, and not our adversarie. For indeed I had much rather, (sith truly I may doe it) shew theyr mistaking of Plato, (under whose Lyons skin they would make an Asselike braying against Poesie,) then goe about to overthrow his authority, whom the wiser a man is, the more just cause he shall find to have in admiration: especially, sith he attributeth unto Poesie, more then my selfe doe; namely, to be a very inspiring of a divine force, farre above mans wit: as in the aforenamed Dialogue is apparent.

Of the other side, who wold shew the honors, have been by the best sort of judgements granted them, a whole Sea of examples woulde present themselves. Alexanders, Cæsars, Scipios, al favorers of Poets. Lelius, called the Romane Socrates, himselfe a Poet: so as part of *Heautontimorumenon* in Terence, was supposed to be made by him. And even the Greek Socrates, whom Apollo confirmed to be the onely wise man, is sayde to have spent part of his old tyme, in putting Esops fables into verses. And therefore, full evill should it become his scholler Plato, to put such words in his Maisters mouth, against Poets. But what need more? Aristotle writes the Arte of Poesie: and why if it should not be written? Plutarch teacheth the use to be gathered of them, and how if they should not be read? And who reades Plutarchs eyther historie or philosophy, shall finde, hee trymmeth both theyr garments, with gards of Poesie. But I list not to defend Poesie, with the helpe of her underling, Historiography. Let it suffise, that it is a fit soyle for prayse to dwell upon: and what dispraise may set upon it, is eyther easily overcome, or transformed into just commendation. So that, sith the excellencies of it, may be so easily, and so justly confirmed, and the lowcreeping objections, so soone troden downe; it not being an Art of lyes, but of true doctrine: not of effeminatenes, but of notable stirring of courage: not of abusing mans witte, but of strengthening mans wit: not banished, but honored by Plato: let us rather plant more Laurels, for to engarland our Poets heads, (which honor of beeing laureat, as besides them, onely tryumphant Captaines weare, is a sufficient authority, to shewe the price they ought to be had in,) then suffer the ill-favouring breath of such wrong-speakers, once to blowe upon the cleere springs of Poesie.

But sith I have runne so long a careere in this matter, me thinks, before I give my penne a fulle stop, it shal be but a little more lost time, to inquire, why England (the Mother of excellent mindes,) shoulde bee growne so hard a step-mother to Poets, who certainly in wit ought to passe all other: sith all onely proceedeth from their wit, being indeede makers of themselves, not takers of others. How can I but exclaime,

> *Musa mihi causas memora, quo numine læso.*
> ["Oh Muse, recount to me what divinity was offended."]

Sweete Poesie that hath aunciently had Kings, Emperors, Senators, great Captaines, such, as besides a thousand others, David, Adrian, Sophocles, Germanicus, not onely to favour Poets, but to be Poets. And of our neerer times, can present for her Patrons, a Robert, king of Sicil, the great king Francis of France, King James of Scotland. Such Cardinals as Bembus, and Bibiena. Such famous Preachers and Teachers, as Beza and Melancthon. So learned Philosophers, as Fracastorius and Scaliger. So great Orators, as Pontanus and Muretus. So piercing wits, as George Buchanan. So grave Counsellors, as besides many, but before all, that Hospitall of Fraunce: then whom, (I thinke) that Realme never brought forth a more accomplished judgement: more firmely builded upon vertue. I say these, with numbers of others, not onely to read others Poesies, but to poetise for others reading, that Poesie thus embraced in all other places, should onely finde in our time, a hard welcome in England, I thinke the very earth lamenteth it, and therefore decketh our Soyle with fewer Laurels then it was accustomed. For heertofore, Poets have in England also florished. And which is to be noted, even in those times, when the trumpet of Mars did sounde loudest. And now, that an overfaint quietnes should seeme to strew the house for Poets, they are almost in as good reputation, as the Mountibancks at Venice. Truly even that, as of the one side, it giveth great praise to Poesie, which like Venus, (but to better purpose) hath rather be troubled in the net with Mars, then enjoy the homelie quiet of Vulcan: so serves it for a peece of reason, why they are lesse gratefull to idle England, which nowe can scarce endure the payne of a pen. Upon this, necessarily followeth, that base men, with servile wits undertake it: who think it inough, if they can be rewarded of the Printer. And so as Epaminondas is sayd, with the honor of his vertue, to have made an office, by his exercising it, which before was contemptible, to become highly respected: so these, no more but setting their names to it, by their owne disgracefulnes, disgrace the most gracefull Poesie. For now, as if all the Muses were gotte with childe, to being foorth bastard Poets, without any commission, they doe poste over the banckes of Helicon, tyll they make the readers more weary than Post-horses: while in the mean tyme, they

> *Queis meliore luto finxit præcordia Titan,*
> ["Whose soul the Titan has shaped of finer clay."]

are better content, to suppresse the out-flowing of their wit, then by publishing them, to bee accounted Knight of the same order. But I, that before ever I durst aspire unto the dignitie, am admitted into the company of the Paper-blurers, doe finde the very true cause of our wanting estimation, is want of desert: taking upon us to be Poets, in despight of Pallas. Nowe, wherein we want desert, were a thanke-worthy labour to expresse: but if I knew, I should have mended my selfe. But I, as I never desired the title, so have I neglected the meanes to come by it. Onely over-mastred by some thoughts, I yeelded an inckie tribute unto them. Mary, they that delight in Poesie it selfe, should seeke to knowe what they doe, and how they doe; and especially, looke themselves in an unflattering Glasse of reason, if they bee inclinable unto it. For Poesie, must not be drawne by the eares, it must bee gently led, or rather, it must lead. Which was partly the cause, that made the auncient-learned affirme, it was a divine gift, and no humaine skill: sith all other knowledges, lie ready for any that hath strength of witte: A Poet, no industrie can make, if his owne Genius bee not carried unto it: and therefore is it an old proverbe, *Orator fit: Poeta nascitur.* Yet confesse I alwayes, that as the firtilest ground must bee manured, so must the highest flying wit, have a Dedalus to guide him. That Dedalus, they say, both in this, and in other, hath three wings, to beare it selfe up into the ayre of due commendation: that is, Arte, Imitation, and Exercise. But these, neyther artificiall rules, nor imitative patternes, we much cumber our selves withall. Exercise indeede wee doe, but that, very fore-backwardly:

for where we should exercise to know, wee exercise as having knowne: and so is oure braine delivered of much matter, which never was begotton by knowledge. For, there being two principal parts, matter to be expressed by wordes, and words to expresse the matter, in neyther, wee use Arte, or Imitation, rightly. Our matter is *Quodlibit* indeed, though wrongly perfourming Ovids verse,

> *Quicquid conabar dicere versus erit:*
> ["Whatever I attempted to say was verse."]

never marshalling it into an assured rancke, that almost the readers cannot tell where to finde themselves.

Chaucer undoubtedly did excellently in hys *Troylus and Cresseid:* of whom, truly I know not, whether to mervaile more, either that he in that mistie time, could see so clearly, or that wee in this cleare age, walke so stumblingly after him. Yet had he great wants, fitte to be forgiven, in so reverent antiquity. I account the *Mirrour of Magistrates*, meetely furnished of beautiful parts; and in the Earle of Surries *Liricks*, many things tasting of a noble birth, and worthy of a noble minde. The *Sheapheards Kalender*, hath much Poetrie in his Eglogues: indeede worthy the reading if I be not deceived. That same framing of his stile, to an old rustick language, I dare not alowe, sith neyther Theocritus in Greeke, Virgill in Latine, nor Sanazar in Italian, did affect it. Besides these, doe I not rmember to have seene but fewe, (to speake boldely) printed, that have poeticall sinnewes in them: for proofe whereof, let but most of the verses bee put in Prose, and then aske the meaning: and it will be found, that one verse did but beget another, without ordering at the first, what should be at the last: which becomes a confused masse of words, with a tingling sound of ryme, barely accompanied with reason.

Our Tragedies, and Comedies, (not without cause cried out against,) observing rules, neyther of honest civilitie, nor of skilfull Poetrie, excepting *Gorboduck*, (againe, I say, of those that I have seen,) which notwithstanding, as it is full of stately speeches, and well sounding Phrases, clyming to the height of Seneca his stile, and as full of notable moralitie, which it doth most delightfully teach; and so obtayne the very end of Poesie: yet in troth it is very defectious in the circumstances; which greeveth mee, because it might not remaine as an exact model of all Tragedies. For it is faulty both in place, and time, the two necessary companions of all corporall actions. For where the stage should alwaies represent but one place, and the uttermost time presupposed in it, should be, both by Aristotles precept, and common reason, but one day: there is both many dayes, and many places, inartificially imagined. But if it be so in *Gorboduck*, how much more in all the rest? where you shal have Asia of the one side, and Affrick of the other, and so many other under-kingdoms, that the Player, when he commeth in, must ever begin with telling where he is: or els, the tale wil not be conceived. Now ye shal have three Ladies, walke to gather flowers, and then we must beleeve the stage to be a Garden. By and by, we heare newes of shipwracke in the same place, and then wee are to blame, if we accept it not for a Rock.

Upon the backe of that, comes out a hideous Monster, with fire and smoke, and then the miserable beholders, are bounder to take it for a Cave. While in the meantime, two Armies flye in, represented with foure swords and bucklers, and then what harde heart will not receive it for a pitched fielde? Now, of time they are much more liberall, for ordinary it is that two young Princes fall in love. After many traverces, she is got with childe, delivered of a faire boy, he is lost, groweth a man, falls in love, and is ready to get another child, and all this in two hours space: which how absurd it is in sence, even sence may imagine, and Arte hath taught, and all auncient examples justified: and at this day' the ordinary Players in Italie, will not erre in. Yet wil some bring in an example of *Eunuchus* in Terence, that containeth matter of two dayes, yet far short of twenty yeeres. True it is, and so was it to be playd in two daies, and so fitted to the time it set forth. And though Plautus hath in one place done amisse, let us hit with him, and not misse with him. But they will say, how then shall we set forth a story, which containeth both many places, and many times? And doe they not knowe, that a Tragedie is tied to the lawes of Poesie, and not of Historie? not bound to follow the storie, but having liberty, either to faine a quite newe matter, or to frame the history, to the most tragicall conveniencie. Againe, many things may be told, which cannot be shewed, if they knowe the difference betwixt reporting and representing. As for example, I may speake, (though I am heere) of Peru, and in speech, digresse from that, to the description of Calicut: but in action, I cannot represent it without Pacolets horse: and so was the manner the Aunciens tooke, by some *Nuncius*, to recount thinges done in former time, or other place. Lastly, if they wil represent an history, they must not (as Horace saith) beginne *Ab ovo* ["From the egg."], but they must come to the principall poynt of that one action, which they will repre-sent. By example this will be best expressed. I have a story of young Polidorus, delivered for safeties sake, with great riches, by his Father Priamus to Polimnestor king of Thrace, in the Troyan war time: Hee after some yeeres, hearing the over-throwe of Priamus, for to make the treasure his owne, murthereth the child: the body of the child is taken up [by] Hecuba; shee the same day, findeth a slight to bee revenged most cruelly of the Tyrant: where nowe would one of our Tragedy writers begin, but with the delivery of the childe? Then should he sayle over into Thrace, and so spend I know not how many yeeres, and travaile numbers of places. But where dooth Euripides? Even with the finding of the body, leaving the rest to be tolde by the spirit of Polidorus. This need no further to be inlarged, the dullest wit may conceive it. But besides these grosse absurdities, how all theyr Playes be neither right Tragedies, nor right Comedies: mingling Kings and Clownes, not because the matter so carrieth it: but thrust in Clownes by head and shoulders, to play a part in majesticall matters, with neither decencie, nor discretion. So as neither the admiration and commiseration, nor the right sportfulnes, is by their mungrell Tragy-comedie obtained. I know Apuleius did some-what so, but that is a thing recounted with space of time, not represented in one moment: and I knowe, the Auncients have one or two examples of Tragy-comedies, as Plautus hath *Amphitrio:* But if we marke them well, we shall find, that they never, or very daintily, match Horn-pypes and Funeralls. So falleth it out, that having indeed no right Comedy, in that comicall part of our Tragedy, we have nothing but scurrility, unwoorthy of any chast ears: or some extreame shew of doltishnes, indeed fit to lift up a loude laughter, and nothing els: where the whole tract of a Comedy, shoulde be full of delight, as the Tragedy shoulde be still maintained, in a well raised admiration. But our Comedians, thinke there is no delight with-out laughter, which is very wrong, for though laughter may come with delight, yet commeth it not of delight: as though delight should be the cause of luaghter, but well may one thing breed both together: nay, rather in themselves, they have as it were, a kind of contrarietie; for delight we scarcely doe, but in things that have a conveniencie to our selves, or to the general nature: laughter, almost ever commeth, of things most disproportioned to our selves, and nature. Delight hath a joy in it, either permanent, or present. Laughter, hath onely a scornful tickling.

For example, we are ravished with delight to see a faire woman, and yet are far from being moved to laughter. We laugh at deformed creatures, wherein certainely we cannot delight. We delight in good chaunces, we laugh at mischaunces; we delight to heare the happines of our friends, or Country; at which he were worthy to be laughed at, that would laugh; wee shall contrarily laugh sometimes, to finde a matter quite mistaken, and goe downe the hill agaynst the byas, in the mouth of some such men, as for the respect of them, one shal be hartely sorry, yet he cannot chuse but laugh; and so is rather pained, then delighted with laughter. Yet deny I not, but that they may goe well together, for as in Alexanders picture well set out, wee delight without laughter, and in twenty mad Anticks we laugh without delight: so in Hercules, painted with his great beard, and furious contenance, in womans attire, spinning at Omphales commaundement, it breedeth both delight and laughter. For the representing of so strange a power in love, procureth delight: and the scornefulnes of the action, stirreth laughter. But I speake to this purpose, that all the end of the comicall part, bee not upon such scornefull matters, as stirreth laughter onely: but mixt with it, that delightful teaching which is the end of Poesie. And the great fault even in that point of laughter, and forbidden plainely by Aristotle, is, that they styrre laughter in sinfull things; which are rather execrable then ridiculous: or in miserable, which are rather to be pittied than scorned. For what is it to make folkes gape at a wretched Begger, or a beggerly Clowne? or against lawe of hospitality, to jest at straungers, because they speake not English so well as wee doe? what do we learne, sith it is certaine

> (*Nil habet infœlix paupertas durius in se,*)
> *Quam quod ridiculos homines facit.*——
> ["Unhappy poverty has nothing harder in it than that it makes men ridiculous."]

But rather a busy loving Courtier, a hartles threatening Thraso. A selfe-wise-seeming schoolemaster. A awry-transformed Traveller. These, if we sawe walke in stage names, which wee play naturally, therein were delightfull laughter, and teaching delightfulnes: as in the other, the Tragedies of Buchanan, doe justly bring forth a divine admiration. But I have lavished out too many wordes of this play matter. I doe it because as they are excelling parts of Poesie, so is there none so much used in England, and none can be more pittifully abused. Which like an unmannerly Daughter, shewing a bad education, causeth her mother Poesies honesty, to bee called in question. Other sorts of Poetry almost have we none, but that Lyricall kind of Songs and Sonnets: which, Lord, if he gave us so good mindes, how well it might be imployed, and with howe heavenly fruite, both private and publique, in singing the prayses of the immortall beauty: the immortall goodnes of that God, who gyveth us hands to write, and wits to conceive, of which we might well want words, but never matter, of which, we could turne our eies to nothing, but we should ever have new budding occasions. But truely many of such writings, as come under the banner of unresistable love, if I were a Mistres, would never perswade mee they were in love: so coldely they apply fiery speeches, as men that had rather red Lovers writings; and so caught up certaine swelling phrases, which hang together, like a man which once tolde mee, the winde was at North, West, and by South, because he would be sure to name windes enowe: then that in truth they feele those passions, which easily (as I think) may be bewrayed, by that same forciblenes, or Energia, (as the Greekes cal it) of the writer. But let this bee a sufficient, though short note, that wee misse the right use of the materiall point of Poesie.

Now, for the out-side of it, which is words, or (as I may tearme it) Diction, it is even well worse. So is that honny-flowing Matron Eloquence, apparelled, or rather disguised, in a Curtizan-like painted affectation: one time with so farre fette words, they may seeme Monsters: but must seeme straungers to any poore English man. Another tyme, with coursing of a Letter, as if they were bound to followe the method of a Dictionary: an other tyme, with figures and flowers, extreamelie winter-starved. But I would this fault were only peculier to Versifiers, and had not as large possession among Prose-printers; and, (which is to be mervailed) among many Schollers, and, (which is to be pittied) among some Preachers. Truly I could wish, if at least I might be so bold, to wish in a thing beyond the reach of my capacity, the diligent imitators of Tullie, and Demosthenes, (most worthy to be imitated) did not so much keep, Nizolian Paper-bookes of their figures and phrases, as by attentive translation (as it were) devoure them whole, and make them wholly theirs: For nowe they cast Sugar and Spice, upon every dish that is served to the table; Like those Indians, not content to weare eareings at the fit and naturall place of the eares, but they will thrust Jewels through their nose, and lippes because they will be sure to be fine.

Tullie, when he was to drive out Cateline, as it were with a Thunder-bolt of eloquence, often used that figure of repitition, *Vivit vivit? imo Senatum venit &c.* ["He lives, he lives? Why, he actually comes into the senate."] Indeed, inflamed with a well-grounded rage, hee would have his words (as it were) double out of his mouth: and so doe that artificially, which we see men doe in choller naturally. And wee, having noted the grace of those words, hale them in sometime to a familer Epistle, when it were to too much choller to be chollerick. Now for similitudes, in certained printed discourses, I thinke all Hebarists, all stories of Beasts, Foules, and Fishes, are rifled up, that they come in multitudes, to waite upon any of our conceits; which certainly is as absurd a surfet to the eares, as is possible: for the force of a similitude, not being to proove anything to a contrary Disputer, but onely to explane to a willing hearer when that is done, the rest is a most tedious pratling: rather over-swaying the memory from the purpose whereto they were applyed, then any whit informing the judgement, already eyther satisfied, or by similitudes not to be satis-fied. For my part, I doe not doubt, when Antonius and Crassus, the great forefathers of Cicero in eloquence, the one (as Cicero testifieth of them) pretended not to know Arte, the other, not to set by it: because with a playne sensiblenes, they might win credit of popular eares; which credit, is the neearest step to perswasion: which perswasion, is the chiefe marke of Oratory; I doe not doubt (I say) but that they used these tracks very sparingly, which who doth generally use, any man may see doth daunce to his owne musick: and so be noted by the audience, more careful to speake curiously, then to speake truly.

Undoubtedly, (at least to my opinion undoubtedly,) I have found in divers smally learned Courtiers, a more sounde stile, then in some pro-fessors of learning: of which I can gesse no other cause, but that the Courtier following that which by practise hee findeth fittest to nature, therein, (though he know it not,) doth according to Art, though not by Art: where the other, using Art to shew Art, and not to hide Art, (as in these cases he should doe) flyeth from nature, and indeede abuseth Art.

But what? me thinkes I deserve to be pounded, for straying from Poetrie to Oratorie: but both have such an affinity in this wordish consideration, that I thinke this digression, will make my meaning receive the fuller understanding: which is not to take upon me to teach Poets howe they should doe, but onely finding my selfe sick among the rest, to shewe some one or two spots of the common infection, growne

among the most part of Writers: that acknowledging our selves somewhat awry, we may bend to the right use both of matter and manner;
whereto our language gyveth us great occasion, beeing indeed capable
of any excellent exercising of it. I know, some will say it is a mingled
language. And why not so much the better, taking the best of both the
other? Another will say it wanteth Grammer. Nay truly, it hath that
prayse, that it wanteth not Grammer: for Grammer it might have, but
it needes it not; beeing so easie of it selfe, and so voyd of those cumber-
some differences of Cases, Genders, Moodes, and Tenses, which I
thinke was a peece of the Tower of Babilons curse, that a man should
be put to schoole to learne his mother-tongue. But for the uttering
sweetly, and properly the conceits of the minde, which is the end of
speech that hath it equally with any other tongue in the world: and is
particulerly happy, in compositions of two or three words together,
neere the Greeke, far beyond the Latine: which is one of the greatest
beauties can be in a language.

Now, of versifying there are two sorts, the one Auncient, the other
Moderne: the Auncient marked the quantitie of each silable, and
according to that, framed his verse: the Moderne, observing onely
number, (with some regarde of the accent,) the chiefe life of it, standeth
in that lyke sounding of the words, which we call Ryme. Whether of
these be the most excellent, would beare many speeches. The Auncient,
(no doubt) more fit for Musick, both words and tune observing quantity,
and more fit lively to expresse divers passions, by the low and lofty
sounde of the well-weyed silable. The latter likewise, with hys Ryme,
striketh a certaine musick to the eare: and in fine, sith it dooth delight,
though by another way, it obtaines the same purpose: there beeing in
eyther sweetnes, and wanting in neither majestie. Truely the English,
before any other vulgar language I know, is fit for both sorts: for, for
the Ancient, the Italian is so full of Vowels, that it must ever be cumbred
with Elisions. The Dutch, so of the other side with Consonants, that
they cannot yeeld the sweet slyding, fit for a Verse. The French, in his
whole language, hath not one word, that hath his accent in the last
silable saving two, called Antepenultima, and little more hath the
Spanish: and therefore, very gracelesly may they use Dactiles. The
English is subject to none of these defects.

Nowe, for the ryme, though wee doe not observe quantity, yet wee
observe the accent very precisely: which other languages, eyther cannot
doe, or will not doe so absolutely. That Cæsura, or breathing place in

the midddest of the verse, neither Italian nor Spanish have, the French, and we, never almost fayle of. Lastly, even the very ryme it selfe, the Italian cannot put in the last silable, by the French named the Masculine ryme, but still in the next to the last, which the French call the Female; or the next before that, which the Italians terme *Sdrucciola*. The example of the former, is *Buono*, *Suono*, of the *Sdrucciola*, *Femina*, *Semina*. The French, of the other side, hath both the Male, as *Bon*, *Son*, and the Female, as *Plaise*, *Taise*. But the *Sdrucciola*, hee hath not: where the English hath all three, as *Due*, *True*, *Father*, *Rather*, *Motion*, *Potion:* with much more which might be sayd, but that I finde already, the triflingnes of this discourse, is much too much enlarged. So that sith the ever-praise-worthy Poesie, is full of vertue-breeding delightfulnes, and voyde of no gyfte, that ought to be in the noble name of learning: sith the blames laid against it, are either false, or feeble: sith the cause why it is not esteemed in Englande, is the fault of Poet-apes, not Poets: sith lastly, our tongue is most fit to honor Poesie, and to bee honored by Poesie, I conjure you all, that have had the evill lucke to reade this incke-wasting toy of mine, even in the name of the nyne Muses, no more to scorn the sacred misteries of Poesie: no more to laugh at the name of Poets, as though they were next inheritours to Fooles: no more to jest at the reverent title of a Rymer: but to beleeve with Aristotle, that they were the auncient Treasurers, of the Græcians Divinity. To beleeve with Bembus, that that they were first bringers in of all civilitie. To beleeve with Scaliger, that no Philosophers precepts can sooner make you an honest man, then the reading of Virgill. To beleeve with Clauserus, the Translator of Cornutus, that it pleased the heavenly Deitie, by Hesiod and Homer, under the vayle of fables, to give us all knowledge, Logick, Rethorick, Philosophy, naturall, and morall; and *Quid non?* To believe with me, that there are many misteries contained in Poetrie, which of purpose were written darkely, least by prophane wits, it should bee abused. To believe with Landin, that they are so beloved of the Gods, that whatsoever they write, proceeds of a divine fury. Lastly, to beleeve themselves, when they tell you they will make you immortall, by their verses.

Thus doing, your name shal florish in the Printers shoppes; thus doing, you shall bee of kinne to many a poetical Preface; thus doing, you shall be most fayre, most ritch, most wise, most all, you shall dwell upon Superlatives. Thus dooing, though you be *Libertino patre natus* ["Born of a freedman."], you shall suddenly grow *Hercules proles*

["Hercules' offspring.":]

> *Si quid mea carmina possunt.*
> ["If my poetry wields any power."]

Thus doing, your soule shal be placed with Dantes Beatrix, or Virgils Anchises. But if, (fie of such a but) you be borne so neere the dull making Cataphract of Nilus, that you cannot heare the Plannet-like Musick of Poetrie, if you have so earth-creeping a mind, that it cannot lift it selfe up, to looke to the sky of Poetry: or rather, by a certaine rusticall disdaine, will become such a Mome, as to be a Momus of Poetry: then, though I will not wish unto you, the Asses eares of Midas, nor to bee driven by a Poets verses, (as Bubonax was) to hang himselfe, nor to be rimed to death, as is sayd to be doone in Ireland: yet thus much curse I must send you in the behalfe of all Poets, that while you live, you live in love, and never get favour, for lacking skill of a Sonnet: and when you die, your memory die from the earth, for want of an Epitaph.

5. DRYDEN

"An Essay of Dramatic Poesy"

John Dryden (1631–1700) was born at Aldwincle in Northampton-shire, England. He attended Trinity School, Cambridge, and then went to London to write. Success seemed to come quickly to him: his plays were praised; he was made a member of the Royal Society in 1662; in 1668 he succeeded Davenant as poet laureate. He became a Catholic on the succession of James II (1685). After James' deposition (1688) Dryden's fortune changed considerably: he lost his position as poet laureate and was forced to support himself by writing again.

Dryden is one of the most prolific English writers and also one of the most versatile. He excels in poetry, drama, and criticism—few writers since him have been superior in all three fields, with the possible exception of T. S. Eliot, one of Dryden's great admirers. Dryden's first poetic success was the long poem *Annus Mirabilis* in 1666. Subsequent poems are varied in length and subject: satires, such as *Absalom and Achitophel* and *MacFleknoe;* religious, such as *Religio Laici, or a Layman's Faith* and *The Hind and the Panther;* occasional (that is, written for a specific occasion), such as *Alexander's Feast, An Ode in Honour of St. Cecilia's Day*, and the previously mentioned *Annus Mirabilis;* translations, such as Virgil's *Aeneid.* Among his verse plays the most famous are: *Marriage à la Mode, The Conquest of Granada, All for Love, or the World Well Lost.*

Not only did Dryden excel in poetry, but he is usually credited with making prose respectable and interesting. He has one of the great prose styles and one on which generations of writers modeled theirs. Thus his critical works can be read for the excellence of both style and thought. Most of his criticism is in the form of prefaces, the most famous of which is Preface to *Fables Ancient and Modern.* In this preface he discusses English poetry from the beginning (Chaucer).

This is the work from which quotations live on to our day: Chaucer is "a diamond in the rough," and that he "followed Nature everywhere"; of Chaucer's poetry he remarks, "Here is God's plenty."

The selection is from another famous critical work, *An Essay on Dramatic Poesy*, first published in 1668. It is representative of Neoclassic attitudes and preoccupations tempered however with good humor, good sense, and grace. It slowly leads the reader into the subject matter—only a bore would rush into difficult arguments. The essay is presented as an exchange of opinions between sophisticated gentlemen who are spending one summer's day on a barge on the Thames to escape the noise of the naval battle between the English and the Dutch. Delicately the scene is set: while one international physical conflict is taking place, another more subtle, mental international struggle is also taking place. The four disputants have long been identified: Crites is Sir Robert Howard, Dryden's brother-in-law; Eugenius is Lord Buckhurst, Dryden's patron; Lisideius is Sir Charles Sedley; and Neander is Dryden himself. The classical names are, of course, significant: Dryden is tackling classical themes.

These four gentlemen dispute at length the major concerns of the age: the superiority of drama over other genres, and the Ancients and Moderns controversy. However, they also manage to touch upon most of the more minor concerns of the age, such as the use of rhyme, the propriety of prose, the mixing of tragedy and comedy, the three unities, the comparative merits of French and English drama, and refinement, unity, and propriety.

The scope and variety of concerns discussed can be seen from an outline of each disputant's arguments. Crites points out the superiority of ancient drama: the Greeks created it; they imitated nature best; we can do no better than to follow in their footsteps. Thus he takes an uncompromising, though by no means unusual, position in this Ancients and Moderns controversy. Sir William Temple argued the same position in "Of Ancient and Modern Learning." Eugenius then replies with arguments for the moderns: poets improve upon each other and the particular improvement of modern literature lies in its refinement—which the ancients sometimes sadly lacked. His second charge against the ancients also includes many of the Neoclassic concerns: the ancients are not regular enough; they do not divide the plays into acts; they do not observe the three unities; they do not have "poetic justice." Eugenius, like Crites, had real influential allies for his views. The best-known essay pleading for the moderns is Edward Young's "Conjectures on Original Composition." The whole controversy was delightfully satirized by Jonathan Swift in "The Battle of the Books."

Lisideius embarks on another current controversy and argues the superiority of the French drama over the English, because the English have tragicomedy. Then Neander, very calmly accepting the truth and good sense of the previous disputants' arguments, presses the excellence of the modern English playwrights. He considers as good the diversity, variety, and experimentation of English drama. Consequently, there is more "lively imitation of nature" in English drama than in French. Thus we are back to the central dividing issue: best imitation of nature.

John Dryden is seen by many to be the founder of serious English criticism. As George Saintsbury points out, for the first time in criticism Dryden used "the constant application of the 'leaden rule,' the taking of book, author, kind, *as it is*, and judging it accordingly, instead of attempting to force everything into agreement or disagreement with a prearranged schedule of rules." (Vol. II, p. 382.) It is a tribute to John Dryden's greatness as a critic that, despite the usual reaction against the work of previous ages in the nineteenth century, he was considered the only Neoclassic poet and critic worth reading.

It was that memorable day, in the first summer of the late war, when our navy engaged the Dutch; a day wherein the two most mighty and best appointed fleets which any age had ever seen, disputed the command of the greater half of the globe, the commerce of nations, and the riches of the universe. While these vast floating bodies, on either side, moved against each other in parallel lines, and our countrymen, under the happy conduct of his Royal Highness, went breaking, by little and little, into the line of the enemies; the noise of the cannon from both navies reached our ears about the City, so that all men being alarmed with it, and in a dreadful suspense of the event which they knew was then deciding, every one went following the sound as his fancy led him; and leaving the town almost empty, some took towards the park, some cross the river, others down it; all seeking the noise in the depth of silence.

Among the rest, it was the fortune of Eugenius, Crites, Lisideius, and Neander, to be in company together; three of them persons whom their wit and quality have made known to all the town; and whom I have chose to hide under these borrowed names, that they may not suffer by so ill a relation as I am going to make of their discourse.

Taking then a barge, which a servant of Lisideius had provided for them, they made haste to shoot the bridge, and left behind them that great fall of waters which hindered them from hearing what they desired: after which, having disengaged themselves from many vessels which rode at anchor in the Thames, and almost blocked up the passage towards Greenwich, they ordered the watermen to let fall their oars more gently; and then, every one favouring his own curiosity with a strict silence, it was not long ere they perceived the air to break about them like the noise of distant thunder, or of swallows in a chimney: those little undulations of sound, though almost vanishing before they reached them, yet still seeming to retain somewhat of their first horror, which they had betwixt the fleets. After they had attentively listened till such time as the sound by little and little went from them, Eugenius, lifting up his head, and taking notice of it, was the first who congratulated to the rest that happy omen of our Nation's victory: adding, that we had but this to desire in confirmation of it, that we might hear no more of that noise, which was now leaving the English coast. When the rest had concurred in the same opinion, Crites, a person of a sharp judgment, and somewhat too delicate a taste in wit, which the world have mistaken in him for ill-nature, said, smiling to us, that if the concernment of this battle had not been so exceeding great, he could scarce have wished the victory at the price he knew he must pay for it, in being subject to the reading and hearing of so many ill verses as he was sure would be made upon it. Adding, that no argument could scape some of those eternal rhymers, who watch a battle with more diligence than the ravens and birds of prey; and the worst of them surest to be first in upon the quarry: while the better able either out of modesty writ not at all, or set that due value upon their poems, as to let them be often called for and long expected! "There are some of those impertinent people you speak of," answered Lisideius, "who to my knowledge are already so provided, either way, that they can produce not only a Panegyric upon the victory, but, if need be, a Funeral Elegy on the Duke; and, after they have crowned his valour with many laurels, they will at last deplore the odds under which he fell, concluding that his courage deserved a better destiny." All the company smiled at the conceipt of Lisideius; but Crites, more eager than before, began to make particular exceptions against some writers, and said, the public magistrate ought to send betimes to forbid them; and that it concerned the peace and quiet of all honest people, that ill poets should be as well silenced as seditious preachers. "In my opinion," replied Eugenius, "you pursue your point too far; for as to my own particular, I am so great a lover of poesy, that I could wish them all rewarded, who attempt but to do well; at least, I would not have them worse used than Sylla the Dictator did one of their brethren heretofore:—*Quem in concione vidimus* (says Tully), *cum ei libellum malus poeta de populo subjecisset, quod epigramma in eum fecisset tantummodo alternis versibus longiusculis, statim ex iis rebus quas tunc vendebat jubere ei praemium tribui, sub ea conditione ne quid postea scriberet.*" ["We saw him once in a popular gathering when from the crowd a bad poet offered him an epigram in elegiac verse which he had just composed attacking him; immediately he ordered the poet to be given a reward out of the articles he was then selling on the condition that he not write anything afterwards."] "I could wish with all my heart," replied Crites, "that many whom we know were as bountifully thanked upon the same condition,— that they would never trouble us again. For amongst others, I have a mortal apprehension of two poets, whom this victory, with the help of both her wings, will never be able to escape." "'Tis easy to guess whom you intend," said Lisideius; "and without naming them, I ask you, if one of them does not perpetually pay us with clenches upon words, and a certain clownish kind of railery? if now and then he does not offer at a catachresis or Clevelandism, wrestling and torturing a word into another meaning: in fine, if he be not one of those whom the French would call *un mauvais buffon;* one that is so much a well-willer to the satire, that he spares not man; and though he cannot strike a blow to hurt any, yet ought to be punished for the malice of the action, as our witches are justly hanged, because they think themselves so; and suffer deservedly for believing they did mischief, because they meant it." "You have described him," said Crites, "so exactly, that I am afraid to come after you with my other extremity of poetry. He is one of those who, having had some advantage of education and converse, knows better than the other what a poet should be, but puts it into practice more unluckily than any man; his style and matter are every where alike: he is the most calm, peaceable writer you ever read: he never disquiets your passions with the least concernment, but still leaves you in as even a temper as he found you; he is a very Leveller in poetry: he creeps along with ten little words in every line, and helps out his numbers with *For to*, and *Unto*, and all the pretty expletives he can find, till he drags them to the end of another line; while the sense is left tired half way behind it: he doubly starves all his verses, first for want of thought, and then of expression; his poetry neither has wit in it, nor seems to have it; like him in Martial:

Pauper videri Cinna *vult, et est pauper.*
["Cinna wants to appear a pauper, and, in fact, he is a pauper."]

"He affects plainness, to cover his want of imagination: when he writes the serious way, the highest flight of his fancy is some miserable antithesis, or seeming contradiction; and in the comic he is still reaching at some thin conceit, the ghost of a jest, and that too flies before him, never to be caught; these swallows which we see before us on the Thames are the just resemblance of his wit: you may observe how near the water they stoop, how many proffers they make to dip, and yet how seldom they touch it; and when they do, it is but the surface: they skim over it but to catch a gnat, and then mount into the air and leave it."

"Well, gentlemen," said Eugenius, "you may speak your pleasure of these authors; but though I and some few more about the town may give you a peaceable hearing, yet assure yourselves, there are multitudes who would think you malicious and then injured: especially him whom you first described; he is the very Withers of the city: they have bought more editions of his works than would serve to lay under all their pies at the Lord Mayor's Christmas. When his famous poem first came out in the year 1660, I have seen them reading it in the midst of 'Change time; nay so vehement they were at it, that they lost their bargain by the candles' ends; but what will you say if he has been received amongst the great ones? I can assure you he is, this day, the envy of one who is lord in the art of quibbling; and who does not take it well, that any man should intrude so far into his province." "All I would wish," replied Crites, "is, that they who love his writings, may still admire him, and his fellow poet: *Qui Bavium non odit, etc.*, ["Who does not hate Bavius."] is curse sufficient." "And farther," added Lisideius, "I believe there is no man who writes well, but would think himself very hardly dealt with, if their admirers should praise anything of his: *Nam quos contemnimus, eorum quoque laudes contemnimus.*" ["For those whom we despise, their praises we despise too."] "There are so few who write well in this age," says Crites, "that methinks any praises should be welcome; they neither rise to the dignity of the last age, nor to any of the Ancients: and we may cry out of the writers of this time, with more reason than Petronius of his, *Pace vestrâ liceat dixisse, primi omnium eloquentiam perdidistis* ["With your permission, may we say that you were the first of all to lose eloquence."]: you have debauched the true old poetry so far, that Nature, which is the soul of it, is not in any of your writings."

"If your quarrel," said Eugenius, "to those who now write, be grounded only on your reverence to antiquity, there is no man more ready to adore those great Greeks and Romans than I am: but on the other side, I cannot think so contemptibly of the age I live in, or so dishonourably of my own country, as not to judge we equal the Ancients in most kinds of poesy, and in some surpass them; neither know I any reason why I may not be as zealous for the reputation of our age as we find the Ancients themselves in reference to those who lived before them. For you hear your Horace saying,

> *Indignor quidquam reprehendi, non quia crasse*
> *Compositum, illepideve putetur, sed quia nuper.*

["I grow indignant when anything is censored not because it is considered to have been written crudely and tastelessly but because it has been written recently."]

And after:

> *Si meliora dies, ut vina, poemata reddit,*
> *Scire veiim, pretim chartis quotus arroget annus?*

["If time improves poems, like wines, I should like to know how many years it takes to bestow value upon writings."]

"But I see I am engaging in a wide dispute, where the arguments are not like to reach close on either side; for Poesy is of so large an extent, and so many both of the Ancients and Moderns have done well in all kinds of it, that in citing one against the other, we shall take up more time this evening than each man's occasions will allow him: therefore I would ask Crites to what part of Poesy he would confine his arguments, and whether he would defend the general cause of the Ancients against the Moderns, or oppose any age of the Moderns against this of ours?"

Crites, a little while considering upon this demand, told Eugenius he approved his propositions, and if he pleased, he would limit their dispute to Dramatic Poesy; in which he thought it not difficult to prove, either that the Ancients were superior to the Moderns, or the last age of this of ours.

Eugenius was somewhat surprised, when he heard Crites make choice of that subject. "For ought I see," said he, "I have undertaken a harder province than I imagined; for though I never judged the plays of the Greek or Roman poets comparable to ours, yet, on the other side, those we now see acted come short of many which were written in the last age: but my comfort is, if we are overcome, it will be only by our own countrymen: and if we yield to them in this one part of poesy, we more surpass them in all the other: for in the epic or lyric way, it will be hard for them to show us one such amongst them, as we have many now living, or who lately were so: they can produce nothing so courtly writ, or which expresses so much the conversation of a gentleman, as Sir John Suckling; nothing so even, sweet, and flowing as Mr. Waller; nothing so majestic, so correct, as Sir John Denham; nothing so elevated, so copious, and full of spirit as Mr. Cowley; as for the Italian, French, and Spanish plays, I can make it evident, that those who now write surpass them; and that the Drama is wholly ours."

All of them were thus far of Eugenius his opinion, that the sweetness of English verse was never understood or practised by our fathers; even Crites himself did not much oppose it; and every one was willing to acknowledge how much our poesy is improved by the happiness of some writers yet living; who first taught us to mould our thoughts into easy and significant words; to retrench the superfluities of expression, and to make our rhyme so properly a part of the verse, that it should never mislead the sense, but itself be led and governed by it.

Eugenius was going to continue this discourse, when Lisideius told him that it was necessary, before they proceeded further, to take a standing measure of their controversy; for how was it possible to be decided who writ the best plays, before we know what a play should be? But, this once agreed on by both parties, each might have recourse to it, either to prove his own advantages, or to discover the failings of his adversary.

He had no sooner said this, but all desired the favour of him to give the definition of a play; and they were the more importunate, because neither Aristotle, nor Horace, nor any other, who had writ of that subject, had ever done it.

Lisideius, after some modest denials, at last confessed he had a rude notion of it; indeed, rather a description than a definition; but which served to guide him in his private thoughts, when he was to make a judgment of what others writ: that he conceived a play ought to be, *A just and lively image of human nature, representing its passions and humours, and the changes of fortune to which it is subject, for the delight and instruction of mankind.*

This definition, though Crites raised a logical objection against it— that it was only *a genere et fine* ["By general classification and purpose."], and not altogether perfect, was yet well received by the rest; and after they had given order to the watermen to turn their barge, and row softly, that they might take the cool of the evening in their return,

Crites, being desired by the company to begin, spoke on behalf of the Ancients, in this manner:

"If confidence presage a victory, Eugenius, in his own opinion, has already triumphed over the Ancients: nothing seems more easy to him, than to overcome those whom it is our greatest praise to have imitated well; for we do not only build upon their foundations, but by their models. . . . Emulation is the spur of wit; and sometimes envy, sometimes admiration, quickens our endeavours.

"But now, since the rewards of honour are taken away, that virtuous emulation is turned into direct malice; yet so slothful, that it contents itself to condemn and cry down others, without attempting to do better: it is a reputation too unprofitable, to take the necessary pains for it; yet, wishing they had it, is incitement enough to hinder others from it. And this, in short, Eugenius, is the reason why you have now so few good poets, and so many severe judges. Certainly, to imitate the Ancients well, much labour and long study is required; which pains, I have already shown, our poets would want encouragement to take, if yet they had ability to go through with it. Those Ancients have been faithful imitators and wise observers of that Nature which is so torn and ill represented in our plays; they have handed down to us a perfect resemblance of her; which we, like all copiers, neglecting to look on, have rendered monstrous, and disfigured. But, that you may know how much you are indebted to those your masters, and be ashamed to have so ill requited them, I must remember you, that all the rules by which we practise the Drama at this day, (either such as relate to the justness and symmetry of the plot, or the episodical ornaments, such as descriptions, narrations, and other beauties, which are not esential to the play,) were delivered to us from the observations which Aristotle made, of those poets, which either lived before him, or were his contemporaries: we have added nothing of our own, except we have the confidence to say our wit is better; of which, none boast in this our age, but such as understand not theirs. Of that book which Aristotle has left us, περὶ τῆς Ποιητικῆς, Horace his *Art of Poetry* is an excellent comment, and, I believe, restores to us that Second Book of his concerning *Comedy*, which is wanting in him.

"Out of these two have been extracted the famous Rules, which the French call *Des Trois Unitez*, or, The Three Unities, which ought to be observed in every regular play; namely, of Time, Place, and Action.

"The Unity of Time they comprehend in twenty-four hours, the compass of a natural day, or as near as it can be contrived; and the reason of it is obvious to every one,—that the time of the feigned action, or fable of the play, should be proportioned as near as can be to the duration of that time in which it is represented: since, therefore, all plays are acted on the theatre in the space of time much within the compass of twenty-four hours, that play is to be thought the nearest imitation of nature, whose plot or action is confined within that time; and, by the same rule which concludes this general proportion of time, it follows, that all the parts of it are to be equally subdivided; as namely, that one act take not up the supposed time of half a day, which is out of proportion to the rest: since the other four are then to be straitened within the compass of the remaining half: for it is unnatural that one act, which being spoke or written is not longer than the rest, should be supposed longer by the audience; it is therefore the poet's duty, to take care that no act should be imagined to exceed the time in which it is represented on the stage; and that the intervals and inequalities of time be supposed to fall out between the acts.

"This rule of time, how well it has been observed by the Ancients, most of their plays will witness; you see them in their tragedies, (wherein to follow this rule is certainly most difficult), from the very beginning of their plays, falling close into that part of the story which they intend for the action or principal object of it, leaving the former part to be delivered by narration: so that they set the audience, as it were, at the post where the race is to be concluded; and, saving them the tedious expectation of seeing the poet set out and ride the beginning of the course, you behold him not till he is in sight of the goal, and just upon you.

"For the second Unity, which is that of Place, the Ancients meant by it, that the scene ought to be continued through the play, in the same place where it was laid in the beginning: for the stage on which it is represented being but one and the same place, it is unnatural to conceive it many, and those far distant from one another. I will not deny but, by the variation of painted scenes, the fancy, which in these cases will contribute to its own deceit, may sometimes imagine it several places, with some appearance of probability; yet it still carries the greater likelihood of truth, if those places be supposed so near each other as in the same town or city; which may all be comprehended under the larger denomination of one place; for a greater distance will bear no proportion to the shortness of time which is allotted in the acting, to pass from one of them to another; for the observation of this, next to the Ancients, the French are to be most commended. They tie themselves so strictly to the Unity of Place that you never see in any of their plays a scene changed in the middle of an act: if the act begins in a garden, a street, or chamber, 'tis ended in the same place; and that you may know it to be the same, the stage is so supplied with persons, that it is never empty all the time: he that enters second, has business with him who was on before; and before the second quits the stage, a third appears who has business with him. This Corneille calls *la liaison des scènes*, the continuity or joining of the scenes; and 'tis a good mark of a well-contrived play, when all the persons are known to each other, and every one of them has some affairs with all the rest.

"As for the third Unity, which is that of Action, the Ancients meant no other by it than what the logicians do by their *finis*, the end or scope of any action; that which is the first in intention, and last in execution: now the poet is to aim at one great and complete action, to the carrying on of which all things in his play, even the very obstacles, are to be subservient; and the reason of this is as evident as any of the former. For two actions, equally laboured and driven on by the writer, would destroy the unity of the poem; it would be no longer one play, but two: not but that there may be many actions in a play, as Ben Jonson has observed in his *Discoveries:* but they must be all subservient to the great one, which our language happily expresses in the name of *under-plots:* such as in Terence's *Eunuch* is the difference and reconcilement of Thais and Phædria, which is not the chief business of the play, but promotes the marriage of Chærea and Chremes's sister, principally intended by the poet. There ought to be but one action, says Corneille, that is, one complete action, which leaves the mind of the audience in a full repose; but this cannot be brought to pass but by many other imperfect actions, which conduce to it, and hold the audience in a delightful suspense of what will be.

"If by these rules (to omit many other drawn from the precepts and practice of the Ancients) we should judge our modern plays, 'tis probable that few of them would endure the trial: that which should be the business of a day, takes up in some of them an age; instead of one action, they are the epitomes of a man's life; and for one spot of ground, which the stage should represent, we are sometimes in more countries than the map can show us.

"But if we allow the Ancients to have contrived well, we must acknowledge them to have writ better. . . ."

Crites had no sooner left speaking, but Eugenius, who had waited with some impatience for it, thus began:

"I have observed in your speech, that the former part of it is convincing as to what the Moderns have profited by the rules of the Ancients; but in the latter you are careful to conceal how much they have excelled them; we own all the helps we have from them, and want neither veneration nor gratitude, while we acknowledge that, to overcome them, we must make use of the advantages we have received from them: but to these assistances we have joined our own industry; for, had we sat down with a dull imitation of them, we might then have lost somewhat of the old perfection, but never acquired any that was new. We draw not therefore after their lines, but those of Nature; and having the life before us, besides the experience of all they knew, it is no wonder if we hit some airs and features which they have missed. I deny not what you urge of arts and sciences, that they have flourished in some ages more than others; but your instance in philosophy makes for me: for if natural causes be more known now than in the time of Aristotle, because more studied, it follows that poesy and other arts may, with the same pains, arrive still nearer to perfection; and, that granted, it will rest for you to prove that they wrought more perfect images of human life than we; which seeing in your discourse you have avoided to make good, it shall now be my task to show you some part of their defects, and some few excellencies of the Moderns. And I think there is none among us can imagine I do it enviously, or with purpose to detract from them; for what interest of fame or profit can the living lose by the reputation of the dead? . . .

"Be pleased then in the first place to take notice, that the Greek poesy, which Crites has affirmed to have arrived to perfection in the reign of the Old Comedy, was so far from it, that the distinction of it into acts was not known to them; or if it were, it is yet so darkly delivered to us that we cannot make it out. . . .

"But since the Spaniards at this day allow but three acts, which they call *Jornadas*, to a play, and the Italians in many of theirs follow them, when I condemn the Ancients, I declare it is not altogether because they have not five acts to every play, but because they have not confined themselves to one certain number: it is building an house without a model; and when they succeeded in such undertakings, they ought to have sacrificed to Fortune, not to the Muses.

"Next, for the plot, which Aristotle called τὸ μῦθος, [*to Muthos*] and often τῶν πραγμάτων σύνθεσις, *tōn Pragmatōn sunthesis* ["the placing together of the actions"], and from him the Romans *Fabula;* it has already been judiciously observed by a late writer, that in their tragedies it was only some tale derived from Thebes or Troy, or at least something that happened in those two ages; which was worn so threadbare by the pens of all the epic poets, and even by tradition, itself of the talkative Greeklings (as Ben Jonson calls them), that before it came upon the stage it was already known to all the audience: and the people, so soon as ever they heard the name of Œdipus, knew as well as the poet, that he had killed his father by a mistake, and committed incest with his mother, before the play; that they were now to hear of a great plague, an oracle, and the ghost of Laius: so that they sat with a yawning kind of expectation, till he was to come with his eyes pulled out, and speak a hundred or two verses in a tragic tone, in complaint of his misfortunes. But one Œdipus, Hercules, or Medea, had been tolerable: poor people, they escaped not so good cheap; they had still the *chapon bouille* [Literally, "Boiled capon" ("tasty dish, luxury").] set before them, till their appetites were cloyed with the same dish, and, the novelty being gone, the pleasure vanished; so that one main end of Dramatic Poesy in its definition, which was to cause delight, was of consequence destroyed.

"In their comedies, the Romans generally borrowed their plots from the Greek poets; and theirs was commonly a little girl stolen or wandered from her parents, brought back unknown to the same city, there [falling into the hands of] some young fellow, who, by the help of his servant, cheats his father; and when her time comes, to cry,—*Juno Lucina, fer opem*, ["Juno, goddess of childbirth, bring help."]—one or other sees a little box or cabinet which was carried away with her, and so discovers her to her friends, if some god do not prevent it, by coming down in a machine, and take the thanks of it to himself.

"By the plot you may guess much of the characters of the persons. An old father, who would willingly, before he dies, see his son well married; his debauched son, kind in his nature to his wench, but miserably in want of money; a servant or slave, who had so much wit to strike in with him, and help to dupe his father; a braggadocio captain, a parasite, and a lady of pleasure.

"As for the poor honest maid, on whom the story is built, and who ought to be one of the principal actors in the play, she is commonly a mute in it: she has the breeding of the old Elizabeth way, for maids to be seen and not to be heard; and it is enough you know she is willing to be married, when the fifth act requires it.

"These are plots built after the Italian mode of houses,—you see through them all at once: the characters are indeed the imitation of Nature, but so narrow, as if they had imitated only an eye or an hand, and did not dare to venture on the lines of a face, or the proportion of a body.

"But in how strait a compass soever they have bounded their plots and characters, we will pass it by, if they have regularly pursued them, and perfectly observed those three Unities of Time, Place, and Action; the knowledge of which you say is derived to us from them. But in the first place give me leave to tell you, that the Unity of Place, however it might be practised by them, was never any of their rules: we neither find it in Aristotle, Horace, or any who have written of it, till in our age the French poets first made it a precept of the stage. The Unity of Time, even Terence himself, who was the best and most regular of them, has neglected: his *Heautontimorumenos*, or *Self-Punisher*, takes up visibly two days, therefore, says Scaliger; the two first acts concluding the first day, were acted overnight; the three last on the ensuing day; and Euripides, in tying himself to one day, has committed an absurdity never to be forgiven him; for in one of his tragedies he has made Theseus go from Athens to Thebes, which was about forty English miles, under the walls of it to give battle, and appear victorious in the next act; and yet, from the time of his departure to the return of the Nuntius, who gives the relation of his victory, Æthra and the Chorus have but thirty-six verses; that is not for every mile a verse.

"The like error is as evident in Terence his *Eunuch*, when Laches, the old man, enters in a mistake the house of Thais; where, betwixt his exit and the entrance of Pythias, who comes to give ample relation of the disorders he has raised within, Parmeno, who was left upon the stage, has not above five lines to speak. *C'est bien employer un temps si court* ["It is well to employ so short a time."], says the French poet, who furnished me with one of the observations: and almost all their tragedies will afford us examples of the like nature.

"'T is true, they have kept the continuity, or, as you called it, *liaison des scènes*, somewhat better: two do not perpetually come in together, talk, and go out together; and other two succeed them, and do the same throughout the act, which the English call by the name of single scenes; but the reason is, because they have seldom above two or three scenes, properly so called in every act; for it is to be accounted a new scene, not every time the stage is empty; but every person who enters, though to others, makes it so; because he introduces a new business. Now the plots of their plays being narrow, and the persons few, one of their acts was written in a less compass then one of our well-wrought scenes; and yet they are often deficient even in this. . . .

"But as they have failed both in laying of their plots, and managing of them, swerving from the rules of their own art by misrepresenting Nature to us, in which they have ill satisfied one intention of a play, which was delight; so in the instructive part they have erred worse: instead of punishing vice and rewarding virtue, they have often shown a prosperous wickedness, and an unhappy piety: they have set before us a bloody image of revenge in Medea, and given her dragons to convey her safe from punishment; a Priam and Astyanes murdered, and Cassandra ravished, and the lust and murder ending in the victory of him who acted them: in short, there is no indecorum in any of our modern plays, which if I would excuse, I could not shadow with some authority from the Ancients.

"And one farther note of them let me leave you: tragedies and comedies were not writ then as they are now, promiscuously, by the same person; but he who found his genius bending to the one, never attempted the other way. This is so plain, that I neet not instance to you, that Aristophanes, Plautus, Terence, never any of them writ a tragedy; Æschylus, Euripides, Sophocles, and Seneca, never meddled with comedy: the sock and buskin were not worn by the same poet. Having then so much care to excel in one kind, very little is to be pardoned them, if they miscarried in it; and this would lead me to the consideration of their wit, had not Crites given me sufficient warning not be too bold in my judgment of it; because, the languages being dead, and many of the customs and little accidents on which it depended lost to us, we are not competent judges of it. But though I grant that here and there we may miss the application of a proverb or a custom, yet a thing well said will be wit in all languages; and though it may lose something in the translation, yet to him who reads it in the original, 'tis still the same: he had an idea of its excellency, though it cannot pass from his mind into any other expression or words than those in which he finds it. . . ."

Eugenius was proceeding in that part of his discourse, when Crites interrupted him. "I see," said he, "Eugenius and I are never like to have this question decided betwixt us; for he maintains, the Moderns have acquired a new perfection in writing; I can only grant they have altered the mode of it. Homer described his heroes men of great appetites, lovers of beef broiled upon the coals, and good fellows; contrary to the practice of the French Romances, whose heroes neither eat, nor drink, nor sleep, for love. Virgil makes Æneas a bold avower of his own virtues:

> *Sum pius Æneas, fama super æthera notus;*
> ["I am dutiful Aeneas, whose fame is known above the heavens."]

which in the civility of our poets is the character of a fanfaron or Hector: for with us the knight takes occasion to walk out, or sleep, to avoid the vanity of telling his own story, which the trusty 'squire is ever to perform for him. So in their love-scenes of which Eugenius spoke last, the ancients were more hearty, we more talkative: they writ love as it was then the mode to make it; and I will grant thus much to Eugenius, that perhaps one of their poets had he lived in our age, *si foret hoc nostrum fato delapsus in ævum* ["If he had been dropped into our age by fate."] (as Horace says of Lucilius), he had altered many things; not that they were not natural before, but that he might accommodate himself to the age he lived in. Yet in the meantime, we are not to conclude anything rashly against those great men, but preserve to them the dignity of masters, and give that honour to their memories, *quos Libitina sacravit* ["Which Libitina has consecrated."], part of which we expect may be paid to us in future times."

This moderation of Crites, as it was pleasing to all the company, so it put an end to that dispute; which Eugenius, who seemed to have the better of the argument, would urge no farther: but Lisideius, after he had acknowledged himself of Eugenius his opinion concerning the Ancient, yet told him, he had forborne, till his discourse were ended, to ask him why he preferred the English plays above those of other nations? and whether we ought not to submit our stage to the exactness of our next neighbours?

"Though," said Eugenius, "I am at all times ready to defend the honour of my country against the French, and to maintain, we are as well able to vanquish them with our pens, as our ancestors have been with their swords; yet, if you please," added he, looking upon Neander, "I will commit this cause to my friend's management; his opinion of our plays is the same with mine: and besides, there is no reason, that Crites and I, who have now left the stage, should reenter so suddenly upon it; which is against the laws of comedy."

"If the question had been stated," replied Lisideius, "who had writ best, the French or English, forty years ago, I should have been of your opinion, and adjudged the honour to our own nation; but since that time" (said he, turning towards Neander), "we have been so long together bad Englishmen that we had not leisure to be good poets. Beaumont, Fletcher, and Jonson (who were only capable of bringing us to that degree of perfection which we have), were just then leaving the world; as if (in an age of so much horror) wit, and those milder studies of humanity, had no farther business among us. But the Muses, who ever follow peace, went to plant in another country: it was then that the great Cardinal Richelieu began to take them into his protection; and that, by his encouragement, Corneille, and some other Frenchmen, reformed their theatre, which before was as much below ours, as it now surpasses it and the rest of Europe. But because Crites in his discourse for the Ancients has prevented me, by touching upon many rules of the stage which the Moderns have borrowed from them, I shall only, in short, demand of you, whether you are not convinced that of all nations the French have best observed them? In the Unity of Time you find them so scrupulous, that it yet remains a dispute among their poets, whether the artificial day of twelve hours, more or less, be not meant by Aristotle, rather than the natural one of twenty-four; and consequently, whether all plays ought not to be reduced into that compass. This I can testify, that in all their dramas writ within these last twenty years and upwards, I have not observed any that have extended the time to thirty hours: in the Unity of Place they are full as scrupulous; for many of their critics limit it to that very spot of ground where the play is supposed to begin; none of them, exceed the compass of the same town or city. The Unity of Action in all plays is yet more conspicuous; for they do not burden them with under-plots, as the English do: which is the reason why many scenes of our tragi-comedies carry on a design that is nothing of kin to the main plot; and that we see two distinct webs in a play, like those in ill-wrought stuffs; and two actions, that is, two plays, carried on together, to the confounding of the audience; who, before they are warm in their concernments for one part, are diverted to another; and by that means espouse the interest of neither. From hence likewise it arises that the one half of our actors are not known to the other. They keep their distances, as if they were Montagues and Capulets, and seldom begin an acquaintance till the last scene of the fifth act, when they are all to meet upon the stage. There is no theatre in the world has anything so absurd as the English tragi-comedy; 'tis a drama of our own invention, and the fashion of it is enough to proclaim it so; here a course of mirth, there another of sadness and passion, and a third of honour, and fourth a duel: thus, in two hours and a half, we run through all the fits of Bedlam. The French affords you as much variety on the same day, but they do it not so unseasonably, or *mal à propos*, as we: our poets present you the play and the farce together; and our stages still retain somewhat of the original civility of the *Red Bull:*

> *Atque ursum et pugiles media inter carmina poscunt.*
> ["And in the middle of plays they ask for a bear and boxers."]

The end of tragedies or serious plays, says Aristotle, is to beget admiration, compassion, or concernment; but are not mirth and compassion things incompatible? and is it not evident that the poet must of necessity destroy the former by intermingling of the latter? that is, he must ruin the sole end and object of his tragedy, to introduce somewhat that is forced in, and is not of the body of it. Would you not think that physician mad, who, having prescribed a purge, should immediately order you to take restringents upon it?

"But to leave our plays, and return to theirs. I have noted one great advantage they have had in the plotting of their tragedies; that is, they are always grounded upon some known history: according to that of Horace, *Ex noto fictum carmen sequar* ["Out of a well-known story, I should bring a poem."], and in that they have so imitated the Ancients that they have surpassed them. For the Ancients, as was observed before, took for the foundation of their plays some poetical fiction, such as under that consideration could move but little concernment in the audience, because they already knew the event of it. But the French goes farther:

> *Atque ita mentitur, sic veris falsa remiscet*
> *Primo ne medium, medio ne discrepet imum.*
> ["And he so lies and so mixes the false with the true that the middle part will not be inconsistent with the first part nor the last part with the middle."]

He so interweaves truth with probable fiction that he puts a pleasing fallacy upon us; mends the intrigues of fate, and dispenses with the severity of history, to reward that virtue which has been rendered to us there unfortunate. Sometimes the story has left the success so doubtful that the writer is free, by the privilege of a poet, to take that which of two or more relations will best suit with his design: as for example, the death of Cyrus, whom Justin and some others report to have perished in the Scythian war, but Xenophon affirms to have died in his bed of extreme old age. Nay more, when the event is past dispute, even then we are willing to be deceived, and the poet, if he contrives it with appearance of truth, has all the audience of his party; at least during the time his play is acting: so naturally we are kind to virtue, when our own interest is not in question, that we take it up as the general concernment of mankind. On the other side, if you consider the historical plays of Shakespeare, they are rather so many chronicles of kings, or the business many times of thirty or forty years, cramped into a representation of two hours and a half; which is not to imitate or paint Nature, but rather to draw her in miniature, to take her in little; to look upon her through the wrong end of a perspective, and receive her images not only much less, but infinitely more imperfect than the life: this, instead of making a play delightful, renders it ridiculous:—

> *Quodcunque ostendis mihi sic, incredulus odi.*
> ["Whatever you show me in this way I find incredible and I hate."]

For the spirit of man cannot be satisfied but with truth, or at least verisimility; and a poem is to contain, if not τὰ ἔτυμα yet ἐτυμοισιν ὁμοῖα ["True things"—"things like the truth."], as one of the Greek poets has expressed it.

"Another thing in which the French differ from us and from the Spaniards, is that they do not embarrass, or cumber themselves with too much plot; they only represent so much of a story as will constitute one whole and great action sufficient for a play; we, who undertake more, do but multiply adventures; which, not being produced from one another, as effects from causes, but barely following, constitute many actions in the drama, and consequently make it many plays.

"But by pursuing close one argument, which is not cloyed with many turns, the French have gained more liberty for verse, in which they write; they have leisure to dwell on a subject which deserves it; and to represent the passions (which we have acknowledged to be the poet's work), without being hurried from one thing to another, as we are in the plays of Calderon, which we have seen lately upon our theatres under the name of Spanish plots. I have taken notice but of one tragedy of ours, whose plot has that uniformity and unity of design in it, which I have commended in the French; and that is *Rollo*, or rather, under the name of Rollo, the Story of Bassianus and Geta in Herodian: there indeed the plot is neither large nor intricate, but just enough to fill the minds of the audience, not to cloy them. Besides, you see it founded upon the truth of history,—only the time of the action is not reduceable to the strictness of the rules; and you see in some places a little farce mingled, which is below the dignity of the other parts; and in this all our poets are extremely peccant: even Ben Jonson himself, in *Sejanus* and *Catiline*, has given us this oleo of a play, this unnatural mixture of comedy and tragedy; which to me sounds just as ridiculously as the history of David with the merry humours of Golias. In *Sejanus* you may take notice of the scene betwixt Livia and the physician, which is a pleasant satire upon the artificial helps of beauty: in *Catiline* you may see the parliament of women; the little envies of them to one another; and all that passes betwixt Curio and Fulvia: scenes admirable in their kind, but of an ill mingle with the rest.

"But I return again to the French writers, who, as I have said, do not burden themselves too much with plot, which has been reproached to them by an *ingenious person* of our nation as a fault; for, he says, they commonly make but one person considerable in a play; they dwell on him, and his concernments, while the rest of the persons are only subservient to set him off. If he intends this by it, that there is one person in the play who is of greater dignity than the rest, he must tax, not only theirs, but those of the Ancients, and which he would be loth to do, the best of ours; for it is impossible but that one person must be more conspicuous in it than any other, and consequently the greatest share in the action must devolve on him. We see it so in the management of all affairs; even in the most equal aristocracy, the balance cannot be so justly poised but some one will be superior to the rest, either in parts, fortune, interest, or the consideration of some glorious exploit; which will reduce the greatest part of business into his hands.

"But, if he would have us to imagine, that in exalting one character the rest of them are neglected, and that all of them have not some share or other in the action of the play, I desire him to produce any of Corneille's tragedies, wherein every person, like so many servants in a well-governed family, has not some employment, and who is not necessary to the carrying on of the plot, or at least to your understanding it.

"There are indeed some protatic persons in the Ancients, whom they make use of in their plays, either to hear or give the relation: but the French avoid this with great address, making their narrations only to, or by such, who are some way interested in the main design. And now I am speaking of relations, I cannot take a fitter opportunity to add this in favour of the French, that they often use them with better judgment and more *à propos* than the English do. Not that I commend narrations in general,—but there are two sorts of them. One, of those things which are antecedent to the play, and are related to make the conduct of it more clear to us. But 'tis a fault to choose such subjects for the stage as will force us on that rock because we see they are seldom listened to by the audience and that is many times the ruin of the play; for, being once let pass without attention, the audience can never recover themselves to understand the plot: and indeed it is somewhat unreasonable that they should be put to so much trouble, as that, to comprehend what passes in their sight, they must have recourse to what was done, perhaps, ten or twenty years ago.

"But there is another sort of relations, that is, of things happening in the action of the play, and supposed to be done behind the scenes; and this is many times both convenient and beautiful; for by it the French avoid the tumult to which we are subject in England, by representing duels, battles, and the like; which renders our stage too like the theatres where they fight prizes. For what is more ridiculous than to represent an army with a drum and five men behind it; all which the hero of the other side is to drive in before him; or to see a duel fought, and one slain with two or three thrusts of the foils, which we know are so blunted, that we might give a man an hour to kill another in good earnest with them.

"I have observed that in all our tragedies, the audience cannot forbear laughing when the actors are to die; it is the most comic part of the whole play. All *passions* may be lively represented on the stage, if to the well-writing of them the actor supplies a good commanded voice, and limbs that move easily, and without stiffness; but there are many *actions* which can never be imitated to a just height: dying especially is a thing which none but a Roman gladiator could naturally perform on the stage, when he did not imitate or represent, but naturally do it; and therefore it is better to omit the representation of it.

"The words of a good writer, which describe it lively, will make a deeper impression of belief in us than all the actor can persuade us to, when he seems to fall dead before us; as a poet in the description of a beautiful garden, or a meadow, will please our imagination more than the place itself can please our sight. When we see death represented, we are convinced it is but fiction; but when we hear it related, our eyes, the strongest witnesses, are wanting, which might have undeceived us; and we are all willing to favour the sleight, when the poet does not too grossly impose on us. They therefore who imagine these relations would make no concernment in the audience, are deceived, by confounding them with the other, which are of things antecedent to the play: those are made often in cold blood, as I may say, to the audience; but these are warmed with our concernments, which were before awakened in the play. What the philosophers say of motion, that, when it is once begun, it continues of itself, and will do so to eternity, without some stop put to it, is clearly true on this occasion: the soul being already moved with the characters and fortunes of those imaginary persons, continues going of its own accord; and we are no more weary to hear what becomes of them when they are not on the stage, than we are to listen to the news of an absent mistress. But it is objected, that if one part of the play may be related, then why not all? I answer, some parts of the action are more fit to be represented, some to be related. Corneille says judiciously, that the poet is not obliged to expose to view all particular actions which conduce to the principal: he ought to select such of them to be seen, which will appear with the greatest beauty, either by the magnificence of the show, or the vehemence of passions, which they produce, or some other charm which they have in them; and let the rest arrive to the audience by narration. 'Tis a great mistake in us to believe the French present no part of the action on the stage; every alteration or crossing of a design, every new-sprung passion, and turn of it, is a part of the action, and much the noblest, except we conceive nothing to be action till they come to blows; as if the painting of the hero's mind were not more properly the poet's work than the strength of his body. Nor does this anything contradict the opinion of Horace, where he tells us,

> *Segnius irritant animos demissa per aurem,*
> *Quam quæ sunt oculis subjecta fidelibus.*

["The things which are transmitted through the ear stir the mind less forcefully than the things which are set before the faithful eyes."]

For he says immediately after,

> *Non tamen intus*
> *Digna geri promes in scenam; multaq; tolles*
> *Ex oculis, quæ mox narret facundia præsens.*

["You shall not bring on the stage things which should be done offstage; and you shall remove from my sight things which a ready eloquence will soon narrate."]

Among which many he recounts some:

> *Nec pueros coram populo Medea trucidet,*
> *Aut in avem Progne mutetur, Cadmus in anguem, etc.*

["And Medea should not cut up her children in front of the audience, nor Procne be changed into a bird, Cadmus into a snake, etc."]

That is, those actions which by reason of their cruelty, will cause aversion in us, or by reason of their impossibility, unbelief, ought either wholly to be avoided by a poet, or only delivered by narration. To which we may have leave to add such as to avoid tumult (as was before hinted), or to reduce the plot into a more reasonable compass of time, or for defect of beauty in them, are rather to be related than presented to the eye. Examples of all these kinds are frequent, not only among all the Ancients, but in the best received of our English poets. We find Ben Jonson using them in his *Magnetic Lady*, where one comes out from dinner, and relates the quarrels and disorders of it, to save the undecent appearance of them on the stage, and to abbreviate the story; and this in express imitation of Terence, who had done the same before him in his *Eunuch*, where Pythias makes the like relation of what had happened within at the Soldier's entertainment. The relations likewise of Sejanus's death, and the prodigies before it, are remarkable; the one of which was hid from sight, to avoid the horror and tumult of the representation; the other, to shun the introducing of things impossible to be believed. In that excellent play, *The King and no King*, Fletcher goes yet farther; for the whole unravelling of the plot is done by narration in the fifth act, after the manner of the Ancients; and it moves great concernment in the audience, though it be only a relation of what was done many years before the play. I could multiply other instances, but these are sufficient to prove that there is no error in choosing a subject which requires this sort of narrations; in the ill managing of them, there may.

"But I find I have been too long in this discourse, since the French have many other excellencies not common to us; as that you never see any of their plays end with a conversion, or simple change of will, which is the ordinary way which our poets use to end theirs. It shows little art in the conclusion of a dramatic poem, when they who have hindered the felicity during the four acts, desist from it in the fifth, without some powerful cause to take them off; and though I deny not but such reasons may be found, yet it is a path that is cautiously to be trod, and the poet is to be sure he convinces the audience that the motive is strong enough. As for example, the conversion of the Usurer in *The Scornful Lady* seems to me a little forced; for, being an Usurer, which implies a lover of money to the highest degree of covetousness (and such the poet has represented him), the account he gives for the sudden change is, that he has been duped by the wild young fellow; which in reason might render him more wary another time, and make him punish himself with harder fare and coarser clothes, to get it up again: but that he should look on it as a judgment, and so repent, we may expect to hear of in a sermon, but I should never endure it in a play.

"I pass by this; neither will I insist on the care they take that no person after his first entrance shall ever appear, but the business which brings him upon the stage shall be evident; which, if observed, must needs render all the events in the play more natural; for there you see the probability of every accident, in the cause that produced it; and that which appears chance in the play, will seem so reasonable to you, that you will there find it almost necessary: so that in the exits of the actors you have a clear account of their purpose and design in the next entrance (though, if the scene be well wrought, the event will commonly deceive you) for there is nothing so absurd, says Corneille, as for an actor to leave the stage only because he has no more to say.

"I should now speak of the beauty of their rhyme, and the just reason I have to prefer that way of writing in tragedies before ours in blank-verse; but because it is partly received by us, and therefore not altogether peculiar to them, I will say no more of it in relation to their plays. For our own, I doubt not but it will exceedingly beautify them; and I can see but one reason why it should not generally obtain, that is, because our poets write so ill in it. This indeed may prove a more prevailing argument than all others which are used to destroy it, and therefore I am only troubled when great and judicious poets, and those who are acknowledged such, have writ or spoke against it: as for others, they are to be answered by that one sentence of an ancient author:—*Sed ut primo ad consequendos eos quos priores ducimus, accendimur, ita ubi aut proeteriri, aut æquari eos posse desperavimus, studium cum spe senescit: quod, scilicet, assequi non potest, sequi desinit: . . . praeteritoque eo in quo eminere non possumus, aliquid in quo nitamur, conquirimus.*"

["But just as we are inflamed to follow those whom we consider foremost, so, when we despair that they can be either surpassed or equalled, our zeal wanes with our hope: for, to be sure, what it cannot attain it stops to follow ... and when that in which we cannot excel is passed, we look for something in which to strive."]

Lisideius concluded in this manner; and Neander, after a little pause, thus answered him:

"I shall grant Lisideius, without much dispute, a great part of what he has urged against us; for I acknowledge that the French contrive their plots more regularly, and observe the laws of comedy, and decorum of the stage (to speak generally), with more exactness than the English. Farther, I deny not but he has taxed us justly in some irregularities of ours, which he has mentioned: yet, after all, I am of opinion that neither our faults nor their virtues are considerable enough to place them above us.

"For the lively imitation of Nature being in the definition of a play, those which best fulfil that law ought to be esteemed superior to the others. 'Tis true, those beauties of the French poesy are such as will raise perfection higher where it is, but are not sufficient to give it where it is not: they are indeed the beauties of a statue, but not of a man, because not animated with the soul of Poesy, which is imitation of humour and passions: and this Lisideius himself, or any other, however biassed to their party, cannot but acknowledge, if he will either compare the humours of our comedies, or the characters of our serious plays, with theirs. He that will look upon theirs which have been written till these last ten years, or thereabouts, will find it an hard matter to pick out two or three passable humours amongst them. Corneille himself, their arch-poet, what has he produced except *The Liar*, and you know how it was cried up in France; but when it came upon the English stage, though well translated, and that part of Dorant acted to so much advantage by Mr. Hart as I am confident it never received in its own country, the most favourable to it would not put it in competition with many of Fletcher's or Ben Jonson's. In the rest of Corneille's comedies you have little humour; he tells you himself, his way is, first to show two lovers in good intelligence with each other; in the working up of the play to embroil them by some mistake, and in the latter end to clear it, and reconcile them.

"But of late years Molière, the younger Corneille, Quinault, and some others, have been imitating afar off the quick turns and graces of the English stage. They have mixed their serious plays with mirth, like our tragi-comedies, since the death of Cardinal Richelieu; which Lisideius and many others not observing, have commended that in them for a virtue which they themselves no longer practise. Most of their new plays are, like some of ours, derived from the Spanish novels. There is scarce one of them without a veil, and a trusty Diego, who drolls much after the rate of *The Adventures*. But their humours, if I may grace them with that name, are so thin-sown, that never above one of them comes up in any play. I dare take upon me to find more variety of them in some one play of Ben Jonson's than in all theirs together; as he who has seen *The Alchemyst*, *The Silent Woman*, or *Bartholomew Fair*, cannot but acknowledge with me.

"I grant the French have performed what was possible on the ground-work of the Spanish plays; what was pleasant before, they have made regular: but there is not above one good play to be writ on all those plots; they are too much alike to please often; which we need not the experience of our own stage to justify. As for their new way of mingling mirth with serious plot, I do not, with Lisideius, condemn the thing, though I cannot approve their manner of doing it. He tells us, we cannot so speedily recollect ourselves after a scene of great passion and concernment, as to pass to another of mirth and humour, and to enjoy it with any relish: but why should he imagine the soul of man more heavy than his senses? Does not the eye pass from an unpleasant object to a pleasant in a much shorter time than is required to this? and does not the unpleasantness of the first commend the beauty of the latter? The old rule of logic might have convinced him, that contraries, when placed near, set off each other. A continued gravity keeps the spirit too much bent; we must refresh it sometimes, as we bait in a journey that we may go on with greater ease. A scene of mirth, mixed with tragedy, has the same effect upon us which our music has betwixt the acts; and that we find a relief to us from the best plots and language of the stage, if the discourses have been long. I must therefore have stronger arguments, ere I am convinced that compassion and mirth in the same subject destroy each other; and in the meantime cannot but conclude, to the honour of our nation, that we have invented, increased, and perfected a more pleasant way of writing for the stage, than was ever known to the Ancients or moderns of any nation, which is tragi-comedy.

"And this leads me to wonder why Lisideius and many others should

cry up the barrenness of the French plots above the variety and copiousness of the English. Their plots are single; they carry on one design,
which is pushed forward by all the actors, every scene in the play
contributing and moving towards it. Our plays, besides the main design,
have under-plots or by-concernments, of less considerable persons and
intrigues, which are carried on with the motion of the main plot: just
as they say the orb of the fixed stars, and those of the planets, though
they have motions of their own, are whirled about by the motion of the
primum mobile, in which they are contained. That similitude expresses
much of the English stage; for if contrary motions may be found in
nature to agree; if a planet can go east and west at the same time;—one
way by virtue of his own motion, the other by the force of the First
Mover, it will not be difficult to imagine how the underplot, which is
only different, not contrary to the great design, may naturally be
conducted along with it.

"Eugenius has already shown us, from the confession of the French
poets, that the Unity of Action is sufficiently preserved, if all the imperfect actions of the play are conducing to the main design; but when
those petty intrigues of a play are so ill ordered, that they have no
coherence with the other, I must grant that Lisideius has reason to tax
that want of due connection; for co-ordination in a play is as dangerous
and unnatural as in a state. In the meantime he must acknowledge, our
variety, if well ordered, will afford a greater pleasure to the audience.

"As for his other argument, that by pursuing one single theme they
gain an advantage to express and work up the passions, I wish any
example he could bring from them would make it good; for I confess
their verses are to me the coldest I have ever read. Neither, indeed, is it
possible for them, in the way they take, so to express passion, as that
the effects of it should appear in the concernment of an audience, their
speeches being so many declamations, which tire us with the length;
so that instead of persuading us to grieve for their imaginary heroes,
we are concerned for our own trouble, as we are in tedious visits of
bad company; we are in pain till they are gone. When the French stage
came to be reformed by Cardinal Richelieu, those long harangues were
introduced to comply with the gravity of a churchman. Look upon the
Cinna and the *Pompey*; they are not so properly to be called plays as
long discourses of reason of state; and *Polieucte* in matters of religion
is a solemn as the long stops upon our organs. Since that time it is grown
into a custom, and their actors speak by the hour-glass, as our parsons

do; nay, they account it the grace of their parts, and think themselves disparaged by the poet, if they may not twice or thrice in a play entertain the audience with a speech of an hundred or two hundred lines. I deny not but this may suit well enough with the French; for as we, who are a more sullen people, come to be diverted at our plays, so they, who are of an airy and gay temper, come thither to make themselves more serious: and this I conceive to be one reason why comedy is more pleasing to us, and tragedies to them. But to speak generally: it cannot be denied that short speeches and replies are more apt to move the passions and beget concernment in us, than the other; for it is unnatural for any one in a gust of passion to speak long together, or for another in the same condition to suffer him, without interruption. Grief and passion are like floods raised in little brooks by a sudden rain; they are quickly up; and if the concernment be poured unexpectedly in upon us, it overflows us: but a long sober shower gives them leisure to run out as they came in, without troubling the ordinary current. As for Comedy, repartee is one of its chiefest graces; the greatest pleasure of the audience is a chase of wit, kept up on both sides, and swiftly managed. And this our forefathers, if not we, have had in Fletcher's plays, to a much higher degree of perfection than the French poets can arrive at.

"There is another part of Lisideius his discourse, in which he has rather excused our neighbours, than commended them; that is, for aiming only to make one person considerable in their plays. 'Tis very true what he has urged, that one character in all plays even without the poet's care, will have advantage of all the others; and that the design of the whole drama will chiefly depend on it. But this hinders not that there may be more shining characters in the play: many persons of a second magnitude, nay, some so very near, so almost equal to the first, that greatness may be opposed to greatness, and all the persons be made considerable, not only by their quality, but their action. 'Tis evident that the more the persons are, the greater will be the variety of the plot. If then the parts are managed so regularly, that the beauty of the whole be kept entire, and that the variety become not a perplexed and confused mass of accidents, you will find it infinitely pleasing to be led in a labyrinth of design, where you see some of your way before you, yet discern not the end till you arrive at it. And that all this is practicable, I can produce for examples many of our English plays: as *The Maid's Tragedy*, *The Alchemyst*, *The Silent Woman:* I was going to have named *The Fox*, but that the unity of design seems not exactly observed in it;

for there appear two actions in the play: the first naturally ending with the fourth act; the second forced from it in the fifth; which yet is the less to be condemned in him, because the disguise of Volpone, though it suited not with his character as a crafty or covetous person, agreed well enough with that of a voluptuary; and by it the poet gained the end he aimed at, the punishment of vice, and the reward of virtue, which that disguise produced. So that to judge equally of it, it was an excellent fifth act, but not so naturally proceeding from the former.

"But to leave this, and pass to the latter part of Lisideius his discourse, which concerns relations: I must acknowledge with him, that the French have reason when they hide that part of the action which would occasion too much tumult on the stage, and choose rather to have it made known by narration to the audience. Farther, I think it very convenient, for the reasons he has given, that all incredible actions were removed; but, whether custom has so insinuated itself into our countrymen, or nature has so formed them to fierceness, I know not; but they will scarcely suffer combats and other objects of horror to be taken from them. And indeed, the indecency of tumults is all which can be objected against fighting: for why may not our imagination as well suffer itself to be deluded with the probability of it, as with any other thing in the play? For my part, I can with as great ease persuade myself that the blows which are struck, are given in good earnest, as I can, that they who strike them are kings or princes, or those persons which they represent. For objects of incredibility, I would be satisfied from Lisideius whether we have any so removed from all appearance of truth, as are those of Corneille's *Andromède*; a play which has been frequented the most of any he has writ. If the Perseus, or the son of an heathen god, the Pegasus, and the Monster, were not capable to choke a strong belief, let him blame any representation of ours hereafter. Those indeed were objects of delight; yet the reason is the same as to the probability: for he makes it not a Ballette or masque, but a play, which is to resemble truth. But for death, that it ought not to be represented, I have, besides the arguments alleged by Lisideius, the authority of Ben Jonson, who has forborne it in his tragedies; for both the death of Sejanus and Catiline are related: though in the latter I cannot but observe one irregularity of that great poet; he has removed the scene in the same act from Rome to Catiline's army, and from thence again to Rome; and besides, has allowed a very inconsiderable time, after Catiline's speech, for the striking of the battle, and the return of Petreius, who is to relate the event of it to the senate: which I should not animadvert on him, who was otherwise a painful observer of τὸ πρέπον, or the *decorum* of the stage, if he had not used extreme severity in his judgment on the incomparable Shakespeare for the same fault.—To conclude on this subject of relations; if we are to be blamed for showing too much of the action, the French are as faulty for discovering too little of it: a mean betwixt both should be observed by every judicious writer, so as the audience may neither be left unsatisfied by not seeing what is beautiful, or shocked by beholding what is either incredible or undecent.

"I hope I have already proved in this discourse, that though we are not altogether so puncatal as the French, in observing the laws of Comedy, yet our errors are so few, and little, and those things wherein we excel them so considerable, that we ought of right to be preferred before them. But what will Lisideius say, if they themselves acknowledge they are too strictly tied up by those laws, for breaking which he has blamed the English? I will allege Corneille's words, as I find them in the end of his Discourse of the Three Unities:—*Il est facile aux spéculatifs d'estre sévères, etc.* ''Tis easy for speculative persons to judge severely; but if they would produce to public view ten or twelve pieces of this nature, they would perhaps give more latitude to the rules than I have done, when by experience they had known how much we are bound up and constrained by them, and how many beauties of the stage they banished from it.' To illustrate a little what he has said: By their servile observations of the Unities of Time and Place, and integrity of scenes, they have brought on themselves that dearth of plot, and narrowness of imagination, which may be observed in all their plays. How many beautiful accidents might naturally happen in two or three days, which cannot arrive with any probability in the compass of twenty-four hours? There is time to be allowed also for maturity of design, which, amongst great and prudent persons, such as are often represented in Tragedy, cannot, with any likelihood of truth, be brought to pass at so short a warning. Farther; by tying themselves strictly to the Unity of Place, and unbroken scenes, they are forced many times to omit some beauties which cannot be shown where the act began; but might, if the scene were interrupted, and the stage cleared for the persons to enter in another place; and therefore the French poets are often forced upon absurdities; for if the act begins in a chamber, all the persons in the play must have some business or other to come thither, or else they are not to be shown that act; and sometimes their characters are very unfitting to appear there. As, suppose it were the king's bed-chamber; yet the meanest man in the tragedy must come and dispatch his business there, rather than in the lobby or courtyard (which is fitter for him), for fear the stage should be cleared, and the scenes broken. Many times they fall by it in a greater inconvenience; for they keep their scenes unbroken, and yet change the place; as in one of their newest plays, where the act begins in the street. There a gentleman is to meet his friend; he sees him with his man, coming out from his father's house; they talk together, and the first goes out: the second, who is a lover, has made an appointment with his mistress; she appears at the window, and then we are to imagine the scene lies under it. This gentleman is called away, and leaves his servant with his mistress; presently her father is heard from within; the young lady is afraid the serving-man should be discovered, and thrusts him in through a door, which is supposed to be her closet. After this, the father enters to the daughter, and now the scene is in a house; for he is seeking from one room to another for this poor Philipin, or French Diego, who is heard from within, drolling and breaking many a miserable conceit upon his sad condition. In this ridiculous manner the play goes on, the stage being never empty all the while: so that the street, the window, the houses, and the closet, are made to walk about, and the persons to stand still. Now what, I beseech you, is more easy than to write a regular French play, or more difficult than to write an irregular English one, like those of Fletcher, or of Shakspeare?

"If they content themselves, as Corneille did, with some flat design, which, like an ill riddle, is found out ere it be half proposed, such plots we can make every way regular, as easily as they; but whene'er they endeavour to rise to any quick turns and counterturns of plot, as some of them have attempted, since Corneille's plays have been less in vogue, you see they write as irregularly as we, though they cover it more speciously. Hence the reason is perspicuous, why no French plays, when translated, have, or ever can succeed on the English stage. For, if you consider the plots, our own are fuller of variety; if the writing, ours are more quick and fuller of spirit; and therefore 'tis a strange mistake in those who decry the way of writing plays in verse, as if the English therein imitated the French. We have borrowed nothing from them; out plots are weaved in English looms: we endeavour therein to follow the variety and greatness of characters which are derived to us from Shakspeare and Fletcher; the copiousness and well-knitting of the intrigues we have from Johnson; and for the verse itself we have English precedents of elder date than any of Corneille's plays. Not to name our old comedies before Shakspeare, which were all writ in verse of six feet, or Alexandrines, such as the French now use, I can show in Shakspeare, many scenes of rhyme together, and the like in Ben Jonson's tragedies: in *Catiline* and *Sejanus* sometimes thirty or forty lines, I mean besides the Chorus, or the monologues; which, by the way, showed Ben no enemy to this way of writing, especially if you look upon his *Sad Shepherd*, which goes sometimes on rhyme, sometimes on blank verse, like an horse who eases himself on trot and amble. You find him likewise commending Fletcher's pastoral of *The Faithful Shepherdess*, which is for the most part rhyme, though not refined to that purity to which it hath since been brought. And these examples are enough to clear us from a servile imitation of the French.

"But to return whence I have digressed: I dare boldly affirm these two things of the English drama;—First, that we have many plays of ours as regular as any of theirs, and which, besides, have more variety of plot and characters; and secondly, that in most of the irregular plays of Shakspeare or Fletcher (for Ben Jonson's are for the most part regular) there is a more masculine fancy and greater spirit in the writing than there is in any of the French. I could produce, even in Shakspeare's and Fletcher's works, some plays which are almost exactly formed; as *The Merry Wives of Windsor*, and *The Scornful Lady:* but because (generally speaking) Shakspeare, who writ first, did not perfectly observe the laws of Comedy, and Fletcher, who came nearer to perfection, yet through carelessness made many faults; I will take the pattern of a perfect play from Ben Jonson, who was a careful and learned observer of the dramatic laws, and from all his comedies I shall select *The Silent Woman*; of which I will make a short examen, according to those rules which the French observe."

As Neander was beginning to examine *The Silent Woman*, Eugenius, looking earnestly upon him; "I beseech you, Neander," said he, "gratify the company, and me in particular, so far, as before you speak of the play, to give us a character of the author; and tell us frankly your opinion, whether you do not think all writers, both French and English, ought to give place to him."

"I fear," replied Neander, "that in obeying your commands I shall draw a little envy on myself. Besides, in performing them, it will be first necessary to speak somewhat of Shakspeare and Fletcher, his rivals in poesy; and one of them, in my opinion, at least his equal, perhaps his superior.

"To begin, then, with Shakspeare. He was the man who of all modern, and perhaps ancient poets, had the largest and most comprehensive soul. All the images of Nature were still present to him, and he drew them, not laboriously, but luckily; when he describes any thing, you more than see it, you feel it too. Those who accuse him to have wanted learning, give him the greater commendation: he was naturally learned; he needed not the spectacles of books to read Nature: he looked inwards, and found her there. I cannot say he is everywhere alike; were he so, I should do him injury to compare him with the greatest of mankind. He is many times flat, insipid; his comic wit degenerating into clenches, his serious swelling into bombast. But he is always great, when some great occasion is presented to him; no man can say he ever had a fit subject for his wit, and did not then raise himself as high above the rest of poets,

> *Quantum lenta solent inter viburna cupressi.*
> ["As cypresses commonly do among pliant shrubs."]

The consideration of this made Mr. Hales of Eaton say, that there was no subject of which any poet ever writ, but he would produce it much better treated of in Shakspeare; and however others are now generally preferred before him, yet the age wherein he lived, which had contemporaries with him Fletcher and Jonson, never equalled them to him in their esteem: and in the last King's court, when Ben's reputation was at highest, Sir John Suckling, and with him the greater part of the courtiers, set our Shakspeare far above him.

"Beaumont and Fletcher, of whom I am next to speak, had, with the advantage of Shakspeare's wit, which was their precedent, great natural gifts, improved by study: Beaumont especially being so accurate a judge of plays, that Ben Jonson, while he lived, submitted all his writing to his censure, and, 'tis thought, used his judgment in correcting, if not contriving, all his plots. What value he had for him, appears by the verses he writ to him; and therefore I need speak no farther of it. The first play that brought Fletcher and him in esteem was their *Philaster:* for before that, they had written two or three very unsuccessfully, as the like is reported of Ben Jonson, before he writ *Every Man in his Humour.* Their plots were generally more regular than Shakspeare's, especially those which were made before Beaumont's death; and they understood and imitated the conversation of gentlemen much better; whose wild debaucheries, and quickness of wit in repartees, no poet can ever paint as they have done. Humour, which Ben Jonson derived from particular persons, they made it not their business to describe: they represented all the passions very likely, but above all, love. I am apt to believe the English language in them arrived to its highest perfection: what words have since been taken in, are rather superfluous than ornamental. Their plays are now the most pleasant and frequent entertainments of the stage; two of theirs being acted through the year for one of Shakspeare's or Jonson's: the reason is, because there is a certain gaiety in their comedies, and pathos in their more serious plays, which suit generally with all men's humours. Shakspeare's language is likewise a little obsolete, and Ben Jonson's wit comes short of theirs.

"As for Jonson, to whose character I am now arrived, if we look upon him while he was himself (for his last plays were but his dotages), I think him the most learned and judicious writer which any theatre ever had. He was a most severe judge of himself, as well as others. One cannot say he wanted wit, but rather that he was frugal of it. In his works you find little to retrench or alter. Wit, and language, and humour also in some measure, we had before him; but something of art was wanting to the Drama till he came. He managed his strength to more advantage than any who preceded him. You seldom find him making love in any of his scenes, or endeavouring to move the passions; his genius was too sullen and saturnine to do it gracefully, especially when he knew he came after those who had performed both to such an height. Humour was his proper sphere; and in that he delighted most to represent mechanic people. He was deeply conversant in the Ancients, both Greek and Latin, and he borrowed boldly from them: there is scarce a poet or historian among the Roman authors of those times whom he had not translated in *Sejanus* and *Catiline*. But he has done his robberies so openly, that one may see he fears not to be taxed by any law. He invades authors like a monarch; and what would be theft in other poets is only victory in him. With the spoils of these writers he so represents old Rome to us, in its rites, ceremonies, and customs, that if one of their poets had written either of his tragedies, we had seen less of it than in him. If there was any fault in his language, 'twas that he weaved it too closely and laboriously, in his serious plays: perhaps, too, he did a little too much Romanise our tongue, leaving the words which he translated almost as much Latin as he found them: wherein, though he learnedly followed the idiom of their language, he did not enough comply with the idiom of ours. If I would compare him with Shakspeare, I must ack-nowledge him the more correct poet, but Shakspeare the greater wit. Shakspeare was the Homer, or father of our dramatic poets; Jonson was the Virgil, the pattern of elaborate writing; I admire him, but I love Shakspeare. To conclude of him; as he has given us the most correct plays, so in the precepts which he has laid down in his *Discoveries*, we have as many and profitable rules for perfecting the stage, as any where-with the French can furnish us.

"Having thus spoken of the author, I proceed to the examination of his comedy, *The Silent Woman*.

"EXAMEN OF *The Silent Woman*

"To begin first with the length of the action; it is so far from exceed-ing the compass of a natural day, that it takes not up an artificial one. 'Tis all included in the limits of three hours and a half, which is no more than is required for the presentment on the stage. A beauty perhaps not much observed; if it had, we should not have looked on the Spanish translation of *Five Hours* with so much wonder. The scene of it is laid in London; the latitude of place is almost as little as you can imagine; for it lies all within the compass of two houses, and after the first act, in one. The continuity of scenes is observed more than in any of our plays, except his own *Fox* and *Alchemyst*. They are not broken above twice or thrice at most in the whole comedy; and in the two best of Corneille's plays, the *Cid* and *Cinna*, they are interrupted once apiece. The action of the play is entirely one; the end or aim of which is the settling Morose's estate on Dauphine. The intrigue of it is the greatest and most noble of any pure unmixed comedy in any language; you see in it many persons of various characters and humours, and all delightful: as first, Morose, or an old man, to whom all noise but his own talking is offen-sive. Some who would be thought critics, say this humour of his is forced: but to remove that objection, we may consider him first to be naturally of a delicate hearing, as many are, to whom all sharp sounds are unpleasant; and secondly, we may attribute much of it to the peevishness of his age, or the wayward authority of an old man in his own house, where he may make himself obeyed; and this the poet seems to allude to in his name Morose. Besides this, I am assured from divers persons, that Ben Jonson was actually acquainted with such a man, one altogether as ridiculous as he is here represented. Others say, it is not enough to find one man of such an humour; it must be common to more, and the more common the more natural. To prove this, they instance in the best of comical characters, Falstaff. There are many men resembling him; old, fat, merry, cowardly, drunken, amorous, vain, and lying. But to convince these people, I need but tell them, that humour is the ridiculous extravagance of conversation, wherein one man differs from all others. If then it be common, or communicated to many, how differs it from other men's? or what indeed causes it to be ridiculous so much as the singularity of it? As for Falstaff, he is not properly one humour, but a miscellany of humours or images, drawn from so many several men: that wherein he is singular is his wit, or those things he says *præter expectatum*, unexpected by the audience; his quick evasions, when you imagine him surprised, which, as they are extremely diverting of themselves, so receive a great addition from his person; for the very sight of such an unwieldy old debauched fellow is a comedy alone. And here, having a place so proper for it, I cannot but enlarge somewhat upon this subject of humour into which I am fallen. The ancients had little of it in their comedies; for the τὸ γελοῖον ["The laughable."] of the Old Comedy, of which Aristophanes was chief, was not so much to imitate a man, as to make the people laugh at some odd conceit, which had commonly somewhat of unnatural or obscene in it. Thus, when you see Socrates brought upon the stage, you are not to imagine him made ridiculous by the imitation of his actions, but rather by making him perform something very unlike himself; something so childish and absurd, as by comparing it with the gravity of the true Socrates, makes a ridiculous object for the spectators. In their New Comedy which succeeded, the poets sought indeed to express the ἦθος *ēthos* ["character"], as in their tragedies the πάθος *pathos* ["emotion"] of mankind. But this ἦθος *ēthos* contained only the general characters of men and manners; as old men, lovers, serving-men, courtezans, parasites, and such other persons as we see in their comedies; all which they made alike: that is, one old man or father, one lover, one courtezan, so like another, as if the first of them had begot the rest of every sort: *ex homine hunc natum dicas* ["You would say that one was born from the other."]. The same custom they observed likewise in their tragedies. As for the French, though they have the word *humour* among them, yet they have small use of it in their comedies or farces; they being but ill imitations of the *ridiculum*, or that which stirred up laughter in the Old Comedy. But among the English 'tis otherwise: where by humour is meant some extravagant habit, passion, or affection, particular (as I said before) to some one person, by the oddness of which, he is immediately distinguished from the rest of men which being lively and naturally represented, most frequently begets that malicious pleasure in the audience which is testified by laughter as all things which are deviations from custom are ever the aptest to produce it: though by the way this laughter is only accidental, as the person represented is fantastic or bizarre; but pleasure is essential to it as the imitation of what is natural. The description of these humours, drawn from the knowledge and observation of particular persons, was the peculiar genius and talent of Ben Jonson; to whose play I now return.

"Besides Morose, there are at least nine or ten different characters and humours in *The Silent Woman;* all which persons have several concernments of their own, yet are all used by the poet to the conducting of the main design to perfection. I shall not waste time in commending the writing of this play; but I will give you my opinion, that there is more wit and acuteness of fancy in it than in any of Ben Jonson's. Besides that he has here described the conversation of gentlemen in the persons of True-Wit, and his friends, with more gaiety, air, and free dom, than in the rest of his comedies. For the contrivance of the plot, 'tis extreme elaborate, and yet withal easy; for the λυσις [lusis], or untying of it, 'tis so admirable, that when it is done, no one of the audience would think the poet could have missed it; and yet it was concealed so much before the last scene, that any other way would sooner have entered into your thoughts. But I dare not take upon me to commend the fabric of it, because it is altogether so full of art, that I must unravel every scene in it to commend it as I ought. And this excellent contrivance is still the more to be admired, because 'tis comedy, where the persons are only of common rank, and their business private, not elevated by passions or high concernments, as in serious plays. Here every one is a proper judge of all he sees, nothing is represented but that with which he daily converses: so that by consequence all faults lie open to discovery, and few are pardonable. 'Tis this which Horace has judiciously observed:

> *Creditur, ex medio quia res arcessit, habere*
> *Sudoris minimum; sed habet Comedia tanto*
> *Plus oneris, quanto veniæ minus.*

["Comedy is thought to require the least work because it draws its subjects from every-day life; but the less indulgence it has the more work it requires."]

"But our poet who was not ignorant of these difficulties, had prevailed himself of all advantages; as he who designs a large leap takes his rise from the highest ground. One of these advantages is that which Corneille has laid down as the geatest which can arrive to any poem, and which he himself could never compass above thrice in all his plays; viz. the making choice of some signal and long-expected day, whereon the action of the play is to depend. This day was that designed by Dauphine for the settling of his uncle's estate upon him; which to compass, he contrives to marry him. That the marriage had been plotted by him long beforehand, is made evident by what he tells True-Wit in the second act, that in one moment he had destroyed what he had been raising many months.

"There is another artifice of the poet, which I cannot here omit, because by the frequent practice of it in his comedies he had left it to us almost as a rule; that is, when he has any character or humour wherein he would show a *coup de Maistre*, or his highest skill, he recommends it to your observation by a pleasant description of it before the person first appears. Thus, in *Bartholomew Fair* he gives you the pictures of Numps and Cokes, and in this those of Daw, Lafoole, Morose, and the Collegiate Ladies; all which you hear described before you see them. So that before they come upon the stage, you have a longing expectation of them, which prepares you to receive them favourably; and when they are there, even from their first appearance you are so far acquainted with them, that nothing of their humour is lost to you.

"I will observe yet one thing further of this admirable plot; the business of it rises in every act. The second is greater than the first; the third than the second; and so forward to the fifth. There too you see, till the very last scene, new difficulties arising to obstruct the action of the play; and when the audience is brought into despair that the business can naturally be effected, then, and not before, the discovery is made. But that the poet might entertain you with more variety all this while, he reserves some new characters to show you, which he opens not till the second and third act. In the second Morose, Daw, the Barber, and Otter; in the third the Collegiate Ladies: all which he moves afterwards in by-walks, or under-plots, as diversions to the main design, lest it should grow tedious, though they are still naturally joined with it, and somewhere or other subservient to it. Thus, like a skilful chess-player, by little and little he draws out his men, and makes his pawns of use to his greater persons.

occasion; and Lisideius, I think, was going to reply, when he was prevented thus by Crites: "I am confident," said he, "that the most material things that can be said have been already urged on either side; if they have not, I must beg of Lisideius that he will defer his answer till another time: for I confess I have a joint quarrel to you both, because you have concluded, without any reason given for it, that rhyme is proper for the stage. I will not dispute how ancient it hath been among us to write this way; perhaps our ancestors knew no better till Shakspeare's time. I will grant it was not altogether left by him, and that Fletcher and Ben Jonson used it frequently in their Pastorals, and sometimes in other plays. Farther, I will not argue whether we received it originally from our own countrymen, or from the French; for that is an inquiry of as little benefit, as theirs who, in the midst of the great Plague, were not so solicitous to provide against it, as to know whether we had it from the malignity of our own air, or by transportation from Holland. I have therefore only to affirm, that it is not allowable in serious plays; for comedies, I find you already concluding with me. To prove this, I might satisfy myself to tell you, how much in vain it is for you to strive against the stream of the people's inclination; the greatest part of which are prepossessed so much with those excellent plays of Shakspeare, Fletcher, and Ben Jonson, which have been written out of rhyme, that except you could bring them such as were written better in it, and those too by persons of equal reputation with them, it will be impossible for you to gain your cause with them, who will still be judges. This it is to which, in fine, all your reasons must submit. The unanimous consent of an audience is so powerful, that even Julius Cæsar (as Macrobius reports of him), when he was perpetual dictator, was not able to balance it on the other side; but when Laberius, a Roman Knight, at his request contended in the Mime with another poet, he was forced to cry out, *Etiam favente me victus es, Laberi* ["Even with me on your side you were defeated, Laberius."]. But I will not on this occasion take the advantage of the greater number, but only urge such reasons against rhyme, as I find in the writings of those who have argued for the other way. First then, I am of opinion, that rhyme is unnatural in a play, because dialogue there is presented as the effect of sudden thought: for a play is the imitation of Nature; and since no man without premeditation speaks in rhyme, neither ought he to do it on the stage. This hinders not but the fancy may be there elevated to an higher pitch of thought than it is in ordinary discourse; for there is a probability that men of excellent and

"If this comedy and some others of his were translated into prose (which would now be no wonder to them, since Moli lately given them plays out of verse, which have not displeased tl believe the controversy would soon be decided betwixt the two na even making them the judges. But we need not call our heroes t aid. Be it spoken to the honour of the English, our nation can want in any age such who are able to dispute the empire of wit with people in the universe. And though the fury of a civil war, and powei twenty years together abandoned to a barbarous race of men, enemies all good learning, had buried the Muses under the ruins of monarcl yet, with the restoration of our happiness, we see revived Poesy liftii up its head, and already shaking off the rubbish which lay so heavy o it. We have seen since his Majesty's return, many dramatic poems whicl yield not to those of any foreign nation, and which deserve all laurels but the English. I will set aside flattery and envy: it cannot be denied but we have had some little blemish either in the plot or writing of all those plays which have been made within these seven years (and perhaps there is no nation in the world so quick to discern them, or so difficult to pardon them, as ours:) yet if we can persuade ourselves to use the candour of that poet, who, though the most severe of critics, has left us this caution by which to moderate our censures—

> *ubi plura nitent in carmine, non ego paucis*
> *Offendar maculis;—*

["Where many beauties shine in a poem, I shall not be offended by little faults."]

if, in consideration of their many and great beauties, we can wink at some slight and little imperfections, if we, I say, can be thus equal to ourselves, I ask no favour from the French. And if I do not venture upon any particular judgment of our late plays, 'tis out of the consideration which an ancient writer gives me: *vivorum, ut magna admiratio, ita censura difficilis* ["Just as admiration for the living is great so is criticism of them difficult."]: betwixt the extremes of admiration and malice, 'tis hard to judge uprightly of the living. Only I think it may be permitted me to say, that as it is no lessening to us to yield to some plays, and those not many, of our own nation in the last age, so can it be no addition to pronounce of our present poets, that they have far surpassed all the Ancients, and the modern writers of other countries."

This, my Lord, was the substance of what was then spoken on that quick parts may speak noble things *extempore:* but those thoughts are never fettered with the numbers or sound of verse without study, and therefore it cannot be but unnatural to present the most free way of speaking in that which is the most constrained. For this reason, says Aristotle, 'tis best to write tragedy in that kind of verse which is the least such, or which is nearest prose: and this amongst the Ancients was the iambic, and with us is blank verse, or the measure of verse kept exactly without rhyme. These numbers therefore are fittest for a play; the others for a paper of verses, or a poem; blank verse being as much below them as rhyme is improper for the Drama. And if it be objected that neither are blank verses made *extempore*, yet, as nearest nature, they are still to be preferred.—But there are two particular exceptions, which many besides myself have had to verse; by which it will appear yet more plainly how improper it is in plays. And the first of them is grounded on that very reason for which some have commended rhyme; they say, the quickness of repartees in argumentative scenes receives an ornament from verse. Now what is more unreasonable than to imagine that a man should not only light upon the wit, but the rhyme too, upon the sudden? This nicking of him who spoke before both in sound and measure, is so great an happiness, that you must at least suppose the persons of your play to be born poets: *Arcades omnes, et cantare pares, et respondere parati* ["Both young Arcadians, both alike inspired To sing, and answer as the song requir'd." (Dryden)]: they must have arrived to the degree of *quicquid conabar dicere* ["(of) singing what they attempted."]—to make verses almost whether they will or no. If they are any thing below this, it will look rather like the design of two, than the answer of one: it will appear that your actors hold intelligence together; that they perform their tricks like fortune-tellers, by confederacy. The hand of art will be too visible in it, against that maxim of all professions, *Ars est celare artem* ["It is an art to conceal art."], that it is the greatest perfection of art to keep itself undiscovered. Nor will it serve you to object, that however you manage it, 'tis still known to be a play; and, consequently, the dialogue of two persons understood to be the labour of one poet. For a play is still an imitation of Nature; we know we are to be deceived, and we desire to be so; but no man ever was deceived but with a probability of truth; for who will suffer a gross lie to be fastened on him? Thus we sufficiently understand, that the scenes which represent cities and countries to us are not really such, but only painted on boards and canvas; but shall that excuse the ill painture or designment of them? Nay, rather ought they not be laboured with so much the more diligence and exactness, to help the imagination? since the mind of man does naturally tend to, and seek after truth; and therefore the nearer any thing comes to the imitation of it, the more it pleases.

"Thus, you see, your rhyme is incapable of expressing the greatest thoughts naturally, and the lowest it cannot with any grace: for what is more unbefitting the majesty of verse, than to call a servant, or bid a door be shut in rhyme? And yet this miserable necessity you are forced upon. But verse, you say, circumscribes a quick and luxuriant fancy, which would extend itself too far on every subject, did not the labour which is required to well-turned and polished rhyme, set bounds to it. Yet this argument, if granted, would only prove that we may write better in verse, but not more naturally. Neither is it able to evince that; for he who wants judgment to confine his fancy in blank verse, may want it as much in rhyme: and he who has it will avoid errors in both kinds. Latin verse was as great a confinement to the imagination of those poets, as rhyme to ours; and yet you find Ovid saying too much on every subject. *Nescivit* (says Seneca) *quod bene cessit relinquere* ["He did not know to leave off where he should have."]: of which he gives you one famous instance in his description of the deluge:

> *Omnia pontus erat, deerant quoque litora ponto*
> Now all was sea, nor had that sea a shore.

Thus Ovid's fancy was not limited by verse, and Virgil needed not verse to have bounded his.

"In our own language we see Ben Jonson confining himself to what ought to be said, even in the liberty of blank verse; and yet Corneille the most judicious of the French poets, is still varying the same sense an hundred ways, and dwelling eternally on the same subject, though confined by rhyme. Some other exceptions I have to verse; but being these I have named are for the most part already public, I conceive it reasonable they should first be answered."

"It concerns me less than any," said Neander (seeing he had ended), "to reply to this discourse; because when I should have proved that verse may be natural in plays, yet I should always be ready to confess, that those which I have written in this kind come short of that perfection which is required. Yet since you are pleased I should undertake this province, I will do it, though with all imaginable respect and deference, both to that person from whom you have borrowed your strongest arguments, and to whose judgment, when I have said all, I finally submit. But before I proceed to answer your objections, I must first remember you, that I exclude all Comedy from my defence; and next that I deny not but blank verse may be also used; and content myself only to assert, that in serious plays where the subject and characters are great, and the plot unmixed with mirth, which might allay or divert these concernments which are produced, rhyme is there as natural and more effectual than blank verse.

"And now having laid down this as a foundation,—to begin with Crites, I must crave leave to tell him, that some of his arguments against rhyme reach no farther than, from the faults or defects of ill rhyme, to conclude against the use of it in general. May not I conclude against blank verse by the same reason? If the words of some poets who write in it, are either ill chosen, or ill placed, which makes not only rhyme, but all kind of verse in any language unnatural, shall I, for their vicious affectation, condemn those excellent lines of Fletcher, which are written in that kind? Is there any thing in rhyme more constrained than this line in blank verse, *I heaven invoke, and strong resistance make?* where you see both the clauses are placed unnaturally, that is, contrary to the common way of speaking, and that without the excuse of a rhyme to cause it: yet you would think me very ridiculous, if I should accuse the stubbornness of blank verse for this, and not rather the stillness of the poet. Therefore, Crites, you must either prove that words, though well chosen and duly placed, yet render not rhyme natural in itself; or that, however natural and easy that rhyme may be, yet it is not proper for a play. If you insist on the former part, I would ask you, what other conditions are required to make rhyme natural in itself, besides an election of apt words, and a right dispositing of them? For the due choice of your words expresses your sense naturally, and the due placing them adapt the rhyme to it. If you object that one verse may be made for the sake of another, though both the words and rhyme be apt, I answer, it cannot possibly so fall out; for either there is a dependance of sense betwixt the first line and the second, or there is none: if there be that connection, then in the natural position of the words the latter line must of necessity flow from the former; if there be no dependance, yet still the due ordering of words makes the last line as natural in itself as the other: so that the necessity of a rhyme never forces any but bad or lost writers to say what they would not otherwise. 'Tis true, there is both care and art required to write in verse. A good poet never concludes upon the first line, till he has sought out such a rhyme as may fit the sense, already prepared to heighten the second: many times the close of the sense falls into the middle of the next verse, or farther off, and he may often prevail himself of the same advantages in English which Virgil had in Latin; he may break off in the hemistich and begin another line. Indeed, the not observing these two last things, makes plays which are writ in verse so tedious: for though, most commonly, the sense is to be confined to the couplet, yet nothing that does *perpetuo tenore fluere*, run in the same channel, can please all ways. 'Tis like the murmuring of a stream, which not varying in the fall, causes at first attention at last drowsiness. Variety of cadences is the best rule; the greatest help to the actors, and refreshment to the audience.

"If then verse may be made natural in itself how becomes it improper to a play? You say the stage is the representation of Nature, and no man in ordinary conversation speaks in rhyme. But you foresaw when you said this, that it might be answered—neither does any man speak in blank verse, or in measure without rhyme. Therefore you concluded, that which is nearest Nature is still to be preferred. But you took no notice that rhyme might be made as natural as blank verse, by the well placing of the words, etc. All the difference between them, when they are both correct, is, the sound in one, which the other wants; and if so, the sweetness of it, and all the advantage resulting from it, which are handled in the Preface to *The Rival Ladies*, will yet stand good. As for that place of Aristotle, where he says, plays should be writ in that kind of verse which is nearest prose, it makes little for you; blank verse being properly but measured prose. Now measure alone, in any modern language, does not constitute verse; those of the Ancients in Greek and Latin consisted in quantity of words, and a determinate number of feet. But when, by the inundation of the Goths and Vandals into Italy, new languages were brought in, and barbarously mingled with the Latin, of which the Italian, Spanish, French, and ours (made out of them and the Teutonic) are dialects, a new way of poesy was practised; new, I say, in those countries, for in all probability it was that of the conquerors in their own nations. This new way consisted in measure or number of feet, and rhyme; the sweetness of rhyme, and observation of accent, supplying the place of quantity in words, which could neither exactly be observed by those Barbarians, who knew not the rules of it, neither was it suitable to their tongues, as it has been to the Greek and Latin.

No man is tied in modern poesy to observe any farther rule in the feet of his verse, but that they be dissyllables; whether spondee, trochee, or iambic, it matters not; only he is obliged to rhyme. Neither do the Spanish, French, Italian, or Germans, acknowledge at all, or very rarely, any such kind of poesy as blank verse amongst them. Therefore, at most 'tis but a poetic prose, a *sermo pedestris:* and as such, most fit for comedies, where I acknowledge rhyme to be improper. Farther; as to that quotation of Aristotle, our couplet verses may be rendered as near prose as blank verse itself, by using those advantages I lately named, as breaks in an hemistich, or running the sense into another line, thereby making art and order appear as loose and free as nature: or not tying ourselves to couplets strictly, we may use the benefit of the Pindaric way practised in *The Siege of Rhodes;* where the numbers vary, and the rhyme is disposed carelessly, and far from often chiming. Neither is that other advantage of the Ancients to be despised, of changing the kind of verse when they please, with the change of the scene, or some new entrance; for they confine not themselves always to iambics, but extend their liberty to all lyric numbers, and sometimes even to hexameter. But I need not go so far to prove that rhyme, as it succeeds to all other offices of Greek and Latin verse, so especially to this of plays, since the custom of all nations at this day confirms it, all the French, Italian, and Spanish tragedies are generally writ in it; and sure the universal consent of the most civilised part of the world ought in this, as it doth in other customs, to include the rest.

"But perhaps you may tell me, I have proposed such a way to make rhyme natural, and consequently proper to plays, as is unpracticable; and that I shall scarce find six or eight lines together in any play, where the words are so placed and chosen as is required to make it natural. I answer, no poet need constrain himself at all times to it. It is enough he makes it his general rule; for I deny not but sometimes there may be a greatness in placing the words otherwise; and sometimes they may sound better, sometimes also the variety itself is excuse enough. But if, for the most part, the words be placed as they are in the negligence of prose, it is sufficient to denominate the way practicable; for we esteem that to be such, which in the trial oftener succeeds than misses. And thus far you may find the practice made good in many plays: where you do not, remember still, that if you cannot find six natural rhymes together, it will be as hard for you to produce as many lines in blank verse, even among the greatest of our poets, against which I cannot make some reasonable exception.

"And this, Sir, calls to my remembrance the beginning of your discourse, where you told us we should never find the audience favourable to this kind of writing, till we could produce as good plays in rhyme as Ben Jonson, Fletcher, and Shakspeare, had writ out of it. But it is to raise envy to the living, to compare them with the dead. They are honoured, and almost adored by us, as they deserve; neither do I know any so presumptuous of themselves as to contend with them. Yet give me leave to say thus much, without injury to their ashes; that not only we shall never equal them, but they could never equal themselves, were they to rise and write again. We acknowledge them our fathers in wit: but they have ruined their estates themselves, before they came to their children's hands. There is scarce an humour, a character, or any kind of plot, which they have not blown upon. All comes sullied or wasted to us: and were they to entertain this age, they could not make so plenteous treatments out of such decayed fortunes. This therefore will be a good argument to us, either not to write at all, or to attempt some other way. There is no bays to be expected in their walks: *tentanda via est, quà me quoque possum tollere humo* ["New ways I must attempt, my grov'ling name/To raise aloft." (Dryden)].

"This way of writing in verse they have only left free to us; our age is arrived to a perfection in it, which they never knew; and which (if we may guess by what of theirs we have seen in verse, as *The Faithful Shepherdess*, and *Sad Shepherd*) 'tis probable they never could have reached. For the genius of every age is different; and though ours excel in this, I deny not but to imitate Nature in that perfection which they did in prose, is a greater commendation than to write in verse exactly. As for what you have added, that the people are not generally inclined to like this way; if it were true, it would be no wonder, that betwixt the shaking off an old habit, and the introducing of a new, there should be difficulty. Do we not see them stick to Hopkins' and Sternhold's psalms, and forsake those of David, I mean Sandys his translation of them? If by the people you understand the multitude, the οἱπολλί [*hoi polloi*], 'tis no matter what they think; they are sometimes in the right, sometimes in the wrong: their judgment is a mere lottery. *Est ubi plebs rectè putat, est ubi peccat* ["There is a time when the people think rightly, there is a time when they err."]. Horace says it of the vulgar, judging poesy. But if you mean the mixed audience of the populace and the noblesse, I dare confidently affirm that a great part of the latter sort are already favourable to verse; and thus no serious plays written since the King's return have been more kindly received by them than *The Siege of Rhodes*, the *Mustapha, The Indian Queen*, and *Indian Emperor*.

"But I come now to the inference of your first argument. You said the dialogue of plays is presented as the effect of sudden thought, but no man speaks suddenly, or *ex tempore*, in rhyme; and you inferred from thence, that rhyme, which you acknowledge to be proper to epic poesy cannot equally be proper to dramatic, unless we could suppose all men born so much more than poets, that verses should be made in them not by them.

"It has been formerly urged by you, and confessed by me, that since no man spoke any kind of verse *ex tempore*, that which was nearer Nature was to be preferred. I answer you, there fore, by distinguishing betwixt what is nearest to the nature of Comedy, which is the imitation of common persons and ordinary speaking, and what is nearest the nature of a serious play: the last is indeed the representation of Nature, but 'tis Nature wrought up to a higher pitch. The plot, the characters, the wit, the passions, the descriptions, are all exalted above the level of common converse, as high as the imagination of the poet can carry them, with proportion to verisimility. Tragedy, we know, is wont to image to us the minds and fortunes of noble persons, and to portray these exactly; heroic rhyme as nearest Nature, as being the noblest kind of modern verse.

> *Indignatur enim privatis et prope socco*
> *Dignis carminibus narrari cœna Thyestæ*
> ["It is offensive for the banquet of Thyestes to be narrated in familiar verses that belong almost to comedy."]

says Horace: and in another place,

> *Effutire leres indigna tragœdia versus.*
> ["It is not fitting for tragedy to babble forth light verse."]

Blank verse is acknowledged to be too low for a poem, nay more, for a paper of verses; but if too low for an ordinary sonnet, how much more for Tragedy, which is by Aristotle, in the dispute betwixt the epic poesy and the dramatic, for many reasons he there alleges, ranked above it?

"But setting this defence aside, your argument is almost as strong against the use of rhyme in poems as in plays; for the epic way is every where interlaced with dialogue, or discoursive scenes; and therefore you must either grant rhyme to be improper there, which is contrary to your assertion, or admit it into plays by the same title which you have given it to poems. For though Tragedy be justly preferred above the other, yet there is a great affinity between them, as may easily be discovered in that definition of a play which Lisideius gave us. The *genus* of them is the same, a just and lively image of human nature, in its actions, passions, and traverses of fortune: so is the end, namely, for the delight and benefit of mankind. The characters and persons are still the same, viz. the greatest of both sorts; only the manner of acquainting us with those actions, passions, and fortunes, is different. Tragedy performs it *viva voce*, or by action, in dialogue; wherein it excels the Epic Poem, which does it chiefly by narration, and therefore is not so lively an image of human nature. However, the agreement betwixt them is such, that if rhyme be proper for one, it must be for the other. Verse, 'tis true, is not the effect of sudden thought; but this hinders not that sudden thought may be represented in verse, since those thoughts are such as must be higher than Nature can raise them without premeditation, especially to a continuance of them, even out of verse; and consequently you cannot imagine them to have been sudden either in the poet or in the actors. A play, as I have said, to be like Nature, is to be set above it; as statues which are placed on high are made greater than the life, that they may descend to the sight in their just proportion.

"Perhaps I have insisted too long on this objection; but the clearing of it will make my stay shorter on the rest. You tell us, Crites, that rhyme appears most unnatural in repartees, or short replies: when he who answers, it being presumed he knew not what the other would say, yet makes up that part of the verse which was left incomplete, and supplies both the sound and measure of it. This, you say, looks rather like the confederacy of two, than the answer of one.

"This, I confess, is an objection which is in every one's mouth, who loves not rhyme: but suppose, I beseech you, the repartee were made only in blank verse, might not part of the same argument be turned against you? for the measure is as often supplied there as it is in rhyme; the latter half of the hemistich as commonly made up, or a second line subjoined as a reply to the former; which any one leaf in Jonson's plays will sufficiently clear to you. You will often find in the Greek tragedians, and in Seneca, that when a scene grows up into the warmth of repartees, which is the close fighting of it, the latter part of the trimeter is supplied by him who answers; and yet it was never observed as a fault in them by any of the ancient or modern critics. The case is the same in our verse, as it was in theirs; rhyme to us being in lieu of quantity to them. But if no latitude is to be allowed a poet, you take from him not only his licence of *quidlibet audendi* ["Of taking any liberty."], but you tie him up in a straiter compass than you would a philosopher. This is indeed *Musas colere severiores* ["To worship the more serious Muses."]. You would have him follow Nature, but he must follow her on foot: you have dismounted him from his Pegasus. But you tell us, this supplying the last half of a verse, or adjoining a whole second to the former, looks more like the design of two, than the answer of one. Suppose we acknowledge it: how comes this confederacy to be more displeasing to you, than in a dance which is well contrived? You see there the united design of many persons to make up one figure: after they have separated themselves in many petty divisions, they rejoin one by one into a gross: the confederacy is plain amongst them, for chance could never produce anything so beautiful; and yet there is nothing in it, that shocks your sight. I acknowledge the hand of art appears in repartee, as of necessity it must in all kind of verse. But there is also the quick and poynant brevity of it (which is an high imitation of Nature in those sudden gusts of passion) to mingle with it; and this, joined with the cadency and sweetness of the rhyme, leaves nothing in the soul of the hearer to desire. 'Tis an art which appears; but it appears only like the shadowings of painture, which being to cause the rounding of it, cannot be absent; but while that is considered, they are lost: so while we attend to the other beauties of the matter, the care and labour of the rhyme is carried from us, or at least drowned in its own sweetness, as bees are sometimes buried in their honey. When a poet has found the repartee, the last perfection he can add to it, is to put it into verse. However good the thought may be, however apt the words in which 'tis couched, yet he finds himself at a little unrest, while rhyme is wanting: he cannot leave it till that comes naturally, and then is at ease, and sits down contented.

"From replies, which are the most elevated thoughts of verse, you pass to the most mean ones, those which are common with the lowest of household conversation. In these, you say, the majesty of verse suffers. You instance in the calling of a servant, or commanding a door to be shut, in rhyme. This, Crites, is a good observation of yours, but no argument: for it proves no more but that such thoughts should be waived, as often as may be, by the address of the poet. But suppose they are necessary in the places where he uses them, yet there is no need to put them into rhyme. He may place them in the beginning of a verse, and break it off, as unfit, when so debased, for any other use: or granting the worst,—that they require more room than the hemistich will allow, yet still there is a choice to be made of the best words, and least vulgar (provided they be apt) to express such thoughts. Many have blamed rhyme in general, for this fault, when the poet with a little care might have redressed it. But they do it with no more justice, than if English Poesy should be made ridiculous for the sake of the Water Poet's rhymes. Our language is noble, full, and significant; and I know not why he who is master of it may not clothe ordinary things in it as decently as the Latin, if he use the same diligence in his choice of words: *delectus verborum origo est eloquentiæ* ["Proper choice of words is the origin of eloquence."]. It was the saying of Julius Cæsar, one so curious in his, that none of them can be changed but for a worse. One would think, *unlock the door*, was a thing as vulgar as could be spoken; and yet Seneca could make it sound high and lofty in his Latin:

> *Reserate clusos regii postes laris.*
> Set wide the palace gates.

"But I turn from this conception, both because it happens not above twice or thrice in any play that those vulgar thoughts are used, and then too, were there no other apology to be made, yet the necessity of them, which is alike in all kind of writing, may excuse them. Besides that the great eagerness and precipitation with which they are spoken makes us rather mind the substance than the dress; that for which they are spoken, rather than what is spoken. For they are always the effect of some hasty concernment and something of consequence depends on them.

"Thus, Crites, I have endeavoured to answer your objections; it remains only that I should vindicate an argument for verse, which you have gone about to overthrow. It had formerly been said that the easiness of blank verse renders the poet too luxuriant, but that the labour of rhyme bounds and circumscribes an over-fruitful fancy; the sense there being commonly confined to the couplet, and the words so ordered that the rhyme naturally follows them, not they the rhyme. To this you answered, that it was no argument to the question in hand; for the dispute was not which way a man may write best, but which is most proper for the subject on which he writes.

"First, give me leave, Sir, to remember you, that the argument against which you raised this objection was only secondary: it was built on this hypothesis, that to write in verse was proper for serious plays. Which supposition being granted (as it was briefly made out in that discourse, by showing how verse might be made natural), it asserted, that this way of writing was an help to the poet's judgment, by putting bounds to a wild overflowing fancy. I think, therefore, it will not be hard for me to make good what it was to prove. But you add, that were this let pass, yet he who wants judgment in the liberty of his fancy, may as well show the defect of it when he is confined to verse; for he who has judgment will avoid errors, and he who has it not, will commit them in all kinds of writing.

"This argument, as you have taken it from a most acute person, so I confess it carries much weight in it: but by using the word judgment here indefinitely, you seem to have put a fallacy upon us. I grant, he who has judgment, that is, so profound, so strong, so infallible a judgment, that he needs no helps to keep it always poised and upright, will commit no faults either in rhyme or out of it. And on the other extreme, he who has a judgment so weak and crazed that no helps can correct or amend it, shall write scurvily out of rhyme, and worse in it. But the first of these judgments is no where to be found, and the latter is not fit to write at all. To speak therefore of judgment as it is in the best poets; they who have the greatest proportion of it, want other helps than from it, within. As for example, you would be loth to say, that he who was endued with a sound judgment had no need of History, Geography, or Moral Philosophy, to write correctly. Judgment is indeed the master-workman in a play; but he requires many subordinate hands, many tools to his assistance. And verse I affirm to be one of these; 'tis a rule and line by which be keeps his building compact and even, which otherwise lawless imagination would raise either irregularly or loosely; at least, if the poet commits errors with this help, he would make greater and more without it: 'tis, in short, a slow and painful, but the purest kind of working. Ovid, whom you accuse for luxuriancy in verse, had perhaps been farther guilty of it, had he writ in prose. And for your instance of Ben Jonson, who, you say, writ exactly without the help of rhyme; you are to remember, 'tis only an aid to a luxuriant fancy, which his was not: as he did not want imagination, so none ever said he had much to spare. Neither was verse then refined so much to be an help to that age, as it is to ours. Thus then the second thoughts being usually the best, as receiving the maturist digestion from judgment, and the last and most mature product of those thoughts being artful and laboured verse, it may well be inferred, that verse is a great help to a luxuriant fancy; and this is what that argument which you opposed was to evince."

Neander was pursuing this discourse so eagerly, that Eugenius had called to him twice or thrice, ere he took notice that the barge stood still, and that they were at the foot of Somerset stairs, where they had appointed it to land. The company were all sorry to separate so soon, though a great part of the evening was already spent; and stood a-while looking back on the water, which the moonbeams played upon and made it appear like floating quick-silver: at last they went up through a crowd of French people, who were merrily dancing in the open air, and nothing concerned for the noise of guns which had alarmed the town that afternoon. Walking thence together to the Piazze, they parted there; Eugenius and Lisideius to some pleasant appointment they had made, and Crites and Neander to their several lodgings.

6. WORDSWORTH

"Observations Prefixed to
Lyrical Ballads"

William Wordsworth (1770–1850) was born in Cockermouth, Cumberland, England. He attended St. John's College, Cambridge. After visiting the continent, he lived as a neighbor to Coleridge with whom he collaborated on *Lyrical Ballads*. He married in 1802 and settled at Grasmere. At the end of his life in 1843 he was appointed poet laureate—an honor that is not necessarily bestowed always on the greatest poets, though it had also been conferred on Dryden.

Wordsworth also is in the long line of English poet critics. The publication in 1798 of the *Lyrical Ballads* in collaboration with Coleridge established both of them as poets with whom the age would have to reckon. Coleridge in his "Occasion of the *Lyrical Ballads*" explains the division of labors: "The thought suggested itself—(to which of us I do not recollect)—that a series of poems might be composed of two sorts. In the one, the incidents and agents were to be, in part at least, supernatural; and the excellence aimed at was to consist in the interesting of the affections by the dramatic truth of such emotions, as would naturally accompany such situations, supposing them real. . . . For the second class, subjects were to be chosen from ordinary life; the characters and incidents were to be such as will be found in every village and its vicinity, where there is a meditative and feeling mind to seek after them, or to notice them, when they present themselves." Coleridge wrote a few poems of the first kind ("The Rime of the Ancient Mariner," "Christabel"), and Wordsworth, who was much more prolific, as Coleridge ruefully admits, wrote the other kind of poems.

Although they remained friends and neighbors for a number of years, they did not collaborate again. Coleridge wrote less and less poetry and more and more criticism, of which the two-volume

Biographia Literaria is the best known. Wordsworth, however, continued to turn his attention to poetry. *Lyrical Ballads* contains some of Wordsworth's finest and best-known long poems, "Lines Composed a Few Miles Above Tintern Abbey," "Michael," as well as short lyrics, such as "To a Skylark," and sonnets. Among later famous poems are "Ode on Intimations of Immortality," "Ode to Duty," "The Excursion," and the "Prelude," subtitled "The Growth of a Poet's Mind," which is really a poetic autobiography.

Although Wordsworth is primarily known as a great and prolific poet, his "Observations Prefixed to *Lyrical Ballads*" is one of the most important and influential documents in the history of criticism. It has often been seen as the dividing line between previous criticism and modern criticism. The selection included is the complete essay, which first appeared in the 1800 edition of *Lyrical Ballads* and as the Appendix in the edition of 1802. Wordsworth's obvious place in the tradition of Aristotle and Longinus has already been noted. Like them, he is also concerned with imitating nature, though his concept of nature differs from previous critics'. (Actually, as should be clear by now, each age insists that it imitates nature most correctly.) Closely tied to the imitation of nature is the second traditional yet new concern with language: real incidents and men should be depicted in language actually spoken by men. Just as Wordsworth agrees basically with Aristotle on what poetry is, they also agree that the end or aim of poetry should be to give pleasure. No longer does art need to teach and delight. Finally, despite the shift from the universal to the concrete, Wordsworth also reaffirms the basic philosophic and therefore universal aspect of poetry.

Let us turn now to the other side of the dividing line: to the new critical concerns which were already slowly being established in the eighteenth century. The basic shift from reason to emotion, or better non-rational faculties of the mind, is really the premise from which everything else follows. Two of the non-rational faculties that fascinated Wordsworth and other Romantics are imagination and the mind's ability to associate ideas. Both these faculties were discussed in the eighteenth century, of course, but primarily in philosophical and scientific contexts, not literary and critical ones. The preoccupation with the definition and function of imagination and how ideas are associated are crucial to the concept of poetry, its source, and its end. Wordsworth explains in his Preface the object of the *Lyrical Ballads*, but this explanation applies to other poems: "The principal object, then, proposed in these Poems was to choose incidents and situations from common life, and to relate or describe them, throughout, as far as possible in a selection of language really used by men, and, at the same time, *to throw over them a certain colouring of imagination*, whereby ordinary things should be presented to the mind in an unusual aspect; and, further, and above all, to make these incidents and situations interesting by tracing in them, truly though not ostentatiously, the primary laws of our nature: chiefly, as far as regards *the manner in which we associate ideas in a state of excitement.*" [my emphases].

The first volume of these Poems has already been submitted to general perusal. It was published, as an experiment, which, I hoped, might be of some use to ascertain, how far, by fitting to metrical arrangement a selection of the real language of men in a state of vivid sensation, that sort of pleasure and that quantity of pleasure may be imparted, which a Poet may rationally endeavour to impart.

I had formed no very inaccurate estimate of the probable effect of those Poems: I flattered myself that they who should be pleased with them would read them with more than common pleasure: and, on the other hand, I was well aware, that by those who should dislike them, they would be read with more than common dislike. The result has differed from my expectation in this only, that a greater number have been pleased than I ventured to hope I should please.

Several of my Friends are anxious for the success of these Poems, from a belief, that, if the views with which they were composed were indeed realized, a class of Poetry would be produced, well adapted to interest mankind permanently, and not unimportant in the quality, and in the multiplicity of its moral relations: and on this account they have advised me to prefix a systematic defence of the theory upon which the Poems were written. But I was unwilling to undertake the task, knowing that on this occasion the Reader would look coldly upon my arguments, since I might be suspected of having been principally influenced by the selfish and foolish hope of *reasoning* him into an approbation of these particular Poems: and I was still more unwilling to undertake the task, because, adequately to display the opinions, and fully to enforce the arguments, would require a space wholly disproportionate to a preface. For, to treat the subject with the clearness and coherence of which it is susceptible, it would be necessary to give a full account of the present state of the public taste in this country, and to determine how far this taste is healthy or depraved; which, again, could not be determined, without pointing out in what manner language and the human mind act and re-act on each other, and without retracing the revolutions, not of literature alone, but likewise of society itself. I have therefore altogether declined to enter regularly upon this defence; yet I am sensible, that there would be something like impropriety in abruptly obtruding upon the Public, without a few words of introduction, Poems so materially different from those upon which general approbation is at present bestowed.

It is supposed, that by the act of writing in verse an Author makes a formal engagement that he will gratify certain known habits of association; that he not only thus apprises the Reader that certain classes of ideas and expressions will be found in his book, but that others will be carefully excluded. This exponent or symbol held forth by metrical language must in different eras of literature have excited very different expectations: for example, in the age of Catullus, Terence, and Lucretius, and that of Statius or Claudian; and in our own country, in the age of Shakespeare and Beaumont and Fletcher, and that of Donne and Cowley, or Dryden, or Pope. I will not take upon me to determine the exact import of the promise which, by the act of writing in verse, an Author in the present day makes to his reader: but it will undoubtedly appear to many persons that I have not fulfilled the terms of an engagement thus voluntarily contracted. They who have been accustomed to the gaudiness and inane phraseology of many modern writers, if they persist in reading this book to its conclusion, will, no doubt, frequently have to struggle with feelings of strangeness and awkwardness: they will look round for poetry, and will be induced to inquire by what species of courtesy these attempts can be permitted to assume that title. I hope therefore the reader will not censure me for attempting to state what I have proposed to myself to perform; and also (as far as the limits of a preface will permit) to explain some of the chief reasons which have determined me in the choice of my purpose: that at least he may be spared any unpleasant feeling of disappointment, and that I myself may be protected from one of the most dishonourable accusations which can be brought against an Author; namely, that of an indolence which prevents him from endeavouring to ascertain what is his duty, or, when his duty is ascertained, prevents him from performing it.

The principal object, then, proposed in these Poems was to choose incidents and situations from common life, and to relate or describe them, throughout, as far as was possible in a selection of language really used by men, and, at the same time, to throw over them a certain colouring of imagination, whereby ordinary things should be presented to the mind in an unusual aspect; and, further, and above all, to make these incidents and situations interesting by tracing in them, truly though not ostentatiously, the primary laws of our nature: chiefly, as far as regards the manner in which we associate ideas in a state of excitement. Humble and rustic life was generally chosen, because, in that condition, the essential passions of the heart find a better soil in which they can attain their maturity, are less under restraint, and speak a plainer and more emphatic language; because in that condition of life our elementary feelings coexist in a state of greater simplicity, and, consequently, may be more accurately contemplated, and more forcibly communicated; because the manners of rural life germinate from those elementary feelings, and, from the necessary character of rural occupations, are more easily comprehended, and are more durable; and, lastly, because in that condition the passions of men are incorporated with the beautiful and permanent forms of nature. The language, too, of these men has been adopted (purified indeed from what appear to be its real defects, from all lasting and rational causes of dislike or disgust) because such men hourly communicate with the best objects from which the best part of language is originally derived; and because, from their rank in society and the sameness and narrow circle of their intercourse, being less under the influence of social vanity, they convey their feelings and notions in simple and unelaborated expressions. Accordingly, such a language, arising out of repeated experience and regular feelings, is a more permanent, and a far more philosophical language, than that which is frequently substituted for it by Poets, who think that they are conferring honour upon themselves and their art, in proportion as they separate themselves from the sympathies of men, and indulge in arbitrary and capricious habits of expression, in order to furnish food for fickle tastes, and fickle appetites, of their own creation.[1]

I cannot, however, be insensible to the present outcry against the triviality and meanness, both of thought and language, which some of my contemporaries have occasionally introduced into their metrical compositions; and I acknowledge that this defect, where it exists, is more dishonourable to the Writer's own character than false refinement or arbitrary innovation, though I should contend at the same time, that it is far less pernicious in the sum of its consequences. From such verses the Poems in these volumes will be found distinguished at least by one mark of difference, that each of them has a worthy *purpose*. Not that I

[1] It is worth while here to observe, that the affecting parts of Chaucer are almost always expressed in language pure and universally intelligible even to this day.

always began to write with a distinct purpose formally conceived; but habits of meditation have, I trust, so prompted and regulated my feelings, that my descriptions of such objects as strongly excite those feelings, will be found to carry along with them a *purpose*. If this opinion be erroneous, I can have little right to the name of a Poet. For all good poetry is the spontaneous overflow of powerful feelings: and though this be true, Poems to which any value can be attached were never produced on any variety of subjects but by a man who, being possessed of more than usual organic sensibility, had also thought long and deeply. For our continued influxes of feeling are modified and directed by our thoughts, which are indeed the representatives of all our past feelings; and, as by contemplating the relation of these general representatives to each other, we discover what is really important to men, so, by the repetition and continuance of this act, our feelings will be connected with important subjects, till at length, if we be originally possessed of much sensibility, such habits of mind will be produced, that, by obeying blindly and mechanically the impulses of those habits, we shall describe objects, and utter sentiments, of such a nature, and in such connexion with each other, that the understanding of the Reader must necessarily be in some degree enlightened, and his affections strengthened and purified.

It has been said that each of these poems has a purpose. Another circumstance must be mentioned which distinguishes these Poems from the popular Poetry of the day; it is this, that the feeling therein developed gives importance to the action and situation, and not the action and situation to the feeling.

A sense of false modesty shall not prevent me from asserting, that the Reader's attention is pointed to this mark of distinction, far less for the sake of these particular Poems than from the general importance of the subject. The subject is indeed important! For the human mind is capable of being excited without the application of gross and violent stimulants; and he must have a very faint perception of its beauty and dignity who does not know this, and who does not further know, that one being is elevated above another, in proportion as he possesses this capability. It has therefore appeared to me, that to endeavour to produce or enlarge this capability is one of the best services in which, at any period, a Writer can be engaged; but this service, excellent at all times, is especially so at the present day. For a multitude of causes, unknown to former times, are now acting with a combined force to blunt the discriminating powers of the mind, and, unfitting it for all voluntary exertion, to reduce it to a state of almost savage torpor. The most effective of these causes are the great national events which are daily taking place, and the increasing accumulation of men in cities, where the uniformity of their occupations produces a craving for extraordinary incident, which the rapid communication of intelligence hourly gratifies. To this tendency of life and manners the literature and theatrical exhibitions of the country have conformed themselves. The invaluable works of our elder writers, I had almost said the works of Shakespeare and Milton, are driven into neglect by frantic novels, sickly and stupid German Tragedies, and deluges of idle and extravagant stories in verse.—When I think upon this degrading thirst after outrageous stimulation, I am almost ashamed to have spoken of the feeble endeavour made in these volumes to counteract it; and, reflecting upon the magnitude of the general evil, I should be oppressed with no dishonourable melancholy, had I not a deep impression of certain inherent and indestructible qualities of the human mind, and likewise of certain powers in the great and permanent objects that act upon it, which are equally inherent and indestructible; and were there not added to this impression a belief, that the time is approaching when the evil will be systematically opposed, by men of greater powers, and with far more distinguished success.

Having dwelt thus long on the subjects and aim of these Poems, I shall request the Reader's permission to apprise him of a few circumstances relating to their *style*, in order, among other reasons, that he may not censure me for not having performed what I never attempted. The Reader will find that personifications of abstract ideas rarely occur in these volumes; and are utterly rejected, as an ordinary device to elevate the style, and raise it above prose. My purpose was to imitate, and, as far as possible, to adopt the very language of men; and assuredly such personifications do not make any natural or regular part of that language. They are, indeed, a figure of speech occasionally prompted by passion, and I have made use of them as such; but have endeavoured utterly to reject them as a mechanical device of style, or as a family language which Writers in metre seem to lay claim to by prescription. I have wished to keep the Reader in the company of flesh and blood, persuaded that by so doing I shall interest him. Others who pursue a different track will interest him likewise; I do not interfere with their claim, but wish to prefer a claim of my own. There will also be found in these volumes little of what is usually called poetic diction; as much pains has been taken to avoid it as is ordinarily taken to produce it; this has been done for the reason already alleged, to bring my language near to the language of men; and further, because the pleasure which I have proposed to myself to impart, is of a kind very different from that which is supposed by many persons to be the proper object of poetry. Without being culpably particular, I do not know how to give my Reader a more exact notion of the style in which it was my wish and intention to write, than by informing him that I have at all times endeavoured to look steadily at my subject; consequently, there is I hope in these Poems little falsehood of description, and my ideas are expressed in language fitted to their respective importance. Something must have been gained by this practice, as it is friendly to one property of all good poetry, namely, good sense: but it has necessarily cut me off from a large portion of phrases and figures of speech which from father to son have long been regarded as the common inheritance of Poets. I have also thought it expedient to restrict myself still further, having abstained from the use of many expressions, in themselves proper and beautiful, but which have been foolishly repeated by bad Poets, till such feelings of disgust are connected with them as it is scarcely possible by any art of association to overpower.

If in a poem there should be found a series of lines, or even a single line, in which the language, though naturally arranged, and according to the strict laws of metre, does not differ from that of prose, there is a numerous class of critics, who, when they stumble upon these prosaisms, as they call them, imagine that they have made a notable discovery, and exult over the Poet as over a man ignorant of his own profession. Now these men would establish a canon of criticism which the Reader will conclude he must utterly reject, if he wishes to be pleased with these volumes. And it would be a most easy task to prove to him, that not only the language of a large portion of every good poem, even of the most elevated character, must necessarily, except with reference to the metre, in no respect differ from that of good prose, but likewise that some of the most interesting parts of the best poems will be found to be strictly the language of prose when prose is well written. The truth of this assertion might be demonstrated by innumerable passages from almost all the poetical writings, even of Milton himself. To illustrate the subject in a general manner, I will here adduce a short composition of Gray, who was at the head of those who, by their reasonings, have attempted to widen the space of separation betwixt Prose and Metrical composition, and was more than any other man curiously elaborate in the structure of his own poetic diction.

> In vain to me the smiling mornings shine,
> And reddening Phœbus lifts his golden fire:
> The birds in vain their amorous descant join,
> Or cheerful fields resume their green attire.
> These ears, alas! for other notes repine;
> *A different object do these eyes require;*
> *My lonely anguish melts no heart but mine;*
> *And in my breast the imperfect joys expire;*
> Yet morning smiles the busy race to cheer,
> And new-born pleasure brings to happier men;
> The fields to all their wonted tribute bear;
> To warm their little loves the birds complain,
> *I fruitless mourn to him that cannot hear,*
> *And weep the more because I weep in vain.*

It will easily be perceived, that the only part of this Sonnet which is of any value is the lines printed in Italics; it is equally obvious, that, except in the rhyme, and in the use of the single word "fruitless" for fruitlessly, which is so far a defect, the language of these lines does in no respect differ from that of prose.

By the foregoing quotation it has been shown that language of Prose may yet be well adapted to Poetry; and it was previously asserted, that a large portion of the language of every good poem can in no respect differ from that of good Prose. We will go further. It may be safely affirmed, that there neither is, nor can be, any *essential* difference between the language of prose and metrical composition. We are fond of tracing the resemblance between Poetry and Painting, and, accordingly, we call them Sisters: but where shall we find bonds of connexion sufficiently strict to typify the affinity betwixt metrical and prose composition? They both speak by and to the same organs; the bodies in which both of them are clothed may be said to be of the same substance, their affections are kindred, and almost identical, not necessarily differing even in degree; Poetry[2] sheds no tears "such as Angels weep,"

---

[2] I here use the word "Poetry" (though against my own judgement) as opposed to the word Prose, and synonymous with metrical composition. But much confusion has been introduced into criticism by this contradistinction of Poetry and Prose, instead of the more philosophical one of Poetry and Matter of Fact, or Science. The only strict antithesis to Prose is Metre; nor is this, in truth, a *strict* antithesis, because lines and passages of metre so naturally occur in writing prose, that it would be scarcely possible to avoid them, even were it desirable.

but natural and human tears; she can boast of no celestial ichor that distinguishes her vital juices from those of prose; the same human blood circulates through the veins of them both.

If it be affirmed that rhyme and metrical arrangement of themselves constitute a distinction which overturns what has just been said on the strict affinity of metrical language with that of prose, and paves the way for other artificial distinctions which the mind voluntarily admits, I answer that the language of such Poetry as is here recommended is, as far as possible, a selection of the language really spoken by men; that this selection, wherever it is made with true taste and feeling, will of itself form a distinction far greater than would at first be imagined, and will entirely separate the composition from the vulgarity and meanness of ordinary life; and, if metre be superadded thereto, I believe that a dissimilitude will be produced altogether sufficient for the gratification of a rational mind. What other distinction would we have? Whence is it to come? And where is it to exist? Not, surely, where the Poet speaks through the mouths of his characters: it cannot be necessary here, either for elevation of style, or any of its supposed ornaments: for, if the Poet's subject be judiciously chosen, it will naturally, and upon fit occasion, lead him to passions the language of which, if selected truly and judiciously, must necessarily be dignified and variegated, and alive with metaphors and figures. I forbear to speak of an incongruity which would shock the intelligent Reader, should the Poet interweave any foreign splendour of his own with that which the passion naturally suggests: it is sufficient to say that such addition is unnecessary. And, surely, it is more probable that those passages, which with propriety abound with metaphors and figures, will have their due effect, if, upon other occasions where the passions are of a milder character, the style also be subdued and temperate.

But, as the pleasure which I hope to give by the Poems now presented to the Reader must depend entirely on just notions upon this subject, and, as it is in itself of high importance to our taste and moral feelings, I cannot content myself with these detached remarks. And if, in what I am about to say, it shall appear to some that my labour is unnecessary, and that I am like a man fighting a battle without enemies, such persons may be reminded, that, whatever be the language outwardly holden by men, a practical faith in the opinions which I am wishing to establish is almost unknown. If my conclusions are admitted, and carried as far as they must be carried if admitted at all, our judgements concerning the works of the greatest Poets both ancient and modern will be far different from what they are at present, both when we praise, and when we censure: and our moral feelings influencing and influenced by these judgements will, I believe, be corrected and purified.

Taking up the subject, then, upon general grounds, let me ask, what is meant by the word Poet? What is a Poet? To whom does he address himself? And what language is to be expected from him?—He is a man speaking to men: a man, it is true, endowed with more lively sensibility, more enthusiasm and tenderness, who has a greater knowledge of human nature, and a more comprehensive soul, than are supposed to be common among mankind; a man pleased with his own passions and volitions, and who rejoices more than other men in the spirit of life that is in him; delighting to contemplate similar volitions and passions as manifested in the goings-on of the Universe, and habitually impelled to create them where he does not find them. To these qualities he has added a disposition to be affected more than other men by absent things as if they were present; an ability of conjuring up in himself passions, which are indeed far from being the same as those produced by real events, yet (especially in those parts of the general sympathy which are pleasing and delightful) do more nearly resemble the passions produced by real events, than anything which, from the motions of their own minds merely, other men are accustomed to feel in themselves:— whence, and from practice, he has acquired a greater readiness and power, in expressing what he thinks and feels, and especially those thoughts and feelings which, by his own choice, or from the structure of his own mind, arise in him without immediate external excitement.

But whatever portion of this faculty we may suppose even the greatest Poet to possess, there cannot be a doubt that the language which it will suggest to him, must often, in liveliness and truth, fall short of that which is uttered by men in real life, under the actual pressure of those passions, certain shadows of which the Poet thus produces, or feels to be produced, in himself.

However exalted a notion we would wish to cherish of the character of a Poet, it is obvious, that while he describes and imitates passions, his employment is in some degree mechanical, compared with the freedom and power of real and substantial action and suffering. So that it will be the wish of the Poet to bring his feelings near to those of the persons whose feelings he describes, nay, for short spaces of time, perhaps, to let himself slip into an entire delusion, and even confound and identify his own feelings with theirs; modifying only the language which is thus suggested to him by a consideration that he describes for a particular purpose, that of giving pleasure. Here, then, he will apply the principle of selection which has been already insisted upon. He will depend upon this for removing what would otherwise be painful or disgusting in the passion; he will feel that there is no necessity to trick out or to elevate nature: and, the more industriously he applies this principle, the deeper will be his faith that no words, which *his* fancy or imagination can suggest, will be to be compared with those which are the emanations of reality and truth.

But it may be said by those who do not object to the general spirit of these remarks, that, as it is impossible for the Poet to produce upon all occasions language as exquisitely fitted for the passion as that which the real passion itself suggests, it is proper that he should consider himself as in the situation of a translator, who does not scruple to substitute excellencies of another kind for those which are unattainable by him; and endeavours occasionally to surpass his original, in order to make some amends for the general inferiority to which he feels that he must submit. But this would be to encourage idleness and unmanly despair. Further, it is the language of men who speak of what they do not understand; who talk of Poetry as of a matter of amusement and idle pleasure; who will converse with us as gravely about a *taste* for Poetry, as they express it, as if it were a thing as indifferent as a taste for rope-dancing, or Frontiniac or Sherry. Aristotle, I have been told, has said, that Poetry is the most philosophic of all writing: it is so: its object is truth, not individual and local, but general, and operative; not standing upon external testimony, but carried alive into the heart by passion; truth which is its own testimony, which gives competence and confidence to the tribunal to which it appeals, and receives them from the same tribunal. Poetry is the image of man and nature. The obstacles which stand in the way of the fidelity of the Biographer and Historian, and of their consequent utility, are incalculably greater than those which are to be encountered by the Poet who comprehends the dignity of his art. The Poet writes under one restriction only, namely, the necessity of giving immediate pleasure to a human Being possessed of that information which may be expected from him, not as a lawyer, a physician a mariner, an astronomer, or a natural philosopher, but as a Man. Except this one restriction, there is no object standing between the Poet and the image of things; between this, and the Biographer and Historian, there are a thousand.

Nor let this necessity of producing immediate pleasure be considered as a degradation of the Poet's art. It is far otherwise. It is an acknowledgement of the beauty of the universe, an acknowledgement the more sincere, because not formal, but indirect; it is a task light and easy to him who looks at the world in the spirit of love: further, it is a homage paid to the native and naked dignity of man, to the grand elementary principle of pleasure, by which he knows, and feels, and lives, and moves. We have no sympathy but what is propagated by pleasure: I would not be misunderstood; but wherever we sympathize with pain, it will be found that the sympathy is produced and carried on by subtle combinations with pleasure. We have no knowledge, that is, no general principles drawn from the contemplation of particular facts, but what has been built up by pleasure, and exists in us by pleasure alone. The Man of science, the Chemist and Mathematician, whatever difficulties and disgusts they may have had to struggle with, know and feel this. However painful may be the objects with which the Anatomist's knowledge is connected, he feels that his knowledge is pleasure; and where he has no pleasure he has no knowledge. What then does the Poet? He considers man and the objects that surround him as acting and reacting upon each other, so as to produce an infinite complexity of pain and pleasure; he considers man in his own nature and in his ordinary life as contemplating this with a certain quantity of immediate knowledge, with certain convictions, intuitions, and deductions, which from habit acquire the quality of intuitions; he considers him as looking upon this complex scene of ideas and sensations, and finding everywhere objects that immediately excite in him sympathies which, from the necessities of his nature, are accompanied by an overbalance of enjoyment.

To this knowledge which all men carry about with them, and to these sympathies in which, without any other discipline than that of our daily life, we are fitted to take delight, the Poet principally directs his attention. He considers man and nature as essentially adapted to each other, and the mind of man as naturally the mirror of the fairest and most interesting properties of nature. And thus the Poet, prompted by his feeling of pleasure, which accompanies him through the whole course of his studies, converses with general nature, with affections akin to those, which, through labour and length of time, the Man of science has raised up in himself, by conversing with those particular parts of nature which are the objects of his studies. The knowledge both of the

Poet and the Man of science is pleasure; but the knowledge of the one cleaves to us as a necessary part of our existence, our natural and unalienable inheritance; the other is a personal and individual acquisition, slow to come to us, and by no habitual and direct sympathy connecting us with our fellow-beings. The Man of science seeks truth as a remote and unknown benefactor; he cherishes and loves it in his solitude: the Poet singing a song in which all human beings join with him, rejoices in the presence of truth as our visible friend and hourly companion. Poetry is the breath and finer spirit of all knowledge; it is the impassioned expression which is in the countenance of all Science. Emphatically may it be said of the Poet, as Shakespeare hath said of man, "that he looks before and after." He is the rock of defence for human nature; and upholder and preserver, carrying everywhere with him relationship and love. In spite of difference of soil and climate, of language and manners, of laws and customs: in spite of things silently gone out of mind, and things violently destroyed; the Poet binds together by passion and knowledge the vast empire of human society, as it is spread over the whole earth, and over all time. The objects of the Poet's thoughts are everywhere; though the eyes and senses of man are, it is true, his favourite guides, yet he will follow wheresoever he can find an atmosphere of sensation in which to move his wings. Poetry is the first and last of all knowledge—it is as immortal as the heart of man. If the labours of Men of science should ever create any material revolution, direct or indirect, in our condition, and in the impressions which we habitually receive, the Poet will sleep then no more than at present; he will be ready to follow the steps of the Man of science, not only in those general indirect effects, but he will be at his side, carrying sensation into the midst of the objects of the science itself. The remotest discoveries of the Chemist, the Botanist, or Mineralogist, will be as proper objects of the Poet's art as any upon which it can employed, if the time should ever come when these things shall be familiar to us, and the relations under which they are contemplated by the followers of these respective sciences shall be manifestly and palpably material to us as enjoying and suffering beings. If the time should ever come when what is now called science, thus familiarized to men, shall be ready to put on, as it were, a form of flesh and blood, the Poet will lend his divine spirit to aid the transfiguration, and will welcome the Being thus produced, as a dear and genuine inmate of the household of man.—It is not, then, to be supposed that any one, who holds that sublime notion of Poetry which I have attempted to convey, will break in upon the sanctity and truth of his pictures by transitory and accidental ornaments, and endeavour to excite admiration of himself by arts, the necessity of which must manifestly depend upon the assumed meanness of his subject.

What has been thus far said applies to Poetry in general; but especially to those parts of composition where the Poet speaks through the mouths of his characters; and upon this point it appears to authorize the conclusion that there are few person of good sense, who would not allow that the dramatic parts of composition are defective, in proportion as they deviate from the real language of nature, and are coloured by a diction of the Poet's own, either peculiar to him as an individual Poet or belonging simply to Poets in general; to a body of men who, from the circumstance of their compositions being in metre, it is expected will employ a particular language.

It is not, then, in the dramatic parts of composition that we look for this distinction of language; but still it may be proper and necessary where the Poet speaks to us in his own person and character. To this I answer by referring the Reader to the description before given of a Poet. Among the qualities there enumerated as principally conducing to form a Poet, is implied nothing differing in kind from other men, but only in degree. The sum of what was said is, that the Poet is chiefly distinguished from other men by a greater promptness to think and feel without immediate external excitement, and a greater power in expressing such thoughts and feelings as are produced in him in that manner. But these passions and thoughts and feelings are the general passions and thoughts and feelings of men. And with what are they connected? Undoubtedly with our moral sentiments and animal sensations, and with the causes which excite these; with the operation of the elements, and the appearances of the visible universe; with storm and sunshine, with the revolutions of the seasons, with cold and heat, with loss of friends and kindred, with injuries and resentments, gratitude and hope, with fear and sorrow. These, and the like, are the sensations and objects which the Poet describes, as they are the sensations of other men, and the objects which interest them. The Poet thinks and feels in the spirit of human passions. How, then, can his language differ in any material degree from that of all other men who feel vividly and see clearly? It might be *proved* that it is impossible. But supposing that this were not the case, the Poet might then be allowed to use a peculiar language when expressing his feelings for his own gratification, or that of men like himself. But Poets do not write for Poets alone, but for men. Unless therefore we are advocates for that admiration which subsists upon ignorance, and that pleasure which arises from hearing what we do not understand, the Poet must descend from this supposed height; and, in order to excite rational sympathy, he must express himself as other men express themselves. To this it may be added, that while he is only selecting from the real language of men, or, which amounts to the same thing, composing accurately in the spirit of such selection, he is treading upon safe ground, and we know what we are to expect from him. Our feelings are the same with respect to metre; for, as it may be proper to remind the Reader, the distinction of metre is regular and uniform, and not, like that which is produced by what is usually called POETIC DICTION, arbitrary, and subject to infinite caprices upon which no calculation whatever can be made. In the one case, the Reader is utterly at the mercy of the Poet, respecting what imagery or diction he may choose to connect with the passion; whereas, in the other, the metre obeys certain laws, to which the Poet and Reader both willingly submit because they are certain, and because no interference is made by them with the passion, but such as the concurring testimony of ages has shown to heighten and improve the pleasure which co-exists with it.

It will now be proper to answer an obvious question, namely, Why, professing these opinions, have I written in verse? To this, in addition to such answer as is included in what has been already said, I reply, in the first place, Because, however I may have restricted myself, there is still left open to me what confessedly constitutes the most valuable object of all writing, whether in prose or verse; the great and universal passions of men, the most general and interesting of their occupations, and the entire world of nature before me—to supply endless combinations of forms and imagery. Now, supposing for a moment that whatever is interesting in these objects may be as vividly described in prose, why should I be condemned for attempting to superadd to such description the charm which, by the consent of all nations, is acknowledged to exist in metrical language? To this, by such as are yet unconvinced, it may be answered that a very small part of the pleasure given by Poetry depends upon the metre, and that it is injudicious to write in metre, unless it be accompanied with the other artificial distinctions of style with which metre is usually accompanied, and that, by such deviation, more will be lost from the shock which will thereby be given to the Reader's associations than will be counterbalanced by any pleasure which he can derive from the general power of numbers. In answer to those who still contend for the necessity of accompanying metre with certain appropriate colours of style in order to the accomplishment of its appropriate end, and who also, in my opinion, greatly underrate the power of metre in itself, it might, perhaps, as far as relates to these Volumes, have been almost sufficient to observe, that poems are extant, written upon more humble subjects, and in a still more naked and simple style, which have continued to give pleasure from generation to generation. Now, if nakedness and simplicity be a defect, that fact here mentioned affords a strong presumption that poems somewhat less naked and simple are capable of affording pleasure at the present day; and, what I wish *chiefly* to attempt, at present, was to justify myself for having written under the impression of this belief.

But various causes might be pointed out why, when the style is manly and the subject of some importance, words metrically arranged will long continue to impart such a pleasure to mankind as he who proves the extent of that pleasure will be desirous to impart. The end of Poetry is to produce excitement in co-existence with an overbalance of pleasure; but, by the supposition, excitement is an unusual and irregular state of the mind; ideas and feelings do not, in that state, succeed each other in accustomed order. If the words, however, by which this excitement is produced be in themselves powerful, or the images and feelings have an undue proportion of pain connected with them, there is some danger that the excitement may be carried beyond its proper bounds. Now the co-presence of something regular, something to which the mind has been accustomed in various moods and in a less excited state, cannot but have great efficacy in tempering and restraining the passion by an inter-texture of ordinary feeling, and of feeling not strictly and necessarily connected with the passion. This is unquestionably true; and hence, though the opinion will at first appear paradoxical, from the tendency of metre to divest language, in a certain degree, of its reality, and thus to throw a sort of half-consciousness of unsubstantial existence over the whole composition, there can be little doubt but that more pathetic situations and sentiments, that is, those which have a greater proportion of pain connected with them, may be endured in metrical composition, especially in rhyme, than in prose. The metre of the old ballads is very artless; yet they contain many passages which would illustrate this opinion; and, I hope, if the following Poems be attentively perused, similar instances will be found in them. This opinion may be further illustrated by appealing to the Reader's own experience of the reluctance with which he comes to the re-perusal of the distressful parts of *Clarissa Harlowe*, or *The Gamester;* while Shakespeare's writings, in the most pathetic scenes, never act upon us, as pathetic, beyond the bounds of pleasure—an effect which, in a much great degree than might at first be imagined, is to be ascribed to small, but continual and regular impulses of pleasurable surprise from the metrical arrangement.—On the other hand (what it must be allowed will much more frequently happen) if the Poet's words should be incommensurate with the passion, and inadequate to raise the Reader to a height of desirable excitement, then (unless the Poet's choice of his metre has been grossly injudicious), in the feelings of pleasure which the Reader has been accustomed to connect with metre in general, and in the feeling, whether cheerful or melancholy, which he has been accustomed to connect with that particular movement of metre, there will be found something which will greatly contribute to impart passion to the words, and to effect the complex end which the Poet proposes to himself.

If I had undertaken a SYSTEMATIC defence of the theory here maintained, it would have been my duty to develop the various causes upon which the pleasure received from metrical language depends. Among the chief of these causes is to be reckoned a principle which must be well known to those who have made any of the Arts the object of accurate reflection; namely, the pleasure which the mind derives from the perception of similitude in dissimilitude. This principle is the great spring of the activity of our minds, and their chief feeder. From this principle the direction of the sexual appetite, and all the passions connected with it, take their origin: it is the life of our ordinary conversation; and upon the accuracy with which similitude in dissimilitude, and dissimilitude in similitude are perceived, depend our taste and our moral feelings. It would not be a useless employment to apply this principle to the consideration of metre, and to show that metre is hence enabled to afford much pleasure, and to point out in what manner that pleasure is produced. But my limits will not permit me to enter upon this subject, and I must content myself with a general summary.

I have said that poetry is the spontaneous overflow of powerful feelings: it takes its origin from emotion recollected in tranquillity: the emotion is contemplated till, by a species of reaction, the tranquillity gradually disappears, and an emotion, kindred to that which was before the subject of contemplation, is gradually produced, and does itself actually exist in the mind. In this mood successful composition generally begins and in a mood similar to this it is carried on; but the emotion of whatever kind and in whatever degree, from various causes, is qualified by various pleasures, so that in describing any passions whatsoever, which are voluntarily described, the mind will, upon the whole, be in a state of enjoyment. If Nature be thus cautious to preserve in a state of enjoyment a being so employed, the Poet ought to profit by the lesson held forth to him, and ought especially to take care, that, whatever passions he communicates to his Reader, those passions, if his Reader's mind be sound and vigorous, should always be accompanied with an overbalance of pleasure. Now the music of harmonious metrical language, the sense of difficulty overcome, and the blind association of pleasure which has been previously received from works of rhyme or metre of the same or similar construction, an indistinct perception perpetually renewed of language closely resembling that of real life, and yet, in the circumstance of metre, differing from it so widely—all these imperceptibly make up a complex feeling of delight, which is of the most important use in tempering the painful feeling always found intermingled with powerful descriptions of the deeper passions. This effect is always produced in pathetic and impassioned poetry; while, in lighter compositions, the ease and gracefulness with which the Poet manages his numbers are themselves confessedly a principal source of the gratification of the Reader. All that it is *necessary* to say, however, upon this subject, may be effected by affirming, what few persons will deny, that, of two descriptions, either of passions, manners, or characters, each of them equally well executed, the one in prose and the other in verse, the verse will be read a hundred times where the prose is read once.

Having thus explained a few of my reasons for writing in verse, and why I have chosen subjects from common life, and endeavoured to bring my language near to the real language of men, if I have been too minute in pleading my own cause, I have at the same time been treating a subject of general interest; and for this reason a few words shall be added with reference solely to these particular poems, and to some defects which will probably be found in them. I am sensible that my associations must have sometimes been particular instead of general, and that, consequently, giving to things a false importance, I may have sometimes written upon unworthy subjects; but I am less apprehensive on this account, than that my language may frequently have suffered from those arbitrary connexions of feelings and ideas with particular words and phrases, from which no man can altogether protect himself. Hence I have no doubt, that, in some instances, feelings, even of the ludicrous, may be given to my Readers by expressions which appeared to me tender and pathetic. Such faulty expressions, were I convinced they were faulty at present, and that they must necessarily continue to be so, I would willingly take all reasonable pains to correct. But it is dangerous to make these alterations on the simple authority of a few individuals, or even of certain classes of men; for where the understanding of an Author is not convinced, or his feelings altered, this cannot be done without great injury to himself: for his own feelings are his stay and support; and, if he set them aside in one instance, he may be induced to repeat this act till his mind shall lose all confidence in itself, and become utterly debilitated. To this it may be added, that the critic ought never to forget that he is himself exposed to the same errors as the Poet, and, perhaps, in a much greater degree: for there can be no presumption in saying of most readers, that it is not probable they will be so well acquainted with the various stages of meaning through which words have passed, or with the fickleness or stability of the relations of particular ideas to each other; and, above all, since they are so much less interested in the subject, they may decide lightly and carelessly.

Long as the Reader has been detained, I hope he will permit me to caution him against a mode of false criticism which has been applied to Poetry, in which the language closely resembles that of life and nature. Such verses have been triumphed over in parodies, of which Dr. Johnson's stanza is a fair specimen:—

> I put my hat upon my head
> And walked into the Strand,
> And there I met another man
> Whose hat was in his hand.

Immediately under these lines let us place one of the most justly admired stanzas of the "Babes in the Wood."

> These pretty Babes with hand in hand
> Went wandering up and down;
> But never more they saw the Man
> Approaching from the Town.

In both these stanzas the words, and the order of the words, in no respect differ from the most unimpassioned conversation. There are words in both, for example, "the Strand," and "the Town," connected with none but the most familiar ideas; yet the one stanza we admit as admirable, and the other as a fair example of the superlatively contemptible. Whence arises this difference? Not from the metre, not from the language, not from the order of the words; but the *matter* expressed in Dr. Johnson's stanza is contemptible. The proper method of treating trivial and simple verses, to which Dr. Johnson's stanza would be a fair parallelism, is not say, this is a bad kind of poetry, or, this is not poetry; but, this wants sense; it is neither interesting in itself nor can *lead* to anything interesting; the images neither originate in that same state of feeling which arises out of thought, nor can excite thought or feeling in the Reader. This is the only sensible manner of dealing with such verses. Why trouble yourself about the species till you have previously decided upon the genus? Why take pains to prove that an ape is not a Newton, when it is self-evident that he is not a man?

One request I must make of my reader, which is, that in judging these Poems he would decide by his own feelings genuinely, and not by reflection upon what will probably be the judgement of others. How common is it to hear a person say, I myself do not object to this style of composition, or this or that expression, but, to such and such classes of people it will appear mean or ludicrous! This mode of criticism, so destructive of all sound unadulterated judgement, is almost universal: let the Reader then abide, independently, by his own feelings, and, if he finds himself affected, let him not suffer such conjectures to interfere with his pleasure.

If an Author, by any single composition, has impressed us with respect for his talents, it is useful to consider this as affording a presumption, that on other occasions where we have been displeased, he, nevertheless, may not have written ill or absurdly; and further, to give him so much credit for this one composition as may induce us to review what has displeased us, with more care than we should otherwise have bestowed upon it. This is not only an act of justice, but, in our decisions upon poetry especially, may conduce, in a high degree, to the improvement of our own taste; for an *accurate* taste in poetry, and in all other arts, as Sir Joshua Reynolds has observed, is an *acquired* talent, which can only be produced by thought and a long continued intercourse with the best models of composition. This is mentioned, not with so ridiculous a purpose as to prevent the most inexperienced Reader from judging for himself (I have already said that I wish him to judge for himself), but merely to temper the rashness of decision, and to suggest, that, if Poetry be a subject on which much time has not been bestowed, the judgement may be erroneous; and that, in many cases, it necessarily will be so.

Nothing would, I know, have so effectually contributed to further the end which I have in view, as to have shown of what kind the pleasure is, and how that pleasure is produced, which is confessedly produced by metrical composition essentially different from that which I have here endeavoured to recommend: for the Reader will say that he has been pleased by such composition; and what more can be done for him? The power of any art is limited; and he will suspect, that, if it be proposed to furnish him with new friends, that can be only upon condition of his abandoning his old friends. Besides, as I have said, the Reader is himself conscious of the pleasure which he has received from such composition, composition to which he has peculiarly attached the endearing name of Poetry; and all men feel an habitual gratitude, and something of an honourable bigotry, for the objects which have long continued to please them: we not only wish to be pleased, but to be pleased in that particular way in which we have been accustomed to be pleased. There is in these feelings enough to resist a host of arguments; and I should be the less able to combat them successfully, as I am willing to allow, that, in order entirely to enjoy the Poetry which I am recommending, it would be necessary to give up much of what is ordinarily enjoyed. But, would my limits have permitted me to point out how this pleasure is produced, many obstacles might have been removed, and the Reader assisted in perceiving that the powers of language are not so limited as he may suppose; and that it is possible for poetry to give other enjoyments, of a purer, more lasting, and more exquisite nature. This part of the subject has not been altogether neglected, but it has not been so much my present aim to prove, that the interest excited by some other kinds of poetry is less vivid, and less worthy of the nobler powers of the mind, as to offer reasons for presuming, that if my purpose were fulfilled, a species of poetry would be produced, which is genuine poetry; in its nature well adapted to interest mankind permanently, and likewise important in the multiplicity and quality of its moral relations.

From what has been said, and from a perusal of the Poems, the Reader will be able clearly to perceive the object which I had in view: he will determine how far it has been attained; and, what is a much more important question, whether it be worth attaining: and upon the decision of these two questions will rest my claim to the approbation of the Public.

7. ARNOLD

"The Study of Poetry"

Matthew Arnold (1822–88) was the son of a famous headmaster at the great English public school Rugby. He attended Balliol College, Oxford, and later became fellow of Oriel College. He spent most of his life working as inspector of schools; he even kept the job when he was made professor of poetry at Oxford in 1857. Toward the end of his life in 1883 he made a year-long lecture tour in the United States.

Unlike most of the English poet critics, Arnold did not engage in both the writing of poetry and criticism at the same time. He wrote most of his poetry before he was thirty-five years old; among his best and best-known poems are "The Scholar-Gipsy," "Rugby Chapel," "Dover Beach," and the long narrative poem "Sohrab and Rustum." Among his famous critical works are *Essays in Criticism* (1865), *On the Study of Celtic Literature* (1867), *Culture and Anarchy* (1869), and "The Study of Poetry," which was written in 1880 as the Introduction to Ward's anthology, *The English Poets*, and is included here in its entirety.

Previous critics stressed the importance of poetry, but few before or since him would make the case for poetry as strongly as he does. Poetry not only teaches and delights, but is at the very center of our culture: "More and more mankind will discover that we have to turn to poetry to interpret life for us, to console us, to sustain us. Without poetry, our science will appear incomplete; and most of what now passes with us for religion and philosophy will be replaced by poetry."

In all his critical writings Arnold is deeply concerned with culture and poetry's important role in it. More than perhaps most critics, Arnold was unusually well educated and had a historical perspective in literature that many lacked. Thus he took most European poetry, not just English, for his province.

In "The Study of Poetry" Arnold does trace only the history of English poetry, but he does so with references to the continental literary works, notably *The Song of Roland* and Dante's *Divine Comedy*. In the process of tracing it he applies his "touchstone" theory: taking a few lines and examining them according to the presence of "the very highest poetical quality." This poetical quality is determined by Aristotle's observation that the best poetry possesses "higher truth and seriousness." Thus Chaucer's verse is found to possess truth but lacks high seriousness, and therefore is not classic (a real classic is a work that "belongs to the class of the very best"). Milton's and Shakespeare's poetry are found to have the two elements, but Dryden's and Pope's are not. It comes as a surprise that Gray is a classic: "He is the scantiest and frailest of classics in our poetry, but he is a classic." Finally, Burns, like Chaucer, falls short in high seriousness.

Despite all the attempts at and avowals of objectivity, Arnold really begins the very modern subjective approach in criticism. The rule of "higher truth and seriousness" appears objective, but its application is surely subjective. Thus Arnold is among the first to give emphasis to value judgments which, as Northrop Frye points out, are very dangerous in criticism: "Rhetorical [dealing with persuasive speech and verbal ornament] value-judgements are closely related to social values, and are usually cleared through a customs-house of moral metaphors: sincerity, economy, subtlety, simplicity, and the like. But because poetics is undeveloped, a fallacy arises from the illegitimate extension of rhetoric into the theory of literature. The invariable mark of this fallacy is the selected tradition, illustrated with great clarity in Arnold's 'touchstone' theory, where we proceed from the intuition of value represented by the touchstone to a system of ranking poets in classes. The practice of comparing poets by weighing their lines (no new invention, as it was ridiculed by Aristophanes in *The Frogs*) is used by both biographical and tropical critics, mainly in order to deny first-class rating to those in favor with the opposite group." (*Anatomy of Criticism*, p. 21.)

But we should not leave Arnold stressing the error of his ways. We should rather leave him as the descendant of Sidney in the sense that "The Study of Poetry," like Arnold's other critical works, is a passionate plea for and affirmation of the greatness and importance of literature.

"The future of poetry is immense, because in poetry, where it is worthy of its high destinies, our race, as time goes on, will find an ever surer and surer stay. There is not a creed which is not shaken, not an accredited dogma which is not shown to be questionable, not a received tradition which does not threaten to dissolve. Our religion has material-ised itself in the fact, in the supposed fact; it has attached its emotion to the fact, and now the fact is failing it. But for poetry the idea is every-thing; the rest is a world of illusion, of divine illusion. Poetry attaches its emotion to the idea; the idea *is* the fact. The strongest part of our religion today is its unconscious poetry."

Let me be permitted to quote these words of my own, as uttering the thought which should, in my opinion, go with us and govern us in all our study of poetry. In the present work it is the course of one great contributory stream to the world-river of poetry that we are invited to follow. We are here invited to trace the stream of English poetry. But whether we set ourselves, as here, to follow only one of the several streams that make the mighty river of poetry, or whether we seek to know them all, our governing thought should be the same. We should conceive of poetry worthily, and more highly than it has been the custom to conceive of it. We should conceive of it as capable of higher uses, and called to higher destinies, than those which in general men have assigned to it hitherto. More and more mankind will discover that we have to turn to poetry to interpret life for us, to console us, to sustain us. Without poetry, our science will appear incomplete; and most of what now passes with us for religion and philosophy will be replaced by poetry. Science, I say, will appear incomplete without it. For finely and truly does Wordsworth call poetry "the impassioned expression which is in the countenance of all science"; and what is a countenance without its expression? Again, Wordsworth finely and truly calls poetry "the breath and finer spirit of all knowledge"; our religion, parading evi-dences such as those on which the popular mind relies now; our philosophy, pluming itself on its reasonings about causation and finite and infinite being; what are they but the shadows and dreams and false shows of knowledge? The day will come when we shall wonder at ourselves for having trusted to them, for having taken them seriously; and the more we perceive their hollowness, the more we shall prize "the breath and finer spirit of knowledge" offered to us by poetry.

But if we conceive thus highly of the destinies of poetry, we must also set our standard for poetry high, since poetry, to be capable of fulfilling such high destinies, must be poetry of a high order of ex-cellence. We must accustom ourselves to a high standard and to a strict judgment. Sainte-Beuve relates that Napoleon one day said, when somebody was spoken of in his presence as a charlatan: "Charlatan as much as you please; but where is there *not* charlatanism?"—"Yes," answers Sainte-Beuve, "in politics, in the art of governing mankind, that is perhaps true. But in the order of thought, in art, the glory, the eternal honour is that charlatanism shall find no entrance; herein lies the inviolableness of that noble portion of man's being." It is admirably said, and let us hold fast to it. In poetry, which is thought and art in one, it is the glory, the eternal honour, that charlatanism shall find no entrance; that this noble sphere be kept inviolate and inviolable. Charlatanism is for confusing or obliterating the distinctions between excellent and inferior, sound and unsound or only half-sound, true and untrue or only half-true. It is charlatanism, conscious or unconscious, whenever we confuse or obliterate these. And in poetry, more than anywhere else, it is unpermissible to confuse or obliterate them. For in poetry the distinction between excellent and inferior, sound and unsound or only half-sound, true and untrue or only half-true, is of paramount importance. It is of paramount importance because of the high destinies of poetry. In poetry, as in criticism of life under the conditions fixed for such a criticism by the laws of poetic truth and poetic beauty, the spirit of our race will find, we have said, as time goes on and as other helps fail, its consolation and stay. But the consolation and stay will be of power in proportion to the power of the criticism of life. And the criticism of life will be of power in proportion as the poetry conveying it is excellent rather than inferior, sound rather than unsound or half-sound, true rather than untrue or half-true.

The best poetry is what we want; the best poetry will be found to have a power of forming, sustaining and delighting us, as nothing else can. A clearer, deeper sense of the best in poetry and of the strength and joy to be drawn from it, is the most precious benefit which we can gather from a poetical collection such as the present. And yet in the very nature and conduct of such a collection there is inevitably something which tends to obscure in us the consciousness of what our benefit should be, and to distract us from the pursuit of it. We should therefore steadily set it before our minds at the outset, and should compel ourselves to revert constantly to the thought of it as we proceed.

Yes; constantly in reading poetry, a sense for the best, the really excellent, and of the strength and joy to be drawn from it, should be present in our minds and should govern our estimate of what we read. But this real estimate, the only true one, is liable to be superseded, if we are not watchful, by two other kinds of estimate, the historic estimate and the personal estimate, both of which are fallacious. A poet or a poem may count to us historically, they may count to us on grounds personal to ourselves, and they may count to us really. They may count to us historically. The course of development of a nation's language, thought, and poetry, is profoundly interesting; and by regarding a poet's work as a stage in this course of development we may easily bring ourselves to make it of more importance as poetry than in itself it really is, we may come to use a language of quite exaggerated praise in criticising it; in short, to over-rate it. So arises in our poetic judgments the fallacy caused by the estimate which we may call historic. Then, again, a poet or poem may count to us on grounds personal to ourselves. Our personal affinities, likings and circumstances, have great power to sway our estimate of this or that poet's work, and to make us attach more importance to it as poetry than in itself it really possesses, because to us it is, or has been, of high importance. Here also we over-rate the object of our interest, and apply to it a language of praise which is quite exaggerated. And thus we get the source of a second fallacy in our poetic judgments—the fallacy caused by an estimate which we may call personal.

Both fallacies are natural. It is evident how naturally the study of the history and development of poetry may incline a man to pause over reputations and works once conspicuous but now obscure, and to quarrel with a careless public for skipping, in obedience to mere tradition and habit, from one famous name or work in its national poetry to another, ignorant of what it misses, and of the reason for keeping what it keeps, and of the whole process of growth in its poetry. The French have become diligent students of their own early poetry, which they long neglected; the study makes many of them dissatisfied with their so-called classical poetry, the court-tragedy of the seventeenth century, a poetry which Pellisson long ago reproached with its want of the true poetic stamp, with its *politesse stérile et rampante*, but which nevertheless has reigned in France as absolutely as if it had been the perfection of classical poetry indeed. The dissatisfaction is natural; yet a lively and accomplished critic, M. Charles d'Héricault, the editor of Clément Marot, goes too far when he says that "the cloud of glory playing round a classic is a mist as dangerous to the future of a literature as it is intolerable for the purposes of history." "It hinders," he goes on, "it hinders us from seeing more than one single point, the culminating and exceptional point; the summary, fictitious and arbitrary, of a thought and of a work. It substitutes a halo for a physiognomy, it puts a statue where there was once a man, and hiding from us all trace of the labour, the attempts, the weaknesses, the failures it claims not study but veneration; it does not show us how the thing is done, it imposes upon us a model. Above all, for the historian this creation of classic personages is inadmissible; for it withdraws the poet from his time from his proper life, it breaks historical relationships, it blinds criticism by conventional admiration, and renders the investigation of literary origins unacceptable. It gives us a human personage no longer but a God seated immovable amidst His perfect work, like Jupiter on Olympus; and hardly will it be possible for the young student to whom such work is exhibited at such a distance from him, to believe that it did not issue ready made from that divine head."

All this is brilliantly and tellingly said, but we must plead for a distinction. Everything depends on the reality of a poet's classic character. If he is a dubious classic, let us sift him; if he is a false classic, let us explode him. But if he is a real classic, if his work belongs to the class of the very best (for this is the true and right meaning of the word *classic, classical*), then the great thing for us is to feel and enjoy his work as deeply as ever we can, and to appreciate the wide difference between it and all work which had not the same high character. This is what is salutary, this is what is formative; this is the great benefit to be got from the study of poetry. Everything which interferes with it, which hinders it, is injurious. True, we must read our classic with open eyes, and not with eyes blinded with superstition; we must perceive when his work comes short, when it drops out of the class of the very best, and we must rate it, in such cases, at its proper value. But the use of this negative criticism is not in itself, it is entirely in its enabling us to have a clearer sense and a deeper enjoyment of what is truly excellent. To trace the labour, the attempts, the weaknesses, the failures of a genuine classic, to acquaint oneself with his time and his life and his historical relationships, is mere literary dilettantism unless it has that clear sense and deeper enjoyment for its end. It may be said that the more we know about a classic the better we shall enjoy him; and, if we lived as long as Methuselah and had all of us heads of perfect clearness and wills of perfect steadfastness, this might be true in fact as it is plausible in theory. But the case here is much the same as the case with the Greek and Latin studies of our schoolboys. The elaborate philological groundwork which we require them to lay is in theory an admirable preparation for appreciating the Greek and Latin authors worthily. The more thoroughly we lay the groundwork, the better we shall be able, it may be said, to enjoy the authors. True, if time were not so short, and schoolboys' wits not so soon tired and their power of attention exhausted; only, as it is, the elaborate philological preparation goes on, but the authors are little known and less enjoyed. So with the investigator of "historic origins" in poetry. He ought to enjoy the true classic all the better for his investigations; he often is distracted from the enjoyment of the best, and with the less good he overbusies himself, and is prone to over-rate it in proportion to the trouble which it has cost him.

The idea of tracing historic origins and historical relationships cannot be absent from a compilation like the present. And naturally the poets to be exhibited in it will be assigned to those persons for exhibition who are known to prize them highly, rather than to those who have no special inclination towards them. Moreover, the very occupation with an author, and the business of exhibiting him, disposes us to affirm and amplify his importance. In the present work, therefore, we are sure of frequent temptation to adopt the historic estimate, or the personal estimate, and to forget the real estimate; which latter, nevertheless, we must employ if we are to make poetry yield us its full benefit. So high is that benefit, the benefit of clearly feeling and of deeply enjoying the really excellent, the truly classic in poetry, that we do well, I say, to set it fixedly before our minds as our object in studying poets and poetry, and to make the desire of attaining it the one principle to which, as the *Imitation* says, whatever we may read or come to know, we always return. *Cum multa legeris et cognoveris, ad unum semper oportet redire principium.*

The historic estimate is likely in especial to affect our judgment and our language when we are dealing with ancient poets; the personal estimate when we are dealing with poets our contemporaries, or at any rate modern. The exaggerations due to the historic estimate are not in themselves, perhaps, of very much gravity. Their report hardly enters the general ear; probably they do not always impose even on the literary men who adopt them. But they lead to a dangerous abuse of language. So we hear Cædmon, amongst our own poets, compared to Milton. I have already noticed the enthusiasm of one accomplished French critic for "historic origins." Another eminent French critic, M. Vitet, comments upon that famous document of the early poetry of his nation, the *Chanson de Roland*. It is indeed a most interesting document. The *joculator* or *jongleur Taillefer*, who was with William the Conqueror's army at Hastings, marched before the Norman troops, so said the tradition, singing "of Charlemagne and of Roland and of Oliver, and of the vassals who died at Roncevaux"; and it is suggested that in the *Chanson de Roland* by one Turoldus or Théroulde, a poem preserved in a manuscript of the twelfth century in the Bodleian Library at Oxford, we have certainly the matter, perhaps even some of the words, of the chant which Taillefer sang. The poem has vigour and freshness; it is not without pathos. But M. Vitet is not satisfied with seeing in it a document of some poetic value, and of very high historic and linguistic value; he sees in it a grand and beautiful work, a monument of epic genius. In its general design he finds the grandiose conception, in its details he finds the constant union of simplicity with greatness, which are the marks, he truly says, of the genuine epic, and distinguish it from the artificial epic of literary ages. One thinks of Homer; this is the sort of praise which is given to Homer, and justly given. Higher praise there cannot well be, and it is the praise due to epic poetry of the highest order only, and to no other. Let us try, then, the *Chanson de Roland* at its best. Roland, mortally wounded, lay himself down under a pine-tree, with his face turned towards Spain and the enemy—

> *De plusurs choses à remembrer li prist,*
> *De tantes teres cume li bers cunquist,*
> *De dulce France, des humes de sun lign,*
> *De Carlemagne sun seignor ki l'nurrit.*

["And he began to recall many things, The many countries the knight had conquered, Sweet France, the men of his lineage, Charlemagne, his lord who brought him up."]

That is primitive work, I repeat, with an undeniable poetic quality of its own. It deserves such praise, and such praise is sufficient for it. But now to Homer—

> *Ōs phato: Tous d'ēdē katechen phusidzoos aia*
> *en Lakedaimoni audi, philē en patridi gaiē.*

["So she said; but the life-giving earth already held them fast in Lacedaemon, their dear native land."]

We are here in another world, another order of poetry altogether; here is rightly due such supreme praise as that which M. Vitet gives to the *Chanson de Roland*. If our words are to have any meaning, if our judgments are to have any solidity, we must not heap that supreme praise upon poetry of an order immeasurably inferior.

Indeed there can be no more useful help for discovering what poetry belongs to the class of the truly excellent, and can therefore do us most good, than to have always in one's mind lines and expressions of the great masters, and to apply them as a touchstone to other poetry. Of course we are not to require this other poetry to resemble them; it may be very dissimilar. But if we have any tact we shall find them, when we have lodged them well in our minds, an infallible touchstone for detecting the presence or absence of higher poetic quality, and also the degree of this quality, in all other poetry which we may place beside them. Short passages, even single lines, will serve our turn quite sufficiently. Take the two lines which I have just quoted from Homer, the poet's comment on Helen's mention of her brothers;—or take his

> *Adeilō, ti sphōï domen Pēlēï anakti*
> *Thnētō? huēis d'eeston agērō t'athanatō te.*
> *ē hina dustēnoisi met' andrasin alge echēton?*

["Ah, wretched pair, why did we give you to King Peleus, a mortal, while you are immortal and forever young? Was it that among ill-fated men you should suffer?"]

the address of Zeus to the horses of Peleus;—or take finally his

> *Kai se, gerun, to Prin men akoumen albion einai:*

["And you, old man, as we have heard, were happy in former times."]

the words of Achilles to Priam, a suppliant before him. Take that incomparable line and a half of Dante, Ugolino's tremendous words—

> *Io no piangeva; sì dentro impietrai.*
> *Piangevan elli . . .*

["I did not weep, so grew to stone within. They wept. . . ."]

take the lovely words of Beatrice to Virgil—

> *Io son fatta da Dio, sua mercè, tale,*
> *Che la vostra miseria non mi tange,*
> *Nè fiamma d'esto incendio non m'assale . . .*

["God, in his mercy, has so made me that your misery does not touch me, nor the flame of this fire assail me."]

take the simple, but perfect, single line—

> *In la sua volontade è nostra pace.*
> ["In His will is our peace."]

Take of Shakespeare a line or two of Henry the Fourth's expostulation with sleep—

> Wilt thou upon the high and giddy mast
> Seal up the ship-boy's eyes, and rock his brains
> In cradle of the rude imperious surge . . .

and take, as well, Hamlet's dying request to Horatio—

> If thou didst ever hold me in thy heart,
> Absent thee from felicity awhile,
> And in this harsh world draw thy breath in pain
> To tell my story . . .

Take of Milton that Miltonic passage:

> Darken'd so, yet shone
> Above them all the archangel; but his face
> Deep scars of thunder had intrench'd, and care
> Sat on his faded cheek . . .

add two such lines as

> And courage never to submit or yield
> And what is else not to be overcome . . .

and finish with the exquisite close to the loss of Proserpine, the loss

> . . . which cost Ceres all that pain
> To seek her through the world.

These few lines, if we have tact and can use them, are enough even of themselves to keep clear and sound our judgments about poetry, to save us from fallacious estimates of it, to conduct us to a real estimate.

The specimens I have quoted differ widely from one another, but they have in common this: the possession of the very highest poetical quality. If we are thoroughly penetrated by their power, we shall find that we have acquired a sense enabling us, whatever poetry may be laid before us, to feel the degree in which a high poetical quality is present or wanting there. Critics give themselves great labour to draw out what in the abstract constitutes the characters of a high quality of poetry. It is much better simply to have recourse to concrete examples;—to take specimens of poetry of the high, the very highest quality, and to say: The characters of a high quality of poetry are what is expressed *there*. They are far better recognized by being felt in the verse of the master, than by being perused in the prose of the critic. Nevertheless if we are urgently pressed to give some critical account of them, we may safely, perhaps, venture on laying down, not indeed how and why the characters arise, but where and in what they arise. They are in the matter and substance of the poetry, and they are in its manner and style. Both of these, the substance and matter on the one hand, the style and manner on the other, have a mark, an accent, of high beauty, worth, and power. But if we are asked to define this mark and accent in the abstract, our answer must be: No, for we should thereby be darkening the question, not clearing it. The mark and accent are as given by the substance and matter of that poetry, by the style and manner of that poetry, and of all other poetry which is akin to it in quality.

Only one thing we may add as to the substance and matter of poetry, guiding ourselves by Aristotle's profound observation that the superiority of poetry over history consists in its possessing a higher truth and a higher seriousness *psilosopsōteron kai spoudaioteron*. Let us add, therefore, to what we have said, this: that the substance and matter of the best poetry acquire their special character from possessing, in an eminent degree, truth and seriousness. We may add yet further, what is in itself evident, that to the style and manner of the best poetry their special character, their accent, is given by their diction, and, even yet more, by their movement. And though we distinguish between the two characters, the two accents, of superiority, yet they are nevertheless vitally connected one with the other. The superior character of truth and seriousness, in the matter and substance of the best poetry, is inseparable from the superiority of diction and movement marking its style and manner. The two superiorities are closely related, and are in steadfast proportion one to the other. So far as high poetic truth and seriousness are wanting to a poet's matter and substance, so far also, we may be sure, will a high poetic stamp of diction and movement be wanting to his style and manner. In proportion as this high stamp of diction and movement, again, is absent from a poet's style and manner, we shall find, also, that high poetic truth and seriousness are absent from his substance and matter.

So stated, these are but dry generalities; their whole force lies in their application. And I could wish every student of poetry to make the application of them for himself. Made by himself, the application would impress itself upon his mind far more deeply than made by me. Neither will my limits allow me to make any full application of the generalities above propounded; but in the hope of bringing out, at any rate, some significance in them, and of establishing an important principle more firmly by their means, I will, in the space which remains to me, follow rapidly from the commencement the course of our English poetry with them in my view.

Once more I return to the early poetry of France, with which our own poetry, in its origins, is indissolubly connected. In the twelfth and thirteenth centuries, the seed-time of all modern language and literature, the poetry of France had a clear predominance in Europe. Of the two divisions of that poetry, its productions in the *langue d'oïl* and its productions in the *langue d'oc*, the poetry of the *langue d'oc*, of southern France, of the troubadours, is of importance because of its effect on Italian literature;—the first literature of modern Europe to strike the true and grand note, and to bring forth, as in Dante and Petrarch it brought forth, classics. But the predominance of French poetry in Europe, during the twelfth and thirteenth centuries, is due to its poetry of the *langue d'oïl*, the poetry of northern France and of the tongue which is now the French language. In the twelfth century the bloom of this romance-poetry was earlier and stronger in England, at the court of our Anglo-Norman kings, than in France itself. But it was a bloom of French poetry; and as our native poetry formed itself, it formed itself out of this. The romance-poems which took possession of the heart and imagination of Europe in the twelfth and thirteenth centuries are French; "they are," as Southey justly says, "the pride of French literature, nor have we anything which can be placed in competition with them." Themes were supplied from all quarters; but the romance-setting which was common to them all, and which gained the ear of Europe, was French. This constituted for the French poetry, literature, and language, at the height of the Middle Age, an unchallenged predominance. The Italian Brunetto Latini, the master of Dante, wrote his *Treasure* in French because, he says, "la parleure en est plus délitable et plus commune à toutes gens." In the same century, the thirteenth, the French romance-writer, Christian of Troyes, formulates the claims, in chivalry and letters, of France, his native country, as follows:—

> *Or vous ert par ce livre apris,*
> *Que Gresse ot de chevalerie*
> *Le premier los et de clergie;*
> *Puis vint chevalerie à Rome,*
> *Et de la clergie la some,*

Qui ore est en France venue.
Diex doinst qu'ele i soit retenue,
Et que li lius li abelisse
Tant que de France n'isse
L'onor qui s'i est arestée!

"Now by this book you will learn that first Greece had the renown for chivalry and letters: then chivalry and the primacy in letters passed to Rome, and now it is come to France. God grant it may be kept there; and that the place may please it so well, that the honour which has come to make stay in France may never depart thence!"

Yet it is now all gone, this French romance-poetry of which the weight of substance and the power of style are not unfairly represented by this extract from Christian of Troyes. Only by means of the historic estimate can we persuade ourselves not to think that any of it is of poetical importance.

But in the fourteenth century there comes an Englishman nourished on this poetry, taught his trade by this poetry, getting words, rhyme, metre from this poetry; for even of that stanza which the Italians used, and which Chaucer derived immediately from the Italians, the basis and suggestion was probably given in France. Chaucer (I have already named him) fascinated his contemporaries, but so too did Christian of Troyes and Wolfram of Eschenbach. Chaucer's power of fascination, however, is enduring; his poetical importance does not need the assistance of the historic estimate; it is real. He is a genuine source of joy and strength, which is flowing still for us and will flow always. He will be read, as time goes on, far more generally than he is read now. His language is a cause of difficulty for us; but so also, and I think in quite as great a degree, is the language of Burns. In Chaucer's case, as in that of Burns, it is a difficulty to be unhesitatingly accepted and overcome.

If we ask ourselves wherein consists the immense superiority of Chaucer's poetry over the romance-poetry—why it is that in passing from this to Chaucer we suddenly feel ourselves to be in another world, we shall find that his superiority is both in the substance of his poetry and in the style of his poetry. His superiority in substance is given by his large, free, simple, clear yet kindly view of human life,—so unlike the total want, in the romance-poets, of all intelligent command of it. Chaucer has not their helplessness; he has gained the power to survey the world from a central, a truly human point of view. We have only to call to mind the Prologue to *The Canterbury Tales*. The right comment upon it is Dryden's: "It is sufficient to say, according to the proverb, that *here is God's plenty*." And again: "He is a perpetual fountain of good sense." It is by a large, free, sound representation of things, that poetry, this high criticism of life, has truth of substance; and Chaucer's poetry has truth of substance.

Of his style and manner, if we think first of the romance-poetry and then of Chaucer's divine liquidness of diction, his divine fluidity of movement, it is difficult to speak temperately. They are irresistible, and justify all the rapture with which his successors speak of his "gold dew-drops of speech." Johnson misses the point entirely when he finds fault with Dryden for ascribing to Chaucer the first refinement of our numbers, and says that Gower also can show smooth numbers and easy rhymes. The refinement of our numbers means something far more than this. A nation may have versifiers with smooth numbers and easy rhymes, and yet may have no real poetry at all. Chaucer is the father of our splendid English poetry; he is our "well of English undefiled," because by the lovely charm of his diction, the lovely charm of his movement, he makes an epoch and founds a tradition. In Spenser, Shakespeare, Milton, Keats, we can follow the tradition of the liquid diction, the fluid movement of Chaucer; at one time it is his liquid diction of which in these poets we feel the virtue, and at another time it is his fluid movement. And the virtue is irresistible.

Bounded as is my space, I must yet find room for an example of Chaucer's virtue, as I have given examples to show the virtue of the great classics. I feel disposed to say that a single line is enough to show the charm of Chaucer's verse; that merely one line like this—

O martyr souded in virginitee!

has a virtue of manner and movement such as we shall not find in all the verse of romance-poetry;—but this is saying nothing. The virtue is such as we shall not find, perhaps, in all English poetry, outside the poets whom I have named as the special inheritors of Chaucer's tradition. A single line, however, is too little if we have not the strain of Chaucer's verse well in our memory; let us take a stanza. It is from *The Prioress's Tale*, the story of the Christian child murdered in a Jewry—

My throte is cut unto my nekke-bone
Saidè this child, and as by way of kinde
I should have deyd, yea, longè time agone;

> But Jesu Christ, as ye in bookès finde,
> Will that his glory last and be in minde,
> And for the worship of his mother dere
> Yet may I sing *O Alma* loud and clere.

Wordsworth has modernised this Tale, and to feel how delicate and evanescent is the charm of verse, we have only to read Wordsworth's first three lines of this stanza after Chaucer's—

> My throat is cut unto the bone, I trow,
> Said this young child, and by the law of kind
> I should have died, yea, many hours ago.

The charm is departed. It is often said that the power of liquidness and fluidity in Chaucer's verse was dependent upon a free, a licentious dealing with language, such as is now impossible; upon a liberty, such as Burns too enjoyed, of making words like *neck*, *bird*, into a dissyllable by adding to them, and words like *cause*, *rhyme*, into a dissyllable by sounding the *e* mute. It is true that Chaucer's fluidity is conjoined with this liberty, and is admirably served by it; but we ought not to say that it was dependent upon it. It was dependent upon his talent. Other poets with a like liberty do not attain to the fluidity of Chaucer; Burns himself does not attain to it. Poets, again, who have a talent akin to Chaucer's, such as Shakespeare or Keats, have known how to attain his fluidity without the like liberty.

  And yet Chaucer is not one of the great classics. His poetry trancends and effaces, easily and without effort, all the romance-poetry of Catholic Christendom; it transcends and effaces all the English poetry contemporary with it, it transcends and effaces all the English poetry subsequent to it down to the age of Elizabeth. Of such avail is poetic truth of substance, in its natural and necessary union with poetic truth of style. And yet, I say, Chaucer is not one of the great classics. He has not their accent. What is wanting to him is suggested by the mere mention of the name of the first great classic of Christendom, the immortal poet who died eighty years before Chaucer,—Dante. The accent of such verse as

In la sua volontade è nostra pace . . .

is altogether beyond Chaucer's reach; we praise him, but we feel that this accent is out of the question for him. It may be said that it was necessarily out of the reach of any poet in the England of that stage of growth. Possibly; but we are to adopt a real, not a historic, estimate of poetry. However we may account for its absence, something is wanting, then, to the poetry of Chaucer, which poetry must have before it can be placed in the glorious class of the best. And there is no doubt what that something is. It is the *spoudaiotēs* the high and excellent seriousness, which Aristotle assigns as one of the grand virtues of poetry. The substance of Chaucer's poetry, his view of things and his criticism of life, has largeness, freedom, shrewdness, benignity; but it has not this high seriousness. Homer's criticism of life has it, Dante's has it, Shakespeare's has it. It is this chiefly which gives to our spirits what they can rest upon; and with the increasing demands of our modern ages upon poetry, this virtue of giving us what we can rest upon will be more and more highly esteemed. A voice from the slums of Paris, fifty or sixty years after Chaucer, the voice of poor Villon out of his life of riot and crime, has at its happy moments (as, for instance, in the last stanza of *La Belle Heaulmière*) more of this important poetic virtue of seriousness than all the productions of Chaucer. But its apparition in Villon, and in men like Villon, is fitful; the greatness of the great poets, the power of their criticism of life, is that their virtue is sustained.

To our praise, therefore, of Chaucer as a poet there must be this limitation; he lacks the high seriousness of the great classics, and therewith an important part of their virtue. Still, the main fact for us to bear in mind about Chaucer is his sterling value according to that real estimate which we firmly adopt for all poets. He has poetic truth of substance, though he has not high poetic seriousness, and corresponding to his truth of substance he has an exquisite virtue of style and manner. With him is born our real poetry.

For my present purpose I need not dwell on our Elizabethan poetry, or on the continuation and close of this poetry in Milton. We all of us profess to be agreed in the estimate of this poetry; we all of us recognise it as great poetry, our greatest, and Shakespeare and Milton as our poetical classics. The real estimate, here, has universal currency. With the next age of our poetry divergency and difficulty begin. An historic estimate of that poetry has established itself; and the question is, whether it will be found to coincide with the real estimate.

The age of Dryden, together with our whole eighteenth century which followed it, sincerely believed itself to have produced poetical classics of its own, and even to have made advance, in poetry, beyond all its predecessors. Dryden regards as not seriously disputable the opinion "that the sweetness of English verse was never understood or practised by our fathers." Cowley could see nothing at all in Chaucer's poetry. Dryden heartily admired it, and, as we have seen, praised its matter admirably; but of its exquisite manner and movement all he can find to say is that "there is the rude sweetness of a Scotch tune in it, which is natural and pleasing, though not perfect." Addison, wishing to praise Chaucer's numbers, compares them with Dryden's own. And all through the eighteenth century, and down even into our own times, the stereotyped phrase of approbation for good verse found in our early poetry has been, that it even approached the verse of Dryden, Addison, Pope, and Johnson.

Are Dryden and Pope poetical classics? Is the historic estimate, which represents them as such, and which has been so long established that it cannot easily give way, the real estimate? Wordsworth and Coleridge, as is well known, denied it; but the authority of Wordsworth and Coleridge does not weigh much with the young generation, and there are many signs to show that the eighteenth century and its judgments are coming into favour again. Are the favourite poets of the eighteenth century classics?

It is impossible within my present limits to discuss the question fully. And what man of letters would not shrink from seeming to dispose dictatorially of the claims of two men who are, at any rate, such masters in letters as Dryden and Pope; two men of such admirable talent, both of them, and one of them, Dryden, a man, on all sides, of such energetic and genial power? And yet, if we are to gain the full benefit from poetry, we must have the real estimate of it. I cast about for some mode of arriving, in the present case, at such an estimate without offence. And perhaps the best way is to begin, as it is easy to begin, with cordial praise.

When we find Chapman, the Elizabethan translator of Homer, expressing himself in his preface thus: "Though truth in her very nakedness sits in so deep a pit, that from Gades to Aurora and Ganges few eyes can sound her, I hope yet those few here will so discover and confirm that, the date being out of her darkness in this morning of our poet, he shall now gird his temples with the sun,"—we pronounce that such a prose is intolerable. When we find Milton writing: "And long it was not after, when I was confirmed in this opinion, that he, who would not be frustrate of his hope to write well hereafter in laudable things, ought himself to be a true poem,"—we pronounce that such a prose has its own grandeur, but that it is obsolete and inconvenient. But when we find Dryden telling us: "What Virgil wrote in the vigour of his age, in plenty and at ease, I have undertaken to translate in my declining years; struggling with wants, oppressed with sickness, curbed in my genius, liable to be misconstrued in all I write,"—then we exclaim that here at last we have the true English prose, a prose such as we would all gladly use if we only knew how. Yet Dryden was Milton's contemporary.

But after the Restoration the time had come when our nation felt the imperious need of a fit prose. So, too, the time had likewise come when our nation felt the imperious need of freeing itself from the absorbing preoccupation which religion in the Puritan age had exercised. It was impossible that this freedom should be brought about without some negative excess, without some neglect and impairment of the religious life of the soul; and the spiritual history of the eighteenth century shows us that the freedom was not achieved without them. Still, the freedom was achieved; the preoccupation, and undoubtedly baneful and retarding one if it had continued, was got rid of. And as with religion amongst us at that period, so it was also with letters. A fit prose was a necessity; but it was impossible that a fit prose should establish itself amongst us without some touch of frost to the imaginative life of the soul. The needful qualities for a fit prose are regularity, uniformity, precision, balance. The men of letters, whose destiny it may be to bring their nation to the attainment of a fit prose, must of necessity, whether they work in prose or in verse, give a predominating, an almost exclusive attention to the qualities of regularity, uniformity, precision, balance. But an almost exclusive attention to these qualities involves some repression and silencing of poetry.

We are to regard Dryden as the puissant and glorious founder, Pope as the splendid high priest, of our age of prose and reason, of our excellent and indispensable eighteenth century. For the purposes of their mission and destiny their poetry, like their prose, is admirable. Do you ask me whether Dryden's verse, take it almost where you will, is not good?

> A milk-white Hind, immortal and unchanged,
> Fed on the lawns and in the forest ranged.

I answer: Admirable for the purposes of the inaugurator of an age of prose and reason. Do you ask me whether Pope's verse, take it almost where you will, is not good?

To Hounslow Heath I point, and Banstead Down
Thence comes your mutton, and these chicks my own.

I answer: Admirable for the purposes of the high priest of an age of
prose and reason. But do you ask me whether such verse proceeds
from men with an adequate poetic criticism of life, from men whose
criticism of life has a high seriousness, or even, without that high
seriousness, has poetic largeness, freedom, insight, benignity? Do you
ask me whether the application of ideas to life in the verse of these men,
often a powerful application, no doubt, is a powerful *poetic* application?
Do you ask me whether the poetry of these men has either the matter or
the inseparable manner of such an adequate poetic criticism; whether
it has the accent of

Absent thee from felicity awhile . . .

or of

And what is else not to be overcome . . .

or of

O Martyr souded in virginitee!

I answer: It has not and cannot have them; it is the poetry of the
builders of an age of prose and reason. Though they may write in verse,
though they may in a certain sense be masters of the art of versification,
Dryden and Pope are not classics of our poetry, they are classics of our
prose.

Gray is our poetical classic of that literature and age; the position of
Gray is singular, and demands a word of notice here. He has not the
volume or the power of poets who, coming in times more favourable,
have attained to an independent criticism of life. But he lived with the
great poets, he lived, above all, with the Greeks, through perpetually
studying and enjoying them; and he caught their poetic point of view for
regarding life, caught their poetic manner. The point of view and the
manner are not self-sprung in him, he caught them of others; and he had
not the free and abundant use of them. But, whereas Addison and Pope
never had the use of them, Gray had the use of them at times. He is the
scantiest and frailest of classics in our poetry, but he is a classic.

And now, after Gray, we are met, as we draw toward the end of the
eighteenth century, we are met by the great name of Burns. We enter
now on times where the personal estimate of poets begins to be rife,

and where the real estimate of them is not reached without difficulty. But in spite of the disturbing pressures of personal partiality, of national partiality, let us try to reach a real estimate of the poetry of Burns.

By his English poetry Burns in general belongs to the eighteenth century, and has little importance for us.

> Mark ruffian Violence, distain'd with crimes,
> Rousing elate in these degenerate times;
> View unsuspecting Innocence a prey,
> As guileful Fraud points out the erring way;
> While subtle Litigation's pliant tongue
> The life-blood equal sucks of Right and Wrong!

Evidently this is not the real Burns, or his name and fame would have disappeared long ago. Nor is Clarinda's love-poet, Sylvander, the real Burns either. But he tells us himself: "These English songs gravel me to death. I have not the command of the language that I have of my native tongue. In fact, I think that my ideas are more barren in English than in Scotch. I have been at *Duncan Gray* to dress it in English, but all I can do is desperately stupid." We English turn naturally, in Burns, to the poems in our own language, because we can read them easily; but in those poems we have not the real Burns.

The real Burns is of course in his Scotch poems. Let us boldly say that of much of this poetry, a poetry dealing perpetually with Scotch drink, Scotch religion, and Scotch manners, a Scotchman's estimate is apt to be personal. A Scotchman is used to this world of Scotch drink, Scotch religion, and Scotch manners; he has a tenderness for it; he meets its poet half way. In this tender mood he reads pieces like the *Holy Fair* or *Halloween*. But this world of Scotch drink, Scotch religion, and Scotch manners is against a poet, not for him, when it is not a partial countryman who reads him; for in itself it is not a beautiful world, and no one can deny that it is of advantage to a poet to deal with a beautiful world. Burns's world of Scotch drink, Scotch religion, and Scotch manners is often a harsh, a sordid, a repulsive world: even the world of his *Cotter's Saturday Night* is not a beautiful world. No doubt a poet's criticism of life may have such truth and power that it triumphs over its world and delights us. Burns may triumph over his world, often he does triumph over his world, but let us observe how and where. Burns is the first case we have had where the bias of the personal estimate tends to mislead; let us look at him closely, he can bear it.

Many of his admirers will tell us that we have Burns, convivial, genuine, delightful, here—

> Leeze me on drink! it gies us mair
> Than either school or college;
> It kindles wit, it waukens lair,
> It pangs us fou o' knowledge.
> Be't whisky gill or penny wheep
> Or ony stronger potion,
> It never fails, on drinking deep,
> To kittle up our notion
>   By night or day.

There is a great deal of that sort of thing in Burns, and it is unsatisfactory, not because it is bacchanalian poetry, but because it has not that accent of sincerity which bacchanalian poetry, to do it justice, very often has. There is something in it of bravado, something which makes us feel that we have not the man speaking to us with his real voice; something, therefore, poetically unsound.

With still more confidence will his admirers tell us that we have the genuine Burns, the great poet, when his strain asserts the independence, equality, dignity, of men, as in the famous song *For a' that and a' that*—

> A prince can mak' a belted knight,
> A marquis, duke, and a' that;
> But an honest man's aboon his might,
> Guid faith he mauna fa' that!
> For a' that, and a' that,
>   Their dignities, and a' that,
>   The pith o' sense, and pride o' worth,
>   Are higher rank than a' that.

Here they find his grand genuine touches; and still more when his puissant genius, who so often set morality at defiance, falls moralising—

> The sacred lowe o' weel-placed love
> Luxuriantly indulge it;
> But never tempt th' illicit rove,
> Tho' naething should divulge it.
> I waive the quantum o' the sin,
> The hazard o' concealing,
> But och! it hardens a' within,
> And petrifies the feeling.

Or in a higher strain—

> Who made the heart, 'tis He alone
>> Decidedly can try us;
> He knows each chord, its various tone;
>> Each spring, its various bias.
> Then at the balance let's be mute,
>> We never can adjust it;
> What's *done* we partly may compute,
>> But know not what's resisted.

Or in a better strain yet, a strain, his admirers will say, unsurpassable—

> To make a happy fire-side clime
> To weans and wife,
> That's the true pathos and sublime
> Of human life.

There is criticism of life for you, the admirers of Burns will say to us; there is the application of ideas to life! There is, undoubtedly. The doctrine of the last-quoted lines coincides almost exactly with what was the aim and end, Xenophon tells us, of all the teaching of Socrates. And the application is a powerful one; made by a man of vigorous understanding, and (need I say?) a master of language.

But for supreme poetical success more is required than the powerful application of ideas to life; it must be an application under the conditions fixed by the laws of poetic truth and poetic beauty. Those laws fix as an essential condition, in the poet's treatment of such matters as are here in question, high seriousness;—the high seriousness which comes from absolute sincerity. The accent of high seriousness, born of absolute sincerity, is what gives to such verse as

In la sua volontade è nostra pace . . .

to such criticism of life as Dante's, its power. Is this accent felt in the passages which I have been quoting from Burns? Surely not; surely, if our sense is quick, we must perceive that we have not in those passages a voice from the very inmost soul of the genuine Burns; he is not speaking to us from these depths, he is more or less preaching. And the compensation for admiring such passages less, from missing the perfect poetic accent in them, will be that we shall admire more the poetry where that accent is found.

No; Burns, like Chaucer, comes short of the high seriousness of the great classics, and the virtue of matter and manner which goes with that high seriousness is wanting to his work. At moments he touches it in a profound and passionate melancholy, as in those four immortal lines taken by Byron as a motto for *The Bride of Abydos*, but which have in them a depth of poetic quality such as resides in no verse of Byron's own—

> Had we never loved sae kindly,
> Had we never loved sae blindly,
> Never met, or never parted,
> We had ne'er been broken-hearted.

But a whole poem of that quality Burns cannot make; the rest, in the *Farewell to Nancy*, is verbiage.

We arrive best at the real estimate of Burns, I think, by conceiving his work as having truth of matter and truth of manner, but not the accent or the poetic virtue of the highest masters. His genuine criticism of life, when the sheer poet in him speaks, is ironic; it is not—

> Thou Power Supreme, whose mighty scheme
> These woes of mine fulfil,
> Here firm I rest, they must be best
> Because they are Thy will!

It is far rather: *Whistle owre the lave o't!* Yet we may say of him as of Chaucer, that of life and the world, as they come before him, his view is large, free, shrewd, benignant,—truly poetic therefore; and his manner of rendering what he sees is to match. But we must note, at the same time, his great difference from Chaucer. The freedom of Chaucer is heightened, in Burns, by a fiery, reckless energy; the benignity of Chaucer deepens, in Burns, into an overwhelming sense of the pathos of things;—of the pathos of human nature, the pathos, also, of non-human nature. Instead of the fluidity of Chaucer's manner, the manner of Burns has spring, boundless swiftness. Burns is by far the greater force, though he has perhaps less charm. The world of Chaucer is fairer, richer, more significant than that of Burns; but when the largeness and freedom of Burns get full sweep, as in *Tam o' Shanter*, or still more in that puissant and splendid production, *The Jolly Beggars*, his world may be what it will, his poetic genius triumphs over it. In the world of *The Jolly Beggars* there is more than hideousness and squalor, there is bestiality; yet the piece is a superb poetic success. It has a breadth, truth, and power which make the famous scene in Auerbach's Cellar, of Goethe's *Faust*, seem artificial and tame beside it, and which are only matched by Shakespeare and Aristophanes.

Here, where his largeness and freedom serve him so admirably, and also in those poems and songs where to shrewdness he adds infinite archness and wit, and to benignity infinite pathos, where his manner is flawless, and a perfect poetic whole is the result,—in things like the address to the mouse whose home he had ruined, in things like *Duncan Gray*, *Tam Glen*, *Whistle and I'll come to you my Lad*, *Auld Lang Syne* (this list might be made much longer),—here we have the genuine Burns, of whom the real estimate must be high indeed. Not a classic, nor with the excellent *spoudaiotēs* of the great classics, nor with a verse rising to a criticism of life and a virtue like theirs; but a poet with thorough truth of substance and an answering truth of style, giving us a poetry sound to the core. We all of us have a leaning towards the pathetic, and may be inclined perhaps to prize Burns most for his touches of piercing, sometimes almost intolerable, pathos; for verse like—

> We twa hae paidl'd i' the burn
> From mornin' sun till dine;
> But seas between us braid hae roar'd
> Sin auld lang syne . . .

where he is as lovely as he is sound. But perhaps it is by the perfection of soundness of his lighter and archer masterpieces that he is poetically most wholesome for us. For the votary misled by a personal estimate of Shelley, as so many of us have been, are, and will be,—of that beautiful spirit building his many-coloured haze of words and images

> pinnacled dim in the intense inane—

no contact can be wholesomer than the contact with Burns at his archest and soundest. Side by side with the

> On the brink of the night and the morning
> My coursers are wont to respire,
> But the Earth has just whispered a warning
> That their flight must be swifter than fire . . .

of *Prometheus Unbound*, how salutary, how very salutary, to place this from *Tam Glen*—

> My minnie does constantly deave me
> And bids me beware o' young men;
> They flatter, she says, to deceive me;
> But wha can think sae o' Tam Glen?

But we enter on burning ground as we approach the poetry of times so near to us—poetry like that of Byron, Shelley, and Wordsworth—of which the estimates are so often not only personal, but personal with passion. For my purpose, it is enough to have taken the single case of Burns, the first poet we come to of whose work the estimate formed is evidently apt to be personal, and to have suggested how we may proceed, using the poetry of the great classics as a sort of touchstone, to correct this estimate, as we had previously corrected by the same means the historic estimate where we met with it. A collection like the present, with its succession of celebrated names and celebrated poems, offers a good opportunity to us for resolutely endeavouring to make our estimates of poetry real. I have sought to point out a method which will help us in making them so, and to exhibit it in use so far as to put any one who likes in a way of applying it for himself.

At any rate the end to which the method and the estimate are designed to lead, and from leading to which, if they do lead to it, they get their whole value,—the benefit of being able clearly to feel and deeply to enjoy the best, the truly classic, in poetry,—is an end, let me say it once more at parting, of supreme importance. We are often told that an era is opening in which we are to see multitudes of a common sort of readers, and masses of a common sort of literature; that such readers do not want and could not relish anything better than such literature, and that to provide it is becoming a vast and profitable industry. Even if good literature entirely lost currency with the world, it would still be abundantly worth while to continue to enjoy it by oneself. But it never will lose currency with the world, in spite of momentary appearances; it never will lose supremacy. Currency and supremacy are insured to it, not indeed by the world's deliberate and conscious choice, but by something far deeper,—by the instinct of self-preservation in humanity.

8. JAMES

"The Art of Fiction"

Henry James (1843–1916) was born in New York City. His older brother, William, became famous as a philosopher and psychologist. After being educated in various places in Europe and at the Harvard Law School, Henry James began to write. He left the United States and settled permanently in Europe in 1875. In 1915, shortly before his death, James became a naturalized English subject.

His first attempts at fiction were in the field of short stories and novellas—genres in which he excelled throughout his life. Among the many novels he wrote are *The American* (1877), *Daisy Miller* (1879), *The Bostonians* (1886), *The Ambassadors* (1903), and *The Golden Bowl* (1905). Besides the critical essay "The Art of Fiction" (1888), James also wrote critical prefaces to his novels when they were reissued in the New York edition. Thus all his life James was interested in both the practice and the theory of the novel, and helped make both respectable.

"The Art of Fiction," reproduced here in its entirety, was really the first thoughtful and intelligent discussion of the genre in England. It was first published in *Longman's Magazine* in 1884 and republished in 1888 in James' *Partial Portraits*. Until James the novel was not considered an appropriate genre for critical discussion. Indeed, as James remarks in the beginning of his essay, so far there has been "a comfortable good-humored feeling abroad that a novel is a novel, as a pudding is a pudding, and that our only business with it could be to swallow it." On the continent Turgenev, Flaubert, and De Maupassant —all of whom James met and whose influence he felt—had already begun to evolve theories about the novel. In England, James, in turn, influenced the novelists Conrad and Ford.

In his witty, informal essay James touches upon a number of

important issues—issues that are still debated today. First he attacks the notion that a novel cannot be serious because it is "make-believe." In refuting this he echoes Aristotle's notions of art by saying, "The only reason for the existence of a novel is that it does attempt to represent life" and "a novel is in its broadest definition a personal, a direct impression of life." He goes against tradition, however, by asserting that the novel is close to history but then joins tradition again with his concern with truth: both the historian and the novelist look for truth.

After the definition of the novel James' concern is with what a novel should be like, what the artist should do, and what the reader's reaction to a novel is. The main obligation a novel has is to be interesting. Then the notion that a novel should have unity and coherence is expressed in the current scientific analogy already familiar from Taine: "A novel is a living thing, all one and continuous, like any other organism, and in proportion as it lives will it be found, I think, that in each of the parts there is something of each of the other parts."

As far as the artist is concerned, James' first premise is that "no good novel will ever proceed from a superficial mind. . . ." Therefore in a statement reminiscent of T. S. Eliot, James advises the novelist: "Try to be one of the people on whom nothing is lost!" He also adds that the artist should be sincere. However, he opposes giving specific rules because "humanity is immense, and reality has a myriad forms. . . ."

Thus James continues the nineteenth-century concern with the artist. He is not, however, interested in the artist's personality, and he does not see the artist as some mad, inspired prophet erupting spontaneously. To James, a writer is really a highly intelligent workman who laboriously collects impressions and facts; indeed, "art" can be taken as a synonym for "skill" and "craft." He stands firmly with later poets, such as Auden and Yeats, who insist on some of the rational bases of literature and implore the artist to strive for completeness and perfection. If James had read *De Vulgari Eloquentia*, he probably would have agreed with much of what Dante says concerning "genius."

James is also concerned with the reader's reaction: specifically with the troublesome matter of value judgments that we already met in Arnold's essay and will again meet in contemporary criticism. James' observation on our reaction is as tolerant as it is shrewd: "Nothing, of course, will ever take the place of the good old fashion of 'liking' a work of art or not liking it: the most improved criticism will not abolish that primitive, that ultimate test." Consequently, he states that the only distinction worth making is between good and bad novels; this distinction obviously depends on liking or not liking a work.

The tolerant mood of the essay is continued to the end when James asserts the greatness of the genre: he advises the student or the beginning novelist "of the magnificence of the form that is open to him, which offers to sight so few restrictions and such innumerable opportunities. . . . Remember that your first duty is to be as complete as possible to make as perfect a work. Be generous and delicate and pursue the prize." Sir Philip Sidney, the eloquent and passionate advocate of poetry, could not have expressed this more movingly.

I should not have fixed so comprehensive a title to these few remarks, necessarily wanting in any completeness upon a subject the full consideration of which would carry us far, did I not seem to discover a pretext for my temerity in the interesting pamphlet lately published under this name by Mr. Walter Besant. Mr. Besant's lecture at the Royal Institution—the original form of his pamphlet—appears to indicate that many persons are interested in the art of fiction, and are not indifferent to such remarks as those who practice it may attempt to make about it. I am therefore anxious not to lose the benefit of this favorable association, and to edge in a few words under cover of the attention which Mr. Besant is sure to have excited. There is something very encouraging in his having put into form certain of his ideas on the mystery of story-telling.

It is a proof of life and curiosity—curiosity on the part of the brotherhood of novelists as well as on the part of their readers. Only a short time ago it might have been supposed that the English novel was not what the French call *discutable*. It had no air of having a theory, a conviction, a consciousness of itself behind it—of being the expression of an artistic faith, the result of choice and comparison. I do not say it was necessarily the worse for that: it would take much more courage than I possess to intimate that the form of the novel as Dickens and Thackeray (for instance) saw it has any taint of incompleteness. It was, however, *naïf* (if I may help myself out with another French word); and evidently if it be destined to suffer in any way for having lost its *naïveté* it has now an idea of making sure of the corresponding advantages. During the period I have alluded to there was a comfortable good-humored feeling abroad that a novel is a novel, as a pudding is a pudding, and that our only business with it could be to swallow it. But within a year or two, for some reason or other, there have been signs of returning animation—the era of discussion would appear to have been to a certain extent opened. Art lives upon discussion, upon experiment, upon curiosity, upon variety of attempt, upon the exchange of views and the comparison of standpoints; and there is a presumption that those times when no one has anything particular to say about it, and has no reason to give for practice or preference, though they may be times of honor, are not times of development—are times, possibly, even a little of dullness. The successful application of any art is a delightful spectacle, but the theory too is interesting; and though there is a great deal of the latter without the former I suspect there has never been a genuine success that has not had a latent core of conviction. Discussion, suggestion, formulation, these things are fertilizing when they are frank and sincere. Mr. Besant has set an excellent example in saying what he thinks, for his part, about the way in which fiction should be written, as well as about the way in which it should be published; for his view of the "art," carried on into an appendix covers that too. Other laborers in the same field will doubtless take up the argument, they will give it the light of their experience, and the effect will surely be to make our interest in the novel a little more what it had for some time threatened to fail to be—a serious, active, inquiring interest, under protection of which this delightful study may, in movements of confidence, venture to say a little more what it thinks of itself.

It must take itself seriously for the public to take it so. The old superstition about fiction being "wicked" has doubtless died out in England; but the spirit of it lingers in a certain oblique regard directed toward any story which does not more or less admit that it is only a joke. Even the most jocular novel feels in some degree the weight of the proscription that was formerly directed against literary levity: the jocularity does not always succeed in passing for orthodoxy. It is still expected, though perhaps people are ashamed to say it, that a production which is after all only a "make-believe" (for what else is a "story"?) shall be in some degree apologetic—shall renounce the pretension of attempting really to represent life. This, of course, any sensible, wide-awake story declines to do, for it quickly perceives that the tolerance granted to it on such a condition is only an attempt to stifle it disguised in the form of generosity. The old evangelical hostility to the novel, which was as explicit as it was narrow, and which regarded it as little less favorable to our immortal part than a stage-play, was in reality far less insulting. The only reason for the existence of a novel is that it does attempt to represent life. When it relinquishes this attempt, the same attempt that we see on the canvas of the painter, it will have arrived at a very strange pass. It is not expected of the picture that it will make itself humble in order to be forgiven; and the analogy between the art of the painter and the art of the novelist is, so far as I am able to see, complete. Their inspiration is the same, their process (allowing for the different quality of the vehicle) is the same, their success is the same. They may learn from each other, they may explain and sustain each other. Their cause is the same, and the honor of one is the honor of another. The Mahometans think a picture an unholy thing, but it is a long time since any Christian did, and it is therefore the more odd that in the Christian mind the traces (dissimulated though they may be) of a suspicion of the sister art should linger to this day. The only effectual way to lay it to rest is to emphasize the analogy to which I just alluded— to insist on the fact that as the picture is reality, so the novel is history. That is the only general description (which does it justice) that we may give of the novel. But history also is allowed to represent life; it is not, any more than painting, expected to apologize. The subject-matter of fiction is stored up likewise in documents and records, and if it will not give itself away, as they say in California, it must speak with assurance, with the tone of the historian. Certain accomplished novelists have a habit of giving themselves away which must often bring tears to the eyes of people who take their fiction seriously. I was lately struck, in reading over many pages of Anthony Trollope, with his want of discretion in this particular. In a digression, a parenthesis or an aside, he concedes to the reader that he and this trusting friend are only "making believe." He admits that the events he narrates have not really happened, and that he can give his narrative any turn the reader may like best. Such a betrayal of a sacred office seems to me, I confess, a terrible crime; it is what I mean by the attitude of apology, and it shocks me every whit as much in Trollope as it would have shocked me in Gibbon or Macaulay. It implies that the novelist is less occupied in looking for the truth (the truth, of course I mean, that he assumes, the premises that we must grant him, whatever they may be) than the historian, and in doing so it deprives him at a stroke of all his standing-room. To represent and illustrate the past, the actions of men, is the task of either writer, and the only difference that I can see is, in proportion as he succeeds, to the honor of the novelist, consisting as it does in his having more difficulty in collecting his evidence, which is so far from being purely literary. It seems to me to give him a great character, that fact that he has at once so much in common with the philosopher and the painter; this double analogy is a magnificent heritage.

It is of all this evidently that Mr. Besant is full when he insists upon the fact that fiction is one of the *fine* arts, deserving in its turn of all the honors and emoluments that have hitherto been reserved for the successful profession of music, poetry, painting, architecture. It is impossible to insist too much on so important a truth, and the place that Mr. Besant demands for the work of the novelist may be represented, a trifle less abstractly, by saying that he demands not only that it shall be reputed artistic, but that it shall be reputed very artistic indeed. It is excellent that he should have struck this note, for his doing so indicates that there was need of it, that his proposition may be to many people a novelty. One rubs one's eyes at the thought; but the rest of Mr. Besant's essay confirms the revelation. I suspect in truth that it would be possible to confirm it still further, and that one would not be far wrong in saying that in addition to the people to whom it has never occurred that a novel ought to be artistic, there are a great many others who, if this principle were urged upon them, would be filled with an indefinable mistrust. They would find it difficult to explain their repugnance, but it would operate strongly to put them on their guard. "Art," in our Protestant communities, where so many things have got so strangely twisted about, is supposed in certain circles to have some vague injurious effect upon those who make it an important consideration, who let it weight in the balance. It is assumed to be opposed in some mysterious manner to morality, to amusement, to instruction. When it is embodied in the work of the painter (the sculptor is another affair!) you know what it is: it stands there before you, in the honesty of pink and green and a gilt frame; you can see the worst of it at a glance, and you can be on your guard. But when it is introduced into literature it becomes more insidious—there is danger of its hurting you before you know it. Literature should be either instructive or amusing, and there is in many minds an impression that these artistic preoccupations, the search for form, contribute to neither end, interfere indeed with both. They are too frivolous to be edifying, and too serious to be diverting; and they are moreover priggish and paradoxical and superfluous. That, I think, represents the manner in which the latent thought of many people who read novels as an exercise in skipping would explain itself if it were to become articulate. They would argue, of course, that a novel ought to be "good," but they would interpret this term in a fashion of their own, which indeed would vary considerably from one critic to another. One would say that being good means representing virtuous and aspiring characters placed in prominent positions; another would say that it depends on a "happy ending," on a distribution at the last of prizes, pensions, husbands, wives, babies, millions, appended paragraphs, and cheerful remarks. Another still would say that it means being full of incident and movement, so that we shall wish to jump ahead, to see who was the mysterious stranger, and if the stolen will was ever found, and shall not be distracted from this pleasure by any tiresome analysis or "description." But they would all agree that the "artistic" idea would spoil some of their fun. One would hold it accountable for all the description, another would see it revealed in the absence of sympathy. Its hostility to a happy ending would be evident, and it might even in some cases render any ending at all impossible. The "ending" of a novel is, for many persons, like that of a good dinner, a course of dessert and ices, and the artist in fiction is regarded as a sort of meddlesome doctor who forbids agreeable after-tastes. It is therefore true that this conception of Mr. Besant's of the novel as a superior form encounters not only a negative but a positive indifference. It matters little that as a work of art it should really be as little or as much of its essence to supply happy endings, sympathetic characters, and an objective tone, as if it were a work of mechanics: the association of ideas, however incongruous, might easily be too much for it if an eloquent voice were not sometimes raised to call attention to the fact that it is at once as free and as serious a branch of literature as any other.

Certainly this might sometimes be doubted in presence of the enormous number of works of fiction that appeal to the credulity of our generation, for it might easily seem that there could be no great character in a commodity so quickly and easily produced. It must be admitted that good novels are much compromised by bad ones, and that the field at large suffers discredit from overcrowding. I think, however, that this injury is only superficial, and that the superabundance of written fiction proves nothing against the principle itself. It has been vulgarized, like all other kinds of literature, like everything else today, and it has proved more than some kinds accessible to vulgarization. But there is as much difference as there ever was between a good novel and a bad one: the bad is swept with all the daubed canvases and spoiled marble into some unvisited limbo, or infinite rubbish-yard beneath the back-windows of the world, and the good subsists and emits its light and stimulates our desire for perfection. As I shall take the liberty of making but a single criticism of Mr. Besant, whose tone is so full of love of his art, I may as well have done with it at once. He seems to me to mistake, in attempting to say so definitely beforehand, what sort of an affair the good novel will be. To indicate the danger of such an error as that has been the purpose of these few pages; to suggest that certain traditions on the subject, applied *a priori*, have already had much to answer for, and that the good health of an art which undertakes so immediately to reproduce life must demand that it be perfectly free. It lives upon exercise, and the very meaning of exercise is freedom. The only obligation to which in advance we may hold a novel, without incurring the accusation of being arbitrary, is that it be interesting. That general responsibility rests upon it, but it is the only one I can think of. The ways in which it is at liberty to accomplish this result (of interesting us) strike me as innumerable, and such as can only suffer from being marked out or fenced in by prescription. They are as various as the temperament of man, and they are successful in proportion as they reveal a particular mind, different from others. A novel is in its broadest definition a personal, a direct impression of life: that, to begin with, constitutes its value, which is greater or less according to the intensity of the impression. But there will be no intensity at all, and therefore no value, unless there is freedom to feel and say. The tracing of a line to be followed, of a tone to be taken, of a form to be filled out, is a limitation of that freedom and a suppression of the very thing that we are most curious about. The form, it seems to me, is to be appreciated after the fact: then the author's choice has been made, his standard has been indicated; then we can follow lines and directions and compare tones and resemblances. Then in a word we can enjoy one of the most charming of pleasures, we can estimate quality, we can apply the test of execution. The execution belongs to the author alone; it is what is most personal to him, and we measure him by that. The advantage, the luxury, as well as the torment and responsibility of the novelist, is that there is no limit to what he may attempt as an executant—no limit to his possible experiments, efforts, discoveries, successes. Here it is especially that he works, step by step, like his brother of the brush, of whom we may always say that he has painted his picture in a manner best known to himself. His manner is his secret, not necessarily a jealous one. He cannot disclose it as a general thing if he would; he would be at a loss to teach it to others. I say this with a due recollection of having insisted on the community of method of the artist who paints a picture and the artist who writes a novel. The painter *is* able to teach the rudiments of his practice, and it is possible, from the study of good work (granted the aptitude), both to learn how to paint and to learn how to write. Yet it remains true, without injury to the *rapprochment*, that the literary artist would be obliged to say to his pupil much more than the other, "Ah, well, you must do it as you can!" It is a question of degree, a matter of delicacy. If there are exact sciences, there are also exact arts, and the grammar of painting is so much more definite that it makes the difference.

I ought to add, however, that if Mr. Besant says at the beginning of his essay that the "laws of fiction may be laid down and taught with as much precision and exactness as the laws of harmony, perspective, and proportion" he mitigates what might appear to be an extravagance by applying his remark to "general" laws, and by expressing most of these rules in a manner with which it would certainly be unaccommodating to disagree. That the novelist must write from his experience, that his "characters must be real and such as might be met with in actual life"; that "a young lady brought up in a quiet country village should avoid descriptions of garrison life," and "a writer whose friends and personal experiences belong to the lower middle-class should carefully avoid introducing his characters into society"; that one should enter one's notes in a common-place book; that one's figures should be clear in outline; that making them clear by some trick of speech or of carriage is a bad method, and "describing them at length" is a worse one; that English Fiction should have a "conscious moral purpose"; that "it is almost impossible to estimate too highly the value of careful workmanship—that is, of style"; that "the most important point of all is the story," that "the story is everything": these are principles with most of which it is surely impossible not to sympathize. That remark about the lower middle-class writer and his knowing his place is perhaps rather chilling; but for the rest I should find it difficult to dissent from any one of these recommendations. At the same time, I should find it difficult positively to assent to them, with the exception, perhaps, of the injunction as to entering one's notes in a common-place book. They scarcely seem to me to have the quality that Mr. Besant attributes to the rules of the novelist—the "precision and exactness" of "the laws of harmony, perspective, and proportion." They are suggestive, they are even inspiring, but they are not exact, though they are doubtless as much so as the case admits of: which is a proof of that liberty of interpretation for which I just contended. For the value of these different injunctions— so beautiful and so vague—is wholly in the meaning one attaches to them. The characters, the situation, which strike one as real will be those that touch and interest one most, but the measure of reality is very difficult to fix. The reality of Don Quixote or of Mr. Micawber is a very delicate shade; it is a reality so colored by the author's vision that, vivid as it may be, one would hesitate to propose it as a model: one would expose one's self to some very embarrassing questions on the part of a pupil. It goes without saying that you will not write a good novel unless you possess the sense of reality; but it will be difficult to give you a recipe for calling that sense into being. Humanity is immense, and reality has a myriad forms; the most one can affirm is that some of the flowers of fiction have the odor of it, and others have not; as for telling you in advance how your nosegay should be composed, that is another affair. It is equally excellent and inconclusive to say that one must write from experience; to our suppositious aspirant such a declaration might savor of mockery. What kind of experience is in- tended, and where does it begin and end? Experience is never limited, and it is never complete; it is an immense sensibility, a kind of huge spider-web of the finest silken threads suspended in the chamber of consciousness, and catching every air-borne particle in its tissue. It is the very atmosphere of the mind; and when the mind is imaginative—much more when it happens to be that of a man of genius—it takes to itself the faintest hints of life, it converts the very pulses of the air into revelations. The young lady living in a village has only to be a damsel upon whom nothing is lost to make it quite unfair (as it seems to me) to declare to her that she shall have nothing to say about the military. Greater miracles have been seen than that, imagination assisting, she should speak the truth about some of these gentlemen. I remember an English novelist, a woman of genius, telling me that she was much commended for the impression she had managed to give in one of her tales of the nature and way of life of the French Protestant youth. She had been asked where she learned so much about this recondite being, she had been congratulated on her peculiar opportunities. These opportunities consisted in her having once, in Paris, as she ascended a staircase, passed an open door where, in the household of a *pasteur*, some of the young Protestants were seated at table round a finished meal. The glimpse made a picture; it lasted only a moment, but that moment was experience. She had got her direct personal impression, and she turned out her type. She knew what youth was, and what Protestantism; she also had the advantage of having seen what it was to be French, so that she converted these ideas into a concrete image and produced a reality. Above all, however, she was blessed with the faculty which when you give it an inch takes an ell, and which for the artist is a much greater source of strength than any accident of residence or of place in the social scale. The power to guess the unseen from the seen, to trace the implication of things, to judge the whole piece by the pattern, the condition of feeling life in general so completely that you are well on your way to knowing any particular corner of it—this cluster of gifts may almost be said to constitute experience, and they occur in country and in town, and in the most differing stages of education. If experience consists of impressions, it may be said that impressions *are* experience, just as (have we not seen it?) they are the very air we breathe. Therefore, if I should certainly say to a novice, "Write from experience and from experience only," I should feel that this was rather a tantalizing monition if I were not careful immediately to add, "Try to be one of the people on whom nothing is lost!"

I am far from intending by this to minimize the importance of exactness—of truth of detail. One can speak best from one's own taste, and I may therefore venture to say that the air of reality (solidity of specification) seems to me to be the supreme virtue of a novel—the merit on which all its other merits (including that conscious moral purpose of which Mr. Besant speaks) helplessly and submissively depend. If it be not there they are all as nothing, and if these be there, they owe their effect to the success with which the author has produced the illusion of life. The cultivation of this success, the study of this exquisite process, form, to my taste, the beginning and the end of the art of the novelist. They are his inspiration, his despair, his reward, his torment, his delight. It is here in very truth that he competes with life; it is here that he competes with his brother the painter in *his* attempts to render the look of things, the look that conveys their meaning, to catch the color, the relief, the expression, the surface, the substance of the human spectacle. It is in regard to this that Mr. Besant is well inspired when he bids him take notes. He cannot possibly take too many, he cannot possibly take enough. All life solicits him, and to "render" the simplest surface, to produce the most momentary illusion, is a very complicated business.

His case would be easier, and the rule would be more exact, if Mr. Besant had been able to tell him what notes to take. But this, I fear, he can never learn in any manual; it is the business of his life. He has to take a great many in order to select a few, he has to work them up as he can, and even the guides and philosophers who might have most to say to him must leave him alone when it comes to the application of precepts, as we leave the painter in communion with his palette. That his characters "must be clear in outline" as Mr. Besant says—he feels that down to his boots; but how he shall make them so is a secret between his good angel and himself. It would be absurdly simple if he could be taught that a great deal of "description" would make them so, or that on the contrary the absence of description and the cultivation of dialogue, or the absence of dialogue and the multiplication of "incident," would rescue him from his difficulties. Nothing, for instance, is more possible than that he be of a turn of mind for which this odd, literal opposition of description and dialogue, incident and description, has little meaning and light. People often talk of these things as if they had a kind of internecine distinctness, instead of melting into each other at every breath, and being intimately associated parts of one general effort existing in a series of blocks, nor conceive, in any novel worth discussing at all, of a passage of description that is not in its intention narrative, a passage of dialogue that is not in its intention descriptive, a touch of truth of any sort that does not partake of the nature of incident, or an incident that derives its interest from any other source than the general and only source of the success of a work of art—that of being illustrative. A novel is a living thing, all one and continuous, like any other organism, and in proportion as it lives will it be found, I think, that in each of the parts there is something of each of the other parts. The critic who over the close texture of a finished work shall pretend to trace a geography of items will mark some frontiers as artificial, I fear, as any that have been known to history. There is an old-fashioned distinction between the novel of character and the novel of incident which must have cost many a smile to the intending fabulist who was keen about his work. It appears to me as little to the point as the equally celebrated distinction between the novel and the romance— to answer as little to any reality. There are bad novels and good novels, as there are bad pictures and good pictures; but that is the only distinction in which I see any meaning, and I can as little imagine speaking of a novel of character as I can imagine speaking of a picture of character.

When one says picture one says of character, when one says novel one says of incident, and the terms may be transposed at will. What is character but the determination of incident? What is incident but the illustration of character? What is either a picture or a novel that is *not* of character? What else do we seek in it and find in it? It is an incident for a woman to stand up with her hand resting on a table and look at you in a certain way; or if it be not an incident I think it will be hard to say what it is. At the same time it is an expression of character. If you say you don't see it (character in *that—allons donc!*), this is exactly what the artist who has reasons of his own for thinking he *does* see it undertakes to show you. When a young man makes up his mind that he has not faith enough after all to enter the Church as he intended, that is an incident, though you may not hurry to the end of the chapter to see whether perhaps he doesn't change once more. I do not say that these are extraordinary or startling incidents. I do not pretend to estimate the degree of interest proceeding from them, for this will depend upon the skill of the painter. It sound almost puerile to say that some incidents are intrinsically much more important than others, and I need not take this precaution after having professed my sympathy for the major ones in remarking that the only classification of the novel that I can understand is into that which has life and that which has it not.

The novel and the romance, the novel of incident and that of character— these clumsy separations appear to me to have been made by critics and readers for their own convenience, and to help them out of some of their occasional predicaments, but to have little reality or interest for the producer, from whose point of view it is of course that we are attempting to consider the art of fiction. The case is the same with another shadowy category which Mr. Besant apparently is disposed to set up—that of the "modern English novel"; unless indeed it be that in this matter he has fallen into an accidental confusion of standpoints. It is not quite clear whether he intends the remarks in which he alludes to it to be didactic or historical. It is as difficult to suppose a person intending to write a modern English as to suppose him writing an ancient English novel: that is a label which begs the question. One writes the novel, one paints the picture, of one's language and of one's time, and calling it modern English will not, alas! make the difficult task any easier. No more, unfortunately, will calling this or that work of one's fellow-artist a romance—unless it be, of course, simply for the pleasantness of the thing, as for instance when Hawthorne gave this heading to his story of

Blithedale. The French, who have brought the theory of fiction to remarkable completeness, have but one name for the novel, and have not attempted smaller things in it, that I can see, for that. I can think of no obligation to which the "romancer" would not be held equally with the novelist; the standard of execution is equally high for each. Of course it is of execution that we are talking—that being the only point of a novel that is open to contention. This is perhaps too often lost sight of, only to produce interminable confusions and cross-purposes. We must grant the artist his subject, his idea, his *donnée:* our criticism is applied only to what he makes of it. Naturally I do not mean that we are bound to like it or find it interesting: in case we do not our course is perfectly simple—to let it alone. We may believe that of a certain idea even the most sincere novelist can make nothing at all, and the event may perfectly justify our belief; but the failure will have been a failure to execute, and it is in the execution that the fatal weakness is recorded. If we pretend to respect the artist at all, we must allow him his freedom of choice, in the face, in particular cases, of innumerable presumptions that the choice will not fructify. Art derives a considerable part of its beneficial exercise from flying in the face of presumptions, and some of the most interesting experiments of which it is capable are hidden in the bosom of common things. Gustave Flaubert has written a story about the devotion of a servant-girl to a parrot, and the production, highly finished as it is, cannot on the whole be called a success. We are perfectly free to find it flat, but I think it might have been interesting; and I, for my part, am extremely glad he should have written it; it is a contribution to our knowledge of what can be done—or what cannot. Ivan Turgénieff has written a tale about a deaf and dumb serf and a lap-dog, and the thing is touching, loving, a little masterpiece. He struck the note of life where Gustave Flaubert missed it—he flew in the face of a presumption and achieved a victory.

Nothing, of course, will ever take the place of the good old fashion of "liking" a work of art or not liking it: the most improved criticism will not abolish that primitive, that ultimate test. I mention this to guard myself from the accusation of intimating that the idea, the subject, of a novel or a picture, does not matter. It matters, to my sense, in the highest degree, and if I might put up a prayer it would be that artists should select none but the richest. Some, as I have already hastened to admit, are much more remunerative than others, and it would be a world happily arranged in which persons intending to treat them should be exempt from confusions and mistakes. This fortunate condition will arrive only, I fear, on the same day that critics become purged from error. Meanwhile, I repeat, we do not judge the artist with fairness unless we say to him, "Oh, I grant you your starting-point, because if I did not I should seem to prescribe to you, and heaven forbid I should take that responsibility. If I pretend to tell you what you must not take, you will call upon me to tell you then what you must take; in which case I shall be prettily caught. Moreover, it isn't till I have accepted your data that I can begin to measure you. I have the standard, the pitch; I have no right to tamper with your flute and then criticize your music. Of course I may not care for your idea at all; I may think it silly or stale, or unclean; in which case I wash my hands of you altogether. I may content myself with believing that you will not have succeeded in being interesting, but I shall, of course, not attempt to demonstrate it, and you will be as indifferent to me as I am to you. I needn't remind you that there are all sorts of tastes: who can know it better? Some people, for excellent reasons, don't like to read about carpenters; other, for reasons even better, don't like to read about courtesans. Many object to Americans. Other (I believe they are mainly editors and publishers) won't look at Italians. Some readers don't like quiet subjects; others don't like bustling ones. Some enjoy a complete illusion, others the consciousness of large concessions. They choose their novels accordingly, and if they don't care about your idea they won't, *a fortiori*, care about your treatment."

So that it comes back very quickly, as I have said, to the liking: in spite of M. Zola, who reasons less powerfully than he represents, and who will not reconcile himself to this absoluteness of taste, thinking that there are certain things that people ought to like, and that they can be made to like. I am quite at a loss to imagine anything (at any rate in this matter of fiction) that people *ought* to like or to dislike. Selection will be sure to take care of itself, for it has a constant motive behind it. That motive is simply experience. As people feel life, so they will feel the art that is most closely related to it. This closeness of relation is what we should never forget in talking of the effort of the novel. Many people speak of it as a factitious, artificial form, a product of ingenuity, the business of which it is to alter and arrange the things that surround us, to translate them into conventional, traditional moulds. This, however, is a view of the matter which carries us but a very short way, condemns the art to an eternal repetition of a few familiar *clichés*, cuts short its development, and leads us straight up to a dead wall. Catching the very note and trick, the strange irregular rhythm of life, that is the attempt whose strenuous force keeps Fiction upon her feet. In proportion as in what she offers us we see life *without* rearrangement do we feel that we are touching the truth; in proportion as we see it *with* rearrangement do we feel that we are being put off with a substitute, a compromise and convention. It is not uncommon to hear an extraordinary assurance of remark in regard to this matter of rearranging, which is often spoken of as if it were the last word of art. Mr. Besant seems to me in danger of falling into the great error with his rather unguarded talk about "selection." Art is essentially selection, but it is a selection whose main care is to be typical, to be inclusive. For many people art means rose-colored window-panes and selection means picking a bouquet for Mrs. Grundy. They will tell you glibly that artistic considerations have nothing to do with the disagreeable, with the ugly; they will rattle off shallow commonplaces about the province of art and the limits of art till you are moved to some wonder in return as to the province and the limits of ignorance. It appears to me that no one can ever have made a seriously artistic attempt without becoming conscious of an immense increase—a kind of revelation—of freedom. One perceives in that case—by the light of a heavenly ray—that the province of art is all life, all feeling, all observation, all vision. As Mr. Besant so justly intimates, it is all experience. That is a sufficient answer to those who maintain that it must not touch the sad things of life, who stick into its divine unconscious bosom little prohibitory inscriptions on the end of sticks, such as we see in public gardens—"It is forbidden to walk on the grass; it is forbidden to touch the flowers; it is not allowed to introduce dogs or to remain after dark; it is requested to keep to the right." The young aspirant in the line of fiction whom we continue to imagine will do nothing without taste, for in that case his freedom would be of little use to him; but the first advantage of his taste will be to reveal to him the absurdity of the little sticks and tickets. If he have taste, I must add, of course he will have ingenuity, and my disrespectful reference to that quality just now was not meant to imply that it is useless in fiction. But it is only a secondary aid; the first is a capacity for receiving straight impressions.

Mr. Besant has some remarks on the question of "the story" which I shall not attempt to criticize, though they seem to me to contain a singular ambiguity, because I do not think I understand them. I cannot see what is meant by talking as if there were a part of a novel which is the story and part of it which for mystical reasons is not—unless indeed the distinction be made in a sense in which it is difficult to suppose that any one should attempt to convey anything. "The story," if it represents anything, represents the subject, the idea, the *donnée* of the novel; and there is surely no "school"—Mr. Besant speaks of a school—which urges that a novel should be all treatment and no subject. There must assuredly be something to treat; every school is intimately conscious of that. This sense of the story being the idea, the starting-point, of the novel, is the only one that I see in which it can be spoken of as something different from its organic whole; and since in proportion as the work is successful the idea permeates and penetrates it, informs and animates it, so that every word and every punctuation-point contribute directly to the expression, in that proportion do we lose our sense of the story being a blade which may be drawn more or less out of its sheath. The story and the novel, the idea and the form, are the needle and thread, and I never heard of a guild of tailors who recommended the use of the thread without the needle, or the needle without the thread. Mr. Besant is not the only critic who may be observed to have spoken as if there were certain things in life which constitute stories, and certain others which do not. I find the same odd implication in an entertaining article in the *Pall Mall Gazette*, devoted, as it happens, to Mr. Besant's lecture. "The story is the thing!" says this graceful writer, as if with a tone of opposition to some other idea. I should think it was, as every painter who, as the time for "sending in" his picture looms in the distance, finds himself still in quest of a subject—as every belated artist not fixed about his theme will heartily agree. There are some subjects which speak to us and others which do not, but he would be a clever man who should undertake to give a rule—an *index expurgatorius*—by which the story and the no-story should be known apart. It is impossible (to me at least) to imagine any such rule which shall not be altogether arbitrary. The writer in the *Pall Mall* opposes the delightful (as I suppose) novel of *Margot la Balafrée* to certain tales in which "Bostonian nymphs" appear to have "rejected English dukes for psychological reasons." I am not acquainted with the romance just designated, and can scarcely forgive the *Pall Mall* critic for not mentioning the name of the author, but the title appears to refer to a lady who may have received a scar in some heroic adventure. I am inconsolable at not being acquainted with this episode, but am utterly at a loss to see why it is a story when the rejection (or acceptance) of a duke is not, and why a reason, psychological or other, is not a subject when a cicatrix is. They are all particles of the multitudinous life with which the novel deals, and surely no dogma which pretends to make it lawful to touch the one and unlawful to touch the other will stand for a moment on its feet. It is the special picture that must stand or fall, according as it seems to possess truth or to lack it. Mr. Besant does not, to my sense, light up the subject by intimating that a story must, under penalty of not being a story, consist of "adventures." Why of adventures more than of green spectacles? He mentions a category of impossible things, and among them he places "fiction without adventure." Why without adventure, more than without matrimony, or celibacy, or parturition, or cholera, or hydropathy, or Jansenism? This seems to me to bring the novel back to the hapless little *role* of being an artificial, ingenious thing—bring it down from its large, free character of an immense and exquisite correspondence with life. And what *is* adventure when it comes to that, and by what sign is the listening pupil to recognize it? It is an adventure—an immense one—for me to write this little article; and for a Bostonian nymph to reject an English duke is an adventure only less stirring, I should say, than for an English duke to be rejected by a Bostonian nymph. I see dramas within dramas in that, and innumerable points of view. A psychological reason is, to my imagination, an object adorably pictorial; to catch the tint of its complexion—I feel as if that idea might inspire one to Titianesque efforts. There are few things more exciting to me, in short, than a psychological reason, and yet, I protest, the novel seems to me the most magnificent form of art. I have just been reading, at the same time, the delightful story of *Treasure Island*, by Mr. Robert Louis Stevenson, and, in a manner less consecutive, the last tale from M. Edmond de Goncourt, which is entitled *Chérie*. One of these works treats of murders, mysteries, islands of dreadful renown, hairbreadth escapes, miraculous coincidences, and buried doubloons. The other treats of a little French girl who lived in a fine house in Paris, and died of wounded sensibility because no one would marry her. I call *Treasure Island* delightful, because it appears to me to have succeeded wonderfully in what it attempts; and I venture to bestow no epithet upon *Chérie*, which strikes me as having failed deplorably in what it attempts—that is, in tracing the development of the moral consciousness of a child. But one of these productions strikes me as exactly as much of a novel as the other, and as having a "story" quite as much. The moral consciousness of a child is as much a part of life as the islands of the Spanish Main, and the one sort of geography seems to me to have those "surprises" of which Mr. Besant speaks quite as much as the other. For myself (since it comes back in the last resort, as I say, to the preference of the individual), the picture of the child's experience has the advantage that I can at succesive steps (an immense luxury, near to the "sensual pleasure" of which Mr. Besant's critic in the *Pall Mall* speaks) say Yes or No, as it may be, to what the artist puts before me. I have been a child in fact, but I have been on a quest for a buried treasure only in supposition, and it is a simple accident that with M. de Goncourt I should have for the most part to say No. With George Eliot, when she painted that country with a far other intelligence, I always said Yes.

The most interesting part of Mr. Besant's lecture is unfortunately the briefest passage—his very cursory allusion to the "conscious moral purpose" of the novel. Here again it is not very clear whether he be recording a fact or laying down a principle; it is a great pity that in the latter case he should not have developed his idea. This branch of the subject is of immense importance, and Mr. Besant's few words point to considerations of the widest reach, not to be lightly disposed of. He will have treated the art of fiction but superficially who is not prepared to go every inch of the way that these considerations will carry him. It is for this reason that at the beginning of these remarks I was careful to notify the reader that my reflections on so large a theme have no pretension to be exhaustive. Like Mr. Besant, I have left the question of the morality of the novel till the last, and at the last I find I have used up my space. It is a question surrounded with difficulties, as witness the very first that meets us, in the form of a definite question, on the threshold. Vagueness, in such a discussion, is fatal, and what is the meaning of your morality and your conscious moral purpose? Will you not define your terms and explain how (a novel being a picture) a picture can be either moral or immoral? You wish to paint a moral picture or carve a moral statue: will you not tell us how you would set about it? We are discussing the Art of Fiction; questions of art are questions (in the widest sense) of execution; questions of morality are quite another affair, and will you not let us see how it is that you find it so easy to mix them up? These things are so clear to Mr. Besant that he has deduced from them a law which he sees embodied in English Fiction, and which is "a truly admirable thing and a great cause for congratulation." It is a great cause for congratulation indeed when such thorny problems become as smooth as silk. I may add that in so far as Mr. Besant perceives that in point of fact English Fiction has addressed itself preponderantly to these delicate questions he will appear to many people to have made a vain discovery. They will have been positively struck, on the contrary, with the moral timidity of the usual English novelist; with his (or with her) aversion to face the difficulties with which on every side the treatment of reality bristles. He is apt to be extremely shy (whereas the picture that Mr. Besant draws is a picture of boldness), and the sign of his work, for the most part, is a cautious silence on certain subjects. In the English novel (by which of course I mean the American as well), more than in any other, there is a traditional difference between that which people know and that which they agree to admit that they know, that which they see and that which they speak of, that which they feel to be a part of life and that which they allow to enter into literature. There is the great difference, in short, between what they talk of in conversation and what they talk of in print. The essence of moral energy is to survey the whole field, and I should directly reverse Mr. Besant's remark and say not that the English novel has a purpose, but that it has a diffidence. To what degree a purpose in a work of art is a source of corruption I shall not attempt to inquire; the one that seems to me least dangerous is the purpose of making a perfect work. As for our novel, I may say lastly on this score that as we find it in England today it strikes me as addressed in a large degree to "young people," and that this in itself constitutes a presumption that it will be rather shy. There are certain things which it is generally agreed not to discuss, not even to mention, before young people. That is very well, but the absence of discussion is not a symptom of the moral passion. The purpose of the English novel—"a truly admirable thing, and a great cause for congratulation"—strikes me therefore as rather negative.

There is one point at which the moral sense and the artistic sense lie very near together; that is in the light of the very obvious truth that the deepest quality of a work of art will always be the quality of the mind of the producer. In proportion as that intelligence is fine will the novel, the picture, the statue partake of the substance of beauty and truth. To be constituted of such elements is, to my vision, to have purpose enough. No good novel will ever proceed from a superficial mind; that seems to me an axiom which, for the artist in fiction, will cover all needful moral ground: if the youthful aspirant take it to heart it will illuminate for him many of the mysteries of "purpose." There are many other useful things that might be said to him, but I have come to the end of my article, and can only touch them as I pass. The critic in the *Pall Mall Gazette*, whom I have already quoted, draws attention to the danger, in speaking of the art of fiction, of generalizing. The danger that he has in mind is rather, I imagine, that of particularizing, for there are some comprehensive remarks which, in addition to those embodied in Mr. Besant's suggestive lecture, might without fear of misleading him be addressed to the ingenuous student. I should remind him first of the magnificence of the form that is open to him, which offers to sight so few restrictions and such innumerable opportunities. The other arts, in comparison, appear confined and hampered; the various conditions under which they are exercised are so rigid and definite. But the only condition that I can think of attaching to the composition of the novel is, as I have already said, that it be sincere. This freedom is a splendid privilege, and the first lesson of the young novelist is to learn to be worthy of it. "Enjoy it as it deserves," I should say to him; "take possession of it, explore it to its utmost extent, publish it, rejoice in it. All life belongs to you, and do not listen either to those who would shut you up into corners of it and tell you that it is only here and there that art inhabits, or to those who would persuade you that this heavenly messenger wings her way outside of life altogether, breathing a super-fine air, and turning away her head from the truth of things. There is no impression of life, no manner of seeing it and feeling it, to which the plan of the novelist may not offer a place; you have only to remember that talents so dissimilar as those of Alexandre Dumas and Jane Austen, Charles Dickens and Gustave Flaubert have worked in this field with equal glory. Do not think too much about optimism and pessimism; try and catch the color of life itself. In France today we see a prodigious effort (that of Emile Zola, to whose solid and serious work no explorer of the capacity of the novel can allude without respect), we see an extraordinary effort, vitiated by a spirit of pessimism on a narrow basis. M. Zola is magnificent, but he strikes an English reader as ignorant; he has an air of working in the dark; if he had as much light as energy, his results would be of the highest value. As for the aberrations of a shallow optimism, the ground (of English fiction especially) is strewn with their brittle particles as with broken glass. If you must indulge in conclusions, let them have the taste of a wide knowledge. Remember that your first duty is to be as complete as possible—to make as perfect a work. Be generous and delicate and pursue the prize."

9. TAINE

Introduction to
History of English Literature

Hippolyte Taine (1828–93) was born in Vouziers, France, in the Ardennes, where his father was a solicitor. He studied at the École Normale Supérieure in Paris but failed the examination for the title of *agrégé de philosophie* presumably because of his revolutionary views. He taught in provincial schools, read so much that he was able to take a doctor's degree in literature, and visited Italy and England. In 1864 he was made professor of aesthetics and of the history of art at the École des Beaux Arts.

Among his publications are: *Essai sur les Fables de la Fontaine* (1853), which is his doctor's thesis; *Les Philosophes français du XIXe siècle* (1857); *Essai de critique et d'histoire* (1858), which already contains the germ of his historical approach to criticism; *De l'intelligence*, 2 vols. (1870), a philosophical work expounding Positivism; *Les origines de la France contemporaine* (1875–93); and *Histoire de la Littérature Anglaise*, 3 vols. (1863). The selection is taken from the Introduction to this work (trans. by Henry Van Laun).

Taine, a most influential critic, though not often read today, is in many ways really a transmitter and elaborator of the eighteenth-century historical approach applied to literature by Herder and the two Schlegel brothers. "Underlying their work was a new, or at least newly definite, concept of a literary work as a human artifact that appears in a particular society at a particular time and—they believed—needs to be understood in this context. Auguste Comte redefined this view in terms of his 'Positive Philosophy,' and added the theory—which Taine was determined to clarify and prove—that, like all other objects, literary works are completely determined by, and therefore in principle fully explainable in terms of, their contexts." (Monroe C. Beardsley, *Aesthetics* [Macmillan, 1966], p. 291.) Taine's qualification and proof are formulated in the famous theory that a literary work is fashioned by or is a product of race, environment (milieu), and moment (epoch).

Taine is at great pains to explain this deterministic approach to literature. Thus race ". . . consists of those innate and hereditary dispositions which man brings with him into the world and which are generally accompanied with marked differences of temperament and of bodily structure. They vary in different nations." Environment consists of the natural surroundings (mountains, sea, etc.), the climate, and political and social (which include religious) conditions. Moment is the particular time at which the writer lives. In his *History of English Literature* he was forced to introduce a fourth element: "The loophole that enables Taine to avoid the strict consequences of his three determinants is a fourth—a loose system of psychology. Psychology takes over where sociology has given up. . . ." (Harry Levin, "Literature as an Institution," *Criticism*, Shorer, Miles, McKenzie, eds. [Harcourt, Brace & World, 1958], p. 547).

Taine is influenced not only by the historical-sociological approach, but by the general scientific ideas of the time as well. Like the French writers of his time—Balzac, Flaubert, and Zola, for example—Taine wants to introduce the scientific method in both the writing and discussing of literature, to reduce literature to a tidy, classified body of facts that could be explained in terms of his three criteria of race, environment, and moment. Thus scientific jargon is introduced: he likes to talk about literature as an artifact or body that can be examined under laboratory conditions. Analogies with the sciences, such as the following, abound: "Just as in an animal, the instincts, teeth, limbs, and bones, and muscular apparatus are bound together in such a way that a variation of one determines a corresponding variation in the others, and out of which a skilful naturalist, with a few bits, imagines and reconstructs an almost complete body, so, in a civilization, do religion, philosophy, the family scheme, literature, and the arts form a system in which each local change involves a general change, so that an experienced historian, who studies one portion apart from the others, sees beforehand and partially predicts the characteristics of the rest."

Here, in a sense, though, Taine is harking back to the old Aristotelian notion of explaining things in terms of the whole, seeing them as forming parts of an organic unity. He also seems to be influenced by the previous confusion, conscious or unconscious, between religion and literature that runs through so much of Western criticism (it is especially pronounced in Sidney and Arnold). Often he uses the phrase "literature or religion," thus indicating their actual interchangeability.

Taine's influence on later criticism has been immense. Besides the important *Main Currents of Nineteenth Century Criticism* by Georg Brandes, many American critics, such as Vernon Louis Parrington in *Main Currents in American Thought* and Granville Hicks in *The Great Tradition*, show their debt to Taine. As Harry Levin in his excellent essay on Taine remarks, these critics of Taine's school commit the fallacy "to equate art with society, to assume a one-to-one correspondence between a book and its subject-matter, to accept the literature of an age as a complete and exact replica of itself."

I

History, within a hundred years in Germany, and within sixty years in France, has undergone a transformation, owing to a study of literatures.

The discovery has been made that a literary work is not a mere play of the imagination, the isolated caprice of an excited brain, but a transcript of contemporary manners and customs and the sign of a particular state of intellect. The conclusion derived from this is that, through literary monuments, we can retrace the way in which men felt and thought many centuries ago. This method has been tried and found successful.

We have meditated over these ways of feeling and thinking and have accepted them as facts of prime significance. We have found that they were dependent on most important events, that they explain these, and that these explain them, and that henceforth it was necessary to give them their place in history, and one of the highest. This place has been assigned to them, and hence all is changed in history—the aim, the method, the instrumentalities, and the conceptions of laws and of causes. It is this change as now going on, and which must continue to go on, that is here attempted to be set forth.

On turning over the large stiff pages of a folio volume, or the yellow leaves of a manuscript, in short, a poem, a code of laws, a confession of faith, what is your first comment? You say to yourself that the work before you is not of its own creation. It is simply a mold like a fossil shell, an imprint similar to one of those forms embedded in a stone by an animal which once lived and perished. Beneath the shell was an animal and behind the document there was a man. Why do you study the shell unless to form some idea of the animal? In the same way do you study the document in order to comprehend the man; both shell and document are dead fragments and of value only as indications of the complete living being. The aim is to reach this being; this is what you strive to reconstruct. It is a mistake to study the document as if it existed alone by itself. That is treating things merely as a pedant, and you subject yourself to the illusions of a book-worm. At bottom mythologies and languages are not existences; the only realities are human beings who have employed words and imagery adapted to their organs and to suit the original cast of their intellects. A creed is nothing in itself. Who made it? Look at this or that portrait of the sixteenth century, the stern, energetic features of an archbishop or of an English martyr. Nothing exists except through the individual; it is necessary to know the individual himself. Let the parentage of creeds be established, or the classification of poems, or the growth of constitutions, or the transformations of idioms, and we have only cleared the ground. True history begins when the historian has discerned beyond the mists of ages the living, active man, endowed with passions, furnished with habits, special in voice, feature, gesture, and costume, distinctive and complete, like anybody that you have just encountered in the street. Let us strive then, as far as possible, to get rid of this great interval of time which prevents us from observing the man with our eyes, the eyes of our own head. What revelations do we find in the calendered leaves of a modern poem? A modern poet, a man like De Musset, Victor Hugo, Lamartine, or Heine, graduated from a college and travelled, wearing a dress-coat and gloves, favored by ladies, bowing fifty times and uttering a dozen witticisms in an evening, reading daily newspapers, generally occupying an apartment on the second story, not over-cheerful on account of his nerves, and especially because, in this dense democracy in which we stifle each other, the discredit of official rank exaggerates his pretensions by raising his importance, and, owing to the delicacy of his personal sensations, leading him to regard himself as a Deity. Such is what we detect behind modern meditations and sonnets.

Again, behind a tragedy of the seventeenth century there is a poet, one, for example, like Racine, refined, discreet, a courtier, a fine talker, with majestic perruque and ribboned shoes, a monarchist and zealous Christian, "God having given him the grace not to blush in any society on account of zeal for his king or for the Gospel," clever in interesting the monarch, translating into proper French "the *gaulois* of Amyot," deferential to the great, always knowing how to keep his place in their company, assiduous and respectful at Marly as at Versailles, amid the formal creations of a decorative landscape and the reverential bows, graces, intrigues, and finesses of the braided seigniors who get up early every morning to obtain the reversion of an office, together with the charming ladies who count on their fingers the pedigrees which entitle them to a seat on a footstool. On this point consult Saint-Simon and the engravings of Perélle, the same as you have just consulted Balzac and the water-color drawings of Eugène Lami.

In like manner, on reading a Greek tragedy, our first care is to figure to ourselves the Greeks, that is to say, men who lived half-naked in the gymnasiums or on a public square under a brilliant sky, in full view of the noblest and most delicate landscape, busy in rendering their bodies strong and agile, in conversing together, in arguing, in voting, in carrying out patriotic piracies, and yet idle and temperate, the furniture of their houses consisting of three earthen jars and their food of two pots of anchovies preserved in oil, served by slaves who afford them the time to cultivate their minds and to exercise their limbs, with no other concern than that of having the most beautiful city, the most beautiful processions, the most beautiful ideas, and the most beautiful men. In this respect, a statue like the "Meleager" or the "Theseus" of the Parthenon, or again a sight of the blue and lustrous Mediterranean, resembling a silken tunic out of which islands arise like marble bodies, together with a dozen choice phrases selected from the works of Plato and Aristophanes, teach us more than any number of dissertations and commentaries.

And so again, in order to understand an Indian Purana, one must begin by imagining the father of a family who, "having seen a son on his son's knees," follows the law and, with axe and pitcher, seeks solitude under a banyan tree, talks no more, multiplies his fastings, lives naked with four fires around him under the fifth fire, that terrible sun which endlessly devours and resuscitates all living things; who fixes his imagination in turn for weeks at a time on the foot of Brahma, then on his knee, on his thigh, on his navel, and so on, until, beneath the strain of this intense meditation, hallucinations appear, when all the forms of being, mingling together and transformed into each other, oscillate to and fro in this vertiginous brain until the motionless man, with suspended breath and fixed eyeballs, beholds the universe melting away like vapor over the vacant immensity of the Being in which he hopes for absorption. In this case the best of teachings would be a journey in India; but, for lack of a better one, take the narratives of travellers along with works in geography, botany, and ethnology. In any event there must be the same research. A language, a law, a creed, is never other than an abstraction; the perfect thing is found in the active man, the visible corporeal figure which eats, walks, fights, and labors. Set aside the theories of consitutions and their results, of religions and their systems, and try to observe men in their workshops or offices, in their fields along with their own sky and soil, with their own homes, clothes, occupations and repasts, just as you see them when, on landing in England or in Italy, you remark their features and gestures, their roads and their inns, the citizen on his promenades and the workman taking a drink. Let us strive as much as possible to supply the place of the actual, personal, sensible observation that is no longer practicable, this being the only way in which we can really know the man; let us make the past present; to judge of an object it must be present; no experience can be had of what is absent. Undoubtedly, this sort of reconstruction is always imperfect; only an imperfect judgment can be based on it; but let us do the best we can; incomplete knowledge is better than none at all, or than knowledge which is erroneous, and there is no other way of obtaining knowledge approximatively of bygone times than by seeing approximately the men of former times.

Such is the first step in history. This step was taken in Europe at the end of the last century when the imagination took fresh flight under the auspices of Lessing and Walter Scott, and a little later in France under Chauteaubriand, Augustin Thierry, Michelet, and others. We now come to the second step.

II

On observing the visible man with your own eyes what do you try to find in him? The invisible man. These words which your ears catch, those gestures, those airs of the head, his attire and sensible operations of all kinds, are, for you, merely so many expressions; these express something, a soul. An inward man is hidden beneath the outward man, and the latter simply manifests the former. You have observed the house in which he lives, his furniture, his costume, in order to discover his habits and tastes, the degree of his refinement or rusticity, his extravagance or economy, his follies or his cleverness. You have listened to his conversation and noted the inflections of his voice, the attitudes he has assumed, so as to judge of his spirit, self-abandonment or gayety, his energy or his rigidity. You consider his writings, works of art, financial and political schemes, with a view to measure the reach and limits of his intelligence, his creative power and self-command, to ascertain the usual order, kind, and force of his conceptions, in what way he thinks and how he resolves. All these exernals are so many avenues converging to one centre, and you follow these only to reach that centre; here is the real man, namely, that group of faculties and of sentiments which produces the rest. Behold a new world, an infinite world; for each visible action involves an infinite train of reasonings and emotions, new or old sensations which have combined to bring this into light and which, like long ledges of rock sunk deep in the earth, have cropped out above the surface and attained their level. It is this subterranean world which forms the second aim, the special object of the historian. If his critical education suffices, he is able to discriminate under every ornament in architecture, under every stroke of the brush in a picture, under each phrase of literary composition, the particular sentiment out of which the ornament, the stroke, and the phrase have sprung; he is a spectator of the inward drama which has developed itself in the breast of the artist or writer; the choice of words, the length or shortness of the period, the species of metaphor, the accent of a verse, the chain of reasoning—all are to him an indication; while his eyes are reading the text his mind and soul are following the steady flow and ever-changing series of emotions and conceptions from which this text has issued; he is working out its psychology. Should you desire to study this operation, regard the promoter and model of all the high culture of the epoch, Goethe, who, before composing his "Iphigenia," spent days in making drawings of the most perfect statues and who, at last, his eyes filled with the noble forms of antique scenery and his mind penetrated by the harmonious beauty of antique life, succeeded in reproducing internally, with such exactness, the habits and yearnings of Greek imagination as to provide us with an almost twin sister of the "Antigone" of Sophocles and of the goddesses of Phidias. This exact and demonstrated divination of bygone sentiments has, in our days, given a new life to history. There was almost complete ignorance of this in the last century; men of every race and of every epoch were represented as about alike, the Greek, the barbarian, the Hindoo, the man of the Renaissance and the man of the eighteenth century, cast in the same mold and after the same pattern, and after a certain abstract conception which served for the whole human species. There was a knowledge of man but not of men. There was no penetration into the soul itself; nothing of the infinite diversity and wonderful complexity of souls had been detected; it was not known that the moral organization of a people or of an age is as special and distinct as the physical structure of a family of plants or of an order of animals. History to-day, like zoölogy, has found its anatomy, and whatever branch of it is studied, whether philology, languages or mythologies, it is in this way that labor must be given to make it produce new fruit. . . .

Such is the second step, and we are now in train to follow it out. Such is the proper aim of contemporary criticism. No one has done this work so judiciously and on so grand a scale as Sainte-Beuve; in this respect, we are all his pupils; literary, philosophic, and religious criticism in books, and even in the newspapers, is to-day entirely changed by his method. Ulterior evolution must start from this point. I have often attempted to expose what this evolution is; in my opinion, it is a new road open to history and which I shall strive to describe more in detail.

III

After having observed in a man and noted down one, two, three and then a multitude of sentiments, do these suffice and does your knowledge of him seem complete? Does a memorandum book constitute a psychology? It is not a psychology, and here, as elsewhere, the search for causes must follow the collection of facts. It matters not what the facts may be, whether physical or moral, they always spring from causes; there are causes for ambition, for courage, for veracity, as well as for digestion, for muscular action, and for animal heat. Vice and virtue are products like vitriol and sugar; every complex fact grows out of the simple facts with which it is affiliated and on which it depends. We must therefore try to ascertain what simple facts underlie moral qualities the same as we ascertain those that underlie physical qualities, and, for example, let us take the first fact that comes to hand, a religious system of music, that of a Protestant church. A certain inward cause has inclined the minds of worshippers towards these grave, monotonous melodies, a cause much greater than its effect; that is to say, a general conception of the veritable outward forms of worship which man owes to God; it is this general conception which has shaped the architecture of the temple, cast out statues, dispensed with paintings, effaced ornaments, shortened ceremonies, confined the members of a congregation to high pews which cut off the view, and governed the thousand details of decoration, posture, and all other externals. This conception itself again proceeds from a more general cause, an idea of human conduct in general, inward and outward, prayers, actions, dispositions of every sort that man is bound to maintain toward the Deity; it is this which has enthroned the doctrine of grace, lessened the importance of the clergy, transformed the sacraments, suppressed observances, and changed the religion of discipline into one of morality. This conception, in its turn, depends on a third one, still more general, that of moral perfection as this is found in a perfect God, the impeccable judge, the stern overseer, who regards every soul as sinful, meriting punishment, incapable of virtue or of salvation, except through a stricken conscience which He provokes and the renewal of the heart which He brings about. Here is the master conception, consisting of duty erected into the absolute sovereign of human life, and which prostrates all other ideals at the feet of the moral ideal. Here we reach what is deepest in man; for, to explain this conception, we must consider the race he belongs to, say the German, the Northman, the formation and character of his intellect, his ways in general of thinking and feeling, that tardiness and frigidity of sensation which keeps him from rashly and easily falling under the empire of sensual enjoyments, that bluntness of taste, that irregularity and those outbursts of conception which arrest in him the birth of refined and harmonious forms and methods; that disdain of appearances, that yearning for truth, that attachment to abstract, bare ideas which develop conscience in him at the expense of everything else. Here the search comes to an end. We have reached a certain primitive disposition, a particular trait belonging to sensations of all kinds, to every conception peculiar to an age or to a race, to characteristics inseparable from every idea and feeling that stir in the human breast. Such are the grand causes, for these are universal and permanent causes, present in every case and at every moment, everywhere and always active, indestructible, and inevitably dominant in the end, since, whatever accidents cross their path, being limited and partial, end in yielding to the obscure and incessant repetition of their energy; so that the general structure of things and all the main features of events are their work, all religions and philosophies, all poetic and industrial systems, all forms of society and of the family, all, in fine, being imprints bearing the stamp of their seal.

IV

There is, then, a system in human ideas and sentiments, the prime motor of which consists in general traits, certain characteristics of thought and feeling common to men belonging to a particular race, epoch, or country. Just as crystals in mineralogy, whatever their diversity, proceed from a few simple physical forms, so do civilizations in history, however these may differ, proceed from a few spiritual forms. One is explained by a primitive geometrical element as the other is explained by a primitive psychological element. In order to comprehend the entire group of mineralogical species we must first study a regular solid in the general, its facets and angles, and observe in this abridged form the innumerable transformations of which it is susceptible. In like manner, if we would comprehend the entire group of historic varieties we must consider beforehand a human soul in the general, with its two or three fundamental faculties, and, in this abridgment, observe the principal forms it may present.

V

Three different sources contribute to the production of this elementary moral state, race, environment, and epoch. What we call race consists of those innate and hereditary dispositions which man brings with him into the world and which are generally accompanied with marked differences of temperament and of bodily structure. They vary in different nations. Naturally, there are varieties of men as there are varieties of cattle and horses, some brave and intelligent, and others timid and of limited capacity; some capable of superior conceptions and creations, and other reduced to rudimentary ideas and contrivances; some specially fitted for certain works, and more richly furnished with certain instincts, as we see in the better endowed species of dogs, some for running and others for fighting, some for hunting and others for guarding houses and flocks. We have here a distinct force; so distinct that, in spite of the enormous deviations which both the other motors impress upon it, we still recognize, and which a race like the Aryan people, scattered from the Ganges to the Hebrides, established under all climates, ranged along every degree of civilization, transformed by thirty centuries of revolutions, shows nevertheless in its languages, in its religions, in its literatures, and in its philosophies, the community of blood and of intellect which still to-day binds together all its offshoots. However they may differ, their parentage is not lost; barbarism, culture and grafting, differences of atmosphere and of soil, fortunate or unfortunate occurrences, have operated in vain; the grand characteristics of the original form have lasted, and we find that the two or three leading features of the primitive imprint are again apparent under the subsequent imprints with which time has overlaid them. There is nothing surprising in this extraordinary tenacity. Although the immensity of the distance allows us to catch only a glimpse in a dubious light of the origin of species,[1] the events of history throw sufficient light on events anterior to history to explain the almost unshaken solidity of primordial traits. At the moment of encountering them, fifteen, twenty, and thirty centuries before our era, in an Aryan, Egyptian, or Chinese, they represent the work of a much greater number of centuries, perhaps the work of many myriads of centuries. For, as soon as an animal is born it must adapt itself to its surroundings; it breathes in another way, it renews itself differently, it is otherwise stimulated according as the atmosphere, the food, and the temperature are different. A different climate and situation create different necessities and hence activities of a different kind; and hence, again, a system of different habits, and, finally a system of different aptitudes and instincts. Man, thus compelled to put himself in equilibrium with circumstances, contracts a corresponding temperament and character, and his character, like his temperament, are acquisitions all the more stable because of the outward impression being more deeply imprinted in him by more frequent repetitions and transmitted to his offspring by more ancient heredity. So that at each moment of time, the character of a people may be considered as a summary of all antecedent actions and sensations; that is to say, as a quantity and as a weighty mass, not infinite,[2] since all things in nature are limited, but disproportionate to the rest and almost impossible to raise, since each minute of an almost infinite past has contributed to render it heavier, and, in order to turn the scale, it would require, on the other side, a still greater accumulation of actions and sensations. Such is the first and most abundant source of these master faculties from which historic events are derived; and we see at once that if it is powerful it is owing to its not being a mere source, but a sort of lake, and like a deep reservoir wherein other sources have poured their waters for a multitude of centuries.

When we have thus verified the internal structure of a race we must consider the environment in which it lives. For man is not alone in the world; nature envelops him and other men surround him; accidental and

---

[1] Darwin, "The Origin of Species." Prosper Lucas, "De l'Hérédité."
[2] Spinosa, "Ethics," part iv., axiom.

secondary folds come and overspread the primitive and permanent fold, while physical or social circumstances derange or complete the natural groundwork surrendered to them. At one time climate has had its effect. Although the history of Aryan nations can be only obscurely traced from their common country to their final abodes, we can nevertheless affirm that the profound difference which is apparent between the Germanic races on the one hand, and the Hellenic and Latin races on the other, proceeds in great part from the differences between the countries in which they have established themselves—the former in cold and moist countries, in the depths of gloomy forests and swamps, or on the borders of a wild ocean, confined to melancholic or rude sensations, inclined to drunkenness and gross feeding, leading a militant and carnivorous life; the latter, on the contrary, living amidst the finest scenery, alongside of a brilliant, sparkling sea inviting navigation and commerce, exempt from the grosser cravings of the stomach, disposed at the start to social habits and customs, to political organization, to the sentiments and faculties which develop the art of speaking, the capacity for enjoyment and invention in the sciences, in art, and in literature. . . . It is with a people as with a plant; the same sap at the same temperature and in the same soil produces, at different stages of its successive elaborations, different developments, buds, flowers, fruits, and seeds, in such a way that the condition of the following is always that of the preceding and is born of its death. Now, if you no longer regard a brief moment, as above, but one of those grand periods of development which embraces one or many centuries like the Middle Ages, or our last classic period, the conclusion is the same. A certain dominating conception has prevailed throughout; mankind, during two hundred years, during five hundred years, have represented to themselves a certain ideal figure of man, in mediæval times the knight and the monk, in our classic period the courtier and refined talker; this creative and universal conception has monopolized the entire field of action and thought, and, after spreading its involuntarily systematic works over the world, it languished and then died out, and now a new idea has arisen, destined to a like domination and to equally multiplied creations. Note here that the latter depends in part on the former, and that it is the former, which, combining its effect with those of national genius and surrounding circumstances will impose their bent and their direction on new-born things. . . .

VI

There remains to be ascertained in what way these causes, applied to a nation or to a century, distribute their effects. Like a spring issuing from an elevated spot and diffusing its waters, according to the height, from ledge to ledge, until it finally reaches the low ground, so does the tendency of mind or of soul in a people, due to race, epoch, or environment, diffuse itself in different proportions, and by regular descent, over the different series of facts which compose its civilization. In preparing the geographical map of a country, starting at its watershed, we see the slopes, just below this common point, dividing themselves into five or six principal basins, and then each of the latter into several others, and so on until the whole country, with its thousands of inequalities of surface, is included in the ramifications of this network. In like manner, in preparing the psychological map of the events and sentiments belonging to a certain human civilization, we find at the start five or six well determined provinces—religion, art, philosophy, the state, the family, and industries; next, in each of these provinces, natural departments, and then finally, in each of these departments, still smaller territories until we arrive at those countless details of life which we observe daily in ourselves and around us. If, again, we examine and compare together these various groups of facts we at once find that they are composed of parts and that all have parts in common. Let us take first the three principal products of human intelligence—religion, art, and philosophy. What is a philosophy but a conception of nature and of its primordial causes under the form of abstractions and formulas? What underlies a religion and an art if not a conception of this same nature, and of these same primordial causes, under the form of more or less determinate symbols, and of more or less distinct personages, with this difference, that in the first case we believe that they exist, and in the second case that they do not exist. . . . A civilization is a living unit, the parts of which hold together the same as the parts of an organic body. Just as in an animal, the instincts, teeth, limbs, bones, and muscular apparatus are bound together in such a way that a variation of one determines a corresponding variation in the others, and out of which a skilful naturalist, with a few bits, imagines and reconstructs an almost complete body, so, in a civilization, do religion, philosophy, the family scheme, literature and the arts form a system in which each local change involves a general change, so that an experienced historian, who studies one portion apart from the others, sees beforehand and partially predicts the characteristics of the rest. There is nothing vague in this dependence. The regulation of all this in the living body consists, first, of the tendency to manifest a certain primordial type, and, next, the necessity of its possessing organs which can supply its wants and put itself in harmony with itself in order to live. The regulation in a civilization consists in the presence in each great human creation of an elementary productor equally present in other surrounding creations, that is, some faculty and aptitude, some efficient and marked disposition, which, with its own peculiar character, introduces this with that into all operations in which it takes part, and which, according to its variations, causes variation in all the works in which it coöperates.

VIII

History has reached this point at the present day, or rather it is nearly there, on the threshold of this inquest. The question as now stated is this: Given a literature, a philosophy, a society, an art, a certain group of arts, what is the moral state of things which produces it? And what are the conditions of race, epoch, and environment the best adapted to produce this moral state? There is a distinct moral state for each of these formations and for each of their branches; there is one for art in general as well as for each particular art; for architecture, painting, sculpture, music, and poetry, each with a germ of its own in the large field of human psychology; each has its own law, and it is by virtue of this law that we see each shoot up, apparently haphazard, singly and alone, amidst the miscarriages of their neighbors, like painting in Flanders and Holland in the seventeenth century, like poetry in England in the sixteenth century, like music in Germany in the eighteenth century. . . .

Nobody has taught one better [than Stendhal] how to observe with one's own eyes, first, to regard humanity around us and life as it is, and next, old and authentic documents; how to read more than merely the black and white of the page; how to detect under old print and the scrawl of the text the veritable sentiment and the train of thought, the mental state in which the words were penned. In his writings, as in those of Sainte-Beuve and in those of the German critics, the reader will find how much is to be derived from a literary document; if this document is rich and we know how to interpret it, we will find in it the psychology of a particular soul, often that of an age, and sometimes that of a race.

In this respect, a great poem, a good novel, the confessions of a superior man, are more instructive than a mass of historians and histories; I would give fifty volumes of charters and a hundred diplomatic files for the memoirs of Cellini, the epistles of Saint Paul, the table-talk of Luther, or the comedies of Aristophanes. Herein lies the value of literary productions. They are instructive because they are beautiful; their usefulness increases with their perfection; and if they provide us with documents, it is because they are monuments. The more visible a book renders sentiments the more literary it is, for it is the special office of literature to take note of sentiments. The more important the sentiments noted in a book the higher its rank in literature, for it is by representing what sort of a life a nation or an epoch leads, that a writer rallies to himself the sympathies of a nation or of an epoch. Hence, among the documents which bring before our eyes the sentiments of preceding generations, a literature, and especially a great literature, is incomparably the best. It resembles those admirable instruments of remarkable sensitiveness which physicists make use of to detect and measure the most profound and delicate changes that occur in a human body. There is nothing approaching this in constitutions or religions; the articles of a code or of a catechism do no more than depict mind in gross and without finesse; if there are documents which show life and spirit in politics and in creeds, they are the eloquent discourses of the pulpit and the tribune, memoirs and personal confessions, all belonging to literature, so that, outside of itself, literature embodies whatever is good elsewhere. It is mainly in studying literatures that we are able to produce moral history, and arrive at some knowledge of the psychological laws on which events depend.

I have undertaken to write a history of a literature and to ascertain the psychology of a people; in selecting this one, it is not without a motive. A people had to be taken possessing a vast and complete literature, which is rarely found. There are few nations which, throughout their existence, have thought and written well in the full sense of the word. Among the ancients, Latin literature is null at the beginning, and afterward borrowed and an imitation. Among the moderns, German literature is nearly a blank for two centuries. Italian and Spanish literatures come to an end in the middle of the seventeenth century. Ancient Greece, and modern France and England, alone offer a complete series of great and expressive monuments. I have chosen the English because, as this still exists and is open to direct observation, it can be better studied than that of an extinct civilization of which fragments only remain; and because, being different, it offers better than that of France very marked characteristics in the eyes of a Frenchman. Moreover, outside of what is peculiar to English civilization, apart from a spontaneous development, it presents a forced deviation due to the latest and most effective conquest to which the country was subject; the three given conditions out of which it issues—race, climate, and the Norman conquest—are clearly and distinctly visible in its literary monuments; so that we study in this history the two most potent motors of human transformation, namely, nature and constraint, and we study them, without any break or uncertainty, in a series of authentic and complete monuments. I have tried to define these primitive motors, to show their gradual effects, and explain how their insensible operation has brought religions and literary productions into full light, and how the inward mechanism is developed by which the barbarous Saxon became the Englishman of the present day.

10. JUNG

"Psychology and Literature"

Carl Gustav Jung (1875–1961), the great Swiss psychologist, was educated in Basel and Zürich. He received his MD degree in 1900 and began his work in psychiatry in the same year at the University of Zürich. He met his great colleague, Sigmund Freud, early in his career —in 1907. An interesting account of his formative years can be found in *Memories, Dreams, Reflections* (Pantheon, 1963).

Throughout his long life Jung was a very prolific writer. The variety of his interests can be seen from this sampling of the titles of his works: *Experimental Observations on Memory* (1905), *Schizophrenia* (1958), *The Relation Between the Ego and the Unconscious* (1928), *On the Nature of Dreams* (1948), *Archetypes of the Collective Unconscious* (1954), *Flying Saucers: A Modern Myth* (1958), *Yoga and the West* (1936), *Religious Ideas in Alchemy* (1937), *Psychotic Conflicts in a Child* (1946). Among his works dealing with the arts are the following: *On the Relation of Analytic Psychology to the Poetic Art* (1922), *Picasso* (1932), "Ulysses" (1932).

The short excerpt from the chapter "Psychology and Literature"* included in this edition is one of the most succinct and objective statements on the relationship between psychology and literature. Most so-called psychological critics tend to be extremely subjective in their approach and often confuses the realms of fiction and of life to such an extent that fictional characters are psychoanalyzed. Jung, on the other hand, insists on the integrity of the work of art and states that "there is a fundamental difference of approach between the psychologist's

* From *Modern Man in Search of a Soul*, trans. by W. S. Dell and Cary F. Baynes (New York, Harcourt, Brace & World, 1956), Chapter 8. Reprinted by permission of Harcourt Brace Jovanovich, Inc. and Routledge & Kegan Paul.

examination of a literary work and that of the literary critic."

Although he is fascinated with the creative impulse in the artist, Jung's interest in the artist's personality is not based on the desire to explain the work of art in terms of the personality. Here again he is unlike most psychologists interested in literature and many literary critics. Indeed, he goes as far as to insist on the impersonality of the work of art: "Art is a kind of innate desire that seizes a human being and makes him its instrument. The artist is not a person endowed with free will who seeks his own ends, but one who allows art to realize its purposes through him." This statement makes the artist simply a medium who transmits the waves going through him.

In the best tradition of literary criticism Jung's essay is finally an affirmation of the greatness and inviolability of art. His definition of art underlines its basic elusiveness: "A great work of art is like a dream; for all its apparent obviousness it does not explain itself and is never unequivocal."

There is a fundamental difference of approach between the psychologist's examination of a literary work, and that of the literary critic. What is of decisive importance and value for the latter may be quite irrelevant for the former. Literary products of highly dubious merit are often of the greatest interest to the psychologist. For instance, the so-called "psychological novel" is by no means as rewarding for the psychologist as the literary-minded suppose. Considered as a whole, such a novel explains itself. It has done its own work of psychological interpretation, and the psychologist can at most criticize or enlarge upon this. The important question as to how a particular author came to write a particular novel is of course left unanswered, but I wish to reserve this general problem for the second part of my essay.

The novels which are most fruitful for the psychologist are those in which the author has not already given a psychological interpretation of his characters, and which therefore leave room for analysis and explanation, or even invite it by their mode of presentation. Good examples of this kind of writing are the novels of Benoît, and English fiction in the manner of Rider Haggard, including the vein exploited by Conan Doyle which yields that most cherished article of mass-production, the detective story. Melville's *Moby Dick*, which I consider the greatest American novel, also comes within this class of writings. An exciting narrative that is apparently quite devoid of psychological exposition is just what interests the psychologist most of all. Such a tale is built upon a groundwork of implicit psychological assumptions, and, in the measure that the author is unconscious of them, they reveal themselves, pure and unalloyed, to the critical discernment. In the psychological novel, on the other hand, the author himself attempts to reshape his material so as to raise it from the level of crude contingency to that of psychological exposition and illumination—a procedure which all too often clouds the psychological significance of the work or hides it from view. It is precisely to novels of this sort that the layman goes for "psychology"; while it is novels of the other kind that challenge the psychologist, for he alone can give them deeper meaning.

I have been speaking in terms of the novel, but I am dealing with a psychological fact which is not restricted to this particular form of literary art. We meet with it in the works of the poets as well, and are confronted with it when we compare the first and second parts of the Faust drama. The love-tragedy of Gretchen explains itself; there is nothing that the psychologist can add to it that the poet has not already said in better words. The second part, on the other hand, calls for explanation. The prodigious richness of the imaginative material has so overtaxed the poet's formative powers that nothing is self-explanatory and every verse adds to the reader's need of an interpretation. The two parts of *Faust* illustrate by way of extremes this psychological distinction between works of literature.

In order to emphasize the distinction, I will call the one mode of artistic creation *psychological*, and the other *visionary*. The psychological mode deals with materials drawn from the realm of human consciousness—for instance, with the lessons of life, with emotional shocks, the experience of passion and the crises of human destiny in general—all of which go to make up the conscious life of man, and his feeling life in particular. This material is psychically assimilated by the poet, raised from the commonplace to the level of poetic experience, and given an expression which forces the reader to greater clarity and depth of human insight by bringing fully into his consciousness what he ordinarily evades and overlooks or senses only with a feeling of dull discomfort. The poet's work is an interpretation and illumination of the contents of consciousness, of the ineluctable experiences of human life with its eternally recurrent sorrow and joy. He leaves nothing over for the psychologist, unless, indeed, we expect the latter to expound the reasons for which Faust falls in love with Gretchen, or which drive Gretchen to murder her child! Such themes go to make up the lot of humankind;

they repeat themselves millions of times and are responsible for the monotony of the police-court and of the penal code. No obscurity whatever surrounds them, for they fully explain themselves.

Countless literary works belong to this class: the many novels dealing with love, the environment, the family, crime and society, as well as didactic poetry, the larger number of lyrics, and the drama, both tragic and comic. Whatever its particular form may be, the psychological work of art always takes its materials from the vast realm of conscious human experience—from the vivid foreground of life, we might say. I have called this mode of artistic creation psychological because in its activity it nowhere transcends the bounds of psychological intelligibility. Everything that it embraces—the experience as well as its artistic expression—belongs to the realm of the understandable. Even the basic experiences themselves, though non-rational, have nothing strange about them; on the contrary, they are that which has been known from the beginning of time—passion and its fated outcome, man's subjection to the turns of destiny, eternal nature with its beauty and its horror.

The profound difference between the first and second parts of Faust marks the difference between the psychological and the visionary modes of artistic creation. The latter reverses all the conditions of the former. The experience that furnishes the material for artistic expression is no longer familiar. It is a strange something that derives its existence from the hinterland of man's mind—that suggests the abyss of time separating us from pre-human ages, or evokes a super-human world of contrasting light and darkness. It is a primordial experience which surpasses man's understanding, and to which he is therefore in danger of succumbing. The value and the force of the experience are given by its enormity. It arises from timeless depths; it is foreign and cold, many-sided, demonic and grotesque. A grimly ridiculous example of the external chaos—*acrimen laesae majestatis humanae* ["Crime of offending human dignity."]; to use Nietzsche's words—it bursts asunder our human standards of value and of aesthetic form. The disturbing vision of monstrous and meaningless happenings that in every way exceed the grasp of human feeling and comprehension makes quite other demands upon the powers of the artist than do the experiences of the foreground of life. These never rend the curtain that veils the cosmos; they never transcend the bounds of the humanly possible, and for this reason are readily shaped to the demands of art, no matter how great a shock to the individual they may be. But the primordial experiences rend from top to bottom the curtain upon which is painted the picture of an ordered world, and allow a glimpse into the unfathomed abyss of what has not yet become. Is it a vision of other worlds, or of the obscuration of the spirit, or of the unborn generations of the future? We cannot say that it is any or none of these. . . .

Creativeness, like the freedom of the will, contains a secret. The psychologist can describe both these manifestations as processes, but he can find no solution of the philosophical problems they offer. Creative man is a riddle that we may try to answer in various ways, but always in vain, a truth that has not prevented modern psychology from turning now and again to the question of the artist and his art. Freud thought that he had found a key in his procedure of deriving the work of art from the personal experiences of the artist. It is true that certain possibilities lay in this direction, for it was conceivable that a work of art, no less than a neurosis, might be traced back to those knots in psychic life that we call the complexes. It was Freud's great discovery that neuroses have a causal origin in the psychic realm—that they take their rise from emotional states and from real or imagined childhood experiences. Certain of his followers, like Rank and Stekel, have taken up related lines of enquiry and have achieved important results. It is undeniable that the poet's psychic disposition permeates his work root and branch. Nor is there anything new in the statement that personal factors largely influence the poet's choice and use of his materials. Credit, however, must certainly be given to the Freudian school for showing how far-reaching this influence is and in what curious ways it comes to expression.

. . . The personal idiosyncrasies that creep into a work of art are not essential; in fact, the more we have to cope with these peculiarities, the less is it a question of art. What is essential in a work of art is that it should rise far above the realm of personal life and speak from the spirit and heart of the poet as man to the spirit and heart of mankind. The personal aspect is a limitation—and even a sin—in the realm of art. When a form of "art" is primarily personal it deserves to be treated as if it were a neurosis. There may be some validity in the idea held by the Freudian school that artists without exception are narcissistic—by which is meant that they are undeveloped persons with infantile and auto-erotic traits. The statement is only valid, however, for the artist as a person, and has nothing to do with the man as an artist. In his capacity of artist he is neither auto-erotic, nor hetero-erotic, nor erotic in any sense. He is objective and impersonal—even inhuman—for as an artist he is his work, and not a human being.

Every creative person is a duality or a synthesis of contradictory aptitudes. On the one side he is a human being with a personal life, while on the other side he is an impersonal, creative process. Since as a human being he may be sound or morbid, we must look at his psychic make-up to find the determinants of his personality. But we can only understand him in his capacity of artist by looking at his creative achievement. We should make a sad mistake if we tried to explain the mode of life of an English gentleman, a Prussian officer, or a cardinal in terms of personal factors. The gentleman, the officer and the cleric function as such in an impersonal role, and their psychic make-up is qualified by a peculiar objectivity. We must grant that the artist does not function in an official capacity—the very opposite is nearer the truth. He nevertheless resembles the types I have named in one respect, for the specifically artistic disposition involves an overweight of collective psychic life as against the personal. Art is a kind of innate drive that seizes a human being and makes him its instrument. The artist is not a person endowed with free will who seeks his own ends, but one who allows art to realize its purposes through him. As a human being he may have moods and a will and personal aims, but as an artist he is "man" in a higher sense—he is "collective man"—one who carries and shapes the unconscious, psychic life of mankind. To perform this difficult office it is sometimes necessary for him to sacrifice happiness and everything that makes life worth living for the ordinary human being.

All this being so, it is not strange that the artist is an especially interesting case for the psychologist who uses an analytical method. The artist's life cannot be otherwise than full of conflicts, for two forces are at war within him—on the one hand the common human longing for happiness, satisfaction and security in life, and on the other a ruthless passion for creation which may go so far as to override every personal desire. The lives of artists are as a rule so highly unsatisfactory—not to say tragic—because of their inferiority on the human and personal side, and not because of a sinister dispensation. There are hardly any exceptions to the rule that a person must pay dearly for the divine gift of the creative fire. It is as though each of us were endowed at birth with a certain capital of energy. The strongest force in our make-up will seize and all but monopolize this energy, leaving so little over that nothing of value can come of it. In this way the creative force can drain the human impulses to such a degree that the personal ego must develop all sorts of bad qualities—ruthlessness, sefishness and vanity (so-called "auto-erotism")—and even every kind of vice, in order to maintain the spark of life and to keep itself from being wholly bereft. The auto-erotism of artists resembles that of illegitimate or neglected children who from their tenderest years must protect themselves from the destructive influence of people who have no love to give them—who develop bad qualities for that very purpose and later maintain an invincible egocentrism by remaining all their lives infantile and helpless or by actively offending against the moral code or the law. How can we doubt that it is his art that explains the artist, and not the insufficiencies and conflicts of his personal life? These are nothing but the regrettable results of the fact that he is an artist—that is to say, a man who from his very birth has been called to a greater task than the ordinary mortal. A special ability means a heavy expenditure of energy in a particular direction, with a consequent drain from some other side of life.

It makes no difference whether the poet knows that his work is begotten, grows and matures with him, or whether he supposes that by taking thought he produces it out of the void. His opinion of the matter does not change the fact that his own work outgrows him as a child its mother. The creative process has feminine quality, and the creative work arises from unconscious depths—we might say, from the realm of the mothers. Whenever the creative force predominates, human life is ruled and moulded by the unconscious as against the active will, and conscious ego is swept along on a subterranean current, being nothing more than a helpless observer of events. The work in process becomes the poet's fate and determines his psychic development. It is not Goethe who creates *Faust*, but *Faust* which creates Goethe. And what is *Faust* but a symbol? By this I do not mean an allegory that points to something all too familiar, but an expression that stands for something not clearly known and yet profoundly alive. Here it is something that lives in the soul of every German, and that Goethe has helped to bring to birth. Could we conceive of anyone but a German writing *Faust* or *Also sprach Zarathustra*? Both play upon something that reverberates in the German soul—a "primordial image," as Jacob Burckhardt once called it—the figure of a physician or teacher of mankind. The archetypal image of the wise man, the saviour or redeemer, lies buried and dormant in man's unconscious since the dawn of culture; it is awakened whenever the times are out of joint and a human society is committed to a serious error. When people go astray they feel the need of a guide or teacher or even of the physician. These primordial images are numerous, but do not appear in the dreams of individuals or in works of art until they are called into being by the waywardness of the general outlook. When conscious life is characterized by one-sidedness and by a false attitude, then they are activated—one might say, "instinctively"—and come to light in the dreams of individuals and the visions of artists and seers, thus restoring the psychic equilibrium of the epoch.

In this way the work of the poet comes to meet the spiritual need of the society in which he lives, and for this reason his work means more to him than his personal fate, whether he is aware of this or not. Being essentially the instrument for his work, he is subordinate to it, and we have no reason for expecting him to interpret it for us. He has done the best that in him lies in giving it form, and he must leave the interpretation to others and to the future. A great work of art is like a dream; for all its apparent obviousness it does not explain itself and is never unequivocal. A dream never says: "You ought," or: "This is the truth." It presents an image in much the same way as nature allows a plant to grow, and we must draw our own conclusions. If a person has a nightmare, it means either that he is too much given to fear, or else that he is too exempt from it; and if he dreams of the old wise man it may mean that he is too pedagogical, as also that he stands in need of a teacher. In a subtle way both meanings come to the same thing, as we perceive when we are able to let the work of art act upon us as it acted upon the artist. To grasp its meaning, we must allow it to shape us as it once shaped him. Then we understand the nature of his experience. We see that he has drawn upon the healing and redeeming forces of the collective psyche that underlies consciousness with its isolation and its painful errors; that he has penetrated to that matrix of life in which all men are embedded, which imparts a common rhythm to all human existence, and allows the individual to communicate his feeling and his striving to mankind as a whole.

The secret of artistic creation and of the effectiveness of art is to be found in a return to the state of *participation mystique*—to that level of experience at which it is man who lives, and not the individual, and at which the weal or woe of the single human being does not count, but only human existence. This is why every great work of art is objective and impersonal, but none the less profoundly moves us each and all.

And this is also why the personal life of the poet cannot be held essential to his art—but at most a help or a hindrance to his creative task He may go the way of a Philistine, a good citizen, a neurotic, a fool or a criminal. His personal career may be inevitable and interesting, but it does not explain the poet.

11. BROOKS

"The Language of Paradox"

Cleanth Brooks (1906–   ) was born in Murray, Kentucky; he was graduated from Vanderbilt University, received an MA from Tulane and a B.Litt. degree from Oxford. He taught at Louisiana State University until 1947; since then he has been at Yale, where he became Gray professor of rhetoric in 1960.

Brooks' influence on modern criticism began in 1935 when with Robert Penn Warren he edited the *Southern Review*. One of his most influential books, *Understanding Poetry* (1938), was also done with Warren's collaboration, as well as the later *Understanding Fiction* (1943). He collaborated with Robert Heilman on *Understanding Drama* (1947), with W. K. Wimsatt, Jr., on the excellent *Literary Criticism: A Short History* (1957), and with John E. Hardy on *Poems of Mr. John Milton* (1952). Besides *The Well-Wrought Urn* (1947), he has also written *Modern Poetry and the Tradition* (1939), *William Faulkner: The Yoknapatawpha Country* (1963), as well as many articles.

Cleanth Brooks is one of the major spokesmen for what has come to be called New Criticism. So influential and successful an approach has, of course, had its share of opponents. The controversy regarding New Criticism has been raging for thirty years and gives little indication of subsiding. The main reason, perhaps, for the animosity this approach elicits is the fact that it goes against most of the other traditional critical approaches—historical, psychological, biographical, etc.

Basically what Brooks attempts is "seeing what the poem is." This "seeing" gives a hint about the approach: a concrete examination of a particular poem, a concrete literary work. Thus there are few general statements about the approach. A few general or universal notions are applied to the particular poem: the analysis of the poem in terms of these notions *is* the critical approach.

Brooks' essay, "The Language of Paradox,"* which is included here in its entirety, is a good example of applying New Criticism. The basic premise is that a writer deals with words and that these must be closely analyzed in order to arrive at an evaluation of the total structure. The words are examined for their connotations and denotations; metaphors are explained; irony and paradoxes are scrutinized. "Paradox," as one can judge from the title of the essay, is obviously important. Brooks himself has this to say about it: "Our prejudices force us to regard paradox as intellectual rather than emotional, clever rather than profound, rational rather than divinely inspired" and yet "apparently the truth which the poet utters can be approached only in terms of paradox" (unlike the truth of the scientist). To illustrate this point Brooks turns to two sonnets by Wordsworth—a poet who insists on simplicity and distrusts sophistry. He finds basic paradoxes underlying both sonnets.

Closely connected with the revealing of paradoxes is a judgment concerning the excellence of a poem. Unlike other contemporary critics, Brooks insists on the necessity for value judgments. He points out that Wordsworth's sonnet, "Composed upon Westminster Bridge," is agreed to be one of his best. Yet an "attempt to account for it on the grounds of nobility of sentiment soon breaks down. . . . The attempt to make a case for the poem in terms of the brilliance of its images also quickly breaks down. . . ." The poem gets its power "from the paradoxical situation out of which it arises." And paradoxes to Brooks "spring from the very nature of the poet's language: it is a language in which the connotations play as great a part as the denotations."

A good poet works by contradiction (paradox), qualification, and analogies. To show this fully Brooks analyzes Donne's poem, "Canonization," as a concrete case and thus does New Criticism rather than talk about New Criticism. Most of the analysis, in fact, is a detailed examination of the poem's metaphors, connotations, irony, tone, and, of course, paradoxes. Brooks finds at the end that Donne could only say what he did say so successfully by way of paradoxes.

No one, not even Aristotle or Longinus, placed so much emphasis on diction as the New Critics do. Indeed, it seems, that one could go no further in this emphasis. Other Aristotelian concerns are also important here. First Brooks points out in his later essay, "Literary Criticism: Poet, Poem, and Reader," that Aristotle was also concerned with form, not with "Sophocles' deep concern for moral values." Like Aristotle, he also insists on the unity of a work of art, as well as the reader's unified experience. His concern with truth also has a familiar ring. How-

---

* From *The Well-Wrought Urn*, copyright 1947, by Cleanth Brooks. Reprinted by permission of Harcourt Brace Jovanovich, Inc.

ever, Brooks belongs to the new tradition risen since James, of not contrasting literature and history but literature and science when proclaiming the truth of literature.

If Brooks' criticism goes as far as possible in focusing on diction, it also goes as far as possible in focusing on the concrete and the particular in a work of art. It is also, perhaps, as far as one can go in applying "objective" standards to a subjective evaluation of literature.

Few of us are prepared to accept the statement that the language of poetry is the language of paradox. Paradox is the language of sophistry, hard, bright, witty; it is hardly the language of the soul. We are willing to allow that paradox is a permissible weapon which a Chesterton may on occasion exploit. We may permit it in epigram, a special subvariety of poetry; and in satire, which though useful, we are hardly willing to allow to be poetry at all. Our prejudices force us to regard paradox as intellectual rather than emotional, clever rather than profound, rational rather than divinely irrational.

Yet there is a sense in which paradox is the language appropriate and inevitable to poetry. It is the scientist whose truth requires a language purged of every trace of paradox; apparently the truth which the poet utters can be approached only in terms of paradox. I overstate the case, to be sure; it is possible that the title of this chapter is itself to be treated as merely a paradox. But there are reasons for thinking that the overstatement which I propose may light up some elements in the nature of poetry which tend to be overlooked.

The case of William Wordsworth, for instance, is instructive on this point. His poetry would not appear to promise many examples of the language of paradox. He usually prefers the direct attack. He insists on simplicity; he distrusts whatever seems sophistical. And yet the typical Wordsworth poem is based upon a paradoxical situation. Consider his celebrated

> *It is a beauteous evening, calm and free,*
> *The holy time is quiet as a Nun*
> *Breathless with adoration. . . .*

The poet is filled with worship, but the girl who walks beside him is not worshipping. The implication is that she should respond to the holy time, and become like the evening itself, nunlike; but she seems less worshipful than inanimate nature itself. Yet

> *If thou appear untouched by solemn thought,*
> *Thy nature is not therefore less divine:*
> *Thou liest in Abraham's bosom all the year;*
> *And worship'st at the Temple's inner shrine,*
> *God being with thee when we know it not.*

The underlying paradox (of which the enthusiastic reader may well be unconscious) is nevertheless thoroughly necessary, even for that reader. Why does the innocent girl worship more deeply than the self-conscious poet who walks beside her? Because she is filled with an unconscious sympathy for *all* of nature, not merely the grandiose and solemn. One remembers the lines from Wordsworth's friend, Coleridge:

> *He prayeth best, who loveth best*
> *All things both great and small.*

Her unconscious sympathy is the unconscious worship. She is in communion with nature "all the year," and her devotion is continual whereas that of the poet is sporadic and momentary. But we have not done with the paradox yet. It not only underlies the poem, but something of the paradox informs the poem, though, since this is Wordsworth, rather timidly. The comparison of the evening to the nun actually has more than one dimension. The calm of the evening obviously means "worship," even to the dull-witted and insensitive. It corresponds to the trappings of the nun, visible to everyone. Thus, it suggests not merely holiness, but, in the total poem, even a hint of Pharisaical holiness, with which the girl's careless innocence, itself a symbol of her continual secret worship, stands in contrast.

Or consider Wordsworth's sonnet, "Composed upon Westminster Bridge." I believe that most readers will agree that it is one of Wordsworth's most successful poems; yet most students have the greatest difficulty in accounting for its goodness. The attempt to account for it on the grounds of nobility of sentiment soon breaks down. On this level, the poem merely says: that the city in the morning light presents a picture which is majestic and touching to all but the most dull of soul; but the poem says very little more about the sight: the city is beautiful in the morning light and it is awfully still. The attempt to make a case for the poem in terms of the brilliance of its images also quickly breaks down: the students searches for graphic details in vain; there are next to no realistic touches. In fact, the poet simply huddles the details together:

> *silent, bare,*
> *Ships, towers, domes, theatres, and temples lie*
> *Open unto the fields. . . .*

We get a blurred impression—points of roofs and pinnacles along the skyline, all twinkling in the morning light. More than that, the sonnet as a whole contains some very flat writing and some well-worn comparisons.

The reader may ask: Where, then, does the poem get its power? It gets it, it seems to me, from the paradoxical situation out of which the poem arises. The speaker is honestly surprised, and he manages to get some sense of awed surprise into the poem. It is odd to the poet that the city should be able to "wear the beauty of the morning" at all. Mount Snowden, Skiddaw, Mont Blanc—these wear it by natural right, but surely not grimy, feverish London. This is the point of the almost shocked exclamation:

> *Never did sun more beautifully steep*
> *In his first splendour*, valley, rock, *or* hill . . .

The "smokeless air" reveals a city which the poet did not know existed: man-made London is a part of nature too, is lighted by the sun of nature, and lighted to as beautiful effect.

> *The river glideth at his own sweet will . . .*

A river is the most "natural" thing that one can imagine; it has the elasticity, the curved line of nature itself. The poet had never been able to regard this one as a real river—now, uncluttered by barges, the river reveals itself as a natural thing, not at all disciplined into a rigid and mechanical pattern: it is like the daffodils, or the mountain brooks, artless, and whimsical, and "natural" as they. The poem closes, you will remember, as follows:

> *Dear God! the very houses seem asleep;*
> *And all that mighty heart is lying still!*

The city, in the poet's insight of the morning, has earned its right to be considered organic, not merely mechanical. That is why the stale metaphor of the sleeping houses is strangely renewed. The most exciting thing that the poet can say about the houses is that they are *asleep*. He has been in the habit of counting them dead—as just mechanical and inanimate; to say they are "asleep" is to say that they are alive, that they participate in the life of nature. In the same way, the tired old metaphor which sees a great city as a pulsating heart of empire becomes revivified. It is only when the poet sees the city under the semblance of death that he can see it as actually alive—quick with the only life which he can accept, the organic life of "nature."

It is not my intention to exaggerate Wordsworth's own consciousness of the paradox involved. In this poem, he prefers, as is usual with him, the frontal attack. But the situation is paradoxical here as in so many of his poems. In his preface to the second edition of the *Lyrical Ballads* Wordsworth stated that his general purpose was "to choose incidents and situations from common life" but so to treat them that "ordinary things should be presented to the mind in an unusual aspect." Coleridge was to state the purpose for him later, in terms which make even more evident Wordsworth's exploitation of the paradoxical: "Mr. Wordsworth . . . was to propose to himself as his object, to give the charm of novelty to things of every day, and to excite a feeling analogous to the supernatural, by awakening the mind's attention from the lethargy of custom, and directing it to the loveliness and the wonders of the world before us . . ." Wordsworth, in short, was consciously attempting to show his audience that the common was really uncommon, the prosaic was really poetic.

Coleridge's terms, "the charm of novelty to things of every day," "awakening the mind," suggest the Romantic preoccupation with wonder—the surprise, the revelation which puts the tarnished familiar world in a new light. This may well be the *raison d'être* of most Romantic paradoxes; and yet the neo-classic poets use paradox for much the same reason. Consider Pope's lines from "The Essay on Man":

> *In doubt his Mind or Body to prefer;*
> *Born but to die, and reas'ning but to err;*
> *Alike in ignorance, his Reason such,*
> *Whether he thinks too little, or too much . . .*
>
> *Created half to rise, and half to fall;*
> *Great Lord of all things, yet a Prey to all;*
> *Sole Judge of Truth, in endless Error hurl'd;*
> *The Glory, Jest, and Riddle of the world !*

Here, it is true, the paradoxes insist on the irony, rather than the wonder. But Pope too might have claimed that he was treating the things of everyday, man himself, and awakening his mind so that he would view himself in a new and blinding light. Thus, there is a certain awed wonder in Pope just as there is a certain trace of irony implicit in the Wordsworth sonnets. There is, of course, no reason why they should not occur together, and they do. Wonder and irony merge in many of the lyrics of Blake; they merge in Coleridge's *Ancient Mariner*. The variations in emphasis are numerous. Gray's "Elegy" uses a typical Wordsworth "situation" with the rural scene and with peasants contemplated in the light of their "betters." But in the "Elegy" the balance is heavily tilted in the direction of irony, the revelation an ironic rather than a startling one:

> *Can storied urn or animated bust*
> *Back to its mansion call the fleeting breath?*
> *Can Honour's voice provoke the silent dust?*
> *Or Flatt'ry sooth the dull cold ear of Death?*

But I am not here interested in enumerating the possible variations; I am interested rather in our seeing that the paradoxes spring from the very nature of the poet's language; it is a language in which the connotations play as great a part as the denotations. And I do not mean that the connotations are important as supplying some sort of frill or trimming, something external to the real matter in hand. I mean that the poet does not use a notation at all—as the scientist may properly be said to do so. The poet, within limits, has to make up his language as he goes.

T. S. Eliot has commented upon "that perpetual slight alteration of language, words perpetually juxtaposed in new and sudden combinations," which occurs in poetry. It *is* perpetual; it cannot be kept out of the poem; it can only be directed and controlled. The tendency of science if necessarily to stabilize terms, to freeze them into strict denotations; the poet's tendency is by contrast disruptive. The terms are continually modifying each other, and thus violating their dictionary meanings. To take a very simple example, consider the adjectives in the first lines of Wordsworth's evening sonnet: *beauteous, calm, free, holy, quiet, breathless*. The juxtapositions are hardly startling; and yet notice this: the evening is like a nun breathless with adoration. The adjective "breathless" suggests tremendous excitement; and yet the evening is not only quiet but *calm*. There is no final contradiction, to be sure: it is *that* kind of calm and *that* kind of excitement, and the two states may well occur together. But the poet has no one term. Even if he had a polysyllabic technical term, the term would not provide the solution for his problem. He must work by contradiction and qualification.

We may approach the problem in this way: the poet has to work by analogies. All of the subtler states of emotion, as I. A. Richards has pointed out, necessarily demand metaphor for their expression. The poet must work by analogies, but the metaphors do not lie in the same plane or fit neatly edge to edge. There is a continual tilting of the planes; necessary overlappings, discrepancies, contradictions. Even the most direct and simple poet is forced into paradoxes far more often than we think, if we are sufficiently alive to what he is doing.

But in dilating on the difficulties of the poet's task, I do not want to leave the impression that it is a task which necessarily defeats him, or even that with his method he may not win to a fine precision. To use Shakespeare's figure, he can

> *with assays of bias*
> *By indirections find directions out.*

Shakespeare had in mind the game of lawnbowls in which the bowl is distorted, a distortion which allows the skillful player to bowl a curve. To elaborate the figure, science makes use of the perfect sphere and its attack can be direct. The method of art can, I believe, never be direct—is always indirect. But that does not mean that the master of the game cannot place the bowl where he wants it. The serious difficulties will only occur when he confuses his game with that of science and mistakes the nature of his appropriate instrument. Mr. Stuart Chase a few years ago, with a touching naîvete, urged us to take the distortion out of the bowl—to treat language like notation.

I have said that even the apparently simple and straightfoward poet is forced into paradoxes by the the nature of his instrument. Seeing this, we should not be surprised to find poets who consciously employ it to gain a compression and precision otherwise unobtainable. Such a method, like any other, carries with it its own perils. But the dangers are not overpowering; the poem is not predetermined to a shallow and glittering sophistry. The method is an extension of the normal language of poetry, not a perversion of it.

I should like to refer the reader to a concrete case. Donne's "Canonization" ought to provide a sufficiently extreme instance. The basic metaphor which underlies the poem (and which is reflected in the title) involves a sort of paradox. For the poet daringly treats profane love as it it were divine love. The canonization is not that of a pair of holy anchorites who have renounced the world and the flesh. The hermitage of each is the other's body; but they do renounce the world, and so their title to sainthood is cunningly argued. The poem then is a parody of Christian sainthood; but it is an intensely serious parody of a sort that modern man, habituated as he is to an easy yes or no, can hardly understand. He refuses to accept the paradox as a serious rhetorical device; and since he is able to accept it only as a cheap trick, he is forced into this dilemma. Either: Donne does not take love seriously; here he is merely sharpening his wit as a sort of mechanical exercise. Or: Donne does not take sainthood seriously; here he is merely indulging in a cynical and bawdy parody.

Neither account is true; a reading of the poem will show that Donne takes both love and religion seriously; it will show, further, that the paradox is here his inevitable instrument. But to see this plainly will require a closer reading than most of us give to poetry.

The poem opens dramatically on a note of exasperation. The "you" whom the speaker addresses is not identified. We can imagine that it is a person, perhaps a friend, who is objecting to the speaker's love affair. At any rate, the person represents the practical world which regards love as a silly affectation. To use the metaphor on which the poem is built, the friend represents the secular world which the lovers have renounced.

Donne begins to suggest this metaphor in the first stanza by the contemptuous alternatives which he suggests to the friend:

> . . . *chide my palsie, or my gout,*
> *My five gray haires, or ruin'd fortune flout. . . .*

The implications are: (1) All right, consider my love as an infirmity, as a disease, if you will, but confine yourself to my other infirmities, my palsy, my approaching old age, my ruined fortune. You stand a better chance of curing those; in chiding me for this one, you are simply wasting your time as well as mine. (2) Why don't you pay attention to your own welfare—go on and get wealth and honor for yourself. What should you care if I do give these up on pursuing my love.

The two main categories of secular success are neatly, and contemptuously epitomized in the line

> *Or the Kings reall, or his stamped face . . .*

Cultivate the court and gaze at the king's face there, or, if you prefer, get into business and look at his face stamped on coins. But let me alone.

This conflict between the "real" world and the lover absorbed in the world of love runs through the poem; it dominates the second stanza in which the torments of love, so vivid to the lover, affect the real world not at all—

> *What merchants ships have my sighs drown'd?*

It is touched on in the fourth stanza in the contrast between the word "Chronicle" which suggests secular history with its pomp and magnificence, the history of kings and princes, and the word "sonnets" with its suggestions of trivial and precious intricacy. The conflict appears again in the last stanza, only to be resolved when the unworldly lovers, love's saints who have given up the world, paradoxically achieve a more intense world. But here the paradox is still contained in, and supported by, the dominant metaphor: so does the holy anchorite win a better world by giving up this one.

But before going on to discuss this development of the theme, it is important to see what else the second stanza does. For it is in this second stanza and the third, that the poet shifts the tone of the poem, modulating from the note of irritation with which the poem opens into the quite different tone with which it closes.

Donne accomplishes the modulation of tone by what may be called an analysis of love-metaphor. Here, as in many of his poems, he shows that he is thoroughly self-conscious about what he is doing. This second stanza, he fills with the conventionalized figures of the Petrarchan tradition: the wind of lovers' sighs, the floods of lovers' tears, etc.— extravagant figures with which the contemptuous secular friend might be expected to tease the lover. The implication is that the poet himself recognizes the absurdity of the Petrarchan love metaphors. But what of it? The very absurdity of the jargon which lovers are expected to talk makes for his argument: their love, however absurd it may appear to the world, does no harm to the world. The practical friend need have no fears: there will still be wars to fight and lawsuits to argue.

The opening of the third stanza suggests that this vein of irony is to be maintained. The poet points out to his friend the infinite fund of such absurdities which can be applied to lovers:

> *Call her one, mee another flye,*
> *We'are Tapers too, and at our owne cost die. . . .*

For that matter, the lovers can conjure up for themselves plenty of such fantastic comparisons: *they* know what the world thinks of them. But these figures of the third stanza are no longer the threadbare Petrarchan conventionalities; they have sharpness and bite. The last one, the likening of the lovers to the phoenix, is fully serious, and with it, the tone has shifted from ironic banter into a defiant but controlled tenderness.

The effect of the poet's implied awareness of the lovers' apparent madness is to cleanse and revivify metaphor; to indicate the sense in which the poet accepts it, and thus to prepare us for accepting seriously the fine and seriously intended metaphors which dominate the last two stanzas of the poem.

The opening line of the fourth stanza,

> *Wee can dye by it, if not live by love,*

achieves an effect of tenderness and deliberate resolution. The lovers are ready to die to the world; they are committed; they are not callow but confident. (The basic metaphor of the saint, one notices, is being carried on; the lovers in their renunciation of the world, have something of the confident resolution of the saint. By the bye, the word "legend"—

> *. . . if unfit for tombes and hearse*
> *Our legend bee—*

in Donne's time meant "the life of a saint.") The lovers are willing to forego the ponderous and stately chronicle and to accept the trifling and insubstantial "sonnet" instead; but then if the urn be well wrought, it provides a finer memorial for one's ashes than does the pompous and grotesque monument. With the finely contemptuous, yet quiet phrase, "halfe-acre tombes," the world which the lovers reject expands into something gross and vulgar. But the figure works further; the pretty sonnets will not merely hold their ashes as a decent earthly memorial. Their legend, their story, will gain them canonization; and approved as love's saints, other lovers will invoke them.

In this last stanza, the theme receives a final complication. The lovers in rejecting life actually win to the most intense life. This paradox has been hinted at earlier in the phoenix metaphor. Here it receives a powerful dramatization. The lovers in becoming hermits, find that they have not lost the world, but have gained the world in each other, now a more intense, more meaningful world. Donne is not content to treat the lovers' discovery as something which comes to them passively, but rather as something which they actively achieve. They are like the saint, God's athlete:

> *Who did the whole worlds soule* contract, *and* drove
> *Into the glasses of your eyes.* . . .

The image is that of a violent squeezing as of a powerful hand. And what do the lovers "drive" into each other's eyes? The "Countries, Townes," and "Courtes," which they renounced in the first stanza of the poem. The unworldly lovers thus become the most "worldly" of all.

The tone with which the poem closes is one of triumphant achievement, but the tone is a development contributed to by various earlier elements. One of the more important elements which works toward our acceptance of the final paradox is the figure of the phoenix, which will bear a little further analysis.

The comparison of the lovers to the phoenix is very skillfully related to the two earlier comparisons, that in which the lovers are like burning tapers, and that in which they are like the eagle and the dove. The phoenix comparison gathers up both: the phoenix is a bird, and like the tapers, it burns. We have a selected series of items: the phoenix figure seems to come in a natural stream of association. "Call us what you will," the lover says, and rattles off in his desperation the first comparisons that occur to him. The comparison to the phoenix seems thus merely another outlandish one, the most outrageous of all. But it is this most fantastic one, stumbled over apparently in his haste, that the poet goes on to develop. It really describes the lovers best and justifies their renunciation. For the phoenix is not two but one, "we two being one, are it"; and it burns, not like the taper at its own cost, but to live again. Its death is life: "Wee dye and rise the same . . ." The poet literally justifies the fantastic assertion. In the sixteenth and seventeenth centuries to "die" means to experience the consummation of the act of love. The lovers after the act are the same. Their love is not exhausted in mere lust. This is their title to canonization. Their love is like the phoenix.

I hope that I do not seem to juggle the meaning of *die*. The meaning that I have cited can be abundantly justified in the literature of the period; Shakespeare uses "die" in this sense; so does Dryden. Moreover, I do not think that I give it undue emphasis. The word is in a crucial position. On it is pivoted the transition to the next stanza,

> *Wee can dye by it, if not live by love,*
> *And if unfit for tombes . . .*

Most important of all, the sexual submeaning of "die" does not contradict the other meanings: the poet is saying: "Our death is really a more intense life"; "We can afford to trade life (the world) for death (love), for that death is the consummation of life"; "After all, one does not expect to live *by* love, one expects, and wants, to die *by* it." But in the total passage he is also saying: "Because our love is not mundane, we can give up the world"; "Because our love is not merely lust, we can give up the other lusts, the lust for wealth and power"; "because," and this is said with an inflection of irony as by one who knows the world too well, "because our love can outlast its consummation, we are a minor miracle, we are love's saints." This passage with its ironical tenderness and its realism feeds and supports the brilliant paradox with which the poem closes.

There is one more factor in developing and sustaining the final effect. The poem is an instance of the doctrine which it asserts; it is both the assertion and the realization of the assertion. The poet has actually before our eyes built within the song the "pretty room" with which he says the lovers can be content. The poem itself is the well-wrought urn which can hold the lovers' ashes and which will not suffer in comparison with the prince's "halfe-acre tomb."

And how necessary are the paradoxes? Donne might have said directly, "Love in a cottage is enough." "The Canonization" contains this admirable thesis, but it contains a great deal more. He might have been as forthright as a later lyricist who wrote, "We'll build a sweet little nest,/ Somewhere out in the West,/ And let the rest of the world go by." He might even have imitated that more metaphysical lyric, which maintains, "You're the cream in my coffee." "The Canonization" touches on all these observations, but it goes beyond them, not merely in dignity, but in precision.

I submit that the only way by which the poet could say what "The Canonization" says is by paradox. More direct methods may be tempting, but all of them enfeeble and distort what is to be said. This statement may seem the less surprising when we reflect on how many of the important things which the poet has to say have to be said by means of paradox: most of the language of lovers is such—"The Canonization" is a good example; so is most of the language of religion—"He who would save his life, must lose it"; "The last shall be first." Indeed, almost any insight important enough to warrant a great poem apparently has to be stated in such terms. Deprived of the character of paradox with its twin concomitants of irony and wonder, the matter of Donne's poem unravels into "facts," biological, sociological, and economic. What happens to Donne's lovers if we consider them "scientifically," without benefit of the supernaturalism which the poet confers upon them? Well, what happens to Shakespeare's lovers, for Shakespeare uses the basic metaphor of "The Canonization" in his *Romeo and Juliet*? In their first conversation, the lovers play with the analogy between the lover and the pilgrim to the Holy Land. Juliet says:

> *For saints have hands that pilgrims' hands do touch*
> *And palm to palm is holy palmers' kiss.*

Considered scientifically, the lovers become Mr. Aldous Huxley's animals, "quietly sweating, palm to palm."

For us today, Donne's imagination seems obsessed with the problem of unity; the sense in which the lovers become one—the sense in which the soul is united with God. Frequently, as we have seen, one type of union becomes a metaphor for the other. It may not be too far-fetched to see both as instances of, and metaphors for, the union which the creative imagination itself effects. For that fusion is not logical; it apparently violates science and common sense; it welds together the discordant and the contradictory. Coleridge has of course given us the classic description of its nature and power. It "reveals itself in the balance or reconcilement of opposite or discordant qualities: of sameness, with difference; of the general, with the concrete; the idea, with the image; the individual, with the representative; the sense of novelty and freshness, with old and familiar objects; a more than usual state of emotion, with more than usual order. . . ." It is a great and illuminating statement, but is a series of paradoxes. Apparently Coleridge could describe the effect of the imagination in no other way.

Shakespeare, in one of his poems, has given a description that oddly parallels that of Coleridge.

> *Reason in it selfe confounded,*
> *Saw Division grow together,*
> *To themselves yet either neither,*
> *Simple were so well compounded.*

I do not know what his "The Phoenix and the Turtle" celebrates. Perhaps it *was* written to honor the marriage of Sir John Salisbury and Ursula Stanley; or perhaps the Phoenix is Lucy, Countess of Bedford; or perhaps the poem is merely an essay on Platonic love. But the scholars themselves are so uncertain, that I think we will do little violence to established habits of thinking, if we boldly pre-empt the poem for our own purposes. Certainly the poem is an instance of that magic power which Coleridge sought to describe. I propose that we take it for a moment as a poem about that power;

> *So they loved as love in twaine,*
> *Had the essence but in one,*
> *Two distincts, Division none,*
> *Number there in love was slaine.*
>
> *Hearts remote, yet not asunder;*
> *Distance and no space was seene,*
> *Twixt this* Turtle *and his* Queene;
> *But in them it were a wonder.* . . . .
>
> *Propertie was thus appalled,*
> *That the selfe was not the same;*
> *Single Natures double name,*
> *Neither two nor one was called.*

Precisely! The nature is single, one, unified. But the name is double, and today with our multiplication of sciences, it is multiple. If the poet is to be true to his poetry, he must call it neither two nor one: the paradox is his only solution. The difficulty has intensified since Shakespeare's day: the timid poet, when confronted with the problem of "Single Natures double name," has too often funked it. A history of poetry from Dryden's time to our own might bear as its subtitle "The Half-Hearted Phoenix."

In Shakespeare's poem, Reason is "in it selfe confounded" at the union of the Phoenix and the Turtle, but it recovers to admit its own bankruptcy:

> *Love hath Reason, Reason none,*
> *If what parts, can so remaine.* . . . .

and it is Reason which goes on to utter the beautiful threnos with which the poem concludes:

> *Beautie, Truth, and Raritie,*
> *Grace in all simplicitie,*
> *Here enclosde, in cinders lie.*
>
> *Death is now the* Phoenix *nest,*
> *And the* Turtles *loyall brest,*
> *To eternitie doth rest. . . .*
>
> *Truth may seeme, but cannot be,*
> *Beautie bragge, but tis not she,*
> *Truth and Beautie buried be.*
>
> *To this urne let those repaire,*
> *That are either true or faire,*
> *For these dead Birds, sigh a prayer.*

Having pre-empted the poem for our own purposes, it may not be too outrageous to go on to make one further observation. The urn to which we are summoned, the urn which holds the ashes of the phoenix, is like the well-wrought urn of Donne's "Canonization" which holds the phoenix-lovers' ashes: it is the poem itself. One is reminded of still another urn, Keats's Grecian urn, which contained for Keats, Truth and Beauty, as Shakespeare's urn encloses "Beautie, Truth, and Raritie." But there is a sense in which all such well-wrought urns contain the ashes of a Phoenix. The urns are not meant for memorial purposes only, though that often seems to be their chief significance to the professors of literature. The phoenix rises from its ashes; or ought to rise; but it will not arise for all our mere sifting and measuring the ashes, or testing them for their chemical content. We must be prepared to accept the paradox of the imagination itself; else "Beautie, Truth, and Raritie" remain enclosed in their cinders and we shall end with essential cinders, for all our pains.

12. AUERBACH

"Odysseus' Scar"

One of the important critics of this century, Erich Auerbach (1892–1957), was born in Berlin, Germany. He studied law, art history, and philology at various German universities, received a PhD in 1921 from Greifswald University, and the degree of Doctor of Laws from Heidelberg in 1930. In 1929 he was made professor of Romance philology at Marburg University, from which he was discharged by the Nazis. He taught at the Turkish State University in Istanbul before coming to America in 1947. Here he taught at Pennsylvania State University, the Princeton Institute for Advanced Study, and finally was the Sterling professor of Romance languages at Yale.

Erich Auerbach has written a number of essays and long works, most of which have been translated into English. Among these are: *Mimesis, Introduction to Romance Languages and Literature*, and *Scenes from the Drama of European Literature*.

In *Mimesis* Auerbach in a sense summarizes all criticism so far. He accepts Aristotle's premise of art as imitation of nature (as the complete title shows: *Mimesis: The Representation of Reality in Western Literature*), and then he shows that each age imitates nature according to its own preconceptions and ideas as to what reality is. However, of all critics considered so far, Auerbach's thought just about defies all efforts at a summary—not that any critic's views are easily summarized. When one summarizes a chapter of *Mimesis*, one wishes to quote him; as one begins to quote, one wishes to continue quoting. This is partly due to his magnificent style, but it is primarily due to the fact that there is too much to be summarized: the reading of one chapter is first the close examination of a literary text, then an extremely suggestive and intelligent examination of various elements in it, and finally a placing of the text within the particular age. René Wellek explains the method in the following way: "Each passage chosen is used as a springboard for comments which start usually with a close reading, an interpretation of meaning, observations on diction, grammar and syntax. But Mr. Auerbach never rests content with an analysis of style but moves from that to reflections on the attitude of a writer toward reality and his technique of reproducing it, and these topics, in turn, lead to reflections about periods and cultures, social conditions and assumptions. The procedure is by no means uniform. Almost every chapter is organized differently, but almost always Mr. Auerbach combines three methods: those of stylistics, of intellectual history, and of historically oriented sociology." ("Auerbach's Special Realism" [A review of *Mimesis*], *Kenyon Review*, vol. XVI, (1954), p. 300.) Later Wellek adds: "The work is a strikingly successful combination of philology, stylistics, history of ideas and sociology, of meticulous learning and artistic taste, of historical imagination and awareness of our own age." (p. 307)

In the first chapter of *Mimesis*, entitled "Odysseus' Scar,"* which is reprinted here in its entirety, Auerbach moves slowly toward a juxtaposition of the Greek vision of reality with that found in the Bible. As his springboard, he takes an Aristotelian recognition scene: Odysseus' nurse, Euryclea, recognizes him as the long-gone king by his childhood scar. Auerbach then proceeds to show how events, past and present, the characters, and even their thoughts are "clearly outlined, brightly and uniformly illuminated." All is presented in the foreground. An examination of the syntax follows after Auerbach points out that "the separate elements of a phenomenon are most clearly placed in relation to one another; a large number of conjunctions, adverbs, particles, and other syntactical tools, all clearly circumscribed and delicately differentiated in meaning, delimit persons, things, and portions of incidents in respect to one another, and at the same time bring them together in a continuous and ever flexible connection. . . ." (p. 6)

For a comparison with the Homeric representation of reality Auerbach turns to the Bible. Here in the story of Abraham's sacrifice of Isaac he finds that the characters are not illuminated and that their thoughts are not externalized. Yet, as a result of their previous history, the persons in the Bible have greater depths of time, fate, and consciousness than do the Homeric characters. Whereas there are horizontal connections in time in Homer, there are vertical ones in the Bible. The Biblical narrators were not writing "objective" truth; they were not concerned with realism and yet produced it.

---

* Erich Auerbach, *Mimesis: The Representation of Reality in Western Literature*, trans. by Willard R. Trask (copyright 1953 by Princeton University Press; Princeton Paperback, 1968), pp. 3–23. Reprinted by permission of Princeton University Press.

This short summary of the first chapter in *Mimesis* does not really give the scope and breadth of the whole work. As Wellek again points out: "It is a book of such scope and breadth, ranging as it does from Homer to Proust, it combines so many methods so skillfully, it raises so many questions of theory, history, and criticism, it displays so much erudition, insight and wisdom, that it has been hailed as 'the most important and brilliant book in the field of aesthetics and literary history that has been published in the last fifty years.'" (p. 299)

Readers of the *Odyssey* will remember the well-prepared and touching scene in book 19, when Odysseus has at last come home, the scene in which the old housekeeper Euryclea, who had been his nurse, recognizes him by a scar on his thigh. The stranger has won Penelope's good will; at his request she tells the housekeeper to wash his feet, which, in all old stories, is the first duty of hospitality toward a tired traveler. Euryclea busies herself fetching water and mixing cold with hot, meanwhile speaking sadly of her absent master, who is probably of the same age as the guest, and who perhaps, like the guest, is even now wandering somewhere, a stranger; and she remarks how astonishingly like him the guest looks. Meanwhile Odysseus, remembering his scar, moves back out of the light; he knows that, despite his efforts to hide his identity, Euryclea will now recognize him, but he wants at least to keep Penelope in ignorance. No sooner has the old woman touched the scar than, in her joyous surprise, she lets Odysseus' foot drop into the basin; the water spills over, she is about to cry out her joy; Odysseus restrains her with whispered threats and endearments; she recovers herself and conceals her emotion. Penelope, whose attention Athena's foresight had diverted from the incident, has observed nothing.

All this is scrupulously externalized and narrated in leisurely fashion. The two women express their feelings in copious direct discourse. Feelings though they are, with only a slight admixture of the most general considerations upon human destiny, the syntactical connection between part and part is perfectly clear, no contour is blurred. There is also room and time for orderly, perfectly well-articulated, uniformly illuminated descriptions of implements, ministrations, and gestures; even in the dramatic moment of recognition, Homer does not omit to tell the reader that it is with his right hand that Odysseus takes the old woman by the throat to keep her from speaking, at the same time that he draws her closer to him with his left. Clearly outlined, brightly and uniformly illuminated, men and things stand out in a realm where everything is visible; and not less clear—wholly expressed, orderly even in their ardor—are the feelings and thoughts of the persons involved.

In my account of the incident I have so far passed over a whole series of verses which interrupt it in the middle. There are more than seventy of these verses—while to the incident itself some forty are devoted before the interruption and some forty after it. The interruption, which comes just at the point when the housekeeper recognizes the scar—that is, at the moment of crisis—describes the origin of the scar, a hunting accident which occurred in Odysseus' boyhood, at a boar hunt, during the time of his visit to his grandfather Autolycus. This first affords an opportunity to inform the reader about Autolycus, his house, the precise degree of the kinship, his character, and, no less exhaustively than touchingly, his behavior after the birth of his grandson; then follows the visit of Odysseus, now grown to be a youth; the exchange of greetings, the banquet with which he is welcomed, sleep and waking, the early start for the hunt, the tracking of the beast, the struggle, Odysseus' being wounded by the boar's tusk, his recovery, his return to Ithaca, his parents' anxious questions—all is narrated, again with such a complete externalization of all the elements of the story and of their interconnections as to leave nothing in obscurity. Not until then does the narrator return to Penelope's chamber, not until then, the digression having run its course, does Euryclea, who had recognized the scar before the digression began, let Odysseus' foot fall back into the basin.

The first thought of a modern reader—that this is a device to increase suspense—is, if not wholly wrong, at least not the essential explanation of this Homeric procedure. For the element of suspense is very slight in the Homeric poems; nothing in their entire style is calculated to keep the reader or hearer breathless. The digressions are not meant to keep the reader in suspense, but rather to relax the tension. And this frequently occurs, as in the passage before us. The broadly narrated, charming, and subtly fashioned story of the hunt, with all its elegance and self-sufficiency, its wealth of idyllic pictures, seeks to win the reader over wholly to itself as long as he is hearing it, to make him forget what has just taken place during the foot-washing. But an episode that will increase suspense by retarding the action must be so constructed that it will not fill the present entirely, will not put the crisis, whose resolution is being awaited, entirely out of the reader's mind, and thereby destroy the mood of suspense; the crisis and the suspense must continue, must remain vibrant in the background. But Homer—and to this we shall have to return later—knows no background. What he narrates is for the time being the only present, and fills both the stage and the reader's mind completely. So it is with the passage before us. When the young Euryclea (vv. 401ff.) sets the infant Odysseus on his grandfather Autolycus' lap after the banquet, the aged Euryclea, who a few lines earlier had touched the wanderer's foot, has entirely vanished from the stage and from the reader's mind.

Goethe and Schiller, who, though not referring to this particular episode, exhanged letters in April 1797 on the subject of "the retarding element" in the Homeric poems in general, put it in direct opposition to the element of suspense—the latter word is not used, but is clearly implied when the "retarding" procedure is opposed, as something proper to epic, to tragic procedure (letters of April 19, 21, and 22). The "retarding element," the "going back and forth" by means of episodes, seems to me, too, in the Homeric poems, to be opposed to any tensional and suspensive striving toward a goal, and doubtless Schiller is right in regard to Homer when he says that what he gives us is "simply the quiet existence and operation of things in accordance with their natures"; Homer's goal is "already present in every point of his progress." But both Schiller and Goethe raise Homer's procedure to the level of a law for epic poetry in general, and Schiller's words quoted above are meant to be universally binding upon the epic poet, in contradistinction from the tragic. Yet in both modern and ancient times, there are important epic works which are composed throughout with no "retarding element" in this sense but, on the contrary, with suspense throughout, and which perpetually "rob us of our emotional freedom"—which power Schiller will grant only to the tragic poet. And besides it seems to me undemonstrable and improbable that this procedure of Homeric poetry was directed by aesthetic considerations or even by an aesthetic feeling of the sort postulated by Goethe and Schiller. The effect, to be sure, is precisely that which they describe, and is, furthermore, the actual source of the conception of epic which they themselves hold, and with them all writers decisively influenced by classical antiquity. But the true cause of the impression of "retardation" appears to me to lie elsewhere—namely, in the need of the Homeric style to leave nothing which it mentions half in darkness and unexternalized.

The excursus upon the origin of Odysseus' scar is not basically different from the many passages in which a newly introduced character, or even a newly appearing object or implement, though it be in the thick of a battle, is described as to its nature and origin; or in which, upon the appearance of a god, we are told where he last was, what he was doing there, and by what road he reached the scene; indeed, even the Homeric epithets seem to me in the final analysis to be traceable to the same need for an externalization of phenomena in terms perceptible to the senses. Here is the scar, which comes up in the course of the narrative; and Homer's feeling simply will not permit him to see it appear out of the darkness of an unilluminated past; it must be set in full light, and with it a portion of the hero's boyhood—just as, in the *Iliad*, when the first ship is already burning and the Myrmidons finally arm that they may hasten to help, there is still time not only for the wonderful simile of the wolf, not only for the order of the Myrmidon host, but also for a detailed account of the ancestry of several subordinate leaders (16, vv. 155ff.). To be sure, the aesthetic effect thus produced was soon noticed and thereafter consciously sought; but the more original cause must have lain in the basic impulse of the Homeric style: to represent phenomena in a fully externalized form, visible and palpable in all their parts, and completely fixed in their spatial and temporal relations. Nor do psychological processes receive any other treatment: here too nothing must remain hidden and unexpressed. With the utmost fullness, with an orderliness which even passion does not disturb, Homer's personages vent their inmost hearts in speech; what they do not say to others, they speak in their own minds, so that the reader is informed of it. Much that is terrible takes place in the Homeric poems, but it seldom takes place wordlessly: Polyphemus talks to Odysseus; Odysseus talks to the suitors when he begins to kill them; Hector and Achilles talk at length, before battle and after; and no speech is so filled with anger or scorn that the particles which express logical and grammatical connections are lacking or out of place. This last observation is true, of course, not only of speeches but of the presentation in general. The separate elements of a phenomenon are most clearly placed in relation to one another; a large number of conjunctions, adverbs, particles, and other syntactical tools, all clearly circumscribed and delicately differentiated in meaning, delimit persons, things, and portions of incidents in respect to one another, and at the same time bring them together in a continuous and ever flexible connection; like the separate phenomena themselves, their relationships—their temporal, local, causal, final, consecutive, comparative, concessive, antithetical, and conditional limitations—are brought to light in perfect fullness; so that a continuous rhythmic procession of phenomena passes by, and never is there a form left fragmentary or half-illuminated, never a lacuna, never a gap, never a glimpse of unplumbed depths.

And this procession of phenomena takes place in the foreground—that is, in a local and temporal present which is absolute. One might think that the many interpolations, the frequent moving back and forth, would create a sort of perspective in time and place; but the Homeric style never gives any such impression. The way in which any impression of perspective is avoided can be clearly observed in the procedure for introducing episodes, a syntactical construction with which every reader of Homer is familiar; it is used in the passage we are considering, but can also be found in cases when the episodes are much shorter. To the word scar (v. 393) there is first attached a relative clause ("which once long ago a boar . . ."), which enlarges into a voluminous syntactical parenthesis; into this an independent sentence unexpectedly intrudes (v. 396: "A god himself gave him . . ."), which quietly disentangles itself from syntactical subordination, until, with verse 399, an equally free syntactical treatment of the new content begins a new present which continues unchallenged until, with verse 467 ("The old woman now touched it . . ."), the scene which had been broken off is resumed. To be sure, in the case of such long episodes as the one we are considering, a purely syntactical connection with the principal theme would hardly have been possible; but a connection with it through perspective would have been all the easier had the content been arranged with that end in view; if, that is, the entire story of the scar had been presented as a recollection which awakens in Odysseus' mind at this particular moment. It would have been perfectly easy to do; the story of the scar had only to be inserted two verses earlier, at the first mention of the word scar, where the motifs "Odysseus" and "recollection" were already at hand. But any such subjectivistic-perspectivistic procedure, creating a foreground and background, resulting in the present lying open to the depths of the past, is entirely foreign to the Homeric style; the Homeric style knows only a foreground, only a uniformly illuminated, uniformly objective present. And so the excursus does not begin until two lines later, when Euryclea has discovered the scar—the possibility for a perspectivistic connection no longer exists, and the story of the wound becomes an independent and exclusive present.

The genius of the Homeric style becomes even more apparent when it is compared with an equally ancient and equally epic style from a different world of forms. I shall attempt this comparison with the account of the sacrifice of Isaac, a homogeneous narrative produced by the so-called Elohist. The King James version translates the opening as follows (Genesis 22:1): "And it came to pass after these things, that God did tempt Abraham, and said to him, Abraham! and he said, Behold, here I am." Even this opening startles us when we come to it from Homer. Where are the two speakers? We are not told. The reader, however, knows that they are not normally to be found together in one place on earth, that one of them, God, in order to speak to Abraham, must come from somewhere, must enter the earthly realm from some unknown heights or depths. Whence does he come, whence does he call to Abraham? We are not told. He does not come, like Zeus or Poseidon, from the Aethiopians, where he has been enjoying a sacrificial feast. Nor are we told anything of his reasons for tempting Abraham so terribly. He has not, like Zeus, discussed them in set speeches with other gods gathered in council; nor have the deliberations in his own heart been presented to us; unexpected and mysterious, he enters the scene from some unknown height or depth and calls: Abraham! It will at once be said that this is to be explained by the particular concept of God which the Jews held and which was wholly different from that of the Greeks. True enough—but this constitutes no objection. For how is the Jewish concept of God to be explained? Even their earlier God of the desert was not fixed in form and content, and was alone; his lack of form, his lack of local habitation, his single-ness, was in the end not only maintained but developed even further in competition with the comparatively far more manifest gods of the surrounding Near Eastern world. The concept of God held by the Jews is less a cause than a symptom of their manner of comprehending and representing things.

This becomes still clearer if we now turn to the other person in the dialogue, to Abraham. Where is he? We do not know. He says, indeed: Here I am—but the Hebrew word means only something like "behold me," and in any case is not meant to indicate the actual place where Abraham is, but a moral position in respect to God, who has called to him—Here am I awaiting thy command. Where he is actually, whether in Beersheba or elsewhere, whether indoors or in the open air, is not stated; it does not interest the narrator, the reader is not informed; and what Abraham was doing when God called to him is left in the same obscurity. To realize the difference, consider Hermes' visit to Calypso, for example, where command, journey, arrival and reception of the visitor, situation and occupation of the person visited, are set forth in many verses; and even on occasions when gods appear suddenly and briefly, whether to help one of their favorites or to deceive or destroy some mortal whom they hate, their bodily forms, and usually the manner of their coming and going, are given in detail. Here, however, God appears without bodily form (yet he "appears"), coming from some unspecified place—we only hear his voice, and that utters nothing but a name, a name without an adjective, without a descriptive epithet for the person spoken to, such as is the rule in every Homeric address; and of Abraham too nothing is made perceptible except the words in which he answers God: *Hinne-ni*, Behold me here—with which, to be sure, a most touching gesture expressive of obedience and readiness is suggested, but it is left to the reader to visualize it. Moreover the two speakers are not on the same level: if we conceive of Abraham in the foreground, where it might be possible to picture him as prostrate or kneeling or bowing with outspread arms or gazing upward, God is not there too: Abraham's words and gestures are directed toward the depths of the picture or upward, but in any case the undetermined, dark place from which the voice comes to him is not in the foreground.

After this opening, God gives his command, and the story itself begins: everyone knows it; it unrolls with no episodes in a few independent sentences whose syntactical connection is of the most rudimentary sort. In this atmosphere it is unthinkable that an implement, a landscape through which the travelers passed, the serving-men, or the ass, should be described, that their origin or descent or material or appearance or usefulness should be set forth in terms of praise; they do not even admit an adjective: they are serving-men, ass, wood, and knife, and nothing else, without an epithet; they are there to serve the end which God has commanded; what in other respects they were, are, or will be, remains in darkness. A journey is made, because God has designated the place where the sacrifice is to be performed; but we are told nothing about the journey except that it took three days, and even that we are told in a mysterious way: Abraham and his followers rose "early in the morning" and "went unto" the place of which God had told him; on the third day he lifted up his eyes and saw the place from afar. That gesture is the only gesture, is indeed the only occurrence during the whole journey, of which we are told; and though its motivation lies in the fact that the place is elevated, its uniqueness still heightens the impression that the journey took place through a vacuum; it is as if, while he traveled on, Abraham had looked neither to the right nor to the left, had suppressed any sign of life in his followers and himself save only their footfalls.

Thus the journey is like a silent progress through the indeterminate and the contingent, a holding of the breath, a process which has no present, which is inserted, like a blank duration, between what has passed and what lies ahead, and which yet is measured: three days! Three such days positively demand the symbolic interpretation which they later received. They began "early in the morning." But at what time on the third day did Abraham lift up his eyes and see his goal? The text says nothing on the subject. Obviously not "late in the evening," for it seems that there was still time enough to climb the mountain and make the sacrifice. So "early in the morning" is given, not as an indication of time, but for the sake of its ethical significance; it is intended to express the resolution, the promptness, the punctual obedience of the sorely tried Abraham. Bitter to him is the early morning in which he saddles his ass, calls his serving-men and his son Isaac, and sets out; but he obeys, he walks on until the third day, then lifts up his eyes and sees the place. Whence he comes, we do not know, but the goal is clearly stated: Jeruel in the land of Moriah. What place this is meant to indicate is not clear—"Moriah" especially may be a later correction of some other word. But in any case the goal was given, and in any case it is a matter of some sacred spot which was to receive a particular consecration by being connected with Abraham's sacrifice. Just as little as "early in the morning" serves as a temporal indication does "Jeruel in the land of Moriah" serve as a geographical indication; and in both cases alike, the complementary indication is not given, for we know as little of the hour at which Abraham lifted up his eyes as we do of the place from which he set forth—Jeruel is significant not so much as the goal of an earthly journey, in its geographical relation to other places, as through its special election, through its relation to God, who designated it as the scene of the act, and therefore it must be named.

In the narrative itself, a third chief character appears: Isaac. While God and Abraham, the serving-men, the ass, and the implements are simply named, without mention of any qualities or any other sort of definition, Isaac once receives an appositive; God says, "Take Isaac, thine only son, whom thou lovest." But this is not a characterization of Isaac as a person, apart from his relation to his father and apart from the story; he may be handsome or ugly, intelligent or stupid, tall or short, pleasant or unpleasant—we are not told. Only what we need to know about him as a personage in the action, here and now, is illuminated, so that it may become apparent how terrible Abraham's temptation is, and that God is fully aware of it. By this example of the contrary, we see the significance of the descriptive adjectives and digressions of the Homeric poems; with their indications of the earlier and as it were absolute existence of the persons described, they prevent the reader from concentrating exclusively on a present crisis; even when the most terrible things are occurring, they prevent the establishment of an overwhelming suspense. But here, in the story of Abraham's sacrifice, the overwhelming suspense is present; what Schiller makes the goal of the tragic poet—to rob us of our emotional freedom, to turn our intellectual and spiritual powers (Schiller says "our activity") in one direction, to concentrate them there—is effected in this Biblical narrative, which certainly deserves the epithet epic.

We find the same contrast if we compare the two uses of direct discourse. The personages speak in the Bible story too; but their speech does not serve, as does speech in Homer, to manifest, to externalize thoughts—on the contrary, it serves to indicate thoughts which remain unexpressed. God gives his command in direct discourse, but he leaves his motives and his purpose unexpressed; Abraham, receiving the command, says nothing and does what he has been told to do. The conversation between Abraham and Isaac on the way to the place of sacrifice is only an interruption of the heavy silence and makes it all the more burdensome. The two of them, Isaac carrying the wood and Abraham with fire and a knife, "went together." Hesitantly, Isaac ventures to ask about the ram, and Abraham gives the well-known answer. Then the text repeats: "So they went both of them together." Everything remains unexpressed.

It would be difficult, then, to imagine styles more contrasted than those of these two equally ancient and equally epic texts. On the one hand, externalized, uniformly illuminated phenomena, at a definite time and in a definite place, connected together without lacunae in a perpetual foreground; thoughts and feeling completely expressed; events taking place in leisurely fashion and with very little of suspense. On the other hand, the externalization of only so much of the phenomena as is necessary for the purpose of the narrative, all else left in obscurity; the decisive points of the narrative alone are emphasized, what lies between is nonexistent; time and place are undefined and call for interpretation; thoughts and feeling remain unexpressed, are only suggested by the silence and the fragmentary speeches; the whole, permeated with the most unrelieved suspense and directed toward a single goal (and to that extent far more of a unity), remains mysterious and "fraught with background."

I will discuss this term in some detail, lest it be misunderstood. I said above that the Homeric style was "of the foreground" because, despite much going back and forth, it yet causes what is momentarily being narrated to give the impression that it is the only present, pure and without perspective. A consideration of the Elohistic text teaches us that our term is capable of a broader and deeper application. It shows that even the separate personages can be represented as possessing "background"; God is always so represented in the Bible, for he is not comprehensible in his presence, as is Zeus; it is always only "something" of him that appears, he always extends into depths. But even the human beings in the Biblical stories have greater depths of time, fate, and consciousness than do the human beings in Homer; although they are nearly always caught up in an event engaging all their faculties, they are not so entirely immersed in its present that they do not remain continually conscious of what has happened to them earlier and elsewhere; their thoughts and feelings have more layers, are more entangled. Abraham's actions are explained not only by what is happening to him at the moment, nor yet only by his character (as Achilles' actions by his courage and his pride, and Odysseus' by his versatility and foresightedness), but by his previous history; he remembers, he is constantly conscious of, what God has promised him and what God has already accomplished for him—his soul is torn between desperate rebellion and hopeful expectation; his silent obedience is multilayered, has background. Such a problematic psychological situation as this is impossible for any of the Homeric heroes, whose destiny is clearly defined and who wake every morning as if it were the first day of their lives: their emotions, though strong, are simple and find expression instantly.

How fraught with background, in comparison, are characters like Saul and David! How entangled and stratified are such human relations as those between David and Absalom, between David and Joab! Any such "background" quality of the psychological situation as that which the story of Absalom's death and its sequel (II Samuel 18 and 19, by the so-called Jahvist) rather suggests than expresses, is unthinkable in Homer. Here we are confronted not merely with the psychological processes of characters whose depth of background is veritably abysmal, but with a purely geographical background too. For David is absent from the battlefield; but the influence of his will and his feelings continues to operate, they affect even Joab in his rebellion and disregard for the consequences of his actions; in the magnificent scene with the two messengers, both the physical and psychological background is fully manifest, though the latter is never expressed. With this, compare, for example, how Achilles, who sends Patroclus first to scout and then into battle, loses almost all "presentness" so long as he is not physically present. But the most important thing is the "multilayeredness" of the individual character; this is hardly to be met with in Homer, or at most in the form of a conscious hesitation between two possible courses of action; otherwise, in Homer, the complexity of the psychological life is shown only in the succession and alternation of emotions; whereas the Jewish writers are able to express the simultaneous existence of various layers of consciousness and the conflict between them.

The Homeric poems, then, though their intellectual, linguistic, and above all syntactical culture appears to be so much more highly developed, are yet comparatively simple in their picture of human beings; and no less so in their relation to the real life which they describe in general. Delight in physical existence is everything to them, and their highest aim is to make that delight perceptible to us. Between battles and passions, adventures and perils, they show us hunts, banquets, palaces and shepherds' cots, athletic contests and washing days—in order that we may see the heroes in their ordinary life, and seeing them so, may take pleasure in their manner of enjoying their savory present, a present which sends strong roots down into social usages, landscape, and daily life, And thus they bewitch us and ingratiate themselves to us until we live with them in the reality of their lives; so long as we are reading or hearing the poems, it does not matter whether we know that all this is only legend, "make-believe." The oft-repeated reproach that Homer is a liar takes nothing from his effectiveness, he does not need to base his story on historical reality, his reality is powerful enough in itself; it ensnares us, weaving its web around us, and that suffices him. And this "real" world into which we are lured, exists for itself, contains nothing but itself; the Homeric poems conceal nothing, they contain no teaching and no secret second meaning. Homer can be analyzed, as we have essayed to do here, but he cannot be interpreted. Later allegorizing trends have tried their arts of interpretation upon him, but to no avail. He resists any such treatment; the interpretations are forced and foreign, they do not crystallize into a unified doctrine. The general considerations which occasionally occur (in our episode, for example, v. 360: that in misfortune men age quickly) reveal a calm acceptance of the basic facts of human existence, but with no compulsion to brood over them, still less any passionate impulse either to rebel against them or to embrace them in an ecstasy of submission.

It is all very different in the Biblical stories. Their aim is not to bewitch the senses, and if nevertheless they produce lively sensory effects, it is only because the moral, religious, and psychological phenomena which are their sole concern are made concrete in the sensible matter of life. But their religious intent involves an absolute claim to historical truth. The story of Abraham and Isaac is not better established than the story of Odysseus, Penelope, and Euryclea; both are legendary. But the Biblical narrator, the Elohist, had to believe in the objective truth of the story of Abraham's sacrifice—the existence of the sacred ordinances of life rested upon the truth of this and similar stories. He had to believe in it passionately; or else (as many rationalistic interpreters believed and perhaps still believe) he had to be a conscious liar—no harmless liar like Homer, who lied to give pleasure, but a political liar with a definite end in view, lying in the interest of a claim to absolute authority.

To me, the rationalistic interpretation seems psychologically absurd; but even if we take it into consideration, the relation of the Elohist to the truth of his story still remains a far more passionate and definite one than is Homer's relation. The Biblical narrator was obliged to write exactly what his belief in the truth of the tradition (or, from the rationalistic standpoint, his interest in the truth of it) demanded of him—in either case, his freedom in creative or representative imagination was severely limited; his activity was perforce reduced to composing an effective version of the pious tradition. What he produced, then, was not primarily oriented toward "realism" (if he succeeded in being realistic, it was merely a means, not an end); it was oriented toward truth. Woe to the man who did not believe it! One can perfectly well entertain historical doubts on the subject of the Trojan War or of Odysseus' wanderings, and still, when reading Homer, feel precisely the effects he sought to produce; but without believing in Abraham's sacrifice, it is impossible to put the narrative of it to the use for which it was written. Indeed, we must go even further. The Bible's claim to truth is not only far more urgent than Homer's, it is tyrannical—it excludes all other claims. The world of the Scripture stories is not satisfied with claiming to be a historically true reality—it insists that it is the only real world, is destined for autocracy. All other scenes, issues, and ordinances have no right to appear independently of it, and it is promised that all of them, the history of all mankind, will be given their due place within its frame, will be subordinated to it. The Scripture stories do not, like Homer's, court our favor, they do not flatter us that they may please us and enchant us—they seek to subject us, and if we refuse to be subjected we are rebels.

Let no one object that this goes too far, that not the stories, but the religious doctrine, raises the claim to absolute authority; because the stories are not, like Homer's, simply narrated "reality." Doctrine and promise are incarnate in them and inseparable from them; for that very reason they are fraught with "background" and mysterious, containing a second, concealed meaning. In the story of Isaac, it is not only God's intervention at the beginning and the end, but even the factual and psychological elements which come between, that are mysterious, merely touched upon, fraught with background; and therefore they require subtle investigation and interpretation, they demand them. Since so much in the story is dark and incomplete, and since the reader knows that God is a hidden God, his effort to interpret it constantly finds something new to feed upon. Doctrine and the search for enlightenment are inextricably connected with the physical side of the narrative—the latter being more than simple "reality"; indeed they are in constant danger of losing their own reality, as very soon happened when interpretation reached such proportions that the real vanished.

If the text of the Biblical narrative, then, is so greatly in need of interpretation on the basis of its own content, its claim to absolute authority forces it still further in the same direction. Far from seeking, like Homer, merely to make us forget our own reality for a few hours, it seeks to overcome our reality: we are to fit our own life into its world, feel ourselves to be elements in its structure of universal history. This becomes increasingly difficult the further our historical environment is removed from that of the Biblical books; and if these nevertheless maintain their claim to absolute authority, it is inevitable that they themselves be adapted through interpretative transformation. This was for a long time comparatively easy; as late as the European Middle Ages it was possible to represent Biblical events as ordinary phenomena of contemporary life, the methods of interpretation themselves forming the basis for such a treatment. But when, through too great a change in environment and through the awakening of a critical consciousness, this becomes impossible, the Biblical claim to absolute authority is jeopardized; the method of interpretation is scorned and rejected, the Biblical stories become ancient legends, and the doctrine they had contained, now dissevered from them, becomes a disembodied image.

As a result of this claim to absolute authority, the method of interpretation spread to traditions other than the Jewish. The Homeric poems present a definite complex of events whose boundaries in space and time are clearly delimited; before it, beside it, and after it, other complexes of events, which do not depend upon it, can be conceived without conflict and without difficulty. The Old Testament, on the other hand, presents universal history: it begins with the beginning of time, with the creation of the world, and will end with the Last Days, the fulfilling of the Covenant, with which the world will come to an end. Everything else that happens in the world can only be conceived as an element in this sequence; into it everything that is known about the world, or at least everything that touches upon the history of the Jews, must be fitted as an ingredient of the divine plan; and as this too became possible only by interpreting the new material as it poured in, the need for interpretation reaches out beyond the original Jewish-Israelitish realm of reality—for example to Assyrian, Babylonian, Persian, and Roman history; interpretation in a determined direction becomes a general method of comprehending reality; the new and strange world which now comes into view and which, in the form in which it presents itself, proves to be wholly unutilizable within the Jewish religious frame, must be so interpreted that it can find a place there. But this process nearly always also reacts upon the frame, which requires enlarging and modifying. The most striking piece of interpretation of this sort occurred in the first century of the Christian era, in consequence of Paul's mission to the Gentiles: Paul and the Church Fathers reinterpreted the entire Jewish tradition as a succession of figures prognosticating the appearance of Christ, and assigned the Roman Empire its proper place in the divine plan of salvation. Thus while, on the one hand, the reality of the Old Testament presents itself as complete truth with a claim to sole authority, on the other hand that very claim forces it to a constant interpretative change in its own content; for millennia it undergoes an incessant and active development with the life of man in Europe.

The claim of the Old Testament stories to represent universal history, their insistent relation—a relation constantly redefined by conflicts—to a single and hidden God, who yet shows himself and who guides universal history by promise and exaction, gives these stories an entirely different perspective from any the Homeric poems can possess. As a composition, the Old Testament is incomparably less unified than the Homeric poems, it is more obviously pieced together— but the various components all belong to one concept of universal history and its interpretation. If certain elements survived which did not immediately fit in, interpretation took care of them; and so the reader is at every moment aware of the universal religio-historical perspective which gives the individual stories their general meaning and purpose. The greater the separateness and horizontal disconnection of the stories and groups of stories in relation to one another, compared with the *Iliad* and the *Odyssey*, the stronger is their general vertical connection, which holds them all together and which is entirely lacking in Homer. Each of the great figures of the Old Testament, from Adam to the prophets, embodies a moment of this vertical connection. God chose and formed these men to the end of embodying his essence and will—yet choice and formation do not coincide, for the latter proceeds gradually, historically, during the earthly life of him upon whom the choice has fallen. How the process is accomplished, what terrible trials such a formation inflicts, can be seen from our story of Abraham's sacrifice. Herein lies the reason why the great figures of the Old Testament are so much more fully developed, so much more fraught with their own biographical past, so much more distinct as individuals, than are the Homeric heroes. Achilles and Odysseus are splendidly described in many well-ordered words, epithets cling to them, their emotions are constantly displayed in their words and deeds—but they have no development, and their life-histories are clearly set forth once and for all. So little are the Homeric heroes presented as developing or having developed, that most of them—Nestor, Agamemnon, Achilles—appear to be of an age fixed from the very first. Even Odysseus, in whose case the long lapse of time and the many events which occurred offer so much opportunity for biographical development, shows almost nothing of it. Odysseus on his return is exactly the same as he was when he left Ithaca two decades earlier. But what a road, what a fate, lie between the Jacob who cheated his father out of his blessing and the old man whose favorite son has been torn to pieces by a wild beast!—between David the harp player, persecuted by his lord's jealousy, and the old king, surrounded by violent intrigues, whom Abishag the Shunnamite warmed in his bed, and he knew her not! The old man, of whom we know how he has become what he is, is more of an individual than the young man; for it is only during the course of an eventful life that men are differentiated into full individuality; and it is this history of a personality which the Old Testament presents to us as the formation undergone by those whom God has chosen to be examples. Fraught with their development, sometimes even aged to the verge of dissolution, they show a distinct stamp of individuality entirely foreign to the Homeric heroes. Time can touch the latter only outwardly, and even that change is brought to our observation as little as possible; whereas the stern hand of God is ever upon the Old Testament figures; he has not only made them once and for all and chosen them, but he continues to work upon them, bends them and kneads them, and, without destroying them in essence, produces from them forms which their youth gave no grounds for anticipating. The objection that the biographical element of the Old Testament often springs from the combination of several legendary personages does not apply; for this combination is a part of the development of the text. And how much wider is the pendulum swing of their lives than that of the Homeric heroes! For they are bearers of the divine will, and yet they are fallible, subject to misfortune and humiliation—and in the midst of misfortune and in their humiliation their acts and words reveal the transcendent majesty of God. There is hardly one of them who does not, like Adam, undergo the deepest humiliation—and hardly one who is not deemed worthy of God's personal intervention and personal inspiration. Humiliation and elevation go far deeper and far higher than in Homer, and they belong basically together. The poor beggar Odysseus is only masquerading, but Adam is really cast down, Jacob really a refugee, Joseph really in the pit and then a slave to be bought and sold. But their greatness, rising out of humiliation, is almost superhuman and an image of God's greatness. The reader clearly feels how the extent of the pendulum's swing is connected with the intensity of the personal history—precisely the most extreme circumstances, in which we are immeasurably forsaken and in despair, or immeasurably joyous and exalted, give us, if we survive them, a personal stamp which is recognized as the product of a rich existence, a rich development. And very often, indeed generally, this element of development gives the Old Testament stories a historical character, even when the subject is purely legendary and traditional.

Homer remains within the legendary with all his material, whereas the material of the Old Testament comes closer and closer to history as the narrative proceeds; in the stories of David the historical report predominates. Here too, much that is legendary still remains, as for example the story of David and Goliath; but much—and the most essential—consists in things which the narrators knew from their own experience or from firsthand testimony. Now the difference between legend and history is in most cases easily perceived by a reasonably experienced reader. It is a difficult matter, requiring careful historical and philological training, to distinguish the true from the synthetic or the biased in a historical presentation; but it is easy to separate the historical from the legendary in general. Their structure is different. Even where the legendary does not immediately betray itself by elements of the miraculous, by the repetition of well-known standard motives, typical patterns and themes, through neglect of clear details of time and place, and the like, it is generally quickly recognizable by its composition. It runs far too smoothly. All cross-currents, all friction, all that is casual, secondary to the main events and themes, everything unresolved, truncated, and uncertain, which confuses the clear progress of the action and the simple orientation of the actors, has disappeared. The historical event which we witness, or learn from the testimony of those who witnessed it, runs much more variously, contradictorily, and confusedly; not until it has produced results in a definite domain are we able, with their help, to classify it to a certain extent; and how often the order to which we think we have attained becomes doubtful again, how often we ask ourselves if the data before us have not led us to a far too simple classification of the original events! Legend arranges its material in a simple and straightforward way; it detaches it from its contemporary historical context, so that the latter will not confuse it; it knows only clearly outlined men who act from few and simple motives and the continuity of whose feelings and actions remains uninterrupted. In the legends of martyrs, for example, a stiff-necked and fanatical persecutor stands over against an equally stiff-necked and fanatical victim; and a situation so complicated—that is to say, so real and historical—as that in which the "persecutor" Pliny finds himself in his celebrated letter to Trajan on the subject of the Christians, is unfit for legend. And that is still a comparatively simple case. Let the reader think of the history which we are ourselves witnessing; anyone who, for example, evaluates the behavior of individual men and groups of men at the time of the rise of National Socialism in Germany, or the behavior of individual peoples and states before and during the last war, will feel how difficult it is to represent historical themes in general, and how unfit they are for legend; the historical comprises a great number of contradictory motives in each individual, a hesitation and ambiguous groping on the part of groups; only seldom (as in the last war) does a more or less plain situation, comparatively simple to describe, arise, and even such a situation is subject to division below the surface, is indeed almost constantly in danger of losing its simplicity; and the motives of all the interested parties are so complex that the slogans of propaganda can be composed only through the crudest simplification—with the result that friend and foe alike can often employ the same ones. To write history is so difficult that most historians are forced to make concessions to the technique of legend.

It is clear that a large part of the life of David as given in the Bible contains history and not legend. In Absalom's rebellion, for example, or in the scenes from David's last days, the contradictions and crossing of motives both in individuals and in the general action have become so concrete that it is impossible to doubt the historicity of the information conveyed. Now the men who composed the historical parts are often the same who edited the older legends too; their peculiar religious concept of man in history, which we have attempted to describe above, in no way led them to a legendary simplification of events; and so it is only natural that, in the legendary passages of the Old Testament, historical structure is frequently discernible—of course, not in the sense that the traditions are examined as to their credibility according to the method of scientific criticism; but simply to the extent that the tendency to a smoothing down and harmonizing of events, to a simplification of motives, to a static definition of characters which avoids conflict, vacillation, and development, such as are natural to legendary structure, does not predominate in the Old Testament world of legend. Abraham, Jacob, or even Moses produces a more concrete, direct, and historical impression than the figures of the Homeric world —not because they are better described in terms of sense (the contrary is the case) but because the confused, contradictory multiplicity of events, the psychological and factual cross-purposes, which true history reveals, have not disappeared in the representation but still remain clearly perceptible. In the stories of David, the legendary, which only later scientific criticism makes recognizable as such, imperceptibly passes into the historical; and even in the legendary, the problem of the classification and interpretation of human history is already passionately apprehended—a problem which later shatters the framework of historical composition and completely overruns it with prophecy; thus the Old Testament, in so far as it is concerned with human events, ranges through all three domains: legend, historical reporting, and interpretative historical theology.

Connected with the matters just discussed is the fact that the Greek text seems more limited and more static in respect to the circle of personages involved in the action and to their political activity. In the recognition scene with which we began, there appears, aside from Odysseus and Penelope, the house keeper Euryclea, a slave whom Odysseus' father Laertes had bought long before. She, like the swineherd Eumaeus, has spent her life in the service of Laertes' family; like Eumaeus, she is closely connected with their fate, she loves them and shares their interests and feelings. But she has no life of her own, no feelings of her own; she has only the life and feelings of her master. Eumaeus too, though he still remembers that he was born a freeman and indeed of a noble house (he was stolen as a boy), has, not only in fact but also in his own feeling, no longer a life of his own, he is entirely involved in the life of his masters. Yet these two characters are the only ones whom Homer brings to life who do not belong to the ruling class. Thus we become conscious of the fact that in the Homeric poems life is enacted only among the ruling class—others appear only in the rôle of servants to that class. The ruling class is still so strongly patriarchal, and still itself so involved in the daily activities of domestic life, that one is sometimes likely to forget their rank. But they are unmistakably a sort of feudal aristocracy, whose men divide their lives between war, hunting, marketplace councils, and feasting, while the women supervise the maids in the house. As a social picture, this world is completely stable; wars take place only between different groups of the ruling class; nothing ever pushes up from below. In the early stories of the Old Testament the patriarchal condition is dominant too, but since the people involved are individual nomadic or half-nomadic tribal leaders, the social picture gives a much less stable impression class distinctions are not felt. As soon as the people completely emerges —that is, after the exodus from Egypt—its activity is always discernible, it is often in ferment, it frequently intervenes in events not only as a whole but also in separate groups and through the medium of separate individuals who come forward; the origins of prophecy seem to lie in the irrepressible politico-religious spontaneity of the people. We receive the impression that the movement emerging from the depths of the people of Israel-Judah must have been of a wholly different nature from those even of the later ancient democracies—of a different nature and far more elemental.

With the more profound historicity and the more profound social activity of the Old Testament text, there is connected yet another important distinction from Homer: namely, that a different conception of the elevated style and of the sublime is to be found here. Homer, of course, is not afraid to let the realism of daily life enter into the sublime and tragic; our episode of the scar is an example, we see how the quietly depicted, domestic scene of the foot-washing is incorporated into the pathetic and sublime action of Odysseus' homecoming. From the rule of the separation of styles which was later almost universally accepted and which specified that the realistic depiction of daily life was incompatible with the sublime and had a place only in comedy or, carefully stylized, in idyl—from any such rule Homer is still far removed. And yet he is closer to it than is the Old Testament. For the great and sublime events in the Homeric poems take place far more exclusively and unmistakably among the members of a ruling class; and these are far more untouched in their heroic elevation than are the Old Testament figures, who can fall much lower in dignity (consider, for example, Adam, Noah, David, Job); and finally, domestic realism, the representation of daily life, remains in

Homer in the peaceful realm of the idyllic, whereas, from the very first, in the Old Testament stories, the sublime, tragic, and problematic take shape precisely in the domestic and commonplace: scenes such as those between Cain and Abel, between Noah and his sons, between Abraham, Sarah, and Hagar, between Rebekah, Jacob, and Esau, and so on, are inconceivable in the Homeric style. The entirely different ways of developing conflicts are enough to account for this. In the Old Testament stories the peace of daily life in the house, in the fields, and among the flocks, is undermined by jealousy over election and the promise of a blessing, and complications arise which would be utterly incomprehensible to the Homeric heroes. The latter must have palpable and clearly expressible reasons for their conflicts and enmities, and these work themselves out in free battles; whereas, with the former, the perpetually smouldering jealousy and the connection between the domestic and the spiritual, between the paternal blessing and the divine blessing, lead to daily life being permeated with the stuff of conflict, often with poison. The sublime influence of God here reaches so deeply into the everyday that the two realms of the sublime and the everyday are not only actually unseparated but basically inseparable.

We have compared these two texts, and, with them, the two kinds of style they embody, in order to reach a starting point for an investigation into the literary representation of reality in European culture. The two styles, in their opposition, represent basic types: on the one hand fully externalized description, uniform illumination, uninterrupted connection, free expression, all events in the foreground, displaying unmistakable meanings, few elements of historical development and of psychological perspective; on the other hand, certain parts brought into high relief, others left obscure, abruptness, suggestive influence of the unexpressed, "background" quality, multiplicity of meanings and the need for interpretation, universal-historical claims, development of the concept of the historically becoming, and preoccupation with the problematic.

Homer's realism is, of course, not to be equated with classical-antique realism in general; for the separation of styles, which did not develop until later, permitted no such leisurely and externalized description of everyday happenings; in tragedy especially there was no room for it; furthermore, Greek culture very soon encountered the phenomena of historical becoming and of the "multilayeredness" of the human problem, and dealt with them in its fashion; in Roman realism, finally, new and native concepts are added. We shall go into these later changes in the antique representation of reality when the occasion arises; on the whole, despite them, the basic tendencies of the Homeric style, which we have attempted to work out, remained effective and determinant down into late antiquity.

Since we are using the two styles, the Homeric and the Old Testament, as starting points, we have taken them as finished products, as they appear in the texts; we have disregarded everything that pertains to their origins, and thus have left untouched the question whether their peculiarities were theirs from the beginning or are to be referred wholly or in part to foreign influences. Within the limits of our purpose, a consideration of this question is not necessary; for it is in their full development, which they reached in early times, that the two styles exercised their determining influence upon the representation of reality in European literature.

13. FRYE

"The Archetypes of Literature"

Northrop Frye (1912–   ) was born in Sherbrooke, Quebec, and educated at the University of Toronto. After receiving his BA degree, he studied theology at Emmanuel College, Toronto, and was ordained a minister of the United Church of Canada in 1936. He returned to the study of literature at Merton College, Oxford. He has taught at Victoria College of the University of Toronto since 1942, where he has also been principal of the college since 1959 and University professor since 1967.

When Northrop Frye published *Fearful Symmetry: A Study of Blake* in 1947, he established his reputation as a good, young critic; in 1957 with the publication of the *Anatomy of Criticism* he became one of the most important contemporary critics. Other works followed: *The Well-Tempered Critic* in 1963, *The Fables of Identity* (a collection of essays of which the one reprinted in this anthology was originally published in 1959) also in 1963, *A Natural Perspective: The Development of Shakespearean Comedy and Romance* (1965), *The Return to Eden: Five Essays on Milton's Epics* (1965), *Fools of Time: Studies in Shakespearean Tragedy* (1967), *The Modern Century* (1967), *A Study of English Romanticism*, and numerous uncollected essays.

A glance at Frye's bibliography testifies to the variety of his interests and breadth of reading. Each volume constitutes major criticism, yet the *Anatomy of Criticism* remains his most influential work and one with which the adherents and opponents of Frye are most concerned. It is a work that defies easy summary, and, except for the "Polemical Introduction," excerpts are difficult to take from the whole. For that reason an earlier essay has been reprinted here which deals with what Frye has been mainly associated with in literary criticism: archetypes of literature.

It should be remembered, however, that in the *Anatomy of Criticism* the archetypal approach is only one of the four suggested ways of organizing literature, or looking at literature as a whole. These approaches are set forth in specific essays. The first is explained in the "Theory of Modes" where Frye delineates two "tendencies" in fiction: (1) the tragic, which basically depicts the isolation of the hero, and (2) the comic, which shows the integration of the hero in the society; in this distinction he is obviously following Aristotle who also divides literature into the tragic and the comic modes and places the emphasis on character. The second essay, "Ethical Criticism: Theory of Symbols," shows the phases in which the symbol may function (a symbol is defined as "any unit of any literary structure that can be isolated for critical attention," p. 71). Third essay, "Archetypal Criticism: Theory of Myths," deals more fully with the same matter contained in the essay included here, while the fourth essay, "Rhetorical Criticism: Theory of Genres," attempts to go beyond the simple generic distinctions and to establish the form, content, and tendency of the genres; here much of the discussion is based on the previous essay.

In "Archetypes of Literature,"* presented here in its entirety, Frye argues that the archetype is the major or ruling matter in all Western literature. It is derived from a body of myths, the foremost of which are from the Bible and Greek mythology, but may be contained anywhere—even in the comic strip. These archetypes form, as it were, a recurrent rhythm in literature. Frye has ordered and classified variously the myths that incorporate the archetypes. Thus, there are what he calls four phases of a myth: (1) the dawn–spring, (2) the zenith–summer, (3) the sunset–autumn, and (4) the darkness–winter. All four phases have their appropriate characters and genres. The format or the "vision" within which the particular world of the myth can be seen is classified as being either human, animal, vegetable, mineral, or unformed (pp. 306–7 of *Anatomy* outline the images, characters, genres and patterns for each one).

With his theory of archetypes Frye has attempted no less than a system of poetics. He insists that criticism can be an organized study and thus can be viewed at least partially as a science: "I suggest that what is at present missing from literary criticism is a coordinating principal, a central hypothesis which, like the theory of evolution in biology, will see the phenomena it deals with as parts of a whole. . . . The first postulate of this hypothesis is the same as that of any science: the assumption of total coherence." ("Archetypes of Literature," p. 9.)

---

* From *Fables of Identity: Studies in Poetic Mythology* (New York, Harcourt Brace Jovanovich, Inc. [A Harbinger Book], 1951), Chapter 1. Used by permission of the publishers.

Thus Frye is in the tradition of critics who endeavor to apply the scientific method to literary criticism. This method is carried as far as to deny the validity of value judgments.

While Frye has an affinity with many modern critics because he draws analogies between science and criticism, he views himself primarily as a follower of Aristotle. This is seen first of all in his insistence on seeing literature as a coherent whole capable of being organized and analyzed in an orderly fashion. Furthermore, he utilizes Aristotelian concepts throughout—from art as imitation, the proper characters for a genre, to the concept of a beginning, middle, and end in a literary work.

Northrop Frye's position and reputation in modern criticism is well assessed by W. J. Bate: "Alone among twentieth-century critics, Northrop Frye offers a comprehensive, closely argued, and systematic theory of literature. This has made him the most controversial, and probably the most influential critic writing in English since the 1950's. In the humanities, as contrasted with sciences based on demonstrative and step-by-step argument, system is always controversial (though this is true only if it is ably presented; otherwise it is simply disregarded). For the very thing that makes system so appealing to some people also creates resistance in others: the fact that it *simplifies*. The question is whether the gains outweigh in importance what the system inevitably has to exclude or disregard for the sake of the system. The controversy intensifies to the degree that what is gained and what is left out are both felt to be significant." (*Criticism: The Major Texts*, enlarged edition [Harcourt Brace Jovanovich, 1970], p. 597.)

Every organized body of knowledge can be learned progressively; and experience shows that there is also something progressive about the learning of literature. Our opening sentence has already got us into a semantic difficulty. Physics is an organized body of knowledge about nature, and a student of it says that he is learning physics, not that he is learning nature. Art, like nature, is the subject of a systematic study, and has to be distinguished from the study itself, which is criticism. It is therefore impossible to "learn literature": one learns about it in a certain way, but what one learns, transitively, is the criticism of literature. Similarly, the difficulty often felt in "teaching literature" arises from the fact that it cannot be done: the criticism of literature is all that can be directly taught. So while no one expects literature itself to behave like a science, there is surely no reason why criticism, as a systematic and organized study, should not be, at least partly, a science. Not a "pure" or "exact" science, perhaps, but these phrases form part of a 19th century cosmology which is no longer with us. Criticism deals with the arts and may well be something of an art itself, but it does not follow that it must be unsystematic. If it is to be related to the sciences too, it does not follow that it must be deprived of the graces of culture.

Certainly criticism as we find it in learned journals and scholarly monographs has every characteristic of a science. Evidence is examined scientifically; previous authorities are used scientifically; fields are investigated scientifically; texts are edited scientifically. Prosody is scientific in structure; so is phonetics; so is philology. And yet in studying this kind of critical science the student becomes aware of a centrifugal movement carrying him away from literature. He finds that literature is the central division of the "humanities," flanked on one side by history and on the other by philosophy. Criticism so far ranks only as a subdivision of literature; and hence, for the systematic mental organization of the subject, the student has to turn to the conceptual framework of the historian for events, and to that of the philosopher for ideas. Even the more centrally placed critical sciences, such as textual editing seem to be part of a "background" that recedes into history or some other non-literary field. The thought suggests itself that the ancillary critical disciplines may be related to a central expanding pattern of systematic comprehension which has not yet been established, but which, if it were established, would prevent them from being centrifugal. If such a pattern exists, then criticism would be to art what philosophy is to wisdom and history to action.

Most of the central area of criticism is at present, and doubtless always will be, the area of commentary. But the commentators have little sense, unlike the researchers, of being contained within some sort of scientific discipline: they are chiefly engaged, in the words of the gospel hymn, in brightening the corner where they are. If we attempt to get a more comprehensive idea of what criticism is about, we find ourselves wandering over quaking bogs of generalities, judicious pronouncements of value, reflective comments, perorations to works of research and other consequences of taking the large view. But this part of the critical field is so full of pseudo-propositions, sonorous nonsense that contains no truth and no falsehood, that it obviously exists only because criticism, like nature, prefers a waste space to an empty one.

The term "pseudo-proposition" may imply some sort of logical positivist attitude on my own part. But I would not confuse the significant proposition with the factual one, nor should I consider it advisable to muddle the study of literature with a schizophrenic dichotomy between subjective-emotional and objective-descriptive aspects of meaning, considering that in order to produce any literary meaning at all one has to ignore this dichotomy. I say only that the principles by which one can distinguish a significant from a meaningless statement in criticism are not clearly defined. Our first step, therefore, is to recognize and get rid of meaningless criticism: that is, talking about literature in a way that cannot help to build up a systematic structure of knowledge. Casual value-judgments belong not to criticism but to the history of taste, and reflect, at best, only the social and psychological compulsions which prompted their utterance. All judgments in which the values are not based on literary experience but are sentimental or derived from religious or political prejudice may be regarded as casual. Sentimental judgments are usually based either on non-existent categories or antitheses ("Shakespeare studied life, Milton books") or to a visceral reaction to the writer's personality. The literary chitchat which makes the reputations of poets boom and crash in an imaginary stock exchange is pseudo-criticism. That wealthy investor Mr. Eliot, after dumping Milton on the market, is now buying him again; Donne has probably reached his peak and will begin to taper off; Tennyson may be in for a slight flutter but the Shelley stocks are still bearish. This sort of thing cannot be part of any systematic study, for a systematic study can only progress: whatever dithers or vacillates or reacts is merely leisure-class conversation.

We next meet a more serious group of critics who say: the foreground of criticism is the impact of literature on the reader. Let us, then, keep the study of literature centripetal, and base the learning process on a structural analysis of the literary work itself. The texture of any great work of art is complex and ambiguous, and in unravelling the complexities we may take in as much history and philosophy as we please, if the subject of our study remains at the center. If it does not, we may find that in our anxiety to write about literature we have forgotten how to read it.

The only weakness in this approach is that it is conceived primarily as the antithesis of centrifugal or "background" criticism, and so lands us in a somewhat unreal dilemma, like the conflict of internal and external relations in philosophy. Antitheses are usually resolved, not by picking one side and refuting the other, or by making eclectic choices between them, but by trying to get past the antithetical way of stating the problem. It is right that the first effort of critical apprehension should take the form of a rhetorical or structural analysis of a work of art. But a purely structural approach has the same limitation in criticism that it has in biology. In itself it is simply a discrete series of analyses based on the mere existence of the literary structure, without developing any explanation of how the structure came to be what it was and what its nearest relatives are. Structural analysis brings rhetoric back to criticism, but we need a new poetics as well, and the attempt to construct a new poetics out of rhetoric alone can hardly avoid a mere complication of rhetorical terms into a sterile jargon. I suggest that what is at present missing from literary criticism is a coordinating principle, a central hypothesis which, like the theory of evolution in biology, will see the phenomena it deals with as parts of a whole. Such a principle, though it would retain the centripetal perspective of structural analysis, would try to give the same perspective to other kinds of criticism too.

The first postulate of this hypothesis is the same as that of any science: the assumption of total coherence. The assumption refers to the science, not to what it deals with. A belief in an order of nature is an inference from the intelligibility of the natural sciences; and if the natural sciences ever completely demonstrated the order of nature they would presumably exhaust their subject. Criticism, as a science, is totally intelligible literature, as the subject of a science, is, so far as we know, an inexhaustible source of new critical discoveries, and would be even if new works of literature ceased to be written. If so, then the search for a limiting principle in literature in order to discourage the development of criticism is mistaken. The assertion that the critic should not look for more in a poem than the poet may safely be assumed to have been conscious of putting there is a common form of what may be called the fallacy of premature teleology. It corresponds to the assertion that a natural phenomenon is as it is because Providence in its inscrutable wisdom made it so.

Simple as the assumption appears, it takes a long time for a science to discover that it is in fact a totally intelligible body of knowledge. Until it makes this discovery it has not been born as an individual science, but remains an embryo within the body of some other subject. The birth of physics from "natural philosophy" and of sociology from "moral philosophy" will illustrate the process. It is also very approximately true that the modern sciences have developed in the order of their closeness to mathematics. Thus physics and astronomy assumed their modern form in the Renaissance, chemistry in the 18th century, biology in the 19th and the social sciences in the 20th. If systematic criticism, then, is developing only in our day, the fact is at least not an anachronism.

We are now looking for classifying principles lying in an area between two points that we have fixed. The first of these is the preliminary effort of criticism, the structural analysis of the work of art. The second is the assumption that there is such a subject as criticism, and that it makes, or could make, complete sense. We may next proceed inductively from structural analysis, associating the data we collect and trying to see larger patterns in them. Or we may proceed deductively, with the consequences that follow from postulating the unity of criticism. It is clear, of course, that neither procedure will work indefinitely without correction from the other. Pure induction will get us lost in haphazard guessing, pure deduction will lead to inflexible and over-simplified pigeon-holing. Let us now attempt a few tentative steps in each direction, beginning with the inductive one.

II

The unity of a work of art, the basis of structural analysis, has not been produced solely by the unconditioned will of the artist, for the artist is only its efficient cause: it has form, and consequently a formal cause. The fact that revision is possible, that the poet makes changes not because he likes them better but because they are better, means that poems, like poets, are born and not made. The poet's task is to deliver the poem in as uninjured a state as possible, and if the poem is alive, it is equally anxious to be rid of him, and screams to be cut loose from his private memories and associations, his desire for self-expression, and all the other navel-strings and feeding tubes of his ego. The critic takes over where the poet leaves off, and criticism can hardly do without a kind of literary psychology connecting the poet with the poem. Part of this may by a psychological study of the poet, though this is useful chiefly in analysing the failures in his expression, the things in him which are still attached to his work. More important is the fact that every poet has his private mythology, his own spectroscopic band or peculiar formation of symbols, of much of which he is quite unconscious. In works with characters of their own, such as dramas and novels, the same psychological analysis may be extended to the interplay of characters, though of course literary psychology would analyse the behavior of such characters only in relation to literary convention.

There is still before us the problem of the formal cause of the poem, a problem deeply involved with the question of genres. We cannot say much about genres, for criticism does not know much about them. A good many critical efforts to grapple with such words as "novel" or "epic" are chiefly interesting as examples of the psychology of rumor. Two conceptions of the genre, however, are obviously fallacious, and as they are opposite extremes, the truth must lie somewhere between them. One is the pseudo-Platonic conception of genres as existing prior to and independently of creation, which confuses them with mere conventions of form like the sonnet. The other is that pseudo-biological conception of them as evolving species which turns up in so many surveys of the "development" of this or that form.

We next inquire for the origin of the genre, and turn first of all to the social conditions and cultural demands which produced it—in other words to the material cause of the work of art. This leads us into literary history, which differs from ordinary history in that its containing categories, "Gothic," "Baroque," "Romantic," and the like are cultural categories, of little use to the ordinary historian. Most literary history does not get as far as these categories, but even so we know more about it than about most kinds of critical scholarship. The historian treats literature and philosophy historically; the philosopher treats history and literature philosophically, and the so-called history of ideas approach marks the beginning of an attempt to treat history and philosophy from the point of view of an autonomous criticism.

But still we feel that there is something missing. We say that every poet has his own peculiar formation of images. But when so many poets use so many of the same images, surely there are much bigger critical problems involved than biographical ones. As Mr. Auden's brilliant essay *The Enchafèd Flood* shows, an important symbol like the sea cannot remain within the poetry of Shelley or Keats or Coleridge: it is bound to expand over many poets into an archetypal symbol of literature. And if the genre has a historical origin, why does the genre of drama emerge from medieval religion in a way so strikingly similar to the way it emerged from Greek religion centuries before? This is a problem of structure rather than origin, and suggests that there may be archetypes of genres as well as of images.

It is clear that criticism cannot be systematic unless there is a quality in literature which enables it to be so, an order of words corresponding to the order of nature in the natural sciences. An archetype should be not only a unifying category of criticism, but itself a part of a total form, and it leads us at once to the question of what sort of total form criticism can see in literature. Our survey of critical techniques has taken us as far as literary history. Total literary history moves from the primitive to the sophisticated, and here we glimpse the possibility of seeing literature as a complication of a relatively restricted and simple group of formulas that can be studied in primitive culture. If so, then the search for archetypes is a kind of literary anthropology, concerned with the way that literature is informed by pre-literary categories such as ritual, myth and folk tale. We next realize that the relation between these categories and literature is by no means purely one of descent, as we find them reappearing in the greatest classics—in fact there seems to be a general tendency on the part of great classics to revert to them. This coincides with a feeling that we have all had: that the study of mediocre works of art, however energetic, obstinately remains a random and peripheral form of critical experience, whereas the profound masterpiece seems to draw us to a point at which we can see an enormous number of converging patterns of significance. Here we begin to wonder if we cannot see literature, not only as complicating itself in time, but as spread out in conceptual space from some unseen center.

This inductive movement towards the archetype is a process of backing up, as it were, from structural analysis, as we back up from a painting if we want to see composition instead of brushwork. In the foreground of the grave-digger scene in *Hamlet*, for instance, is an intricate verbal texture, ranging from the puns of the first clown to the *danse macabre* of the Yorick soliloquy, which we study in the printed text. One step back, and we are in the Wilson Knight and Spurgeon group of critics, listening to the steady rain of images of corruption and decay. Here too, as the sense of the place of this scene in the whole play begins to dawn on us, we are in the network of psychological relationships which were the main interest of Bradley. But after all, we say, we are forgetting the genre: *Hamlet* is a play, and an Elizabethan play. So we take another step back into the Stoll and Shaw group and see the scene conventionally as part of its dramatic context. One step more, and we can begin to glimpse the archetype of the scene, as the hero's *Liebestod* and first unequivocal declaration of his love, his struggle with Laertes and the sealing of his own fate, and the sudden sobering of his mood that marks the transition to the final scene, all take shape around a leap into and return from the grave that has so weirdly yawned open on the stage.

At each stage of understanding this scene we are dependent on a certain kind of scholarly organization. We need first an editor to clean up the text for us, then the rhetorician and philologist, then the literary psychologist. We cannot study the genre without the help of the literary social historian, the literary philosopher and the student of the "history of ideas," and for the archetype we need a literary anthropologist. But now that we have got our central pattern of criticism established, all these interests are seen as converging on literary criticism instead of receding from it into psychology and history and the rest. In particular, the literary anthropologist who chases the source of the Hamlet legend from the pre-Shakespeare play to Saxo, and from Saxo to nature myths, is not running away from Shakespeare: he is drawing closer to the archetypal form which Shakespeare recreated. A minor result of our new perspective is that contradictions among critics, and assertions that this and not that critical approach is the right one, show a remarkable tendency to dissolve into unreality. Let us now see what we can get from the deductive end.

III

Some arts move in time, like music; others are presented in space, like painting. In both cases the organizing principle is recurrence, which is called rhythm when it is temporal and pattern when it is spatial. Thus we speak of the rhythm of music and the pattern of painting; but later, to show off our sophistication, we may begin to speak of the rhythm of painting and the pattern of music. In other words, all arts may be conceived both temporally and spatially. The score of a musical composition may be studied all at once; a picture may be seen as the track of an intricate dance of the eye. Literature seems to be intermediate between music and painting: its words form rhythms which approach a musical sequence of sounds at one of its boundaries, and form patterns which approach the hieroglyphic or pictorial image at the other. The attempts to get as near to these boundaries as possible form the main body of what is called experimental writing. We may call the rhythm of literature the narrative, and the pattern, the simultaneous mental grasp of the verbal structure, the meaning or significance. We hear or listen to a narrative, but when we grasp a writer's total pattern we "see" what he means.

The criticism of literature is much more hampered by the representational fallacy than even the criticism of painting. That is why we are apt to think of narrative as a sequential representation of events in an outside "life," and of meaning as a reflection of some external "idea." Properly used as critical terms, an author's narrative is his linear movement; his meaning is the integrity of his completed form. Similarly an image is not merely a verbal replica of an external object, but any unit of a verbal structure seen as part of a total pattern or rhythm. Even the letters an author spells his words with form part of his imagery, though only in special cases (such as alliteration) would they call for critical notice. Narrative and meaning thus become respectively, to borrow musical terms, the melodic and harmonic contexts of the imagery.

Rhythm, or recurrent movement, is deeply founded on the natural cycle, and everything in nature that we think of as having some analogy with works of art, like the flower or the bird's song, grows out of a profound synchronization between an organism and the rhythms of its environment, especially that of the solar year. With animals some expressions of synchronization, like the mating dances of birds, could almost be called rituals. But in human life a ritual seems to be something of a voluntary effort (hence the magical element in it) to recapture a lost rapport with the natural cycle. A farmer must harvest his crop at a certain time of year, but because this is involuntary, harvesting itself is not precisely a ritual. It is the deliberate expression of a will to synchronize human and natural energies at that time which produces the harvest songs, harvest sacrifices and harvest folk customs that we call rituals. In ritual, then, we may find the origin of narrative, a ritual being a temporal sequence of acts in which the conscious meaning or significance is latent: it can be seen by an observer, but is largely concealed from the participators themselves. The pull of ritual is toward pure narrative, which, if there could be such a thing, would be automatic and unconscious repetition. We should notice too the regular tendency of ritual to become encyclopedic. All the important recurrences in nature, the day, the phases of the moon, the seasons and solstices of the year, the crises of existence from birth to death, get rituals attached to them, and most of the higher religions are equipped with a definitive total body of rituals suggestive, if we may put it so, of the entire range of potentially significant actions in human life.

Patterns of imagery, on the other hand, or fragments of significance, are oracular in origin, and derive from the epiphanic moment, the flash of instantaneous comprehension with no direct reference to time, the importance of which is indicated by Cassirer in *Myth and Language*. By the time we get them, in the form of proverbs, riddles, commandments and etiological folk tales, there is already a considerable element of narrative in them. They too are encyclopedic in tendency, building up a total structure of significance, or doctrine, from random and empiric fragments. And just as pure narrative would be unconscious act, so pure significance would be an incommunicable state of consciousness, for communication begins by constructing narrative.

The myth is the central informing power that gives archetypal significance to the ritual and archetypal narrative to the oracle. Hence the myth *is* the archetype, though it might be convenient to say myth only when referring to narrative, and archetype when speaking of significance. In the solar cycle of the day, the seasonal cycle of the year, and the organic cycle of human life, there is a single pattern of significance, out of which myth constructs a central narrative around a figure who is partly the sun, partly vegetative fertility and partly a god or archetypal human being. The crucial importance of this myth has been forced on literary critics by Jung and Frazer in particular, but the several books now available on it are not always systematic in their approach, for which reason I supply the following table of its phases:

1   The dawn, spring and birth phase. Myths of the birth of the hero, of revival and resurrection, of creation and (because the four phases are a cycle) of the defeat of the powers of darkness, winter and death. Subordinate characters: the father and the mother. The archetype of romance and of most dithyrambic and rhapsodic poetry.

2   The zenith, summer, and marriage or triumph phase. Myths of apotheosis, of the sacred marriage, and of entering into Paradise. Subordinate characters: the companion and the bride. The archetype of comedy, pastoral and idyll.

3   The sunset, autumn and death phase. Myths of fall, of the dying god, of violent death and sacrifice and of the isolation of the hero. Subordinate characters: the traitor and the siren. The archetype of tragedy and elegy.

4 The darkness, winter and dissolution phase. Myths of the triumph of these powers; myths of floods and the return of chaos, of the defeat of the hero, and Götterdämmerung myths. Subordinate characters: the ogre and the witch. The archetype of satire (see, for instance, the conclusion of *The Dunciad*).

The quest of the hero also tends to assimilate the oracular and random verbal structures, as we can see when we watch the chaos of local legends that results from prophetic epiphanies consolidating into a narrative mythology of departmental gods. In most of the higher religions this in turn has become the same central quest-myth that emerges from ritual, as the Messiah myth became the narrative structure of the oracles of Judaism. A local flood may beget a folk tale by accident, but a comparison of flood stories will show how quickly such tales become examples of the myth of dissolution. Finally, the tendency of both ritual and epiphany to become encyclopedic is realized in the definitive body of myth which constitutes the sacred scriptures of religions. These sacred scriptures are consequently the first documents that the literary critic has to study to gain a comprehensive view of his subject. After he has understood their structure, then he can descend from archetypes to genres, and see how the drama emerges from the ritual side of myth and lyric from the epiphanic or fragmented side, while the epic carries on the central encyclopedic structure.

Some words of caution and encouragement are necessary before literary criticism has clearly staked out its boundaries in these fields. It is part of the critic's business to show how all literary genres are derived from the quest-myth, but the derivation is a logical one within the science of criticism: the quest-myth will constitute the first chapter of whatever future handbooks of criticism may be written that will be based on enough organized critical knowledge to call themselves "introductions" or "outlines" and still be able to live up to their titles. It is only when we try to expound the derivation chronologically that we find ourselves writing pseudo-prehistorical fictions and theories of mythological contract. Again, because psychology and anthropology are more highly developed sciences, the critic who deals with this kind of material is bound to appear, for some time, a dilettante of those subjects. These two phases of criticism are largely undeveloped in comparison with literary history and rhetoric, the reason being the later development of the sciences they are related to. But the fascination which *The Golden Bough* and Jung's book on libido symbols have for literary critics is not based on dilettantism, but on the fact that these books are primarily studies in literary criticism, and very important ones.

In any case the critic who is studying the principles of literary form has a quite different interest from the psychologist's concern with states of mind or the anthropologist's with social institutions. For instance: the mental response to narrative is mainly passive; to significance mainly active. From this fact Ruth Benedict's *Patterns of Culture* develops a distinction between "Apollonian" cultures based on obedience to ritual and "Dionysiac" ones based on a tense exposure of the prophetic mind to epiphany. The critic would tend rather to note how popular literature which appeals to the inertia of the untrained mind puts a heavy emphasis on narrative values, whereas a sophisticated attempt to disrupt the connection between the poet and his environment produces the Rimbaud type of *illumination*, Joyce's solitary epiphanies, and Baudelaire's conception of nature as a source of oracles. Also how literature, as it develops from the primitive to the self-conscious, shows a greater shift of the poet's attention from narrative to significant values, this shift of attention being the basis of Schiller's distinction between naive and sentimental poetry.

The relation of criticism to religion, when they deal with the same documents, is more complicated. In criticism, as in history, the divine is always treated as a human artifact. God for the critic, whether he finds him in *Paradise Lost* or the Bible, is a character in a human story; and for the critic all epiphanies are explained, not in terms of the riddle of a possessing god or devil, but as mental phenomena closely associated in their origin with dreams. This once established, it is then necessary to say that nothing in criticism or art compels the critic to take the attitude of ordinary waking consciousness towards the dream or the god. Art deals not with the real but with the conceivable, and criticism, though it will eventually have to have some theory of conceivability, can never be justified in trying to develop, much less assume, any theory of actuality. It is necessary to understand this before our next and final point can be made.

We have identified the central myth of literature, in its narrative aspect, with the quest-myth. Now if we wish to see this central myth as a pattern of meaning also, we have to start with the workings of the subconscious where the epiphany originates, in other words in the dream.

The human cycle of waking and dreaming corresponds closely to the natural cycle of light and darkness, and it is perhaps in this correspondence that all imaginative life begins. The correspondence is largely an antithesis: it is in daylight that man is really in the power of darkness, a prey to frustration and weakness; it is in the darkness of nature that the "libido" or conquering heroic self awakes. Hence art, which Plato called a dream for awakened minds, seems to have as its final cause the resolution of the antithesis, the mingling of the sun and the hero, the realizing of a world in which the inner desire and the outward circumstance coincide. This is the same goal, of course, that the attempt to combine human and natural power in ritual has. The social function of the arts, therefore, seems to be closely connected with visualizing the goal of work in human life. So in terms of significance, the central myth of art must be the vision of the end of social effort, the innocent world of fulfilled desires, the free human society. Once this is understood, the integral place of criticism among the other social sciences, in interpreting and systematizing the vision of the artist, will be easier to see. It is at this point that we can see how religious conceptions of the final cause of human effort are as relevant as any other to criticism.

The importance of the god or hero in the myth lies in the fact that such characters, who are conceived in human likeness and yet have more power over nature, gradually build up the vision of an omnipotent personal community beyond an indifferent nature. It is this community which the hero regularly enters in his apotheosis. The world of this apotheosis thus begins to pull away from the rotary cycle of the quest in which all triumph is temporary. Hence if we look at the quest-myth as a pattern of imagery, we see the hero's quest first of all in terms of its fulfillment. This gives us our central pattern of archetypal images, the vision of innocence which sees the world in terms of total human intelligibility. It corresponds to, and is usually found in the form of, the vision of the unfallen world or heaven in religion. We may call it the comic vision of life, in contrast to the tragic vision, which sees the quest only in the form of its ordained cycle.

We conclude with a second table of contents, in which we shall attempt to set forth the central pattern of the comic and tragic visions. One essential principle of archetypal criticism is that the individual and the universal forms of an image are identical, the reasons being too complicated for us just now. We proceed according to the general plan of the game of Twenty Questions, or, if we prefer, of the Great Chain of Being:

1   In the comic vision the *human* world is a community, or a hero who represents the wish-fulfillment of the reader. The archetype of images of symposium, communion, order, friendship and love. In the tragic vision the human world is a tyranny or anarchy, or an individual or isolated man, the leader with his back to his followers, the bullying giant of romance, the deserted or betrayed hero. Marriage or some equivalent consummation belongs to the comic vision, the harlot, witch and other varieties of Jung's "terrible mother" belongs to the tragic one. All divine, heroic, angelic or other superhuman communities follow the human pattern.

2   In the comic vision the *animal* world is a community of domesticated animals, usually a flock of sheep, or a lamb, or one of the gentler birds, usually a dove. The archetype of pastoral images. In the tragic vision the animal world is seen in terms of beasts and birds of prey, wolves, vultures, serpents, dragons and the like.

3   In the comic vision the *vegetable* world is a garden, grove or park, or a tree of life, or a rose or lotus. The archetype of Arcadian images, such as that of Marvell's green world or of Shakespeare's forest comedies. In the tragic vision it is a sinister forest like the one in *Comus* or at the opening of the *Inferno*, or a heath or wilderness, or a tree of death.

4   In the comic vision the *mineral* world is a city, or one building or temple, or one stone, normally a glowing precious stone—in fact the whole comic series, especially the tree, can be conceived as luminous or fiery. The archetype of geometrical images: the "starlit dome" belongs here. In the tragic vision the mineral world is seen in terms of deserts, rocks and ruins, or of sinister geometrical images like the cross.

5   In the comic vision the *unformed* world is a river, traditionally fourfold, which influenced the Renaissance image of the temperate body with its four humors. In the tragic vision this world usually becomes the sea, as the narrative myth of dissolution is so often a flood myth. The combination of the sea and beast images gives us the leviathan and similar water-monsters.

Obvious as this table looks, a great variety of poetic images and forms will be found to fit it. Yeats's "Sailing to Byzantium," to take a famous example of the comic vision at random, has the city, the tree, the bird, the community of sages, the geometrical gyre and the detachment from the cyclic world. It is, of course, only the general comic or tragic context that determines the interpretation of any symbol; this is obvious with relatively neutral archetypes like the island, which may be Prospero's island or Circe's.

Our tables are, of course, not only elementary but grossly oversimplified, just as our inductive approach to the archetype was a mere hunch. The important point is not the deficiencies of either procedure, taken by itself, but the fact that, somewhere and somehow, the two are clearly going to meet in the middle. And if they do meet, the ground plan of a systematic and comprehensive development of criticism has been established.

Suggestions for Further Reading

General Reference Works:

ATKINS, J. W. H., *English Literary Criticism*, I. *The Medieval Phase.* Cambridge University Press, 1943; II. *The Renascence.* London, Methuen & Co., 1947; III.*The Seventeenth and Eighteenth Centuries.* London, Methuen & Co., 1951.

BATE, WALTER JACKSON, *Criticism: the Major Texts*, enlarged ed. New York, Harcourt, Brace, Jovanovich, 1970.

CRANE, R. S., ed., *Critics and Criticism.* Chicago, Chicago University Press, 1952.

SAINTSBURY, GEORGE, *A History of Criticism and Literary Taste in Europe*, 3 vols., 4th ed. Edinburgh and London, William Blackwood & Sons, 1949.

WELLEK, RENÉ, *Concepts of Criticism*, Stephen G. Nichols, Jr., ed. New Haven, Connecticut, Yale University Press, 1963.

————, and WARREN, AUSTIN, *Theory of Literature.* New York, Harcourt Brace, 1949.

WIMSATT, WILLIAM K., JR., and BROOKS, CLEANTH, *Literary Criticism: A Short History.* New York, Knopf, 1957.

Specific Reference Works:

Aristotle:

COOPER, LANE, *The Poetics of Aristotle: Its Meaning and Influence.* Ithaca, New York, Cornell University Press, 1956.

ELSE, GERALD F., *Aristotle's Poetics: The Argument.* Cambridge, Massachusetts, Harvard University Press, 1957.

GOLDEN, LEON, and HARDISON, O. B., JR., *Aristotle's Poetics.* Englewood Cliffs, New Jersey, Prentice-Hall, 1968.

HOUSE, HUMPHREY, *Aristotle's Poetics.* London, Rupert Hart-Davis Ltd., 1966, revised with Prefaces.

McKEON, RICHARD, "Literary Criticism and the Concept of Imitation in

Antiquity." *Modern Philology*, vol. XXXIV (1936).

OLSON, ELDER, ed., *Aristotle's Poetics and English Literature: A Collection of Essays*. Chicago, University of Chicago Press, 1965.

Longinus:

ATKINS, J. W. H., *Literary Criticism in Antiquity*, Vol. II. Cambridge University Press, 1934, Chapter 6.

BRODY, JULES, *Boileau and Longinus*. Geneva, E. Droz, 1958.

HENN, T. R., *Longinus and English Criticism*. Cambridge University Press, 1934.

MONK, S. H., *The Sublime: A Study of Critical Theories in Eighteenth Century England*. Ann Arbor, Michigan, University of Michigan Press, 1960.

TATE, ALLEN, "Longinus," in Elliott Coleman, ed., *Lectures in Criticism* (New York, Harper, 1961), pp. 45–70.

Dante:

AUERBACH, ERICH, *Dante: Poet of the Secular World*, trans. by Ralph Manheim. Chicago, University of Chicago Press, 1961.

BERGIN, THOMAS C., *Dante*. Boston, Houghton, Mifflin, 1965.

TOYNBEE, PAGET, *Dante Alighieri: His Life and Works*, Charles S. Singleton, ed. New York, Harper & Row, 1965.

Sidney:

KROUSE, F. M., "Plato and Sidney's *Defense of Poetrie*." *Comparative Literature*, vol. VI (1954), pp. 138–47.

MYRICK, K. O., *Sir Philip Sidney as a Literary Craftsman*. Cambridge, Massachusetts, Harvard University Press, 1935.

SPINGARN, J. E., *Literary Criticism in the Renaissance*. New York, Harcourt, Brace & World, 1963.

Dryden:

BREDVOLD, L. I., *Intellectual Milieu of John Dryden*. Ann Arbor, Michigan, University of Michigan Press, 1934.

CRANE, R. S., "English Neoclassical Criticism: An Outline Sketch," in R. S. Crane, ed., *Critics and Criticism: Ancient and Modern* (Chicago, University of Chicago Press, 1952), pp. 375–88.

ELIOT, T. S., *Homage to John Dryden*. New York, privately printed, 1924.

———, *John Dryden: The Poet, The Dramatist, The Critic*. New York, Haskell House, 1966.

MOORE, F. H., *The Nobler Pleasure: Dryden's Comedy in Theory and Practice*.

Chapel Hill, North Carolina, University of North Carolina Press, 1936.

VERRALL, A. W., *Lectures on Dryden*. Cambridge University Press, 1914.

Wordsworth:

BEATTY, ARTHUR, *William Wordsworth: His Doctrine and Art in Their Historical Relations*. Madison, Wisconsin, University of Wisconsin Press, 1922.

HAVENS, R. D., *The Mind of a Poet: A Study of Wordsworth's Thought with Particular Reference to "The Prelude."* Baltimore, Maryland, Johns Hopkins Press, 1941.

HEFFERMAN, J. A., *Wordsworth's Theory of Poetry*. Ithaca, New York, Cornell University Press, 1969.

OWEN, W. J. B., *Wordsworth as Critic*. Toronto, University of Toronto Press, 1969.

PERKINS, DAVID, *Wordsworth and the Poetry of Sincerity*. Cambridge, Massachusetts, Harvard University Press, 1964.

Arnold:

ANDERSON, W. D., *Matthew Arnold and the Classical Tradition*. Ann Arbor, Michigan, University of Michigan Press, 1965.

BUCKLEY, VINCENT, *Poetry and Morality: Studies in the Criticism of Matthew Arnold, T. S. Eliot, and F. R. Leavis*. London, Chatto & Windus, Ltd., 1959.

JAMES, D. G., *Matthew Arnold and the Decline of English Romanticism*. London, Oxford University Press, 1961.

MADDEN, W. A., *Matthew Arnold: A Study of the Aesthetic Temperament*. Bloomington, Indiana, Indiana University Press, 1967.

PERKINS, DAVID, "Arnold and the Function of Literature." *Journal of English Literary History*, vol. XVIII (1951), pp. 287–309.

ROBBINS, WILLIAM, *The Ethical Idealism of Matthew Arnold*. Toronto, University of Toronto Press, 1959.

SHUMAKER, WAYNE, "Matthew Arnold's Humanism: Literature as Criticism of Life," *Studies in English Literature*, vol. II (1962), pp. 385–402.

James:

JAMES HENRY, *The Art of the Novel: Critical Prefaces*, Introduction by Richard P. Blackmur. New York, Scribner, 1962.

SUTTON, WALTER, *Modern American Criticism*. Englewood Cliffs, New Jersey, Prentice-Hall, 1963.

ZABEL, MORTON D., *Literary Opinion in America*, revised and enlarged ed., New York, Harper 1951.

Taine:

BABBITT, IRVING, *Masters of Modern French Criticism.* New York, Noonday Press, 1963.

EUSTIS, A. A., *Hippolyte Taine and the Classical Genius.* Berkeley, California, University of California Press, 1951.

GATES, LEWIS E., "Taine's Influence as a Critic," in *Studies and Appreciations* New York, Macmillan, 1900, pp. 192–204.

KAHN S. J., *Science and Aesthetic Judgment: A Study in Taine's Critical Method.* New York, Columbia University Press, 1953.

LEVIN, HARRY, "Literature as an Institution." *Accent,* vol. VI (1946), pp. 159–68; reprinted in *Criticism: The Foundations of Modern Literary Judgment,* Schore, Miles, McKenzie, eds. New York, Harcourt, Brace & World, 1958, pp. 546–53.

Jung:

FRAIBERG, LOUIS, *Psychoanalysis and American Literary Criticism.* Detroit, Wayne State University Press, 1960.

JACOBI, JOLANDE, *Complex, Archetype, Symbol in the Psychology of C. G. Jung,* trans. by Ralf Manheim. New York, Pantheon, 1959.

———, *The Psychology of C. G. Jung.* New Haven, Connecticut, Yale University Press, 1962.

LESSER, SIMON O., *Fiction and the Unconscious.* Boston, Beacon, 1957.

SHUMAKER, WAYNE, *Literature and the Irrational: A Study of Anthropological Backgrounds.* Englewood Cliffs, New Jersey, Prentice-Hall, 1960.

Brooks:

CALHOUN, RICHARD C., "The New Criticism Ten Years After." *South Atlantic Bulletin,* vol. XXVI (1960), pp. 1–6.

KENNER, HUGH, *The Art of Poetry.* New York, Holt, Rinehart & Winston, 1959.

KRIEGER, MURRAY, *The New Apologists for Poetry.* Bloomington, Indiana, Indiana University Press, 1963.

MOORMAN, CHARLES, "The Vocabulary of the New Criticism." *American Quarterly,* vol. IX (1957), pp. 180–184.

RANSOM, JOHN CROWE, *The World's Body.* New York, Charles Scribner's Sons, 1938.

STALLMAN, ROBERT W., "The New Critics," in *Critiques and Essays in Criticism* (New York, Ronald Press, 1949), pp. 488–506.

Auerbach:

HASSAN, IHAB, "Criticism as Mimesis." *South Atlantic Quarterly,* vol. LV (1956), pp. 473–86.

WELLEK, RENÉ, "Auerbach's Special Realism." *Kenyon Review*, vol. XVI (1954), pp. 299–307.

————, "Obituary: Erich Auerbach (1892–1957)." *Comparative Literature*, vol. X (1958), pp. 93–94.

Frye:

BODKIN, MAUD, *Archetypal Patterns in Poetry*. London, Oxford University Press, 1963.

KRIEGER, MURRAY, *Northrop Frye in Modern Criticism: Selected Papers from the English Institute*. New York, Columbia University Press, 1966.

SHUMAKER, WAYNE, *Literature and the Irrational: A Study of Anthropological Backgrounds*. Englewood Cliffs, New Jersey, Prentice-Hall, 1960.

SUTTON, WALTER, *Modern American Criticism*. Englewood Cliffs, New Jersey, Prentice-Hall, 1963.